connect feelings c̄ overt behavior
∴ child says insight into behav

Final Exam

CH 2 — 3

CH 3-12 — 1   10 pts each

14 — 3   focus on counseling

16 — 2   ) you can generalize
                what would be unique about (Hierarchy)
17 — 1   ) certain one.
————————
        10

no 18/19

Look for pictorial projections

COUNSELING
CHILDREN

COUNSELING CHILDREN

Charles L. Thompson

The University of Tennessee

Linda B. Rudolph

Austin Peay State University

Brooks/Cole Publishing Company

Monterey, California

Brooks/Cole Publishing Company
A Division of Wadsworth, Inc.

Printed in the United States of America

10 9 8 7 6 5 4 3 2

Library of Congress Cataloging in Publication Data

Thompson, Charles Lowell.
Counseling Children.

Bibliography: p.
Includes index.
1. Child psychotherapy.   2. Children—
Counseling of.   I. Rudolph, Linda B.,
date.   II. Title.
RJ504.T49   618.92′8914   82-4415
ISBN 0-534-01151-9   AACR2

Subject Editor: *Claire Verduin*
Production Editor: *Suzanne Ewing*
Manuscript Editor: *Susan Weisberg*
Interior and Cover Design: *Vicki Van Deventer from Visalia*
Illustrations: *Ryan Cooper*
Photographs: *Courtesy of Cookie DeFenderfer and Bill Minor*
Typesetting: *Graphic Typesetting Service, Los Angeles, California*

Dedicated to our children:

Charles, Cynthia, Marcia   *John, Steve, Andy*

PREFACE

Counseling Children was written to fill the need for a contemporary text book designed to put theory into practice for counseling children. *Counseling Children* is written for people preparing themselves for a career in working with children and for professionals seeking to upgrade skill areas they are not presently using. Counselors, psychologists, teachers, social workers, and parents should find the book useful in developing approaches for teaching children how to find better ways to meet their needs. The book brings together ideas from research journals, counseling theorists, books, and practice. We have attempted to present practical, up-to-date methods for helping children with specific developmental, social, or behavior problems such as fighting, stealing, lying, cheating, withdrawal, shyness, and behaviors destructive to self or others. Also included are specific suggestions for counseling children who are "exceptional" or who may be experiencing special concerns resulting from societal problems—divorce, death, abuse.

The three-part book begins with an explanation of what causes our children's problems. Exploring the commonalities shared by effective counselors, we take the point of view that counseling may have a remedial, preventive, or developmental focus. Part II is a presentation of ten counseling theories and the ways each may be adapted to counseling children. The ten theories range from a psychodynamic counseling method developed from Sigmund Freud's psychoanalytic theory to a behavioral counseling method developed from B. F. Skinner's behavioral technology. Counseling methods based on Carl Rogers's person-centered counseling and Viktor Frankl's logotherapy followed Freud's and Skinner's models as a third-force approach to counseling. The remaining six counseling approaches include two methods for working with children and their families, Virginia Satir's conjoint family therapy and Alfred Adler's individual psychology. Part II is rounded out with presentations of William Glasser's reality therapy, Albert Ellis's rational emotive therapy, Eric Berne's transactional analysis, and Fritz Perls's Gestalt therapy. Presentation of each theory includes a biographical sketch of the theorist, a philosophical statement of the nature of people, a discussion of the theory and the technique used in practice, a case history demonstrating application of the method with children, and a final summation of research and reactions related to the theory.

Part III of the book focuses mainly on practical counseling, consulting, and intervention techniques for specific problems children experience. These problems range from divorce, alcoholism, and death and dying to school-related concerns such as discipline problems, learning problems, conflict with peers, and exceptionality. The problems treated in Part III of the book were identified from a survey of approximately 1000 teachers and counselors from all areas of the United States. Part III also includes a chapter on counseling children in groups and a final chapter on the legal and ethical considerations for counseling children.

We realize that the efficacy of any strategies for changing children's behavior depends on many variables—the severity of the problems, the resistance or cooperation of the child and significant adults, the orientation of the counselor, and so on. This book is our way of sharing with readers the ideas and methods we have found useful for changing children's ineffective behavior and helping them to become more responsible and fully functioning persons.

We would like to acknowledge the contributions of the following people: Lawrence DeRidder, chairperson of the Department of Educational and Counseling Psychology at the University of Tennessee for allowing one author the freedom and time for research and writing, and the administration of Austin Peay State University for their support and encouragement. We thank the manuscript reviewers for their thoughtful comments: Helen B. Moore, James Madison University; Karen A. Paulsen, University of Arizona; and Herman J. Peters, Ohio State University. We also thank Terry Conkin, University of Tennessee, for the excellent art work; Flo Plemmons, Oak Ridge, Tennessee school system, for assistance in obtaining photographs; our editors, Susan Weisberg, and Sue Ewing of Brooks/Cole, for their special way of giving us expert criticism while helping us maintain our sense of self-esteem; Clare Dwan Wylie, for helping to read galleys; all our students who contributed their reactions, ideas, and counseling cases to our work; our spouses, Harriet and Bill, for their support, understanding, and encouragement; and our children, for being patient with our attempts to use them as test cases for our counseling techniques.

Charles L. Thompson
Linda B. Rudolph

CONTENTS

CONTENTS

COUNSELING
CHILDREN

INTRODUCTION TO COUNSELING CHILDREN

CHAPTER
1

INTRODUCTION

The year 1979 was proclaimed as the International Year of the Child by the United Nations. Americans like to talk about their interest and concern for their children, and one of the purposes of this special year was to point out advancements in working with children and to focus on problems of children yet unresolved and the progress needed.

Many children are born into warm and loving homes. Many are born with genetic traits and into environmental conditions that contribute to their growth and development. Many pass through the developmental stages of childhood and adolescence successfully and become effective and productive adults. Maslow (1970) would say such children become self-actualizing because their physical, safety, love and belonging, and esteem needs are met. Erikson (1960) would claim that these fortunate children successfully pass through the psychosocial stages of childhood and adolescence: trust versus mistrust; autonomy versus doubt and shame; initiative versus guilt; industry versus inferiority; identity versus self-diffusion. Behaviorists believe that people learn to respond appropriately because of conditioning. Glasser (1969) feels they are successful because their needs for love and respect have been met and they have learned the "three R's" of right and wrong, reality, and responsibility.

A number of theories seek to explain human growth and development and to predict success in life. Yet, with all the knowledge our society possesses concerning growth and development, the number of children encountering difficulties as they progress toward adulthood continues to grow. In addition to inherent developmental problems, the home environment or the larger society often contributes to children's difficulties.

3

Urie Bronfenbrenner (1977) expressed his concern about the family's ability to raise children and the country's commitment to the development of its children. He points out that the "United States is now the only industrialized nation that does not insure health care or a minimum income for every family with young children, and the only one that has not yet established a program of child care for working mothers" (p. C3). He finds that we are more concerned about our environment and football than the family situation and children. In fact, he contends, the American family is falling apart, as indicated by the following statistics:

1. Accidents are the chief cause of death for children under 18; approximately 15 million school days per year are lost because of accidents.
2. In 1970, it was projected that 200,000 infants would be killed by adults and at least 2 million children would be battered. Evidence makes it highly probable that these figures are increasing with the years rather than decreasing.
3. Arrests of children under 18 years of age for serious crimes (murder, assault, robbery) increased 200% in the 15 years preceding 1977. Arrests for juvenile prostitution increased 286%, and arrests for drug abuse and trafficking increased 4600%.
4. In the 25 years preceding 1977, illegitimacy increased from 4 per 100 live births to 10 per 100 live births; it is estimated that, in 1976, 65,000 teenagers had abortions.
5. The suicide rate for children 15 to 19 years increased from 2.3 per 100,000 in 1956 to 7.1 in 1974. Suicide is the third leading cause of death for white children. The rate for black children is lower but climbing faster.[1]

The problems of children are increasing with serious rapidity, giving cause for grave concern. Intense consideration must be given to the factors contributing to these statistics, and methods for individuals and society to help these children must be found.

It has been and continues to be a source of frustration to clinical, agency, and school counselors that little has been written to suggest specific counseling procedures for specific learning and behavioral problems of children. Most counseling books describe theories and techniques and their application in general terms, with little emphasis given to the problems of children; however, most counselors have neither the time nor facilities available to search the literature for these techniques. The present book will be an attempt to provide counselors in the clinic, agency, school, or other counseling settings with a source of suggestions for counseling with specific learning and/or behavioral problems.

[1]From "The Calamitous Decline of the American Family," by U. Bronfenbrenner. In *The Washington Post*, January 2, 1977, 3. Reprinted by permission of the author.

The organization of the book is practical. Background information on counseling theories and issues is followed by a step-by-step description of ideas for working with children's problems. Illustrations have been employed throughout the book in order to demonstrate the application of important points. No attempt has been made to discuss all of the problem areas mentioned above, but many have been addressed and suggestions made for helping such children.

WHAT CAUSES OUR CHILDREN'S PROBLEMS?

Sherrie is a second grader who is shy, withdrawn, and rejected by her classmates. Her class work has deteriorated rapidly during the past three months. She has just told you that her parents are getting a divorce.

Bob is a bright young man intellectually. However, he is extremely overweight, and he is teased and rejected by his peers. Bob is beginning to retaliate by fighting with his friends. He has become quite a behavior problem at school and in the neighborhood.

Lucy is the only child of an older couple who are extremely wealthy. She is bright and mature for her age. She is also very authoritarian in her manner and attempts to boss other children. She is resented and rejected by her peers.

Jerry has just been diagnosed as learning disabled. His first five years in school have been unsuccessful, and he has given up.

Debbie comes to school unkempt and often without her lunch or lunch money. She frequently has cuts, bruises, and abrasions over her body. She explains that she is clumsy and falls a lot. Her teacher is concerned about the possibility of child abuse.

A child's world

How wonderful it would be to return to the carefree, irresponsible days of childhood, with no financial worries, job pressures, societal problems—so the fantasy goes. Unfortunately, childhood is not the carefree, light-hearted, playful time remembered by many adults. Normal child development involves a series of cognitive, physical, emotional, and social changes. Almost all children, at some time during their development, will experience difficulty in adjusting to the changes, and the accompanying stress or conflict may lead to learning or behavior problems. Normal childhood development brings tasks of achieving independence, learning to relate to peers, developing confidence in self, coping with an ever-changing physical body, forming basic values, and mastering new ways of thinking and new information. Add the stresses and conflict of a rapidly changing society—a society even adults find difficult to understand—and the child's world does not look so appealing.

The American home

According to developmental psychologists, children need warm, loving, and stable home environments in order to grow and develop in a healthy manner. At one time, most children lived in large and stable extended families. If mothers or fathers had no time for the children, there was an older brother or sister, grandmother or grandfather, aunt or uncle who considered the child to be special. Today, the extended family has been replaced by the nuclear family, which too often is unable to meet the needs of the child. Writing in the *Washington Post*, Bronfenbrenner (1977) reported that in 1920 half the homes in Massachusetts had at least one adult besides the parents in residence. As of 1977, only 4% of these homes included an adult other than parents. With grandparents, aunts, uncles, and cousins often many miles away, there may be no one to provide the warmth and stability so necessary for healthy growth and development.

Furthermore, today's home may be broken by separation, divorce, or death. The number of divorces in 1976 exceeded 1 million (Bronfenbrenner, 1977). Single parenthood is growing in frequency; as of 1977, one out of six children lived with only one parent. And even when both parents are physically present in the home, career demands plus family responsibilities often drain the adults, leaving them with little time and energy to devote to their children. A majority of mothers of school-age children held jobs outside the home in 1975, while 39% of mothers with children 6 years and under were working outside the home. Nearly one in three mothers of children under age 3 were working outside the home (Bronfenbrenner, 1977). There may be few people the child can turn to for comfort and guidance.

Societal crises

Not only are many of our children facing insecure and unstable homes, but they are also continually confronted by an unstable and conflict-ridden society. The rising inflation rate and the high cost of life's necessities—food, shelter, clothing—are reported almost daily by the media. Children hear the continual argument over energy. Is there a true energy shortage? What will be our sources of energy for heating and transportation in the future? Unemployment rates are high, and new graduates are having difficulties finding jobs. Job opportunities change rapidly, and career planning is filled with uncertainties about the future demand for specific skills. Those adults with jobs are often dissatisfied and engage in slow-downs, strikes, or contract negotiations. The crime rate is on the upswing, and often neighborhoods are no longer safe for children or adults. The cost of vandalism to schools and other private and public property is astronomical. There is a growing cynicism and distrust of local, state, and federal government. Once respected public figures and governmental agencies have been found to be engaging in criminal or highly unethical practices. Finally, we live under the threat of world war and the potential total destruction such a war could bring.

Changing values

While change can be quite frightening or confusing, especially for a child, it can also be wondrous. A changing world can be exciting. It can bring new discoveries in medicine, new ideas for recreation, new and different jobs, new ways of living—all areas of life may be affected.

Children of today are forming values in a constantly and rapidly changing world. Our concept of what is "right" or "wrong" seems to change daily or vary with the person we are talking to. Who is right concerning standards of sexuality, cohabitation, alternative lifestyles, or abortion? Are the various "liberation movements" good or bad? How does a person behave in a world with changing sex roles? Will drugs seriously harm a person? Should society condone mercy killing? Is capital punishment justified? Adults with mature thinking processes and years of life experience have trouble making rational judgments on such ethical and moral issues.

The frustrations of childhood

Parents often give their children glowing reports of "when I was a child . . . ," but we must question whether adults truly remember what it is like to be ordered to obey; to have rights and privileges extended only at the whim of an adult; to be treated as an object, or perhaps a prisoner; to try to understand a world that is inconsistent and continually changing; to feel the pressures of conforming to the dictates of parents, school, and other authority figures without understanding; or to have feelings or emotions totally ignored.

How many adults would trade their present life for a world in which they were told what to eat and how to dress; in which they spent seven hours moving, working, and speaking at the orders or instructions of others; in which they were told where they could or could not go, when to be in and with whom they could associate; in which someone constantly labeled them "good" or "bad"; in which daily events left them feeling insecure, anxious, and many times helpless and hopeless. Increasing incidences of school vandalism are one expression of the unhappiness and frustration children experience in school and perhaps in life in general. Imagine yourself as a 4 foot, 6 inch person looking up and out at a world you do not understand. Take away your present learning and life experiences from this small person, and then defend the idea that "happiness is a child's world" or that America is a child-centered society.

Obviously, there are children in today's world who have very secure and loving childhoods that are preparing them well to meet our present-day society. The purpose of this pessimistic presentation of childhood is simply to discourage the idea that childhood is a totally carefree and irresponsible period of one's life and to encourage adults to seek to understand the reasons for the increase of learning and behavior problems, emotional problems, drinking and drug abuse, runaways, suicides, lack of commitment, and the multitude of other problems in today's population of children. Although every adult was once a child, a "generation gap" exists in understanding. As early as the days of Socrates and Aristotle, adults felt that the growing generation was "going to the dogs." However, past generations did not have to deal with a gap so compounded by complexities as are present in today's society.

THE PERSONAL WORLD OF THE CHILD

The various social and cultural conditions we have been discussing can have a profound effect on the child's personal and psychological world.

Maslow (1970) believes that we all have certain basic needs that must be met in order for us to become "self-actualizing," or to reach our potential in all areas of development. If our lower-level basic needs are not met, we will be unable to meet higher-order needs. His ideas suggest some possible reasons why our children are experiencing an increased number of learning and behavior problems.

The first level of Maslow's hierarchy is physiological needs—the need for food, shelter, water, and warmth. We might be tempted to pass this need by, feeling that children of today are fed well and have adequate shelter and clothes. However, we must consider, for example, the number of children who participate in breakfast programs in schools or who do not get breakfast either at home or at school, and the poor diet of some children who may have an adequate quantity of food. We are just beginning to learn about the relationship between diet and academic/behavioral problems. There is evidence to support the idea that a poor diet may be related to such problems as hyperactivity and inability to learn; recent research has suggested that an inadequate diet may contribute to mental illness in adolescents. Are we truly meeting the physiological needs of our children?

Maslow's second level is the need for safety. Again, we may be tempted to ignore this need at first glance. However, can we say that our children really feel safe, that they have little to fear? Some children feel afraid in their own homes; they fear for their very physical safety. Parents, frustrated that their own needs are not adequately met, may take their frustration out on the child through physical or psychological abuse. Some adults who would not think of hurting a child physically will psychologically abuse children with demeaning and damaging words. Children may receive similar treatment in school, where teachers who are frustrated personally or professionally may use children as a safe target for their frustration. And not only are children afraid of adults, some are also afraid of their peers. Consider Cliff, who is small for his age, rather shy, and has few friends. As Cliff enters school one morning, several of the "bigger guys" tell him they will be waiting "to get him" this afternoon. Cliff cannot be expected to learn 6 × 6 with this problem weighing on his mind!

Even if bullies do not threaten Cliff, his learning or behavior may be influenced by another need. The need to feel loved and to belong is the first higher-order need, emerging after physiological and safety needs have been met. Humans are social beings and want to feel part of a group. We see this need being fulfilled in children's cliques, gangs, clubs, and other groups. The family also helps to satisfy the need for love and belonging. Wherever we are, most of us want to be loved and accepted, and we want to fit in with the group. Cliff may not be getting positive attention from adults or peers, and he may think that no one likes him. Children sometimes attempt to hide their feelings of rejection or to compensate for the rejection with antisocial behavior; either defense can be destructive to learning and personal relationships.

Perhaps the need that our society has the most trouble fulfilling for children is the need for self-esteem, the fourth need in Maslow's hierarchy. Children are ordered, directed, commanded, criticized, devalued, ignored, and put down. You may have had the experience of being treated like a child. Your feelings probably included annoyance, inferiority, defensiveness, and anger. When adults are treated like children, they rebel, fight, or leave the scene. Such responses are not considered acceptable in children. All people—adults and children—need to be respected as worthwhile individuals, capable of feeling, thinking, and behaving in responsible ways. Children are developing their cognitive abilities and widening their range of experiences. They can be treated with the warmth and respect needed to encourage their learning within firm guidelines and expectations. Cruel and thoughtless remarks can be avoided; criticisms can be reduced; positive interactions can be accentuated to build self-respect and self-confidence.

The satisfaction of needs at the first four levels contributes to the achievement of the fifth need in Maslow's hierarchy—self-actualization. Maslow states that a self-actualized person is moving toward the fulfillment of his or her inherent potential. Thompson and Poppen define self-actualization as the need to "become all that one can become in all areas of life" (1972, p. 14). Fulfilling this need implies that lower needs have been met; the child is not blocked by hunger, fear, low self-esteem, lack of love or feelings of belonging. The child is not problem free, but has learned problem-solving skills and can move forward to becoming all that he or she can.

Glasser (1969) believes that society is not meeting our children's needs. He contends that children are failing in school academically and behaviorally because their needs for love and self-worth are not being met. Glasser believes that children's problems are related to the inability to fulfill these needs. He emphasizes the teaching of reality, right and wrong, and responsibility.

Dinkmeyer and Dinkmeyer (1978) and Dreikurs (1968), Adlerian psychologists, believe that children often attempt to meet their needs in a mistaken direction. They suggest that adults examine the "goals of misbehavior" and attempt to redirect the behavior to achieve more satisfying results.

Behavioral psychologists see academic and behavior problems as resulting from faulty learning. The child has learned inappropriate ways of behaving through such methods as reinforcement for the behavior or from poor models. Helping the child to succeed is a matter of unlearning or "extinguishing" the inappropriate pattern and learning more appropriate behaviors.

We could hypothesize for pages concerning the factors contributing to children's problems in today's society. Whatever the cause, the problems are present. A more immediate concern seems to be what to do about these problems.

WHAT COUNSELING CAN DO

Ask elementary classroom teachers to estimate the number of students in their rooms who are experiencing learning, emotional, or behavioral problems. Ask these teachers to predict how many of the approximately 30 students in each class will experience serious trouble with the law or other adjustment problems in the future. Multiply these figures by the number of classrooms throughout the United States. The estimates will be overwhelming. We can change these statistics if we become more effective helpers.

Counseling with children is a growing area of interest for people in the helping professions. Developmental theorists have studied children's growth and development and the effect of childhood experiences on the adult. Child psychiatry has focused on seriously disturbed children. However, children experiencing learning, social, or behavioral problems not serious enough to be classified as severely disturbed have been largely overlooked. Counseling can be a tool for preventing "normal" problems from becoming more serious and resulting in delinquency, school failure, and emotional disturbance. It can be a method for creating a healthy environment to assist children in coping with the stresses and conflicts of their growth and development. Counseling can also be a major remedial force for helping children in trouble through appraisal, individual or group counseling, parent or teacher consultation, or environmental changes.

The principles of counseling with children are the same as those used with adults; however, the counselor needs to be aware of the world as it is seen by the child client. The counselor must adjust counseling procedures to consider the child's cognitive level, emotional and social development, and physical abilities. Each child is a unique individual with unique characteristics and needs.

Childhood should be a time for healthy growth, for establishing warm and rewarding relationships, for exploring a widening world, for developing confidence in self and others, for learning and experiencing. It should contain some fun and carefree times. And it should also provide a foundation and guidance for the maturing person.

REFERENCES

Bronfenbrenner, U. The calamitous decline of the American family. *The Washington Post*, January 2, 1977.

Dinkmeyer, D., and Dinkmeyer, D. *Adlerian counseling and psychotherapy*. Monterey, Calif.: Brooks/Cole, 1978.

Dreikurs, R. *Psychology in the classroom* (2nd ed.). New York: Harper & Row, 1968.

Erikson, E. H. Youth and the life cycle. *Children*, 1960, 7, 43–49.

Glasser, W. *Schools without failure*. New York: Harper & Row, 1969.

Maslow, A. *Motivation and personality* (2nd ed.). New York: Harper & Row, 1970.

Thompson, C., and Poppen, W. *For those who care: Ways of relating to youth*. Columbus, Ohio: Charles E. Merrill, 1972.

CHAPTER

2

THE COUNSELING
PROCESS

WHAT IS COUNSELING?

The American Psychological Association, Division of Counseling Psychology, Committee on Definition (1956, p. 283) defined counseling as a process "to help individuals toward overcoming obstacles to their personal growth, wherever these may be encountered, and toward achieving optimum development of their personal resources."

How does counseling differ from psychotherapy?

Distinctions between counseling and psychotherapy may be superficial in that both processes have similar objectives and techniques. Pallone (1977) and Patterson (1973) have outlined some of the differences between counseling and psychotherapy, which are summarized in Table 2-1. Differences between the two processes of counseling and psychotherapy are often lost in the common ground they share. The key question about the domain of each process rests with counselors and therapists, who must restrict their practice to their areas of competence.

What is an appropriate working definition of counseling?

Counseling is a process involving a relationship between two people who are meeting so that one person can help the other to resolve a problem. One of these people, by virtue of his or her training, is the counselor; the person receiving the help is the client. The terms *counselor* and *client*, which are viewed by some as dehumanizing, may be replaced by words such as *helper* and *helpee, child, adolescent, adult,* or *person*. In

12

TABLE 2-1 Comparison of counseling and psychotherapy

Counseling is for:	Psychotherapy is for:
1. Clients	1. Patients
2. The less seriously disturbed	2. The more seriously disturbed
3. Vocational, educational, and decision-making problems	3. Personality problems
4. Preventive and developmental concerns	4. Remedial concerns
5. Educational and nonmedical settings	5. Medical settings
6. Conscious concerns	6. Unconscious concerns
7. Teaching methods	7. Healing methods

fact, Carl Rogers has recently referred to his client-centered counseling approach as *person-centered.* We believe the word *cocounselor* best describes the child's role in the counseling process—or the role of anybody who is seeking counseling—as we see counseling as a shared process. Counseling may also be a group process, in which the roles of helper and helpee can be shared and interchanged among the group members. The group counselor would then function as a facilitator as well as counselor.

Coleman (1979, p. 405) credits the Student Counseling Center at UCLA with the following definition of counseling:

> To be listened to
> & to be heard . . .
> to be supported
> while you gather your
> forces & get your bearings.
>
> A fresh look at alternatives
> & some new insights;
> learning some needed skills.
>
> To face your lion—your fears.
> To come to a decision—
> & the courage to act on it
> & to take the risks
> that living demands.

What specific types of assistance can be expected from the counseling session?

Counseling generally involves three areas: (1) thoughts and feelings about where you are in your life at present; (2) thoughts and feelings about where you would like to be in your life; and (3) if there is a discrepancy between (1) and (2), plans to reduce this discrepancy. The amount of emphasis given to each of these three areas varies according to the counseling approach being used. Nevertheless, most counseling approaches seem to share the ultimate goal of behavior change, although they may differ in the method used to attain that goal.

Perhaps the most important outcome for counseling occurs when clients learn how to be their own counselors. By teaching children the counseling process, we help them to become more skilled in solving their problems, which in turn helps them to become less dependent on others. In our view, counseling is a re-educative process designed to replace faulty learning with better strategies for getting what the child wants out of life. Regardless of the counseling approach employed, we believe that it is necessary to listen for three pieces of information children bring to the counseling session: (1) their problem or concern, (2) their feelings about the problem, and (3) their expectations for what they want the counselor to do. Failure to complete this listening process will make further counseling a waste of valuable time and human resources.

Most problems brought to the counselor by children may be classified in one or more of five categories (Callis, 1965):

1. *Conflict with others:* the child has difficulty in relating with parents, siblings, teachers, or peers and is seeking a better way to do this.
2. *Conflict with self:* the child has a decision-making problem and needs some help in clarifying alternatives and consequences involved in the conflict.
3. *Lack of information about self:* the child needs to learn more about his or her abilities, strengths, interests, or values.
4. *Lack of information about the environment:* the child needs information about what it takes to succeed in school or information concerning career development and general career education.
5. *Lack of skill:* the child needs to learn a specific skill, such as effective study methods, assertive behavior, listening skills, or how to make friends.

In summary, counseling goals and objectives may range from becoming one's own counselor to positive behavior change, problem solving, decision making, awareness, personal growth, remediation, and self-acceptance. A significant part of the counseling process for children involves training in life skills, such as communication, assertion, and effective study; however, counselors will choose the counseling focus that seems most appropriate to them. The counselor's orientation will be determined by the proportionate counseling time given to people working in various areas. Figure 2-1 represents the possible areas of focus that counseling may take. Some counselors prefer to work with the general area of developing meaning and purpose in everyday living, while other counselors prefer working with specific problem solving. Of course, many counselors try to accomplish both ends. Conceivably, Child A could start at point −5 on both the x- and the y-axis and move toward +5 on both axes.

In counseling with children in their middle childhood years (ages 5–12), for example, counselors may choose to work with problem areas in any or all four quadrants represented in Figure 2-1. Some counselors prefer to work with developmental and personal growth concerns, found in quadrant one. The children in quadrant one are solving their problems and seem to be finding considerable purpose in living. They are sometimes referred to as "stars" because they get along so well with their friends, teachers, and family. Quadrant one children seem to have a winner's script that spells success for them in achieving their goals. They usually do well in academic, athletic, social, and artistic endeavors. Working with those children is often a matter of staying out of their way. The primary focus of counseling would be to help these winners develop their full potential. The counselor's job would necessarily include some consultation and coordination to ensure that these children receive the appropriate teaching and parenting necessary for the development of their gifts and talents.

Quadrant two children find purpose in life and probably are finding meaning in the suffering they experience from not being able to solve a lot of their problems. The counselor's role with these children is remedial in the sense that counseling will be directed toward estab-

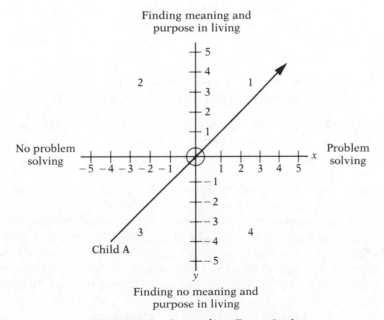

FIGURE 2-1   Counseling Focus Scale

lishing problem-solving strategies. Frequently, these quadrant two children have good interpersonal relationships but experience problems with academic achievement and self-concept. They lack the success identity found in quadrant one children.

Quadrant four children are the people who do very well with their everyday problem solving but do not seem to find life very exciting or challenging. Frequently, these children, being more introverted than extroverted, have little fun and few high points in their lives. A recent fourth-grade classroom discussion on the topic "My high points from last week," led by one of the authors, revealed that 20% of the class had difficulty in finding just one high point! Counseling plans for this group will be more developmental than remedial in that they will be directed toward building high points for each day of the child's life.

Quadrant three children represent the toughest counseling cases. They are not solving their problems and they find little value in living their lives. Children in this group suffer from depression, have a very low self-concept, and may be potential suicide victims. Frequently, the children in quadrant three have no one who really loves and cares about them, and consequently they have no one to love and care for in return. These are the children who have experienced a world of failure at home and at school. They are often in trouble with school and community authorities. Counseling with these children will be a highly remedial process with a great amount of effort directed toward encouragement and the establishment of a positive, caring relationship between counselor and child. This is not to say that the counseling relationship is not important to the children in the other three quadrants; it still remains the key ingredient to any counseling process. Once a helpful relationship is established, the counseling focus may be directed toward building success experiences in the child's life.

APPROACHES TO COUNSELING

The type of help offered to children via counseling varies according to the model utilized by the counselor. Counseling theories often differ more in name and description than they do in actual practice. However, some counseling situations and children are better suited to one approach rather than another. Counseling is basically a learning situation, and we all have our favorite style of learning.

Studies supporting the effectiveness of one counseling approach over another do not hold up well in light of the research by Smith and Glass (1977). They found in their review of several counseling research studies that the typical client of any form of counseling or therapy is better off than 75% of matched, untreated individuals and that no difference in effectiveness existed between the behavioral and nonbehavioral therapies. Therefore, this text will support an eclectic approach to counseling children—one that requires the counselor to match the method to the child and the situation rather than vice versa.

Considerable support exists for using an eclectic counseling approach. Dimond, Havens, and Jones (1978) and Assagioli (1965) point out that an individualized counseling plan is superior, but it is possible only when the counselor is able to draw upon a vast array of theory and technique and is not bound by any single approach. Lazarus (1978) makes essentially the same point in his argument that not only is behavior therapy not behaviorism, but neither behavior therapy nor behaviorism can account for all the events that occur in the counseling process. He recommends a multimodal, or comprehensive, eclectic framework for counseling that can be adapted to meet the needs of individual children. Lazarus developed his BASIC ID model to describe seven problem areas often treated in counseling:

BASIC ID Model for Problem Areas

B—Behavior
- Fighting
- Disruption
- Talking
- Stealing
- Procrastination

A—Affect
- Expression of anger
- Anxiety
- Phobias
- Depression

S—Sensation–School
- Headaches
- Back and stomach aches
- School failure
- Perceptual-motor problems

I—Imagery
- Nightmares
- Low self-concept
- Fear of rejection
- Excessive daydreaming and fantasizing

C—Cognition
- Irrational thinking
- Difficulty in setting goals
- Decision-making problems
- Problem-solving difficulties

I—Interpersonal relationships
Withdrawing from others (shyness)
Conflict with adults
Conflict with peers
Family problems

D—Drugs–Diet
Hyperactivity
Weight-control problems
Drug abuse
Addictions to smoking, alcohol, and other drugs

The Lazarus BASIC ID model covers most counseling problems likely to be encountered by counselors working with children.

Dealing with blocks to development

A key point in counseling children in the middle childhood years is awareness of the child's level of cognitive development (see Table 2-2). The work of Piaget and Inhelder (1969) has established that children in the 5 to 12 age group may be functioning in as many as three stages of cognitive development. Though age is no guarantee of a child's stage of development, it is helpful to remember that we can expect 5- and 6-year-olds to be on the verge of moving from the preoperational to the concrete stage of cognitive development and that 11-year-old children will be moving into the formal stage. In the early stages of concrete cognitive thought, children face four blocks to further development of their thought processes. These are as follows:

1. Egocentrism block—the inability to see another's point of view. For example, children believe that everyone thinks the same way and the same things they do. The egocentrism block prevents children from questioning their own thoughts and behaviors even in the face of conflicting evidence. The development of a sense of empathy in the child is made difficult by the egocentrism block.
2. Centration block—the inability to focus on more than one aspect of a problem. For example, a long line of five coins may be perceived to have more coins than a short line of six coins. Children are perception bound and cannot see the trees for the forest. The centration block makes problem solving in counseling more difficult; thus more detail and explanation by the counselor are necessary.
3. Reversibility block—the inability to work from front to back and then back to front in solving a problem. Children may have difficulty in working mathematics problems such as $17 - \_\_ = 8$. The reversibility block is also characterized by being perception bound. Children often lose track of quantity when the shape of a substance is changed, believing, for example, that a clay ball flattened into a pancake contained more clay when it was in the

TABLE 2-2 Piaget's four stages of cognitive development

Stage	Type of development	Age	Cognitive traits
Infancy	Sensorimotor	0–2	Children learn through their senses by touching, hitting, biting, tasting, smelling, observing, and listening. They begin to learn about the invariants in their environment (for instance, chairs are for sitting). Language begins to take form, habits develop, and children begin to communicate symbolically.
Childhood	Preoperational	2–7	Children are not able to conserve when solving problems. For example, children are not able to account for the quantity of a solid or liquid when it changes shape. This is the period of greatest language growth during childhood. Children are trial-and-error problem solvers in this stage and tend to focus on only one stimulus at a time. These children are able to classify objects more than one way (for instance, size, shape, color, and texture). They do have trouble with reversible thinking and prefer to learn things in ascending order before descending order. They tend to be egocentric thinkers, and play with other children can serve as a basic way to overcome this egocentrism.
Preadolescence	Concrete	7–11	Children in this stage have conservation skills and can do reversible thinking. Reasoning is based on perception, which causes these children difficulty with abstract reasoning, but they are able to appreciate the viewpoint of others. Concrete objects, pictures, diagrams, and examples are helpful learning aids.
Adulthood	Formal	11+	There is no need for manipulation of objects for these children to solve problems. They are capable of abstract thought and scientific experimentation, which includes generation of hypotheses and alternatives, plus the ability to design and implement a series of problem-solving procedures.

form of a "taller" ball. Once again, any block to formal thinking would require a better "teaching" job by the counselor.

4. Transformation block—the inability to put events in the proper order or sequence. Children often have difficulty in seeing the relationship between events or understanding cause and effect. Children may find it hard to predict the consequences of their behavior and to evaluate the effect of their behavior on themselves and others. In addition, children faced with the transformation block have difficulty in seeing the gray areas in a given situation and view events as black or white or right or wrong regardless of the situation.

The counselor must know the level or stage of the child's cognitive development if successful learning is to result from the counseling experience. Most important is the degree to which a child is able to engage in abstract reasoning, a characteristic of the formal thinking stage. Children in the concrete thinking stage will need explicit examples, learning aids, and directions that are not required for formal stage thinkers. The concrete thinker is able to walk through a series of directions but has difficulty in drawing a map of the same route.

Counseling methods need to be matched with the child's cognitive ability if counseling is to be effective. For example, a child limited by the egocentrism block will have great difficulty in empathizing with another person's situation. Piaget characterizes the preoperational child's behavior and thinking as egocentric; that is, the child cannot take the role of or see the viewpoint of another (see Wadsworth, 1971). Preoperational children believe that everyone thinks the same way and the same things they do. As a result, children never question their own thoughts; as far as they are concerned, they are the only thoughts possible and consequently must be correct. When they are confronted with evidence that is contradictory to their thoughts, they conclude the evidence must be wrong because their thoughts cannot be. Thus, from the children's point of view, their thinking is always quite logical and correct. This egocentrism of thought is not egocentric by intent; children remain unaware that they are egocentric and consequently never seek to resolve it.

Wadsworth (1971) adds that it is not until around age 6 or 7, when children's thoughts and those of their peers clearly conflict, that children begin to accommodate to others and egocentric thought begins to give way to social pressure. Peer group social interaction, the repeated conflict of one's own thoughts with those of others, eventually jars the child to question and seek verification of his or her thoughts. The very source of conflict—social interaction—becomes the child's source of verification. To be sure, verification of one's thoughts comes about only through comparison with the thoughts of others. Thus, peer social interaction is the primary factor that acts to dissolve cognitive egocentrism. The work of Piaget strongly supports the use of group counseling to assist children with the egocentrism block.

Cognitive versus affective approaches

The ten counseling approaches presented in this book were chosen because each offers possibilities for helping counselors work with one or more of the seven areas presented in the BASIC ID model.

Rating ten contemporary theories of counseling on a cognitive/affective continuum has about the same significance as picking and placing the top ten teams in football or basketball; raters' opinions are as numerous and varied as are the raters. Nevertheless, this has not discouraged us from adding our ratings to the list (see Figure 2-2).

Transactional analysis gets our vote for the most cognitively oriented therapy because of the heavy emphasis placed on learning all the terms, ego-states, games, roles, transactions, and so on. Psychodynamic counseling ranks second on the cognitive side of our continuum because so much time and attention is given to the analysis and explanation of why we behave the way we do. Behavioral counseling, with its emphasis on counting behaviors and developing reinforcement contingencies, also favors the cognitive side of the scale. Adlerian counseling is included in the cognitive group because considerable attention is given to instructing parents, teachers, and counselors in how to work with children's goals of misbehavior. However, the Adlerians are near the center of the continuum because they do emphasize adult feelings as indicators of which goal of misbehavior a child may be using. Reality therapy is placed next on the continuum because children's feelings are used as indicators to determine whether or not they are on the right track in meeting their needs. Reality therapy is still quite cognitive in the attention that is given to evaluating behavior against the criterion of helpfulness or usefulness to the child. Planning and decision making are also heavily emphasized in reality therapy.

Rational emotive therapy, thought by many to be the most cognitive of counseling theories, actually relies heavily on feeling as the prime indicator of how well or how badly a child may be handling a particular problem or conflict. The rational emotive therapy process begins with the examination of the feeling resulting from some activating event in the child's life. The next step is examining the self-message the child is

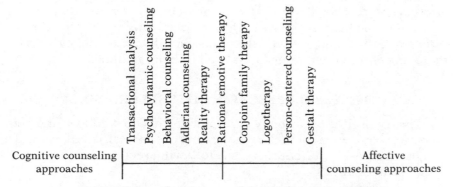

FIGURE 2-2   Continuum of Counseling Approaches

using to achieve the feeling. For these reasons, we place rational emotive therapy on the center point of our continuum. Like rational emotive therapy, conjoint family therapy, as designed by Virginia Satir, is directed toward how various types of family communication patterns make children and their parents feel.

Logotherapy is one of the more difficult placements on the continuum. We have placed it on the affective side because the technique seems well adapted for children suffering from depression and discouragement with their lives. The logotherapy process has the counselor assisting the child in finding ways to make life each day more meaningful and happy. Children may meet this goal by improving their record of achievement, making good friends, and/or finding meaning in unavoidable suffering.

Person-centered counseling has traditionally been considered the most affective counseling approach. The method focuses primarily on the understanding, clarification, and reflection of the child's feelings. The child is given more responsibility than the counselor in directing the counseling interview. However, we have reserved the most affective counseling slot for Gestalt therapy. Fritz Perls's (1969) recommendation that we "lose our minds and come to our senses" was the factor that tipped the scales in favor of Gestalt therapy over person-centered counseling. The Gestalt counselor focuses on ways to help children verbalize and express their feelings and to give voice to their inner conflicts.

We do recognize the area of disagreement in the profession of how to classify counseling theories. L'Abate (1981) proposes his E-R-A model of classification in which he groups counseling theories according to emotionality, rationality, and activity. Under emotionality L'Abate groups person-centered counseling (Rogers), Gestalt therapy (Perls), and logotherapy (Frankl). Under rationality he includes transactional analysis (Berne), rational emotive therapy (Ellis), and psychodynamic counseling (Freud). Under the activity category he lists Adlerian psychology (Dreikurs) and behavioral counseling (Wolpe and Dollard & Miller). Our purpose in classifying the various approaches to counseling is to provide the reader with a system for examining the similarities and differences among the approaches discussed in the text. We believe the ten approaches presented provide a variety of techniques that can be adapted to the learning styles of the children being counseled. The cognitive, affective, and activity classifications should help counselors in matching children with appropriate counseling methods.

WHAT DO EFFECTIVE COUNSELORS DO?

The counseling philosophy expressed in this book follows the point of view that effective counselors have many practices in common regardless of their specific orientation. The following section is a summary of these commonalities.

Beginning the counseling interview

Effective counselors are skilled in creating a relaxed counseling environment and in building rapport with their clients. Making friends with the children you counsel may be the key to the entire counseling process. Play media have been effective in developing a relaxed atmosphere with younger children. A few counselors of children have employed large friendly dogs as ice breakers, with child and counselor sitting on a rug playing with the dog during the session (Levinson, 1962). We might add that, if you choose to use chairs in the counseling office, children prefer chairs that are low enough to allow them to keep their feet on the floor if they want to.

Counseling seems to work better if children can control the distance between them and the counselor. Adults are often too aggressive in trying to initiate conversations with children. Children prefer to talk with adults at the same eye level, so some care needs to be given to seating arrangements that allow for eye-to-eye contact and feet on the floor. Of the various seating arrangements (see Figure 2-3), two seem to be *least* effective: (1) having a desk between the counselor and child, and (2) having no barrier at all between counselor and child. The preferred seating arrangement (3) is to use the corner of a desk or table as an optional barrier for the child, allowing children to retreat behind the desk or table corner or to move out around the corner when they feel comfortable doing so.

The way the counselor listens to the child is an important factor in building rapport. An open and relaxed body posture is recommended as the best way to invite a child to talk. It is often helpful to suggest a

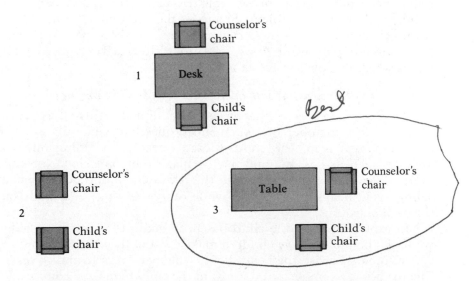

FIGURE 2-3 Seating Arrangements for Counseling Children

time limit for your interview; the time will vary according to the attention span of the child. One way to start might be to say, "Jimmy, we have 20 minutes today to talk about anything you'd like to discuss." In fact, several 20 minute periods might be used to build a friendship with Jimmy. We want to stress the importance of individualizing the counseling process to fit each child you counsel.

When the child wishes to discuss a concern or problem with you, it is necessary that you listen for three significant points. Each child seeking help from a counselor has three things in mind: (1) a problem that has not been solved, (2) feelings about the problem, and (3) expectations of what the counselor should do about the problem. It is helpful if the counselor assumes the role of a student and lets the child teach the counselor about these three topics. We believe that people learn best when they teach something to another person.

Counselors have the responsibility of letting the child know what they have learned as they help the child teach them. For example, the counselor should periodically respond with a statement such as: "In other words, you are feeling _____ because _____, and you want _____." This feedback to the child is referred to as *active listening;* it has the double effect of promoting better communication and of letting the child know you are paying attention. The active listening process continues throughout the interview, but it is most important in helping to clarify the nature of the child's problem. When the child confirms your response as an accurate understanding of the problem, counseling can move to the next phase.

Counselors also need to let children know if they can meet their expectations for counseling. The counselor probably cannot have an unpopular teacher fired, for example. However, counselors can inform children what they are able to do and let the children determine if they want to accept or reject the service available. If the service is rejected, the counselor may want to explore other alternatives with the child about where or how service can be obtained.

Exploring what has been done to solve the problem

As we begin to look at what has been attempted to solve the problem, it is good to remember that open-ended questions generally elicit the best responses from the child. Closed questions yielding one-word answers such as yes, no, and maybe make the counselor's job much more difficult. As you will note in the text, many approaches to counseling avoid heavy questioning, while others rely quite strongly on a series of questions.

In exploring what the child has been doing to solve the problem, we find it helpful to have children make a list of these behaviors if they can write; otherwise they can dictate their answers to the counselor. The list becomes important if we want the child to make a commitment to stop those behaviors that are not helping to solve the problem.

It is helpful to explore the possible rewards or pay-offs the child gets from the ineffective or unhelpful behaviors. Change is facilitated when both the pluses and the minuses are examined. A "profit-and-loss statement" can be prepared to see if the behavior is actually worth the cost the child is paying. If the child decides it is not, the behavior may be discarded in favor of a more productive alternative.

Exploring what new things could be done to solve the problem

The next step could be a brainstorming session, where the child is encouraged to develop as many problem-solving alternatives as possible. Judgment is reserved until the list is finished; quantity of ideas comes before quality in this first step. Thompson and Poppen (1979) recommend drawing a number of empty circles on a sheet of paper and seeing how many circles the child can fill with ideas. Many children may be blocked on thinking of possible new ideas. When this happens, we recommend that the counselor fill two circles with ideas as a way of encouraging the child to get started. The counselor thus allows the child to become a partner in the problem-solving process by choosing one of the two counselor suggestions. Children seem to do best with a plan they have made or helped to make. For example, if the plan involves learning a new skill such as assertion, effective study, or making friends, the counseling interview can be used for teaching and role-play rehearsal.

After the brainstorming list is complete, children are asked to evaluate each alternative in light of its expected success in helping them get what they want.

Obtaining a commitment to try one of the problem-solving ideas

Building commitment to try a new plan may be one of the most difficult things to do in the counseling process. It is important that children achieve success with their first plan because they may be quite discouraged with previous failures to solve the problem. We suggest that the child not set impossible goals in this first attempt; the first plan should be achievable. Children will do better if they are asked to report the results of their plan to the counselor. When plans do not work, the counselor helps the child write a new one until the child achieves success. Plans may include a program of reinforcement when the child is successful in meeting daily and/or weekly goals.

Closing the counseling interview

A good way to close the interview is to ask the child to summarize or review what was discussed in the session. For example, what progress was made and what plans were developed? Summarizing by the child is also helpful when the interview becomes bogged down, and children cannot think of things to say. Because the process seems to stimulate new thoughts, summarizing at the close of the interview should be limited to two to four minutes. We also recommend asking the child to summarize the last counseling interview at the start of each new interview. These counselor requests to summarize help to teach children to pay attention in the session and to review counseling plans between sessions. They have the effect of an oral quiz without the threat of a failing grade. The summary also helps counselors evaluate their own effectiveness. Finally, plans are made for the next counseling interview or for some type of maintenance plan if counseling is to be terminated.

Evaluation

The five-step plan presented above is an eclectic method that borrows from each of the ten theories that will be discussed in Part 2. We believe the plan will be most beneficial if counselors regularly evaluate the effectiveness of their counseling. One method of evaluation is goal attainment scaling, which has the double advantage of facilitating the counseling process and evaluating counseling outcomes. Goal attainment scaling, developed by Kiresuk (1973, 1976) is a process that allows the counselor and client the opportunity to establish counseling goals cooperatively. The counselor's task is to help children clarify their goals in measurable terms as a way of evaluating the distance between what "I" have and what "I" would like to have. The tabulation and calculation of the data are the counselor's responsibility. Generally one to five goals are set, with five levels of attainment defined for each goal (see Table 2-3). In addition, each goal is given a weight to represent its importance to the client. Clients establish priorities for their goals, assigning weights to the most important and least important. For instance, goal number one may be three times more important than goal number two. Intermediate goals are assigned weights representing their relative importance to the client. For example, if the most important goal is three times more important than the least important goal, it would receive a weight of 30 compared to a weight of 10 for the least important goal. Goals are weighted on a scale of 10 to 30.

Levels of attainment for each goal range from a +2 for the best anticipated success to a −2 for the most unfavorable outcome. A 0 value is assigned for the middle level or expected outcome success. Values of +1 and −1 represent "more than" and "less than" expected levels of success, respectively.

The goals are defined in measurable and observable terms, with the level of entry checked on the goal attainment follow-up guide. Following counseling, an asterisk is placed on the guide indicating where the client is after counseling. Follow-up data also can be recorded periodically on the chart.

Goal attainment scores can be calculated for both the intake and follow-up levels. A follow-up goal attainment score of 50 or better is considered successful. The formulas below are used to derive the goal attainment scores for the guide in Table 2-3 (Kiresuk & Sherman, 1968).

TABLE 2-3 Goal attainment follow-up guide

Level at intake: √
Level at follow-up: *

Scale Attainment Level	Scale 1: Worked on task $w_1 = 20$	Scale 2: Disruptive behavior $w_2 = 30$	Scale 3: Completed assignments $w_3 = 25$	Scale 4: Peer and teacher relationships $w_4 = 30$	Scale 5: Grade improvement $w_5 = 10$
a. Most unfavorable counseling outcome thought likely (−2)	Daydreams, does not remain in seat; ignores work	Pushes, hits, leaves room, talks without permission √	Does not bring proper materials to class; never completes work	Child is rude, unfriendly and discourteous; interrupts teacher daily	Child continues to fail
b. Less than expected success with counseling (−1)	Does not work 80% of the time √	Talks without permission	Occasionally brings materials; is late in completing assignments √	Child does not relate favorably 80% of the time √	Child demonstrates "D" work √
c. Expected level of counseling success (0)	Works at seat 75% of the time	Engages in appropriate behavior 75% of the time	Completes work on time 75% of the time	Child is friendly, courteous, and helpful 75% of the time	Child demonstrates "C" work
d. More than expected success with counseling (+1)	Works at seat 85% of the time *	Engages in appropriate behavior 85% of the time *	Completes work on time 85% of the time	Child is friendly, courteous, and helpful 85% of the time *	Child demonstrates "B" work *
e. Best anticipated success with counseling (+2)	Conscientiously works 100% of the time	Engages in appropriate behavior 100% of the time	Consistently completes all work on time *	Child relates well to both teacher and peers 100% of the time	Child demonstrates "A" work

Percentage figures based on spot check observations during the school day

GOAL ATTAINMENT SCORE CALCULATION
(Level at intake)

w = weight value $\qquad\qquad$ x = 50
x = scale value $\qquad\qquad$ s = 10 (standard deviation)
p = probability $\qquad\qquad$ p = .3
s = standard deviation $\qquad\qquad$ $1 - p$ = .7

$$\text{Goal Attainment Score} = 50 + \frac{10\Sigma w_1 x_1}{\sqrt{(.7\Sigma w_1^2) + .3(\Sigma w_1)^2}}$$

$$50 + 10(20 \times -2) + (30 \times -1) + (25 \times -2) + (30 \times -2) + (10 \times -2)$$

$$50 + \frac{10 \times -200}{\sqrt{.7(20^2 + 30^2 + 25^2 + 30^2 + 10^2) + .3(20 + 30 + 25 + 30 + 10)^2}}$$

$$50 + \frac{10 \times -200}{\sqrt{.7(2925) + .3(13225)}}$$

$$50 + \frac{10 \times -200}{\sqrt{6015}}$$

$$50 + \frac{10 \times -200}{77.56}$$

$$50 + \frac{(-2000)}{77.56}$$

$$50 + (-25.78)$$

$$= 24.23$$

$$z \text{ score} = \frac{50 - 24.23}{10} = 2.57 \text{ deviations from the mean}$$

GOAL ATTAINMENT SCORE CALCULATION
(Level at follow-up)

w = weight value $\qquad\qquad$ x = 50
x = scale value $\qquad\qquad$ s = 10 (standard deviation)
p = probability $\qquad\qquad$ p = .3
s = standard deviation $\qquad\qquad$ $1 - p$ = .7

$$\text{Goal Attainment Score} = 50 + \frac{10\Sigma w_1 x_1}{\sqrt{(.7\Sigma w_1{}^2) + .3(\Sigma w_1)^2}}$$

$$50 + 10(20 \times 1) + (30 \times 1) + (25 \times 2) + (30 \times 1) + (10 \times 1)$$

$$50 + \frac{10 \times 140}{\sqrt{.7(20^2 + 30^2 + 25^2 + 30^2 + 10^2) + .3(20 + 30 + 25 + 30 + 10)^2}}$$

$$50 + \frac{10 \times 140}{\sqrt{.7(2925) + .3(13225)}}$$

$$50 + \frac{10 \times 140}{\sqrt{6015}}$$

$$50 + \frac{10 \times 140}{77.56}$$

$$50 + \frac{(1400)}{77.56}$$

$$50 + (18)$$

$$= 68$$

$$z \text{ score} = \frac{68 - 50}{10} = \frac{18}{10} = 1.8 \text{ deviations from the mean}$$

Goal attainment scaling (Dowd & Kelly, 1975) can be graphed to show progress on a weekly basis (see Figure 2-4). The graph can also be used to chart the results of periodic follow-up checks on the maintenance of counseling gains.

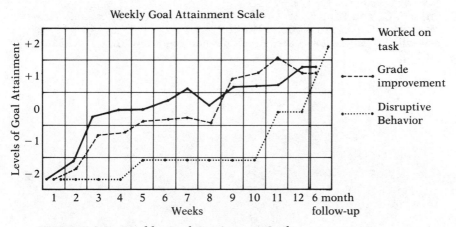

FIGURE 2-4 Weekly Goal Attainment Scale

REFERENCES

American Psychological Association, Division of Counseling Psychology, Committee on Definition. Counseling psychology as a specialty. *American Psychologist*, 1956, *11*, 282–285.

Assagioli, R. *Psychosynthesis*. New York: Viking Press, 1965.

Callis, R. Diagnostic classification as a research tool. *Journal of Counseling Psychology*, 1965, *12*, 238–243.

Coleman, J. *Contemporary psychology and effective behavior*. Glenview, Ill.: Scott, Foresman, 1979.

Dimond, R., Havens, R., and Jones, A. A conceptual framework for the practice of prescriptive eclecticism in psychotherapy. *American Psychologist*, 1978, *33*, 239–248.

Dowd, E., and Kelly, F. The use of goal attainment scaling in single case study research. *Goal Attainment Review*, 1975, *2*, 11–21.

Kiresuk, T. Goal attainment scaling at a county mental health service. *Evaluation*, 1973, Special Monograph Number 1, 12–18.

Kiresuk, T. *Guide to goals: Goal setting for children* (Format two). Minneapolis: Program Evaluation Resource Center, 1976.

Kiresuk, T., and Sherman, R. Goal attainment scaling: A general method for evaluating comprehensive community mental health programs. *Community Mental Health Journal*, 1968, *4*, 443–453.

L'Abate, L. Toward a systematic classification of counseling and therapy theorists, methods, processes and goals: The E-R-A model. *Personnel and Guidance Journal*, 1981, *59*, 263–265.

Lazarus, A. What is multimodal therapy? A brief overview. *Elementary School Guidance and Counseling*, 1978, *13*, 6–11.

Levinson, B. The dog as co-therapist. *Mental Hygiene*, 1962, *46*, 59–65.

Pallone, N. Counseling psychology: Toward an empirical definition. *The Counseling Psychologist*, 1977, 7, 29–32.

Patterson, C. *Theories of counseling and psychotherapy*. New York: Harper & Row, 1973.

Perls, F. *In and out the garbage pail*. New York: Bantam, 1969.

Piaget, J., and Inhelder, B. *The psychology of the child*. New York: Basic Books, 1969.

Smith, M., and Glass, G. Meta-analysis of psychotherapy outcome studies. *American Psychologist*, 1977, *32*, 752–760.

Thompson, C., and Poppen, W. *Guidance activities for counselors and teachers*. Monterey, Calif.: Brooks/Cole, 1979.

Wadsworth, B. *Piaget's theory of cognitive development*. New York: David McKay, 1971.

PART

II

COUNSELING THEORIES: THEIR APPLICATION TO CHILDREN

CHAPTER
3

REALITY THERAPY

WILLIAM GLASSER

William Glasser graduated from Case Institute of Technology as a chemical engineer in 1944, at the age of 19. Later, he enrolled at Case Western Reserve University and, at age 23, earned a master's degree in clinical psychology. At 28 he received a medical degree from the same institution. While serving his last year of residency at the UCLA School of Psychiatry and in a Veterans Administration hospital, Glasser discovered that traditional psychotherapy was not for him. Glasser voiced reservations about psychoanalysis to his last teacher, who reputedly responded "Join the club," although such an attitude was not common or popular among most of his colleagues. Denied a promised teaching position because of his rebellion against Freudian concepts, Glasser is quoted as saying that, if he had had to rely on referrals from his alma mater, as most beginning psychiatrists do, he would have made about $8,000 in the first 16 years of his practice.

In 1956, Glasser became consulting psychiatrist to the Ventura School for Girls, an institution operated by the State of California for the treatment of seriously delinquent adolescent girls. His first book, *Mental Health or Mental Illness?* (1961), laid the basic foundation for the techniques and concepts of reality therapy. For 12 years Glasser conducted a very successful program at the Ventura School, out of which the theory and concepts of reality therapy evolved. Glasser used the term *reality therapy* for the first time in April 1964 in a manuscript entitled "Reality Therapy, A Realistic Approach to the Young Offender." His widely read book *Reality Therapy* was published in 1965. In 1966, Glasser began consulting in California public schools for the purpose of applying reality therapy in education. These new ideas for applying reality therapy to teaching later became his third book, *Schools Without Failure* (1969).

In 1968 Glasser founded the Institute for Reality Therapy in Los Angeles. The Institute offers training courses for selected professionals such as physicians, probation officers, police officers, nurses, lawyers, judges, teachers, and counselors. Both introductory and advanced courses and programs are offered on a regular and continuing basis. Teams of consultants provide a broad base for teaching the application of reality therapy in a variety of settings. Following the publication of *Schools Without Failure*, the Educator Training Center, a special division of the Institute for Reality Therapy, was also established in Los Angeles in 1971. In 1970, the William Glasser LaVerne College Center was established at the University of LaVerne in Southern California to provide teachers with an off-campus opportunity to gain graduate and in-service credits while at the same time working within their own schools to provide an exciting educational environment for children.

The Schools Without Failure Seminars, sponsored by the Educator Training Center, continue to draw large followings across the country. Glasser's two latest books include *The Identity Society* (1972) and *Positive Addiction* (1976). He makes approximately 75 speaking appearances a year in addition to television interviews, writing, and filming.

William Glasser is married and has three children. He enjoys sports such as water skiing, sailing, and tennis. Glasser views himself as a person who enjoys being a helper, one who takes an optimistic view of life and who is good at solving problems. He loves to daydream and has little use for intellectuals who make understandable ideas difficult to grasp. Glasser has a great sense of humor, which he uses skillfully in his teaching and counseling. It is not surprising that he enjoys Clarence Day's *Life with Father* and the humor of Charles Schulz in "Peanuts."

THE NATURE OF PEOPLE

Glasser believes that, despite varying manifestations of psychological problems, problems are the result of one factor: an inability to fulfill one's basic needs. Glasser (1965) believes that there is a correlation between patients' lack of success in meeting their needs and the degree of their distress. He maintains that all psychological problems can be summed up by the fact that people deny the reality of the world around them.

Glasser adheres somewhat to Maslow's theory of the hierarchy of needs and bases his theory on teaching patients to fulfill the need of being loved and loving and the need of feeling worthwhile to oneself and others. Like Rogers's optimistic view of human nature, Glasser's belief is that people have the ability to learn to fulfill their needs and to become responsible people. He bases his system on what he calls the "three R's:" responsibility, right and wrong, and reality. We believe that two other R's could be added: relatedness and respect. Mutual respect and relationship are the keys to a successful counseling partnership.

Glasser views adjusted people as those who are responsible, who can fulfill their needs without infringing on the needs or rights of others. One main product of becoming a responsible person is an increased feeling of self-worth.

THEORY OF COUNSELING

William Glasser was reacting against some of the principles of psychoanalytic theory when he developed reality therapy. Reality therapy differs from traditional psychoanalytic therapy in six ways.

First, the concept of mental illness is discarded in favor of the concept of responsibility. Traditionally, it has been proposed that people behave irresponsibly because they are mentally ill. Glasser believes that people become mentally ill because they behave irresponsibly.

Second, reality therapy focuses on the moral issue of right and wrong—an issue often ignored in counseling because it is believed that people already feel too guilty about various unresolved conflicts. In Freud's time, everybody talked about doing the right thing, so Freud thought it best to make psychotherapy a sanctuary free of moral judgments in order not to increase feelings of guilt in his patients. In reality therapy, moral issues are addressed head on.

Third, the past is largely ignored in favor of dealing with the present and future. Most of the discussion in reality therapy is directed toward evaluating how present behavior is helping to meet one's needs. If present behavior is not working, future alternatives are examined and commitments to change are made.

A fourth difference involves the idea of transference. In traditional psychoanalytic practice, transference is frequently used as a therapeutic mechanism for living through unresolved conflicts. In reality therapy the counselor relates to the client or person on a person-to-person basis. There is no attempt to encourage the client to relate to the counselor as someone other than a counselor; for example, the child does not relate to the counselor as a parent, teacher, or some other authority figure.

Fifth, the unconscious is largely ignored in reality therapy, whereas it is generally the primary focus in psychoanalytic practice. According to Glasser, the unconscious is a fertile ground for excuses for misbehavior. He prefers to look at *what* is going on rather than at *why*.

Perhaps the most significant difference of reality therapy from traditional practice is the aspect that is most dear to educators. It is our philosophy that the counseling we do with children will largely be a teaching/learning situation. This is exactly what Glasser says about reality therapy: it is a teaching process, not a healing process. Counselors are in the business of teaching children a better way to meet their needs. From the reality therapy point of view, counseling is a matter of learning how to solve problems—teaching children, in effect, to become their own counselors.

COUNSELING METHOD

The practice of reality therapy follows eight steps. The first step concerns the most significant issue for all counseling—building good relationships with the children we counsel. Glasser calls this first step becoming involved with the people we counsel, although *involvement* may not be the best word to describe this stage of counseling as it implies entangled or complex relationships, and counselors want to develop positive relationships that are honest, open, and unencumbered. In any approach to counseling children, the goal is to build the kind of trust and climate in which children feel free to express their innermost fears, anxieties, and concerns.

Step two is an examination of present behavior in a nonpunitive way. In the third step, children are asked to evaluate what is going on in their lives and how they are helping themselves. In other words, is their behavior helping them get what they want out of life? If it is not, then there will be a chance to ask, "Do you want to change what is going on?"

This leads to the fourth step in reality therapy. The counselor and child now begin to look at the possible alternatives for getting what the child wants out of life. Step four follows a brainstorming format, in which children are asked to look at better ways of going about meeting their needs. Step five involves selecting an alternative for reaching the child's goals. In addition, the child makes a commitment to try the alternative. A key process in counseling children is helping them to make commitments. When they are able to carry out present commitments, counselors can help them to build on these to get more out of life. Therefore, children are first asked to make a rather small commitment in which success can be achieved so they can have a basis on which to build.

In step six, counselor and client look at the results of the commitment. Often children will come back for a second interview and say, "Well, I made a commitment to turn in one homework paper a day, and I did not meet my commitment," and begin to list all the reasons they failed. Reality therapy does not dwell on rationalizing "whys." At this point, the counselor and child will want to talk about writing a new contract that the child can handle; maybe one homework paper per day is too much for right now, and a less demanding contract is needed. Counselors do not accept excuses if a child does not meet the commitments made. Excuses are designed to avoid punishment, and when children learn they do not get punished for not meeting a commitment and for talking about what they do, there will be no need for excuses.

Step seven entails the use of logical consequences—for instance, receiving a lower grade for failing to turn in a homework paper. Additional penalties that are not logical or natural consequences of failing to turn in the paper, such as paddling, are considered neither effective nor humane; however, logical and natural consequences are not to be permissively removed.

Step eight requires that we do not get discouraged with our counseling failures and give up too soon. How long should we stick with children who seem bent on destroying our self-concepts as effective counselors? Glasser recommends that we work with these children three or four more times than they expect. We are not talking about a lifelong commitment when we say never give up. Build on whatever involvement has been established in step one and continue this through the entire eight-step process.

There are three key terms in reality therapy, which have been mentioned only briefly so far: *reality*, *responsibility*, and *right and wrong*. In reality therapy, *reality* is generally defined as willingness to accept the logical and natural consequences of one's behavior. When we try to avoid these consequences, we deny reality and are prone to act in an irresponsible manner. Glasser defines *responsibility* as the ability to meet one's needs without infringing on other people's rights to meet their needs. The third term is difficult to define, and Glasser leaves us on somewhat shaky ground with his definition. *Right and wrong* is defined as something you know by how you feel and thus is one of the few areas where Glasser works with the concept of feelings. He would say that our feelings are good indicators of when we are behaving in responsible and correct ways. For example, if we feel good about what we are doing and most other people also feel good about it, then we are probably on the right track and doing the right thing. One problem with defining right and wrong in terms of others' opinions is that many people have made significant contributions in the face of mass criticism.

At this point, we should look at some of the basic questions that are asked in the counseling process. The first step—and one that must continue throughout the counseling process—is building a warm relationship that helps you become friends with the child. A number of things can help you do this, but being genuinely interested in the child is the key ingredient.

There is a series of five questions often asked in reality therapy that may be posed in different ways: (1) What are you doing? (2) Is what you are doing helping you get what you want? (3) If not, what might be some other things you could try? (4) Which idea would you like to try first? (5) When? The dialogue below is an example of how you can begin.

Counselor (Co): Mary, can you tell me a little bit about your life right now here at school?

Mary: What do you mean?

Co: Well, Mary, it seems like you get sent to the office a lot to talk to me about problems you're having with your teachers. Tell me what you're doing, and let's talk about it.

Mary: Well, I guess I talk out of turn in class too much sometimes. But my classes are so boring.

Co: OK, so you talk out a lot in class, and the teachers don't like what you're doing. Do you do anything else that seems to get you in trouble with Mr. Thompson and Mrs. Rudolph?

Mary: No, I don't think so.

Co: Are you happy with what happens to you when you do these things?

Mary: I do the same old things that keep getting me in trouble, but I feel good for the moment.

Co: I know you do feel better for a while. Are the good feelings worth the price you have to pay for them?

Mary: I guess not, because I'm sure tired of spending so much time in the office.

Co: Would you like to work on a better plan?

Mary: OK. Why not?

Co: Let's start by thinking of some things you could do to get along better in your classes and some ways to make them less boring, too.

Mary: Well, I could stop talking out of turn! I know the teachers would like that.

Co: Stopping unhelpful things is usually a good way to start. What about some things you could begin doing in class?

Mary: Doing more assignments would please the teachers, but I don't like all the work.

Co: Your two suggestions will probably help you with the teachers, but they won't do much to make the class more enjoyable for you. Can you think of something to help you like school more?

Mary: Some of the kids get free time or get to go to the library when they turn in their work. Could I do this too?

Co: We can ask your teachers about that today. That might be a way to please both you and the teachers. Can you think of other ideas to try?

Mary: I guess that's about all for now.

Co: OK, Mary, how many of these ideas do you want to try?

Mary: I think I can do all of them if I can get free time, too.

Co: When do you want to start?

Mary: Today, if I can.

Co: We can try. Can you go over these with me one time before we leave?

Mary: I think so. No more talking out of turn and do enough work to earn some free time.

Co: That sounds good to me. Do you want to shake hands and make this an agreement between you and me?

Mary: OK.
Co: Good. I'd like to talk with you a little each day to see how
    your plan is working. If it doesn't work, we'll have to write
    another plan. See you tomorrow?
Mary: OK, see you.

The above is a typical interview following the reality therapy philosophy and technique. Identifying and evaluating present behavior is followed by making a plan and building commitment to follow through on it. Each step in the reality therapy process is supported by a relationship of trust, caring, and friendship between the counselor and the child.

Below, as for each theory presented in Part 2, we have included an actual transcript from a case brought to a counselor as a way of demonstrating how the theory can be put into practice.

CASE STUDY

Identification of the problem

Wendy Smith is a 12-year-old girl in the seventh grade at White Oak School. She was referred to the counselor because she was cheating on a mathematics test.

Individual and background information

Academic. School records indicate that Wendy is a high achiever, with an overall "A" average on her elementary school record. She also has an "A" average for the first two grading periods in the seventh grade. During the third grading period, which is almost over, Wendy has had some erratic test scores in mathematics. The test she was caught cheating on was an important test that could have brought up her low grades had she done well on it.

Family. Wendy is the only child of older parents, both of whom are professionals. Teachers have indicated that the parents seem to expect Wendy to make the highest grades in her class.

Social. According to teachers' reports on cumulative records, Wendy was well liked by most of the children in her classes in elementary school. She did not seem to have a close friend then, but this year she has developed a close friendship with a girl in her class. A sociogram done in her sixth-grade class last fall shows she is well accepted by her peers.

Counseling method

The counselor used the reality therapy counseling method to help Wendy evaluate her behavior and try to identify some things she could do to meet more of her needs socially and emotionally without creating problems in other areas of her life.

The five basic steps followed by the counselor in this case are: (1) establishment of a relationship; (2) identification of present behavior—what is being done, or has been done; (3) evaluation of present behavior—is it helping you get what you want?; (4) development of plans that will help; and (5) commitment from the counselee to try at least one of the plans.

Transcript

Counselor (Co): Wendy, I understand that there has been a problem in your math class. Would you like to talk about it?

Wendy: I guess so.

Co: You're feeling somewhat embarrassed about the problem and uncomfortable about talking with me.

Wendy: Yes, I am, but I know I need to talk about it.

Co: Would you like to tell me what happened?

Wendy: Miss Waters caught me cheating on my math test. I have some bad grades in math this period. I knew I had to do well on this test, but I wasn't ready for it.

Co: How did you see cheating as helping you?

Wendy: I was feeling a lot of pressure because I wasn't prepared, and my parents expect me to do well.

Co: Can you tell me what you've been doing that kept you from being prepared for the test?

Wendy: I'm just getting to know Susan, and I've been spending a lot of time talking with her and not enough time studying.

Co: Susan's friendship is very important to you.

Wendy: Yes. I've never had a really close friend before.

Co: What might be some ways that you could still be friends with Susan and also keep up with your studies?

Wendy: Well, I guess I could spend less time talking to her and more time studying.

Co: You believe that you can spend less time with Susan and still be close friends?

Wendy: Yes, I'm sure she'd understand.

Co: What are some other things that you could do that might help?

Wendy: Maybe we could spend time together studying instead of talking so much.

Co: Would you like to try one of these plans for the next week and see how it works?

Wendy: OK. I'd like to try studying with Susan.

Co: All right. Let's meet next Tuesday at 1:00 and see how well your plan worked.

SUMMARY: RESEARCH AND REACTIONS

Perhaps the best validation of reality therapy is found in the success Glasser had at the Ventura School for Girls. Before Glasser's tenure at Ventura, the school recidivism rate approached 90%; in a rather short time this rate was reduced to 10%. What was the secret of changing the orientation of these young women into success identities? Glasser gave them the experience of personal responsibility and success by assigning them tasks they could handle and by making each girl responsible for her own behavior. Punishment was discarded in favor of logical consequences. Generous amounts of praise were given and sincere interest in each girl's welfare displayed. Regardless of one's theoretical outlook, it would be difficult to argue with Glasser's formula for success. In fact, most counseling approaches will be effective if applied under Glasser's conditions, as have been described earlier.

Three research studies conducted at the University of Tennessee may be cited in support of reality therapy. Poppen and Welch (1976) found reality therapy to be effective in group counseling in a weight-loss program for adolescent women. Treatment consisted of six weekly group sessions following the reality therapy counseling format. Two treatment groups of eight subjects each both lost weight, which represented a change significant at the .05 level of confidence. However, no change in self-concept accompanied the weight loss.

A second study conducted by Gang (1976) was directed toward improving classroom behavior of disruptive children. Teachers were trained in using reality therapy counseling techniques. Frequency of undesirable behavior decreased as desirable behavior increased over baseline conditions during treatment and follow-up phases of the study. Building a better relationship with the students proved to be one of the most successful things the teachers did to effect positive change in their children. Gains in desirable behavior ranged from 69% to 222%, while decreases in undesirable behavior ranged from 17% to 56%.

A third study reported by Thompson and Cates (1976) was directed toward examining the effectiveness of a ten-step process for teaching discipline to six primary school children who were nominated by their respective teachers as the number 1 behavior problem in their class. The ten-step process was based on principles and techniques consistent with reality therapy. The results of the study were consistent with those of Gang's work with percentage difference scores ranging from +27 to +122 for appropriate behavior and from -82 to -53 for inappropriate behavior. Thompson (1980) also completed another study using reality therapy with students experiencing learning and behavior problems. Fifteen teachers, representing grade levels K–12, each worked with four students, using a modified version of reality therapy principles. Each of the 60 students improved in their learning or behavior over an eight-week period, with some students experiencing large gains. An updated version of the ten-step method has been written and successfully tested by Thompson and Poppen (1979).

The Reality Therapy Reader, edited by Bassin, Bratter, and Rachin (1976), is a survey of work on reality therapy. The articles supporting and elaborating on Glasser's theory are discussed briefly below.

In an article that was written before Glasser developed his reality therapy, Patterson (1976) indicated that a major goal of the counselor should be to help the client improve his or her self-respect and self-esteem. He suggested that the client should be made to feel worthwhile and be respected as a person who could make responsible decisions. Furthermore, counselors should be humane and give of themselves by getting involved with the client. Patterson is a strong proponent of Rogerian theory, yet many of his major foci are in keeping with the philosophy of reality therapy—feeling worthwhile, taking responsibility, and getting involved. Patterson's research in many ways correlates with Glasser's theory.

An article by W. Easson (1976), "After Psychotherapy," emphasizes a proposition somewhat similar to Glasser's idea of involvement with the client. Easson indicates that, if a situation should develop naturally whereby the client and therapist can become friends, then the therapist should allow him- or herself to enter into the relationship. In addition to enhancing the counseling relationship, it gives counselors an opportunity to solicit feedback on their performance.

Bassin (1976) developed a theory of marriage counseling called *IRT therapy*, which represents a combination of integrity, reality, and transparency theories. Bassin leans heavily on the ideas that a person must (1) love and be loved and must feel worthwhile, and (2) fill personal needs without depriving others of their needs. In his article "IRT Therapy in Marriage Counseling," Bassin (1976) emphasizes Glasser's methods. In addition, he states that the emphasis should be on current evaluation of behavior in terms of its contribution to a satisfactory marriage and on working out plans to correct any apparent deficiencies.

Mainored (1976) sees behavior as an ability to make choices. People who make the wrong choices behave irresponsibly. Like Glasser, Mainored says that a client can choose responsibly or irresponsibly; the former choice is much more healthy.

More of a traditionalist than Glasser, Schofield (1976) stresses that, for effective therapy, the patient should feel that the therapist is a friend. Schofield describes this "friend" in such a way as to indicate there must be a high degree of involvement between the counselor and client—the counselor being a person who cares if the client is victorious or defeated, who will be truly happy in the client's gain, sad in the client's loss. This characterizes and stresses the involvement that Glasser believes is so necessary.

Discussing the methods of self-help groups, Hurvitz (1976) outlines some of their methods and goals. (1) Peers hold each other responsible for their behavior regardless of its causes, (2) peers focus on behavior and try to help each other become more responsible and productive, and (3) peers use a reality based on the here-and-now orientation. This point of view is in strong agreement with Glasser's ideas of responsibility, focusing on behavior for changes, and working in a present orientation.

Swensen (1976) agrees with Glasser in his article "The Successful Therapist," emphasizing that the crucial element is the therapist's commitment to the client. As stated previously, this is Glasser's basic idea about the nature of the counselor/counselee relationship—involvement.

Greenberg and Bassin (1976) compare Moreno's theory of psychodrama with Glasser's reality therapy. Although there are a number of ways in which the two men differ, some of Moreno's ideas greatly support the premises of reality therapy. Role playing, a technique basic to psychodrama, is present in Glasser's research. Glasser stresses certain role-playing methods (such as acting out significant events in one's life).

Some theorists are not supportive of Glasser's approach. Just as Glasser attacks some traditional practices in psychotherapy, so do other people attack reality therapy.

Masserman (1975) suggests that many contemporary individual and group psychotherapies need clarification and integration. Included on his lengthy list is Glasser's reality therapy. Masserman implies that these therapies may offer illusory comfort to the patient and therapist at the time they are involved in therapy but not in actual day-to-day living.

In his book *A Complete Guide to Therapy*, Kovel (1976) scoffs at Glasser's theory of reality therapy. According to Kovel, Glasser is using a form of directive therapy that relies on morals. If people behave more responsibly, their neuroses will go away. In other words, they should conform to the established order, be good citizens, and shape up. Since neurosis consists of the breaking through of profoundly antisocial impulses, the moral approach is bound to have some efficacy. Kovel believes that moral imperatives do not work too well in themselves as an aid to repressing unhelpful behavior; if they did, we wouldn't have to make new resolutions each New Year's. Kovel continues by suggesting that the only way reality therapy could be partially effective is if it were backed up by an authority. For this reason, he says, reality therapy will probably remain popular with clergy, law enforcement agencies, and the like.

Levy and Faltico (1977) report an attempt to apply reality therapy and therapeutic-community principles—mutual support and caring—in beginning a community among college students. This community, called the Caring Community, was set up within the larger university with the purpose of developing personal responsibility and responsible concern. Encounter groups and confrontation were used to develop communication. Although the Caring Community flourished for a while, it ultimately dissolved. The authors discuss many difficulties that should be avoided in future projects.

Moravec (1965) believes that the Freudian approach may actually strengthen rather than weaken responsibility, and he criticizes Glasser for not showing the good points of conventional psychology. He believes the emphasis should not be on "right or wrong," which is a moral concept, but rather on appropriate or inappropriate behavior.

Wahler (1965) questions Glasser's strict behavioral approach. He does not believe the counselor should have to help develop plans for better behavior. Rather, the counselor should help the client discover better ways of thinking and perceiving so that the client will be inwardly motivated to behave more appropriately.

As is true with all counseling approaches, reality therapy has its supporters and critics. In any case, the research basis for reality therapy, starting with Glasser's success at the Ventura School for Girls, is becoming quite solid.

REFERENCES

Bassin, A. IRT therapy in marriage counseling. In A. Bassin, T. Bratter, and R. Rachin (Eds.), *The reality therapy reader*. New York: Harper & Row, 1976.

Bassin, A., Bratter, T., and Rachin, R. *The reality therapy reader*. New York: Harper & Row, 1976.

Easson, W. After psychotherapy. In A. Bassin, T. Bratter, and R. Rachin (Eds.), *The reality therapy reader*. New York: Harper & Row, 1976.

Gang, M. Enhancing student–teacher relationships. *Elementary School Guidance and Counseling*, 1976, *11*, 131–134.

Glasser, W. *Mental health or mental illness?* New York: Harper & Row, 1961.

Glasser, W. *Reality therapy*. New York: Harper & Row, 1965.

Glasser, W. *Schools without failure*. New York: Harper & Row, 1969.

Glasser, W. *The identity society*. New York: Harper & Row, 1972.

Glasser, W. *Positive addiction*. New York: Harper & Row, 1976.

Greenberg, I., and Bassin, A. Reality therapy and psychodrama. In A. Bassin, T. Bratter, and R. Rachin (Eds.), *The reality therapy reader*. New York: Harper & Row, 1976.

Hurvitz, N. Peer self-help groups. In A. Bassin, T. Bratter, and R. Rachin (Eds.), *The reality therapy reader*. New York: Harper & Row, 1976.

Kovel, J. *A complete guide to therapy: From psychoanalysis to behavior modification*. New York: Pantheon, 1976.

Levy, E., and Faltico, G. Reading, writing, and responsibility. *Together*, 1977, *2*, 101–110.

Mainored, W. A therapy. In A. Bassin, T. Bratter, and R. Rachin (Eds.), *The reality therapy reader*. New York: Harper & Row, 1976.

Masserman, J. *Current psychiatric therapies*. New York: Grune & Stratton, 1975.

Moravec, M. Letters to the science editor. *Saturday Review*, May 1, 1965, 64.

Patterson, C. Counseling as a relationship. In A. Bassin, T. Bratter, and R. Rachin (Eds.), *The reality therapy reader*. New York: Harper & Row, 1976.

Poppen, W., and Welch, R. Work with adolescent girls. In A. Bassin, T. Bratter, and R. Rachin (Eds.), *The reality therapy reader*. New York: Harper & Row, 1976.

Schofield, W. The psychotherapist as friend. In A. Bassin, T. Bratter, and R. Rachin (Eds.), *The reality therapy reader*. New York: Harper & Row, 1976.

Swensen, C. The successful therapist. In A. Bassin, T. Bratter, and R. Rachin (Eds.), *The reality therapy reader*. New York: Harper & Row, 1976.

Thompson, C. *Reality therapy as a consultation method with teachers*. Paper presented at the American Personnel and Guidance Association Convention, Atlanta, March 1980.

Thompson, C., and Cates, J. Teaching discipline to students in an individualized teaching–counseling approach. *Focus on Guidance*, 1976, 9, 1–12.

Thompson, C., and Poppen, W. *Guidance activities for counselors and teachers*. Monterey, Calif.: Brooks/Cole, 1979.

Wahler, H. Letters to the science editor. *Saturday Review*, May 1, 1965, *64*.

PERSON-CENTERED COUNSELING

CARL ROGERS

Carl Rogers was born in Illinois in 1902, the fourth of six children. His early home life was marked by close family ties, a strict religious and moral atmosphere, and appreciation of the virtue of hard work. During this period, Carl had the feeling the Rogers' were different from everyone else because their family did not mix socially with other people. In fact, Carl had only two dates in all his high school years.

When Carl was 12, his parents moved to a farm to get the young family away from "the temptations" of suburban life. From raising lambs, pigs, and calves, Carl learned about matching experimental conditions with control conditions and about randomization procedures, and he acquired knowledge and respect for the methods of science. Rogers's thinking was influenced by a number of teachers, from high school through graduate school, who encouraged him to be unique and original in thought.

Rogers started college at the University of Wisconsin in the field of scientific agriculture. After two years, however, he switched to the ministerial field as a result of attending some emotionally charged religious conferences. In his junior year, he was chosen to go to China for six months for an international World Student Christian Federation conference. During this period, two important things happened that were a great influence on his life. First, at the expense of great pain and stress within his family relationships, he freed himself from the religious thinking of his parents and became an independent person, though he did not abandon religion entirely. Second, he fell in love with a girl he had known most of his life. He married her as soon as he finished college, with reluctant parental consent, so they could attend graduate school together.

Rogers chose to go to graduate school at Union Theological Seminary, a very liberal school, to prepare for religious work. While at Union, he became interested in courses and lectures on psychological and psychiatric work, taught by Goodwin Watson and Marian Kenworthy, and he began to take courses at Teachers College, Columbia University, across the street from Union. He found himself drawn into child guidance while working there under Leta Hollingsworth. He applied for a fellowship at the Institute of Child Guidance and was accepted. He was well on his way to a career in psychology.

At the end of his internship at the Institute for Child Guidance, Rogers accepted a job in Rochester, New York, at the Society for the Prevention of Cruelty to Children, even though he had not completed his doctorate. Rogers spent the next 12 years in Rochester. His son and daughter grew through infancy and childhood there. Rogers has said that his children taught him far more about the development and relationships of individuals than he ever learned professionally.

Rogers spent his first eight years in Rochester completely immersed in his work, conducting treatment interviews and trying to be effective with clients. Gradually, he began teaching in the Sociology Department at the University of Rochester. He was also involved in developing a guidance center and writing a book, *The Clinical Treatment of the Problem Child* (1939). Rogers's belief about individuals and their ability to solve their own problems given the proper climate was influenced by Otto Rank, with whose work he became acquainted while at the child guidance center.

In 1940, Rogers accepted a full professorship at the Ohio State University. There he began to realize that he had developed a distinctive viewpoint, and so he wrote the then-controversial book *Counseling and Psychotherapy* in 1942. In this new book, Rogers proposed a counseling relationship based on the warmth and responsiveness of the therapist. Rogers believed that, with such a relationship, clients would feel free to express their feelings and thoughts. This was a radical change in the field of psychotherapy, which had been dominated by psychoanalysis and directive counseling. In fact, Rogers developed the first truly American system of psychotherapy. He and his students at Ohio State made detailed analyses of counseling sessions and began to publish cases utilizing what Rogers called client-centered therapy. The theory developed as Rogers and his colleagues began testing the hypotheses formed from their case studies.

In 1945, Rogers moved on to the University of Chicago, where he organized the counseling center and spent the next 12 years doing research. It was while he was associated with the University of Chicago that he wrote his famous *Client-Centered Therapy*, published in 1951. Rogers describes his years at Chicago as very satisfying, but when an opportunity at the University of Wisconsin became available, he accepted; he saw himself as essentially a frontiersman.

At the University of Wisconsin, he was able to work in both the departments of psychology and psychiatry. This was especially pleasing because he had long wanted to work with psychotic individuals who had been hospitalized.

Rogers left the University of Wisconsin in 1966, moving to the Western Behavioral Science Institute in La Jolla, California. In 1968, he and several colleagues formed the Center for Studies of the Person, also in La Jolla. Through the 1970s and into the 1980s, Rogers has spent most of his time working with and writing about the use of person-centered therapy with groups. As we explained in Chapter 2, Rogers now prefers the term *person-centered* to *client-centered* in writing about his approach.

THE NATURE OF PEOPLE

Carl Rogers and his person-centered school of thought view people as rational, socialized, forward-moving, and realistic beings. Negative, antisocial emotions do exist, but they are only a result of frustrated basic impulses, an idea that is related to Maslow's hierarchy of needs. For instance, extreme aggressive action toward other people would result from failure to meet needs of love and belonging. Once people are free from their defensive behavior, their reactions are positive and progressive.

People possess the capacity to experience—that is, to express rather than repress—their own maladjustment to life and to move toward a more adjusted state of mind. Rogers believes that, in moving toward psychological adjustment, people are moving toward self-actualization. Because people possess the capacity to regulate and control their own behavior, the counseling relationship is merely a means of tapping personal resources and developing human potential. It is believed that people will learn from their external therapy experience how to internalize and provide their own form of psychotherapy.

In summary, a person-centered counselor believes that people:

have worth and dignity in their own right and therefore deserve respect;

have the capacity and right to self-direction and, when given the opportunity, will make wise judgments;

can select their own values if allowed to do so;

can learn to make constructive use of responsibility;

have the capacity to deal with their own feelings, thoughts, and behavior; and

have the potential for constructive change and personal development toward a full and satisfying life.

THEORY OF COUNSELING

Person-centered therapy was first called *nondirective therapy* because of the therapist's encouraging and listening role. Later, the term *client-centered* was adopted because of the complete responsibility that is given to clients for their own growth. Only recently has the name *person-centered* been used in hopes of further humanizing the counseling process.

Reflecting Rogers's view of human nature, if a warm and accepting climate can be created in the counseling interviews, people will trust the counselor enough to risk sharing their ideas about their lives and the problems they face. During this sharing with a nonjudgmental counselor, people will feel free to explore their feelings, thoughts, and behaviors as these relate to their personal growth, development, and adjustment. Such explorations should, in turn, lead to more effective decision making and productive behavior by the client. Rogers (1951) writes that the counselor operates from the point of view that people have the capacity to work effectively with all aspects of their lives that come into conscious awareness. Expansion of this conscious awareness occurs when the counseling climate meets Rogers's standards and when clients realize that the counselor accepts them as people competent to direct their own lives.

Person-centered counseling deals primarily with the organization and functioning of self. The counselor becomes an objective, unemotional "mirror," which reflects the inner world of the person with warmth, acceptance, and trust. This mirroring allows people to judge their thoughts and feelings and to begin to explore their effects on behavior. Thus, people are enabled to reorganize their thoughts, feelings, and behaviors so that they function in a more integrated fashion.

The Rogerian model for helping, as modified by Carkhuff (1973), involves three general stages through which the client proceeds. In the first phase, self-exploration, people are encouraged to examine exactly where they are in their lives. This includes a type of searching of self in which people question themselves concerning their status at the moment—in the present. In the second phase, people begin to understand the relationship between where they are in life and where they would like to be. In other words, they move from a type of discovery in self-exploration to an understanding. The third area involves action. In this context action is goal directed; people engage in some program or plan in order to reach the point where they want to be. The only exception to the logical order of the three areas might be in helping a learning-disabled child, for whom movement through the process might be more meaningful if action were followed by understanding and then self-exploration. Learning-disabled students find it easier to move from the concrete to the abstract in problem solving, and in Rogers's system self-exploration is the most abstract area of the process.

Client-centered or person-centered counseling can be thought of in two dimensions: responsive/facilitative, which includes attending, observing, and listening; and initiative, which includes initiating, personalizing, and responding. The counselor must remain in control of the counseling process, becoming an "expert" in creating the nonthreatening environment that is vital to the counseling process. Empathy, respect, warmth, concreteness, genuineness, and self-disclosure all facilitate change in client behavior. The process works best when the counselor lets the client direct the interview—a first step in teaching clients how to direct their lives. Clients are viewed as experts whose task is to teach the counselor about their life situation. They thereby learn more about themselves as teaching generally helps the teacher to learn. This may be the main reason client-centered therapy is helpful to many people.

The main goal of client-centered therapy is to assist people in becoming more autonomous, spontaneous, and confident (Rogers, 1969). As people move to an awareness of what is going on inside themselves, they can cease fearing and defending their inner feelings. They learn to accept their own values and trust their own judgment rather than live by the values of others. Expectations of client-centered therapy include: discussion of plans, behavioral steps to be taken, and the outcome of the steps; a change from immature behavior to mature behavior; a decrease in current defensive behaviors; an increased tolerance for frustration; and improved functioning in life tasks (Poppen & Thompson, 1974, p. 44).

The ultimate goal of client-centered therapy is to produce fully functioning people who have learned to be free. According to Rogers, learning to be free is the essential goal of education "if the civilized culture is to survive and if individuals in the culture are to be worth saving" (1969, p. 12). People who have learned to be free can confront life and face problems; they trust themselves to choose their own way and accept their own feelings without forcing them on others. Such individuals prize themselves and others as having dignity, worth, and value.

COUNSELING METHOD

Perhaps the vital techniques in the person-centered counselor's repertoire are really attitudes toward people: congruence (genuineness), unconditional positive regard (respect), and empathy. Congruence implies that counselors are able to maintain a sense of their self-identity and are able to convey this identity to their clients. In other words, they are not playing an artificial role. Unconditional positive regard implies that the counselor accepts clients as people who have the potential to become good, rational, and free. Because people have self-worth, dignity, and unique traits as individuals, they require individualized counseling approaches. Thus, people direct their own counseling sessions.

For the process to succeed, clients must feel they can reveal the person they are to the counselor in an air of complete acceptance. Empathy is the attitude that holds the counseling process together. By attempting to understand, the counselor is helping to convince people that they are worth hearing and understanding.

In general, the person-centered counselor refrains from giving advice or solutions, moralizing, and making judgments. Diagnosis and interpretations are considered detrimental to the counseling process. To do any of the above would defeat the plan for teaching clients how to do these things for themselves. It would also imply that the counselors know and understand their clients better than the clients do them-selves—an assumption common to many approaches but totally out of line with Rogers's view. Instead, person-centered counselors will use the methods of (1) active and passive listening, (2) reflection of thoughts and feelings, (3) clarification, (4) summarization, (5) confrontation of contradictions, and (6) general or open leads that help client self-explo-ration (Poppen & Thompson, 1974, p. 43).

The major technique for person-centered counseling is active lis-tening, which lets your client know that you are hearing and under-standing correctly all that is being said to you. As we saw in Chapter 2, active listening is especially important for counseling children. If the counselor fails to get the correct message, the child attempts to reteach it to the counselor. Once counselor and child are in agreement that the counselor has the story straight and that the counseling service will be helpful, counseling can continue.

Carkhuff (1973, 1981) has systematized Rogers's concept of active listening (reflection) into a highly understandable and usable model (see Table 4-1). He believes that counselors typically respond on any one of five levels relating to the three phases of counseling: (I) where you are in your life; (II) where you would like to be; and (III) planning how to get from phase I to phase II. He classifies levels 1 and 2 as harmful, level

TABLE 4-1 Five levels of communication[a]

Levels	Phase I	Phase II	Phase III
	Thoughts and feelings about where you are now	*Thoughts and feelings about where you would like to be*	*Plans for getting from where you are to where you would like to be*
1			
2			X
3	X		
4	X	X	
5	X	X	X

[a]The X's indicate which phase of counseling is treated by each of the five levels of com-munication.

3 as break-even, and levels 4 and 5 as helpful. It is often assumed that the worst thing that can happen in counseling is that clients will show no change. However, this is not true. If clients receive a preponderance of level 1 and 2 responses, they could get worse as the result of counseling.

Level 1 and 2 responses in Carkhuff's model also show up in Gordon's (1974) "dirty dozen" list of responses that tend to close or inhibit further communication:

1. Ordering; directing
2. Warning; threatening; stating consequences
3. Moralizing; shoulds, oughts
4. Advising; giving suggestions and solutions
5. Messages of logic; counterarguments
6. Judging; criticizing
7. Praising; buttering up
8. Name calling; ridiculing
9. Psychoanalyzing
10. Reassuring; giving sympathy; consoling
11. Probing: "who, what, when, where, why?"
12. Humor; distracting; withdrawing

Level 1 responses tend to deny a person's feeling and thinking with statements such as:

1. "Oh don't worry about that. Things will work out."
2. "If you think you have a problem, listen to this."
3. "You must have done something to make Mrs. Jones treat you that way."

As such, level 1 responses do not help with any of the three counseling phases in Table 4-1.

Level 2 responses are messages of advice and solutions to problems. These responses are relevant in phase III, but they are not considered helpful because they do not allow the counselor and client to fully explore the problem situation. Clients are deprived of the opportunity of working out their own solutions to their problems because the active listening process is totally ignored. Level 2 responses keep clients dependent on the authority of the counselor and prevent clients from learning how to counsel themselves. Typical level 2 responses include:

1. "You need to study harder."
2. "You should eat better."
3. "You should be more assertive."
4. "Why don't you make more friends?"
5. "How would you like to have your brother treat you the way you treat him?"

Even though the advice may be excellent, the client—child or adult—may not have the skill to do what you suggest. Moreover, rebellious children may work especially hard to show that your advice is ineffective, receiving some satisfaction from knowing that an "expert" counselor is no more successful than they in trying to solve day-to-day problems.

Level 3 responses are classified as break-even points in the counseling process—neither harmful nor helpful. However, these responses provide bridges to further conversation and exploration in the counseling process; they are the door-openers and invitations to discuss concerns in more depth.

Level 3 responses reflect what the client is thinking and feeling about the present status of the problem—for example: You are feeling *discouraged* because *you haven't been able to make good grades in math*. Such responses are checkpoints for counselors in determining if they are hearing and understanding the client's problem. Either the client acknowledges that the counselor has understood the message correctly, or another attempt is made to relate the concern to the counselor. At this point in counseling, clients are teaching the counselor about their problem and are thereby learning more about their problem themselves.

According to Carkhuff's model, an aid to counselors in making level 3 responses is to ask themselves if the client is expressing pain or pleasure. The next task is to find the correct feeling word describing the pain or pleasure. Below are listed seven feeling words. To help build your counseling vocabulary in order to be able to describe feelings as precisely as possible, add three synonyms of your own under each word. In reflecting the client's feeling and thoughts, be sure to avoid parroting the exact words of the client. It is often helpful to call time out for a summary and say to your client, "Let's see if I understand what you have told me up to now."

strong	happy	sad	angry	scared	confused	weak

Level 4 responses reflect an understanding of phases I and II in Carkhuff's model. For example: You are feeling *discouraged* because *you haven't been able to make good grades in math*, and you want *to find a way to do better*. It is best to rephrase the responses in your own words as you summarize the client's thoughts and feelings.

Level 5 responses are appropriate when the client agrees that the counselor understands the problem or concern. Now it is time to assist the client in developing a plan of action. We find that reality therapy provides a good plan—after client-centered counseling has been employed to help the client relate the concern to the counselor. Together, reality therapy and client-centered counseling provide a most helpful method to the counselor. An example of a level 5 response would be:

> Client-centered therapy: You feel _____because _____, and you want _____.
> Reality therapy: Let's look at what you have been doing to solve your problem.
> You feel *discouraged* because you *haven't been able to make good grades in math*, and you want to *find a way to do better*. Let's look at what you have been trying to do *to make good grades in math*.

We do not want to imply that the entire counseling interview can be accomplished in one response. Several sessions of level 3 and 4 responses may be necessary before the problem is defined well enough for solving.

Since the success of the client-centered approach to therapy is so dependent upon the relationship between therapist and client, many therapists are likely to find themselves unsuccessful in using the approach with young children. Not every adult is capable of establishing true empathy with children or even of liking children. Children, to a greater degree than adults, are sensitive to the real feelings and attitudes of others. They intuitively trust and open up to those who like and understand them. Phony expressions of understanding will not fool a child for very long. An example of a person-centered, relationship counseling method is reported in Virginia Axline's (1964) *Dibs: In Search of Self*.

In order to help children effectively, the counselor must provide a warm, caring environment in which children may explore their emotions and verbally act out the consequences of alternative means of expressing these emotions. Together, counselor and child, or the child alone if he or she possesses sufficient maturity, can evaluate the alternatives and select the one that is most likely to be appropriate and productive.

In using the client-centered approach with young children, the counselor may be required to assume a somewhat more active role than in working with adults. Still, it is assumed that even young children can distinguish between positive and negative behaviors and that they are able to choose the positive once the counselor has established an open dialogue in which feelings and emotions can be aired and conflicts resolved.

It is important to stress once again that the counselor should employ active listening when dealing with children and that the child be given the opportunity to release feelings without feeling threatened by the counselor. Listening carefully and observing the child will increase the counselor's ability to understand what the child is trying to communicate. Both verbal and nonverbal messages are conveyed by all clients, and the counselor needs to be alert to them. With children, whose verbal skills may be relatively limited, nonverbal messages may be the most important clue to what the child is really feeling and trying to communicate.

CASE STUDY[1]

Identification of the problem

Ginger Wood, an 11-year-old girl in the sixth grade at Hill Middle School, was referred to the school counselor because her grades had recently fallen and she seemed depressed.

Individual and background information

Academic.   School records show that Ginger is an "A" student and was chosen to be in an advanced group in third grade. On her last report card, however, her grades dropped to a "C" average.

Family.   Ginger is the older of two children, having a younger brother who is 9. Her mother is an elementary school teacher, and her father is a systems analyst. Her parents have recently separated.

Social.   Ginger is approximately 30 pounds overweight. She has a friendly personality, and teacher reports do not show that she has a problem in relating to her peers.

Counseling method

The counselor chose to use Rogers's (1965) client-centered counseling method. The counselor believes that Ginger's problem originates from emotional blocks. Her goal is to establish a warm relationship with Ginger and aid her in clarifying her thoughts and feelings so she might be better able to solve her problems.

The five basic techniques used by the counselor in this method are:

1. Unconditional positive regard
2. Active listening
3. Reflection
4. Clarification
5. Summarization

Transcript

Counselor (Co): Hi, Ginger, I'm Susan Morgan. Your teacher,
    Ms. Lowe, told me that you might come to talk to me.
Ginger: Yeah, I decided to.

---

[1] The case of Ginger was written by Anne Harvey, a student in Counseling Theories and Techniques at the University of Tennessee in 1980.

Co: Do you know what a counselor's job is?

Ginger: Yeah, Ms. Lowe told me that you help people with their problems.

Co: That's right. I try to teach people how to solve their own problems. Do you have something on your mind that you'd like to talk about?

Ginger: Well, I haven't been doing so well in school lately.

Co: Yes, Ms. Lowe said you are normally an "A" student.

Ginger: I used to be, but not now. I made "C's" on my last report card. My mom was really upset with me; she yelled at me and then grounded me.

Co: It sounds like she was angry with you because your grades went down.

Ginger: Well, not so much angry as unhappy. She looked like she was about to cry.

Co: So she was disappointed that you weren't doing as well in school as you usually do, and this made you feel bad, too.

Ginger: I guess so; she probably blamed herself some, too, and that could have made her feel worse.

Co: You mean that she felt responsible for your grades going down.

Ginger: Well, maybe. Things aren't going so well at home. Mom and Dad aren't living together right now, and they may get a divorce. She hasn't had a lot of time for us lately. I guess she's really been worried.

Co: The problem at home has made it tougher for you to do well at school because you are worried about what's happening.

Ginger: Yeah. I think about it a lot. It's harder to study when I'm worrying about it.

Co: It would be for me, too. This must be a very hard situation for you to go through.

Ginger: It sure is; everybody's mad. My little brother doesn't understand what's going on, and he cries a lot. Mom does, too.

Co: So the whole family is upset.

Ginger: Well, I guess so. My dad doesn't seem to be, but why should he be? It's all his fault. He's getting what he wants.

Co: I guess he's the one who wants the divorce. It doesn't seem fair to the rest of you.

Ginger: Yeah. He's got a girlfriend. My mom didn't even know anything about her till Daddy said he was leaving. I hate him! (Starts to cry.) And that makes me feel even worse cause I know I shouldn't hate my father. I wish he were dead!

Co: (Handing her a tissue) So you're all torn up between the way you feel and the way you think you should feel.

Ginger: Yeah. It's so hard to sort everything out. Do you think that makes me a bad person for me to hate my father?

Co: I think you are a good person who doesn't know what to do with all of her feelings right now. I'm wondering if you think you are a bad person.

Ginger: No, I guess not. I mean, I think most of my friends would feel about the same way I do if they were in my shoes.

Co: Sure, it's a tough thing to handle.

Ginger: And I guess they're not all bad people. Thanks, Ms. Morgan. I'm glad we talked about it. I feel a little better now.

Co: I'm glad, Ginger. It sounds like you're beginning to work out your problems. Would you like to make another appointment to talk with me?

Ginger: OK. Could I come back during free time next week?

Co: That will be fine. You can see me any day when you want to talk.

Ginger: Bye, Ms. Morgan, and thanks.

Co: You're welcome.

SUMMARY: RESEARCH AND REACTIONS

Numerous studies have been conducted on person-centered therapy that lend support to it. One of the most productive contributions to validating the approach was the process scale developed by Rogers and Rablen (1958), which provided seven progress stages descriptive of the therapy process. Studies using the process scale showed that significant behavior variations were discernible over the course of therapy. Walker, Rablen, and Rogers (1960) and Tomlinson and Hart (1962) showed that counseling cases prejudged as more successful were highly distinguishable when ratings were made on the process scale; this would indicate a positive correlation between therapist ratings and the process scale.

Rogers (1967b), by listening to numerous recordings of successful client-centered cases, also noted a consistent pattern of change in clients: the most successful clients moved from a rather rigid and impersonal type of functioning to a level of functioning marked by change and acceptance of personal feelings.

Rogers (1967a) also tested his methods in settings other than individual psychotherapy by becoming involved in the Project for Educational Innovation. In that situation, Rogers applied client-centered principles in an educational institution that was seeking positive and productive change. Plans were devised for small groups (including parents, faculty, students, and administrators) to meet on an intensive basis. The results showed:

1. There was a loosening of the categories of student, faculty, and administrator that enhanced communication.
2. There was more student participation in decision making at all levels and more student-centered teaching.
3. There was more experimentation and innovation.

In addition to Rogers, many other researchers have investigated client-centered therapy. Cartwright (1957) provides an annotated bibliography of 122 studies that investigated both the process and the outcome of client-centered therapy. Shlien and Zimring (1970) published a similar overview of person-centered research supporting Rogers's theory. A few representative studies are mentioned below.

Raskin (1952) and Rosenman (1955) produced evidence that the client shifts his emphasis from others as a source of evaluation to himself during the course of client-centered therapy. Positive evaluation of self increases, and evaluation of others decreases.

Bergman (1951) also provided support for the client-centered approach when he found that structuring and interpretation by the counselor were significantly followed by an abandonment of self-exploration by the client, and reflection by the counselor was significantly followed by continued client self-exploration.

Gallagher (1953b) presented evidence that for 42 clients of client-centered therapy, anxiety, as measured on four different anxiety scales, decreased significantly. He also found that significant improvement occurred as measured on four scales from the Minnesota Multiphasic Personality Inventory (MMPI).

Brown (1957) used a different technique, the Q-sort, to rank client/counselor pairs on their perceptions of the actual therapeutic relationship and the ideal relationship. High agreement was found between the client and counselor for the ideal relationship, but only moderate similarity was found in the actual relationship. The outcome of counseling highly correlated with the ability of the client and therapist to perceive their relationship in similar terms.

Rogers and Dymond (1954) also investigated why a case might fail and found that success is less likely if therapy lasts a "short" time rather than a "long" time. Furthermore, the more deeply disturbed the client is, the less likely it is that therapy will be successful.

Aaronson (1953) wanted to investigate how differences in counselor personality might affect the therapeutic relationship. Four counselors rated themselves and were rated by peers on 24 personality variables. The results indicated that, while counselors did differ on some personality variables, they did not differ on the measures of understanding of self or understanding of the client. No significant differences in client outcome were found, indicating that the counselor's understanding of him- or herself and the client is the key to client-centered therapy.

Baehr (1954) studied 66 hospitalized veterans to see if the type of client-centered therapy they received made any difference. One group of veterans received individual therapy, one group received group therapy, and one group received both individual and group therapy. Although all three groups showed improvement, the combined group (both individual and group) showed the most change.

Halkides (1958) studied the relationship between the therapist's characteristics of congruence, positive regard, and empathy to the success of therapy. Judges rated ten cases found to be successful and ten found to be unsuccessful. Halkides found that the presence of the three therapist characteristics was significantly associated with success in therapy.

Perhaps the most conclusive support for Rogers's method rests with the study done comparing psychotics (schizophrenics), neurotics, and normals (Rogers, 1967b). Rogers compared these three groups to see how effective client-centered therapy would be with each. Although the findings were complex, some are summarized here:

1. Empathic understanding of therapists and the extent to which they were perceived as genuine by schizophrenics were associated with involvement and constructive personality changes in clients.
2. Both psychotics and normals had more realistic perceptions of the therapeutic relationship than the therapist did.
3. The same qualities in the counseling relationship are facilitative for the schizophrenic as for the neurotic.
4. It is possible to identify the qualities of the client in-therapy behavior that indicate change is in progress.
5. The process of change involves a chain of events. The quality of the therapeutic relationship facilitates improved inner integration in the client, which in turn facilitates a reduction in pathological behavior, which facilitates an improvement in social adjustment.
6. Early assessment of the relationship qualities provides a good indicator of whether or not constructive change will result.

Many other studies are available that support client-centered therapy; the ones presented here are a representative sample. Conclusions drawn from these studies would be:

1. Consistent patterns of change are discernible over the course of therapy—successful clients move from rigid to more flexible functioning.
2. Client-centered therapy can be helpful in educational settings.
3. Clients increase their positive evaluation of self as a result of therapy.
4. Improved versus nonimproved clients show more relief from symptoms and more insight into self.
5. Reflection of feelings leads to continued client self-exploration.
6. Significant decrements in anxiety as well as increased signs of adjustment occur as a result of successful therapy.
7. The success of therapy rests partially with the ability of the client and therapist to perceive their relationship in similar terms.
8. A case is less likely to be successful if the client is seen for a short amount of time.

9. Successful therapists have an ability to understand themselves as well as the client.
10. A combination of group and individual counseling is most effective.
11. It is unnecessary to develop different theories and procedures for schizophrenic clients. They were found to respond constructively to client-centered therapy.

More recently, studies have been conducted on the relationship of empathy to social cognitive development. Shantz (1975) summarized a variety of these studies on children and concluded that children have empathy for situations and people who are most similar to them. In other words, they show empathy for other children more readily than they do for adults—a finding that comes as no surprise to parents. Shantz did find that reliable accuracy in judging emotions does not usually appear until middle childhood. These are findings the person-centered counselor must consider when using an empathy-based counseling method with children.

Criticisms of person-centered counseling center around the idea that it is too abstract both for young children and for adults who have not attained the ability to do formal thinking. The perfect clients for person-centered counseling have often been described as having the Yavis syndrome; that is, they are young, attractive, verbal, intelligent, and sensitive. Such people may not need much counseling. Who, then, we might ask, will counsel the tough, nonverbal children? Others criticize the person-centered approach as being one that becomes "bogged down" in feelings and does not move quickly enough into planned behavioral change. Another critical point directed to Rogers's system concerns his distaste for diagnostic tools and tests; critics argue that valuable data may be lost to counselors who do not use diagnostic methods. Hand in hand with Rogers's refusal to use diagnostic tests is his equally strong aversion to prognostication and prescription. Critics of person-centered counseling hold that the counselors are the experts who can dispense valuable advice as well as predict future behavioral patterns and personality development in their clients.

In rebuttal, Rogers (1977), writing about himself, points out how person-centered counseling relates to a wide variety of individual and group concerns spanning diverse populations, including the areas of family counseling, couple relationships, education, politics, government, and business administration.

REFERENCES

Aaronson, M. A study of relationship between certain counselor and client characteristics in client-centered therapy. In W. U. Snyder (Ed.), *Group report of a program of research in psychotherapy*. University Park, Pa.: Pennsylvania

State University, 1953. Reprinted in *Journal of Counseling Psychology*, 1957, *4*, 95.

Axline, V. M. *Dibs: In search of self*. Boston: Houghton Mifflin, 1964.

Baehr, G. D. The comparative effectiveness of individual psychotherapy, group psychotherapy, and a combination of these methods. *Journal of Consulting Psychology*, 1954, *18*, 179–183.

Bergman, D. V. Counseling methods and client responses. *Journal of Consulting Psychology*, 1951, *15*, 216–224.

Brown, O. H. *An investigation of the therapeutic relationship in client-centered therapy*. Unpublished doctoral dissertation, University of Chicago, 1954. Reprinted in *Journal of Counseling Psychology*, 1957, *4*, 93.

Carkhuff, R. *Human achievement, educational achievement, career achievement: Essential ingredients of elementary school guidance*. Paper presented at the Second Annual National Elementary School Guidance Conference, Louisville, Kentucky, March 30, 1973.

Carkhuff, R. *Creating and researching community based helping programs*. Paper presented at the American Personnel and Guidance Association Convention, St. Louis, Missouri, April 14, 1981.

Cartwright, D. Annotated bibliography of research and theory construction in client-centered therapy. *Journal of Counseling Psychology*, 1957, *4*, 82–100.

Gallagher, J. J. MMPI changes concomitant with client-centered therapy. *Journal of Consulting Psychology*, 1953, *17*, 334–338. (a)

Gallagher, J. J. Manifest anxiety changes concomitant with client-centered therapy. *Journal of Consulting Psychology*, 1953, *17*, 443–446. (b)

Gordon, T. *Teacher effectiveness training*. New York: Wyden, 1974.

Halkides, G. *An experimental study of four conditions necessary for therapeutic change*. Unpublished doctoral dissertation, University of Chicago, 1958.

Patterson, C. H. *Theories of counseling and psychotherapy*. New York: Harper & Row, 1966.

Poppen, W. A., and Thompson, C. L. *School counseling: Theories and concepts*. Lincoln, Nebr.: Professional Educators Publications, 1974.

Raskin, N. J. An objective study of the locus-of-evaluation factor in psychotherapy. In W. Wolff and J. A. Precker (Eds.), *Success in psychotherapy*. New York: Grune & Stratton, 1952. Reprinted in *Journal of Counseling Psychology*, 1957, *4*, 85.

Rogers, C. R. *The clinical treatment of the problem child*. Boston: Houghton-Mifflin, 1939.

Rogers, C. R. *Counseling and Psychotherapy*. Boston: Houghton-Mifflin, 1942.

Rogers, C. R. *Client-centered therapy*. Boston: Houghton-Mifflin, 1951.

Rogers, C. R. *Client-centered therapy: Its current practice, implications, and theory*. Boston: Houghton Mifflin, 1965.

Rogers, C. R. A plan for self-directed change in an educational system. *Educational Leadership*, 1967, *24*, 717–731. (a)

Rogers, C. R. *The therapeutic relationship and its impact: A study of psychotherapy with schizophrenics*. Madison: University of Wisconsin Press, 1967. (b)

Rogers, C. R. *Freedom to learn*. Columbus, Ohio: Charles E. Merrill, 1969.

Rogers, C. R. *Carl Rogers on personal power: Inner strength and its revolutionary impact*. New York: Delacorte, 1977.

Rogers, C. R., and Dymond, R. F. *Psychotherapy and personality change*. Chicago: University of Chicago Press, 1954.

Rogers, C. R., and Rablen, R. A. A scale of process in psychotherapy. Unpublished manuscript, University of Wisconsin, 1958. Reprinted in R. Corsini (Ed.), *Current Psychotherapies*. Itasca, Ill.: F. E. Peacock, 1979.

Rogers, C. R., and Stevens, B. *Person to person: The problem of being human*. New York: Pocket Books, 1971.

Rosenman, S. Changes in the representation of self, others, and interrelationships in client-centered therapy. *Journal of Counseling Psychology*, 1955, *2*, 271–277.

Shantz, C. U. Empathy in relation to social cognitive development. *The Counseling Psychologist*, 1975, *5*, 18–21.

Shlien, J., and Zimring, F. Research directives and methods in client centered therapy. In J. T. Hart and T. M. Tomlinson (Eds.), *New directions in client-centered therapy*. Boston: Houghton Mifflin, 1970.

Tomlinson, T. M., and Hart, J. T. A validation study of the process scale. *Journal of Consulting Psychology*, 1962, *26*, 74–78.

Walker, A., Rablen, R., and Rogers, C. Development of a scale to measure process changes in psychotherapy. *Journal of Clinical Psychology*, 1960, *16*, 79–85.

5

GESTALT THERAPY

FRITZ PERLS

Fritz Perls's estranged wife, Laura, once referred to him as half prophet and half bum; Perls considered this an accurate description. In his autobiography (Perls, 1971), *In and Out the Garbage Pail*, he wrote that, at the age of 75, he liked his reputation as being both a dirty old man and a guru. Unfortunately, he continued, the first reputation was on the wane and the second ascending.

Born in a Jewish ghetto on the outskirts of Berlin on July 8, 1893, Friedrich Solomon Perls was the third child of Amelia Rund and Nathan Perls. He later anglicized his first name to Frederick but is remembered more commonly as Fritz.

Perls disliked his eldest sister, Else. He thought of her as a clinger and was uncomfortable in her presence. Else also had severe eye trouble, and Perls disliked the thought that he might have to take care of her someday. He did not mourn much when he heard of her death in a concentration camp. Shepard (1975) speculates that Perls resented the extra attention and favor that his mother offered Else because of her partial blindness. He did seem to enjoy and was close to his second sister, Grete.

After a difficult first few weeks of life, Perls seems to have led a happy and healthy life for his first nine years. Around the age of 10, Perls became rebellious. His parents were having bitter fights, and his father was away from home quite often. He even began to doubt his paternity and suspected that his actual father was a much respected uncle; this remained an open question for Fritz until his death. His marriage was not much happier than his childhood, although he and his wife, Laura, remained married and worked together in the development of Gestalt therapy. Perls came to realize that the roles of husband and father gave him little satisfaction.

After some hard times in Europe, Perls found success as a training analyst in Johannesburg, South Africa. While there, he founded the South Africa Institute for Psychoanalysis. He learned to fly and got his pilot's license. During this time, in 1936, he flew to Czechoslovakia to deliver a paper to the Psychoanalytic Congress. He intended to meet with his hero, Freud, but he was given a cool four-minute audience while standing in Freud's doorway. Another disappointment was the icy reception his paper received from most of the other analysts attending the Congress. From this point on, for 30 years Perls challenged the assumptions and directions of Freud and the psychoanalysts. In his final years, many people began to listen. Perls thought he had four main unfinished situations in his life: not being able to sing well, never having made a parachute jump, never having tried skin diving, and never having the opportunity to show Freud the mistakes he made.

Perls spent 12 years in South Africa, during which time he formulated all the basic ideas that underlined what he would later call Gestalt therapy. At the age of 53, he moved his family to New York, where the "formal birth" of Gestalt therapy took place. Several people were involved with this birth, and a great debate developed among them to determine what to call the new theory. Perls held out for *Gestalt*. The new therapy took its name from a German term. *Gestalt* cannot be translated exactly into English, but the meaning of the concept can be grasped.

> [Gestalt is] a form, a configuration or a totality that has, as a unified whole, properties which cannot be derived by summation from the parts and their relationships. It may refer to physical structures, to physiological and psychological functions, or to symbolic units. (English & English, 1958, p. 225)

In late 1951, Perls's book *Gestalt Therapy* was first published. Perls is listed as author, although Ralph Hefferline wrote nearly all of the first half of the book and Paul Goodman the second. At first, the new therapy had almost no impact. Perls began traveling to cities like Cleveland, Detroit, Toronto, and Miami to run groups for professionals and lay people interested in the new idea. As he traveled about the country, he discovered that he was received far better on the road than he was at home in New York. At the end of ten years in New York, Fritz decided to leave that city, and his wife, for the warmth of Miami. Laura Perls's interpretation of why Fritz left was because he was not the leading psychotherapist, nor even the leading Gestaltist, in New York.

Miami was very important to Fritz because there he met "the most significant woman in my life," Marty Fromm. In Florida he also found LSD and became involved in the drug subculture. From Florida he moved to California, eventually Big Sur, where he became widely known. At the Esalen Institute, he had to compete with people like Virginia Satir, Bernard Gunther, and Will Schutz. His opinion of techniques used by Gunther and Schutz was that they used other people's ideas and offered "instant joy." Perls was against quick cures and respected only originality, so he established the Gestalt Institute of Canada at Cowichan.

Nine months after the center in Canada was begun, Fritz Perls died. He died as he had lived. Two biopsies the doctors took during a very long operation both came back as negative, although an autopsy disclosed that he did have a most advanced cancer of the pancreas. On the last evening of his life, March 14, 1970, Perls was attempting to get out of bed against the wishes of his nurse. "Don't tell me what to do," he said to her, fell back, and died.

Perls viewed the state of Gestalt theory as being in progress at the time of his death. Perls viewed theory development, like human development, as a process of becoming. He was not one to close the book on his theory and treat it as gospel. Rather, Perls revised the theory to fit his observations of human behavior.

THE NATURE OF PEOPLE

According to Gestalt theory, the most important area of concern is the thoughts and feelings people are experiencing at the moment. Normal and healthy behavior occurs when people act and react as total organisms. Many people tend to fragment their lives, distributing their concentration and attention among several variables and events at one time. The results of such fragmentation can be seen in an ineffective living style, with outcomes ranging from low productivity to serious accidents. The Gestalt view of human nature is positive in that people are viewed as capable of becoming self-regulating beings who can achieve a sense of unity and integration in their lives.

Perls (1969) referred to the person as a total organism—not just the brain. His saying that people would be better off losing their minds and coming to their senses meant that our bodies and feelings are better indicators of the truth than our words, which we use to hide ourselves from the truth. Body signs such as headaches, rashes, neck strain, and stomach pains may indicate that we need to change our behavior. Perls believed that awareness alone can be curative. With full awareness, a state of organismic self-regulation develops, and the total person takes control.

Mentally healthy people are viewed as people who can maintain their awareness without being distracted by the various environmental stimuli that constantly vie for our attention. Such people can fully and clearly experience their own needs and the environmental alternatives for meeting these needs. Healthy people still experience their share of inner conflicts and frustrations, but, having achieved increased levels of concentration and awareness, they are able to solve their problems without complicating them with fantasy elaborations. Conflicts with others are likewise resolved when it is possible and dismissed when it is not. People ,with high levels of awareness of their needs and their environment know which problems and conflicts are solvable and which are not. The key to successful adjustment in Perls's theory is the development of personal responsibility—responsibility for one's life and response to one's environment. Much of the Perls doctrine is summarized in his famous Gestalt Prayer (Perls, 1969, p. 4):

> I do my thing and you do your thing.
> I am not in this world to live up to your expectations,
> And you are not in this world to live up to mine.
> You are you and I am I
> And if by chance we find each other, it's beautiful.
> If not, it can't be helped.

The healthy person focuses sharply on one need (the figure) at a time while relegating other needs to the background. When the need is met—or the Gestalt is closed or completed—it is relegated to the background, and a new need comes into focus (becomes the figure). The smoothly functioning figure/ground relationship characterizes the healthy personality. The dominant need of the organism at any time becomes the foreground figure, and the other needs recede, at least temporarily, into the background. The foreground is the need that presses most sharply for satisfaction, whether it is the need to preserve life or is related to less physically or psychologically vital areas. For individuals to be able to satisfy their needs and close the Gestalt in order to move on to other things, they must be able to determine what they need, and they must know how to manipulate themselves and their environment; even the purely physiological needs can be satisfied only through the interaction of the organism and the environment (Perls, 1976).

Perls defined neurotic people as those who try to attend to too many needs at one time with the result being failure to satisfy any one need fully. Neurotic people also use their potential to manipulate others to do for them what they have not done for themselves. Rather than running their own lives, they turn them over to those who will take care of their needs. In summary, people cause themselves additional problems by not handling their lives appropriately in the following six categories.

1. Lacking contact with the environment. People may become so rigid that they cut themselves off from others or from resources in the environment.
2. Confluence. People may incorporate too much of themselves into others or incorporate so much of the environment into themselves

that they lose touch with where they are. Then the environment takes control.

3. Unfinished business. People may have unfulfilled needs, unexpressed feelings, or some uncompleted situations that clamor for their attention. (This may manifest itself in dreams.)

4. Fragmentation. People may try to discover or deny a need such as aggression. The inability to find and obtain those things one needs may be the result of fragmenting one's life.

5. Topdog/underdog. People may experience a split in their personalities between what they think they "should" do (topdog) and what they "want" to do (underdog) (see Passons, 1975).

6. Polarities (dichotomies). People tend to flounder at times between existing, natural dichotomies in their lives such as: body/mind, self/external world, emotional/real, infantile/mature, biological/cultural, poetry/prose, spontaneous/deliberate, personal/social, love/aggression, and unconscious/conscious (Sahakian, 1969). Much of everyday living seems to be involved in resolving conflicts posed by these competing polarities. Five types have been identified by Assagioli (1965):

   a. Physical polarities—masculinity/femininity and parasympathetic/sympathetic nervous system
   b. Emotional polarities—pleasure/pain, excitement/depression, love/hate
   c. Mental polarities—parent/child, eros (feeling)/logos (reason), topdog/underdog
   d. Spiritual polarities—intellectual doubt/dogmatism
   e. Interindividual polarities—man/woman, black/white, Christian/Jew

THEORY OF COUNSELING

Any adaption of Perls's system to counseling children would incorporate the five layers of neuroses proposed by Perls (1971; see also Fagan & Shepard, 1970). These five layers were devised to picture how people fragment their lives and prevent themselves from succeeding and maturing. The five layers form a series of counseling stages or benchmarks for the counseling process; in fact, they could be considered as five steps to a better Gestalt way of life.

1. The phony layer. Many people find themselves trapped in trying to be what they are not. The phony layer is characterized by many conflicts that are never resolved.

2. The phobic layer. As people become aware of their phony games, they become aware of their fears that maintain the games. This is often a frightening experience.

3. The impasse layer. This is the layer reached when people shed the environmental support of their games and find themselves not knowing a better way to cope with their fears and dislikes. People often get stuck here and refuse to move on.
4. The implosive layer. People become aware of how they limit themselves, and they begin to experiment with new behaviors.
5. The explosive layer. If experiments with new behaviors are successful, people are able to reach the explosive layer, where they find much unused energy that had been tied up in maintaining a phony existence.

Perls believed that progress through the five layers of neuroses could best be achieved by observing how psychological defenses might be associated with muscular position or what he called body armor. He believed the body language of the client would be a better indicator of the truth than the client's words. He also believed that awareness of hidden material could be facilitated by acting out feelings. Perls asked people to project their thoughts and feelings upon empty chairs representing significant people in their lives. People were often asked to play several roles in attempting to identify who was experiencing conflict. Perls expanded on Rogers's idea of feedback as a therapeutic agent by including body posture, voice tone, eye movements, feelings, and gestures.

Gestalt therapy emphasizes direct experiences. The focus is on achieving the awareness of the here and now and frustrating the client in any attempt to break out of this awareness. As an experiential approach, Gestalt therapy is not concerned with symptoms and analysis, but rather with total existence and integration. Integration and maturation, according to Perls, are never-ending processes directly related to a person's awareness of the here and now. A "Gestalt" is formed in a person as a new need arises. If a need is satisfied, the destruction of that particular Gestalt is achieved, and new Gestalts can be formed. This is a basic concept of Gestalt therapy. Incomplete Gestalts are referred to as unfinished situations.

Perls (1969) wrote that the aim of his therapy was to help people help themselves to grow up, and mature, take charge of their lives, and become responsible for themselves. The central goal in Gestalt therapy is the deepening of awareness, which promotes a sense of living fully in the here and now. Other goals are to teach people to assume responsibility for themselves and to facilitate their achievement of personal integration. These goals are consistent with those of most counseling systems.

The aim of integration is to help people become systematic, whole persons, whose inner state and behavior match so that little energy is wasted within the system. Such integration would allow people to give their full attention and energy to meeting their needs appropriately.

The ultimate measure of success in Gestalt therapy would be the extent to which clients grow in awareness, take responsibility for their actions, and are able to move from environmental to self-support.

COUNSELING METHOD

The function of the Gestalt counselor is to facilitate the client's awareness in the now. Awareness is the capacity to focus, to attend, to be in touch with the now. The Gestalt counselor is an aggressive therapist, one who frustrates any attempt on the part of the learner to break out of the awareness of here and now. Retreats to the past and jumps into the future are either stopped or related to the immediate present.

Gestalt techniques

In order to maintain the present time orientation of the counseling interview, several language, game, and fantasy methods may be used. Helpful resources available to the counselor include books by Lederman (1969), Passons (1975), and Fagan and Shepard (1970). Some of the following techniques have been used successfully by the present authors and their students with children in the 5 to 12 age group.

"I" language.   The use of the word *I* is encouraged when the client uses a generalized *you* when talking. For example: *"You* know how it is when *you* can't get math and the teacher gets on *your* back." When *I* is substituted for *you*, the message becomes, *"I* know how it is when *I* can't get math and the teacher gets on *my* back." Such substitutions of *I* for *you* are tried on like a pair of shoes to see how they fit. They help children to take responsibility for their feelings, thoughts, and behaviors.

Substituting *won't* for *can't*.   Again, the "shoes" are tried on for comfort: "I won't pass math" rather than "I can't pass math." How much of the responsibility the child will own is the question to be answered.

Substituting *what* and *how* for *why*.   *"How* do you feel about what you have just done?" *"What* are you doing with your foot as we talk about your behavior?"

No gossiping.   If the child must talk about somebody not present in the room, let the talk be directed to the person in an empty chair in the present tense. For example, "I think you treat me unfairly, Miss Clark. I wish you would be as nice to me as you are to the other kids." The child can then move to the other chair and answer for Miss Clark. "Joan, I would find it easier to like you if you would be more helpful to me during the day."

The dialogue would continue until the child was finished with the interaction. Person-to-person dialogues not only update the material into the present but also serve to increase the child's awareness of the problem. Side benefits include a better picture of the situation for the counselor and rehearsal time for the child, who may wish to discuss the problem later with the teacher. Some appreciation for the teacher's side of the conflict may also emerge from the dialogue.

Changing questions into statements.   This method has the effect of helping children to be more authentic and direct in expressing their thoughts and feelings. For example: Rather than, "Don't you think I should stop hanging around those guys?" the child should say, "I think I should stop hanging around those guys," or "I think you want me to stop hanging around those guys." Perls believed that most questions were phony in that they were really disguised statements.

Taking responsibility.   Clients are asked to fill in the sentence blanks as another way of examining personal responsibility for the way they manage their lives. For example, "Right now I'm feeling _____, and I take responsibility for how I feel." The exercise is quite an eye-opener for those clients who tend to view outside sources as the total cause of their good and bad feelings.

Incomplete sentences.   These exercises, like "I take responsibility," help clients to become aware of how they help and hurt themselves. Some examples:

I help myself when I _____

_____

_____

I block or hurt myself when I _____

_____

_____

Bipolarities.   Perls applies the term *differential thinking* to the concept of thinking in terms of opposites. Much everyday living appears to be spent in resolving conflicts posed by competing polarities. One of the most common bipolarities consists of what Perls calls the topdog and the underdog. Perls (1969) describes the topdog/underdog in the following way:

The topdog is righteous and authoritarian; he knows best. The topdog is a bully and works with "you should" and "you should not."

The underdog manipulates by being defensive or apologetic, wheedling, and playing crybaby. The underdog works with "I want" and makes excuses such as "I try hard," "I have good intentions." The underdog is cunning and usually gets the better of the topdog because the underdog position appeals to the pleasure-seeking side of our personality.

The purpose of working with these bipolarities or splits in the personality is to bring each side into awareness so that a reorganization can take place that does not exclude either side. Gestalt therapy is concerned with making life easier by integrating the splits in existence; each side is necessary and has its place in the well-integrated personality.

The topdog/underdog technique can be used individually or in a group situation. If the technique is used in a group, the counselor could divide the clients into two subgroups, the topdogs and the underdogs. The topdog group will make a list of reasons they *should* do a certain thing, while the underdog group will think of reasons they *want* to do something. After the lists are compiled, the activity should lend itself to much discussion. Children respond very well to this activity.

The best outcomes from the topdog/underdog debate occur when the client is able to identify areas where the "I shoulds" and "I wants" are the same. These are synergistic solutions that help people integrate their lives. For example, I love my job, I want to go to work, and I should go to work.

In another exercise, clients are asked to name their greatest weakness and then to write a short paragraph on how their weakness is really their greatest strength. For example, "My greatest weakness is procrastination, but I'll never give it up because by putting things off I create motivation I need for completing unpleasant tasks."

Another exercise involves listing the three people that the client is closest to and, for each of the three, thinking of one thing that is resented, one thing that is demanded, and one thing that is appreciated. For example:

Name	I resent	I demand	I appreciate
John	that you don't spend enough time with me	more time	your company and friendship
Mary			
Sue			

Such an exercise helps clients to become more aware of the mixed feelings they have about others and how it is possible to resent and appreciate one person at the same time.

Fantasy games. Fantasy games can be great fun for children of all ages and can let them become aware of their feelings right now. As a group activity, have the children pick an animal they would like to be. Allow them to move around as they feel this animal would. Then have the children sit down in pairs and discuss what they would feel if they were this particular animal. As a culmination to the activity, they could write a story about how they would feel if they were actually the animal.

By this time, children should have a real awareness of how they feel and can discuss this with the counselor, teacher, or parent.

Fantasy games can be devised from almost any object or situation. The rosebush and wise person fantasies are two favorites. In the first, the clients are asked to fantasize or pretend they are rosebushes. Each client focuses on one rosebush and is asked to consider the following points:

1. Type of bush—strong or weak
2. Root system—deep or shallow
3. Number of roses—too many or too few
4. Amount of thorns—too many or too few
5. Environment—bad or good for growing
6. Does your rosebush stand out?
7. Does it have enough room?
8. How does it get along with the other plants?
9. Does it have a good future?

The wise person fantasy involves asking one's wise man or woman one question, which is pondered for a few minutes before the wise person answers—speaking through the client, of course. Both question and answer should add some awareness and understanding to the client's life. For example, a client might ask, "What should I do with my life?" and answer, as the wise person, "Develop all of your talents and skills as much as you can."

Clients are asked to discuss their fantasies in depth with the counselor in individual sessions and with groups of two to four if a group is meeting. A good follow-up procedure is to have clients respond to the statement: "I learned that _____" after each exercise. The fantasy games are enhanced when clients are given relaxation exercises before the experience and are allowed to lie down in a comfortable spot during the exercises.

Dreamwork.   Dreaming is a way of becoming aware of the world in the here and now. And since awareness is the dominant theme of Gestalt, they seem to work well together. Dreaming is a guardian of one's existence because the content of dreams is always found to be related to one's survival, well-being, and growth; therefore, Gestalt therapists have been able to help clients overcome impasses in their lives through serious consideration of dreams. The Gestalt approach in analyzing dreams is helpful not only to people suffering from dilemmas in their lives but also to the average "healthy" person. Most people spend much of their waking hours out of touch with the here and now by worrying compulsively about the future or doting on memories of failure and past pleasures.

Spontaneity is a very important feature of Gestalt therapy, and according to Perls, dreams are the most spontaneous expression of the existence of the human being. The Gestalt approach is concerned with integration rather than analysis of dreams. Such integration is achieved by consciously reliving a dream, taking responsibility for being the objects and people in the dream, and becoming aware of the messages the dream holds. According to Perls, all the different parts of the dream are fragments of the dreamer's personality that must be put together to form a whole. These projected fragmented parts must be reowned, and thus hidden potential that appears in the dream will be reowned. As clients play the part of all the various objects and persons in the dream, they may become more aware of the message the dream holds. They may act out the dream until two conflicting roles emerge—for instance, the topdog and the underdog. This conflict is essentially the conflict the dreamer is suffering from.

Gestaltists believe that there are hidden existential messages in dreams that, once discovered, can fill the voids in people's personalities. In the Gestalt framework, dreamwork holds many possibilities for solving the problems of life or for developing a better self-awareness.

Variations of the dreamwork method can be used with children. A volunteer can describe a dream, and other students can role play the objects and people in the dream by expressing their thoughts and feelings. The volunteer can serve as the director of the dream enactment. The task of the therapist in the integration of dreams is to concentrate on what clients are avoiding in their present existence and to help them act out painful situations and reintegrate the alienated parts of their personality into their lives.

Gestalt activities adapted for children

Polster and Polster (1973) discuss contact functions that expand the luster of everyday communication. *Contact* usually implies touching in the physical sense. However, the seven processes of contact functioning—looking, listening, touching, talking, moving, smelling, and tasting—are not all physical contact in the direct sense. The contact can be made through space. For example, seeing is being touched by lightwaves; hearing is being touched, along the basilar membrane, by soundwaves; and so on. Although physical contact is one of the most obvious ways of reaching people, the opportunities for reaching people through space are certainly more available and can be very effective. Application of the contact function can be useful in the elementary school classroom. Children can become more aware of their present actions and feelings by participating in various activities that will bring about contact functioning. Listening activities are particularly appropriate for creating a classroom atmosphere conducive to learning.

Music.   Teachers or counselors can play a melody on the piano or phonograph. They ask the children to listen carefully to it and then to write down how the music makes them feel, what they think of when they hear it, and whether they like it or not. When they have finished writing their ideas, the counselor can ask different children to read their papers and discuss their reactions. This exercise should allow the children to get in touch with their present feelings and evaluate what they hear and think as well.

Musical instruments.   These can be very helpful in allowing emotions to come forth that might otherwise be repressed. A shy child may be chosen by the counselor to sit in the center of a circle of the other children. The child may select one of several noisy instruments such as cymbals or drums for leading the group in lively, strong-sounding music. The other children may either have instruments as well or clap hands and stamp their feet in time to the music. Shy children, hopefully, will lose themselves in the activity and, by banging away, express some emotions they usually hide. Leading the group may help their self-confidence as well. This activity can also be used for the opposite effect with a hyperactive or overly aggressive child. The child could lead the group with a very quiet instrument (perhaps the triangle) and play it during a soft song or lullaby. The counselor can encourage the rest of the group to close their eyes, think of peaceful things, and sway slowly to the music. This would give the child the experience of being peaceful and soothed.

Tone of voice, body movement.   This activity involves listening and looking at contact functions. The counselor would ask the children to select partners for role playing certain emotions or feelings. The activity could be initiated because of some altercation between two youngsters. The group can discuss what emotions the two children were feeling or even role play the actual situation that took place. The counselor asks the children to notice not only the words that are spoken but also the tones of voice and the body movements that express the emotion. After working out the bad feelings between the two children involved, the counselor can ask the children to think of other emotions and practice role playing with their partners. When they have had a few minutes to practice a short scene that will display an emotion, the counselor can select different partners to demonstrate for the class, each time making the class aware of tones of voice and body actions. This way the children become aware of the fact that emotion is expressed in many ways and learn to recognize how they show emotion.

Awareness-enhancing activities.
1. "Feely Feely." Directions for child: "For five minutes or so, focus your attention on the way things feel on your skin . . . the way you feel as your weight presses on the chair . . . the feel of your feet in your shoes and against the floor . . . the places where clothing is tight. . . . Can you feel any draft? Are some places warmer or colder than others? Now reach out and touch different things." (Have a variety of objects and

textured surfaces available for touching.) The child could be asked to verbalize descriptions ("I don't like this, it feels squishy"; "this feels rough"; and so on).

2. "Taste Time." Directions for child: "For five minutes or so, focus your attention on the way several mouthfuls of food feel, change, and taste. Try not to talk to yourself as you do this. Feel the texture of the food with your tongue, lips, teeth, mouth. Try the difference between bland, soft foods and crisp, strong-tasting foods. Toward the end of the exercise, take one bite of food and chew it, focusing your awareness on it all the time until it is liquefied. Don't swallow it until it is absolutely liquefied." (Have several bite-sized bits of different foods available— carrots, apples, turnips, meat, and so on.)

3. "Mirror Mirror." Directions: Bring a good-sized mirror to the group and have the children look into it one at a time. Have each child look without any comment at all for 30 seconds or so, and then ask the child to tell you what he or she sees. Ask for more and more description. Be gentle but persistent. When it gets difficult, shift to another child. Polaroid snapshots, videotaping, even movies could also be used in the same way to build self-awareness.

4. "Now." Directions for child: "As you sit quietly, make statements to yourself about exactly what you are aware of at this very moment. Make every statement begin with 'Now I . . .' Be aware of as many things as you can. Try writing things down. Then just talk to yourself. Then try to be aware without talking to yourself."

Art activities. For disturbed children who cannot verbalize emotions, many art media may be utilized. The child can smear fingerpaint with hands or feet, create and destroy images with clay, draw or paint pictures to express confusing feelings. When appropriate, the child can be encouraged to verbalize after the art work is completed ("Tell me about your picture").

Self-confidence building activities.

1. Touching games. There is great variety in touching games. Counselor and child can have a one-to-one game (pseudowrestling, bear-hugging, and the like), or group games can involve several children and several teachers or counselors. The group can lift up one person, lower and lift again, have a conga line, do partner pull-pushes, partner massages, partner face touching, and so on. Children need to be touched, to touch others playfully and affectionately, and to realize their partners in the group will catch them as they start to fall.

2. "Applause! Applause!" Group gathers and sits in a circle with space cleared in the center of the floor. One at a time, children go to the cleared space and say their names aloud. At this, the rest of the group loudly cheers, claps, shouts "bravo!" and so forth. Children acknowledge the applause in whatever way they choose.

3. "Confidence Courses." This is a gentle form of obstacle course, designed to build confidence. Use combinations of pit jumps, incline balances, boxes, barrels, ladder climbs, rope slides, and the like. (Children can also be involved in constructing such a course.) As children attain better motor coordination and balance, they form better self-images, a feeling of mastery, an "I can do it" attitude about themselves. They begin to feel they can solve problems and can deal with their world competently.

CASE STUDIES

Many short-term counseling sessions can be done with children using the empty chair technique. For example, consider the following method for working with anger.

> Child: I hate my dad. He's mean. I hate his guts.
>
> Counselor (Co): Let's pretend your dad is sitting in that empty chair. What do you want to say to him? You can walk over there and say whatever you want.
>
> Child: Get off my back. Leave me alone! I cleaned my room just as good as I could.
>
> Co: Now sit in the other chair. Pretend to be your dad.
>
> Child: I've told you and told you that this room looks like a pig pen.
>
> Co: Now be yourself again.
>
> Child: I cleaned my room good, Dad! Then you came in and said it still isn't good enough. Nothing was left out in the room but my toys!
>
> Co: Now be your dad.
>
> Child: This is the last time I'm telling you, Son. The room better be finished when I get back. That means toys, too.
>
> Co: Now be you.
>
> Child: You don't care about me! You don't care about how I feel. You just worry about the house being messed up. You get mad when I get out my toys. Kids are supposed to have toys! It's MY ROOM! Quit buggin' me! (accompanied by much non-verbal expression of anger as well as the overt angry verbal content).

The child has expressed his strong feelings that his room should be his "territory," that it should be OK to have his toys out. A global "hatred" for the father has been narrowed down to anger about a specific recurring problem (the differing standards for the room held by the parent and the child). After release of the built-up anger, some problem solving could be undertaken to perhaps achieve a compromise about the room situation.

Another sample counseling session involves the topdog/underdog debate, using an empty chair for each "dog." This technique is useful when the child has a decision-making problem. Most decision-making problems involve a debate between the inner voice of "I should do ..." (topdog) versus "Yes, but I want to do ..." (underdog). An empty chair is assigned to each point of view.

Identification of the problem

Susan is experiencing a conflict over whether to live with her mother or father when their divorce is final.

Individual and background information

Susan Adams is a 10-year-old in the fourth grade. Her mother and father are getting a divorce, and she has to choose between living with her mother or her father. Susan is the second of three children. This is the second marriage for Susan's mother and the first marriage for her husband. Her older brother is not the son of her mother's present husband. Both parents work in factory jobs, but their income seems to be limited by the fact that Susan's father drinks up most of his paycheck. Susan is an average student in school, quiet, and has never been a behavior problem. She gets along well with her peers at school. Susan's physical health is good, but she does have a vision problem that requires a new pair of glasses. Susan's parents say they do not have the money to buy a new pair.

Transcript

Counselor (Co): Susan, we have the next 30 minutes for our talk. Where would you like to start?

Susan: Well, you know my problem about having to decide whether to live with Mom or Daddy after their divorce is final. I just don't know what I'm going to do.

Co: I know that when we talked about this the other day, you were feeling really upset about this situation of having to choose between your mom and dad. I can tell you still feel this way.

Susan: Yes, I do. I did all the things we talked about ... like talking to both of them. That made it even harder to decide because they both want me. I still don't know what to do. I wish they would stop the divorce.

Co: Well, it's a good feeling to know that they both want you, but a bad feeling to know you have to choose. You would really like to have them stay together.

Susan: Yes, I really would, but that's impossible. I've tried every way I can to keep them together.

Co: Susan, would you try an exercise with me that might help clarify your thinking about this decision?

Susan: I'll try anything to help.

Co: (Explains and demonstrates the topdog/underdog technique.) So, when you are in the topdog chair, you say "I should ..." and when you are in the underdog chair, you say "I want...." OK?

Susan: OK (goes to the topdog chair first).

> Topdog: I should go with Daddy because he'll be all alone.
>
> Underdog: Yes, but I want to stay with Mom because I hate to give up my room, and I want to stay with my sister.
>
> Topdog: What is Daddy going to do without anyone to cook for him and clean house?
>
> Underdog: Why can't he hire a maid, and I can visit him a lot, too?
>
> Topdog: If I don't live with Daddy, he won't have anybody, because he doesn't want Jake, and Sally is too young to move away from Mom.
>
> Underdog: Well, Daddy goes out and drinks a lot with his friends, and sometimes he gets sick and is not nice to be around when he gets drunk.
>
> Topdog: I think I should take care of him when he gets sick.
>
> Underdog: I think it is better not to be near him when he drinks. I would like to visit him when he is not drinking.
>
> Topdog: How can I live with Mom and help Daddy, too?
>
> Underdog: I just know things will be better if I live with Mom in my room and see Daddy as often as I can.

Co: Do you think you've finished with this argument, Susan?

Susan: Yes, I've said all I can think of.

Co: I'm wondering what you learned from doing this exercise.

Susan: Well, I think things will be better if I stay where I am with Mom. But I'll need to see a lot of Daddy—as much as I can. I love them both so much (starts to cry).

Co: I know this has to be a sad and rough time for you. It really hurts doesn't it?

Susan: It sure does. I need to be brave about this and not let it make me so sad.

Co: It's OK to feel sad about this. You can always come in here to talk to me when you want to.

(Counselor terminates the interview and schedules another session for the next day.)

SUMMARY: RESEARCH AND REACTIONS

Fritz Perls took pride in the fact that Gestalt therapists were doers and not researchers and writers. One of his pet four-letter descriptive terms was reserved for the material turned out by researchers and writers on the topic of psychotherapy. However, an attempt will be made to summarize what research and reactions are available on Gestalt therapy.

Passons (1975) writes that, during the past several years, Gestalt therapy has emerged as a major force in the field of mental health. Evidence for this is readily noted in the increase in publications in response to the request for more knowledge on the theory and practice of Gestalt therapy. Gestalt has a broad appeal.

Fagan and Shepard (1970) have noted that the directory of the American Academy of Psychotherapists lists Gestalt therapy as the sixth most common affiliation, with more members than better known or more extensively published schools such as Jungian and rational-emotive therapies.

Simkin (1979) reports the following results of his research in Gestalt therapy. In an attempt to assess the effectiveness of his Gestalt therapy workshops, Simkin found that 75% of the patients who attended the residential Gestalt workshops reported that they received what they wanted or even more. The same claim was made by 66% of those who were in weekly therapy. Approximately 14% of both groups reported that they received no help or became worse as a result of their experiences. The remaining people in both groups claimed they got something positive from the experience. The people surveyed reported that they preferred (9 to 1) treatment on a massed basis (workshop) to treatment on a spaced basis (groups and individual therapy). Simkin's sample was limited to 200 people who had attended both workshops and traditional therapy.

Simkin (1976) has also reported the results of massing 300 hours of intensive training of Gestalt therapy into a three-month period for five therapists in a residential setting. The number of training hours was equal to or exceeded those required in more formal training centers. Personality inventories, peer group ratings, the A. B. therapist scale, and trainees' clinical impressions were utilized as measures of training effectiveness. Data from these measures supported the possibility of successfully massing training in Gestalt therapy in a three-month period. A follow-up study seven months after training, in which the five therapists returned for a week's evaluation, indicated that the positive direction of change continued in the quality of their work (as rated by their patients and supervisors).

Fagan and Shepard (1970) offer a few words of caution concerning the Gestalt approach to severely disturbed or psychotic clients that are worth noting here. They recommend caution, sensitivity, and patience. They believe it is preferable in the initial stages of therapy to limit therapeutic activity to procedures that strengthen clients' contact with reality, their confidence in their own being, and the good will and competence of the counselor, rather than involving them in role playing or reenactment of past experiences of pain or conflict. This seems to be sensible advice. Fagan and Shepard endorse activities that increase sensory, perceptual, and motor capacities toward self-support. Such activities could be useful adjuncts to many other therapies with children and employed in a wide variety of settings.

The most immediate limitation of Gestalt therapy, as with any other therapy, is the skill, training, experience, and judgment of the therapist. A counselor using this approach must be neither afraid nor inept in allowing the patient to follow through and finish the experience of grief, rage, fear, or joy. Without such skill, the counselor may leave the client aborted, unfinished, opened, and vulnerable (Fagan & Shepard, 1970).

Another issue hinges on the questions of when, with whom, and in what situation. In general, Gestalt therapy is most effective with overly socialized, restrained, constricted individuals. With less organized, more severely disturbed clients, long-term counseling is required. Limiting activities at first to those that strengthen a client's contact with reality is preferable to role-playing situations further removed from the here and now.

Individuals whose problems lie in lack of impulse control, acting out, delinquency, and the like require a different approach. Gestalt therapy can serve to reinforce the activities that are causing the problems.

Since Gestalt techniques facilitate the discovering, facing, and resolution of the client's major conflict in an often dramatically short time, the inexperienced therapist-observer or client may assume that Gestalt therapy offers "instant cure." Even in experienced counselors, the temptation is to push the client to a stance of self-support too fast, too soon. The use of Gestalt therapy with groups is common, but frequently it amounts to individual counseling in a group setting. Another hazard is the counselor's assuming excessive responsibility for the direction of the group by too much activity, thus fostering patient passivity and defeating the goal of patient self-support. Extensive experience with Gestalt therapy may make clients more unfit for or unadjusted to contemporary society. At the same time, however, they may be motivated to work toward changing the world into a more compassionate and productive milieu in which human beings can develop, work, and enjoy their full humanness.

Perls seems to have done well in his attempt to establish the philosophy and practice of Gestalt therapy. The approach is well grounded in and consistent with the principles of human behavior. Perls, by removing the mystique created by professional jargon, has made Gestalt therapy comprehensible to the general public.

REFERENCES

Assagioli, R. *Psychosynthesis.* New York: Viking, 1965.

English, H., and English, A. *A comprehensive dictionary of psychological terms.* New York: Longmans, Green, 1958.

Fagan, J., and Shepard, I. *Gestalt therapy now*. Palo Alto, Calif.: Science and Behavior Books, 1970.

Lederman, J. *Anger and the rocking chair: Gestalt awareness with children*. New York: McGraw-Hill, 1969.

Passons, W. *Gestalt approaches in counseling*. New York: Holt, Rinehart and Winston, 1975.

Perls, F. *Gestalt therapy verbatim*. Moab, Utah: Real People Press, 1969.

Perls, F. *In and out the garbage pail*. New York: Bantam, 1971.

Perls, F. *The Gestalt approaches and eye witnesses to therapy*. New York: Bantam, 1976.

Polster, E., and Polster, M. *Gestalt therapy integrated: Contours of theory and practice*. New York: Brunner/Mazel, 1973.

Sahakian, W. (Ed.). *Psychotherapy and counseling studies in technique*. Chicago: Rand McNally, 1969.

Shepard, M. *Fritz*. New York: Saturday Review Press, 1975.

Simkin, J. *Gestalt therapy mini-lectures*. Millbrae, Calif.: Celestial Arts, 1976.

Simkin, J. Gestalt therapy. In R. Corsini (Ed.), *Current psychotherapies*. Itasca, Ill.: F. E. Peacock, 1979.

CHAPTER

6

RATIONAL EMOTIVE THERAPY

ALBERT ELLIS

Albert Ellis is currently executive director of the Institute for Advanced Study in Rational Psychotherapy in New York, a community agency chartered by the regents of The State University of New York. He is widely known as the founder or developer of rational emotive therapy.

For the past 15 years, Ellis has given individualized remedial instruction—or what he calls emotional education—to several thousand adults, adolescents, and children. In addition, he has done group therapy with over 2000 adults and adolescents.

Ellis was born in Pittsburgh, Pennsylvania, in 1913 and grew up in New York City. In spite of a difficult childhood, he managed to earn a degree in business administration from the City University of New York in 1934. He earned his living during the Depression first by working with his brother in a business that located matching pants for still-usable suit coats. Later he worked as the personnel manager in a gift and novelty firm.

Ellis's ambition was to write, which he did in his spare time. He collected materials for two books on sexual adjustment, which were eventually published: *The American Sexual Tragedy* (1954) and *The Case for Sexual Liberty* (1965). His friends began to regard him as an expert on the subject and often asked his advice. He discovered he enjoyed counseling people as much as writing and decided to return to school. In 1942, Ellis entered the clinical psychology program at Columbia University and in 1947 was awarded his doctorate.

Ellis's early professional work as a therapist in state institutions in New Jersey employed classical psychoanalytic methods, but within ten years Ellis had set psychoanalysis aside almost completely. His change in philosophy came about when he discovered that clients treated once a week or even every other week progressed as well as those he saw daily. Ellis found that a more active role, interjecting advice and direct interpretation, yielded faster results than passive psychoanalytic procedures. His own theory of counseling, however, did not emerge until after he had received his doctorate from Columbia and later received training as a traditional psychoanalytic therapist. Consequently, some of the origins of rational emotive therapy (RET) can be traced to Freud as well as to disillusionment with Freudian psychoanalysis.

After discovering that rationalist philosophy fit his temperament and taste, Ellis began concentrating on changing people's behavior by confronting them with their irrational beliefs and persuading them to adopt more rational ones. He now considers himself a philosophical or educational therapist and sees RET as a system that is uniquely didactic, cognition oriented, and explicative. He believes that RET places people at the center of the universe and gives them almost full responsibility for their fate.

Over 400 books and articles, in addition to his Institute for Rational Living, have proceeded from Ellis's conceptualization of rational emotive therapy. From its early days up to the present, RET has continued to undergo modifications. Ellis (1977) recently noted that, while RET was once a limited rational-persuasive therapy, it has grown into a cognitive-behavior therapy that consciously uses cognitive, emotive, and behavioral techniques to help clients. It may be said that Ellis was quite good at turning his failures into successes. While not successful as a clothing salesman or a novelist, Ellis did develop an effective approach to counseling and proceeded to write volumes about the technique with a great deal of success. In 1957, he published his first book on RET, *How to Live with a Neurotic*, and in 1960 his first really successful book, *The Art of Science and Love*.

THE NATURE OF PEOPLE

Rational emotive therapy is based on the philosophy of Epictetus (born ca. AD 50): "What disturbs men's minds is not events, but their judgment of events." Generally speaking, very young children and animals have limited emotional repertoires and tend to emote in a quick, unsustained manner. When children get old enough to use language effectively, they acquire the ability to sustain their emotions and possibly keep themselves emotionally upset. RET does not concentrate upon the past events in one's life, but rather the present events and how one reacts to them. RET theory stresses that, as human beings, we have choices. We control our ideas, attitudes, feelings, and actions, and we arrange our lives according to our own dictates. We have little control over what happens or what actually exists, but we do have both choices and control over how we view the world and how we react to the difficulties, regardless of how we have been taught to respond.

RET theory holds that people are neither good nor bad if they respond to others with a rational belief system. If individuals react with irrational beliefs, however, they will view themselves and others as evil, awful, and horrible whenever they or others fall short of their expectations. The human being is viewed by Ellis as a naturally irrational, self-defeating individual who needs to be taught otherwise. He has also stated that people can be "naturally" helpful and loving *as long as they do not think irrationally*. In other words, Ellis has described a circular process, as depicted in Figure 6-1. Irrational thinking leads to self-hate, which leads to self-destructive behavior and eventually to hatred of others, which will in turn cause others to act irrationally toward the individual, and thus begin the cycle again.

Ellis believes that some of our irrational thoughts are biological in origin, but the majority stem from our upbringing (parents, teachers, and clergy). Ellis has described three problem areas in which people hold irrational beliefs: they must be perfect; others must be perfect; and/or the world must be a perfect place to live. The following examples describe in a nutshell what people tell themselves when interpreting events with an irrational belief system. A more rational replacement thought follows each irrational self-message.

1. Because it would be highly preferable if I were outstandingly competent, I absolutely should and must be; it is awful when I am not, and I am therefore a worthless individual.

   (alternative) It would sure be nice if I were outstanding in whatever I do, but if I am not, it is OK, and I will try my best anyway.

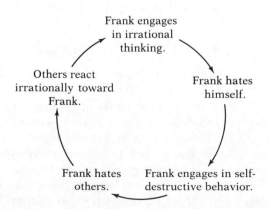

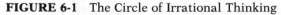

FIGURE 6-1 The Circle of Irrational Thinking

2. Because it is highly desirable that others treat me considerately and fairly, they absolutely should and must, and they are rotten people who deserve to be utterly damned when they do not.

   (alternative)   I would prefer people to treat me considerately. However, I realize that this is not always the case, so I will not take it personally when they do not, *and* I will make it my business to be considerate.

3. Because it is preferable that I experience pleasure rather than pain, the world should absolutely arrange this, and life is horrible and I can't bear it when the world doesn't.

   (alternative)   I realize that in life there are both pleasurable moments and painful moments. Therefore, I will try to make the painful moments a positive, learning experience so that I can endure trials and even benefit from them.

THEORY OF COUNSELING

When interpreting daily events with one or more irrational philosophies, the individual is likely to feel angry or hostile toward others, or to internalize these feelings with resulting anxiety, guilt, and/or depression. In essence, RET theory holds that people are primarily responsible for their feelings about themselves, others, the environment, and whether or not they want to be perpetually disturbed by them.

In their book *A New Guide to Rational Living*, Ellis and Harper (1975) write that, because humans naturally and easily think crookedly, emote inappropriately, and behave self-defeatingly, it seems best to use all possible educational modes dramatically, strongly, and persistently to teach them how to do otherwise. They have compiled a list of irrational beliefs that get people into trouble. These are:

1. It is a dire necessity for people to be loved or approved by almost everyone for virtually everything they do.
2. One should be thoroughly competent, adequate, and achieving in all possible respects.
3. Certain people are bad, wicked, or villainous, and they should be severely blamed and punished for their sins.
4. It is terrible, horrible, and catastrophic when things are not going the way one would like them to go.
5. Human unhappiness is externally caused, and people have little or no ability to control their sorrows or rid themselves of their negative feelings.
6. If something is or may be dangerous or fearsome, one should be terribly occupied with and upset about it.
7. It is easier to avoid facing many life difficulties and self-responsibilities than to undertake more rewarding forms of self-discipline.

8. The past is all-important, and because something once strongly affected one's life, it should do so indefinitely.
9. People and things should be different from the way they are, and it is catastrophic if perfect solutions to the grim realities of life are not immediately found.
10. Maximum human happiness can be achieved by inertia and inaction, or by passively and uncommittedly enjoying oneself.
11. My child is delinquent/emotionally disturbed/mentally retarded; therefore, I'm a failure as a parent.
12. My child is emotionally disturbed/mentally retarded; therefore, he is severely handicapped and will never amount to anything.
13. I cannot give my children everything they want; therefore, I am inadequate.

Goodman and Maultsby (1974) have drawn up a list of consequences that may result from irrational thinking. A sampling follows:

1. High degree of interpersonal difficulties
2. Persistence of emotionalism in reacting to daily problems
3. Desiring what one cannot have or is unlikely to get
4. Not wanting or appreciating what one has or could get
5. Tendency to attribute all one's difficulties to others
6. Tendency to see one's self as worthless
7. Pursuit of contradictory goals or behavior inconsistent with professed goals
8. Tolerating bad situations rather than taking steps to rectify or improve them
9. Remaining dependent on others past the point when it is necessary
10. Remaining angry or hurt past a reasonable period of time
11. Demand for perfection in one's own behavior or in that of others
12. Indulgence in behavior that injures one's body or mind or impedes their functioning
13. Needless self-torment over past events or presumed failures
14. Chronic or intermittent states of depression or anxiety
15. Unreasonable fears
16. Excessive anger

In an article entitled "What Rational-Emotive Therapy Is and Is Not," Ellis (1974) makes the following points about RET.

1. RET views anxiety not as an "irrational" but as an inappropriate feeling that stems largely from irrational ideas. Feelings are not to be confused with ideas.
2. Clients have almost full or complete responsibility for their ideas and consequently their feelings.
3. Clients, not early environment or conditioning or contemporary conditions, mainly choose to create their irrational ideas and consequent feelings. They can choose to change their ideas.

4. RET teaches that people are not to be blamed, damned, denigrated, or condemned for choosing irrational ideas, inappropriate feelings, or defeating behaviors.
5. RET discourages the use of absolutes, such as *must*, *should*, and *ought*, in clients' thinking. There are no absolutes (pun intended).
6. RET therapists definitely do not determine whether clients' ideas or behaviors are rational or irrational.

The goal of rational emotive therapy is to teach people to think and behave in a more personally satisfying way by making them realize that they have a choice between self-defeating, negative behavior and efficient, enhancing, positive behavior. RET teaches people to take the responsibility for their own logical thinking and the consequence or behavior that follows it.

COUNSELING METHOD

In the past, counseling has concentrated upon either the developmental events in one's life or the feelings one had about these events. Ellis did not believe that these two main methods were totally erroneous, but he did not find either approach very effective. Neither approach explained why some people are rather well adjusted (that is, not too unhappy too much of the time regardless of the passage of events) and others are emotionally dysfunctional a good deal of the time with the same passage of events.

Ellis theorized that individuals' responses or feelings toward the same events are predicated upon individuals' belief systems. These individual belief systems are what people tell themselves about an event—in particular, an unfortunate incident. For example, 100 people may get rejected by their true love. Some of these people will respond: "I can't go on; I've lost my purpose in life. Because I've been rejected by such a wonderful person, I must really be a worthless slob. My only solution for getting rid of the unbearable pain I feel is to kill myself." Others will respond: "What a pain in the neck! I had dinner reservations and tickets for the show. Now I have to get another date for Saturday night. This surely sets me back. What an inconvenience!" Between these two extreme reactions are several other degrees of bad feelings growing from the various self-messages of the rejected 100. Such a wide variety of reactions to the same basic event suggests that one's view of the event and consequent self-message is the key to the counseling strategy. The same process happens to children who experience bad feelings from school failure, peer conflicts, and conflicts with adults.

The main goal of RET is to increase happiness and decrease pain. In order to achieve a prevailing happier state, RET has two main objectives. The first is to show the emotionally disturbed child how irrational beliefs or attitudes create dysfunctional consequences. Some of these consequences might include anger, depression, or anxiety. The second objective is to directively and intellectually teach children how to dispute or crumble their irrational beliefs and replace them with rational beliefs. Once counselors lead the children to dispute the irrational ideas, they guide them into adopting new expectations for themselves, others, and the environment. Ellis reasons that, if the irrational and absolute philosophies and resultant feelings are replaced with more rational and productive thoughts, children will no longer be trapped into a repetitious cycle of negative feelings. When children are no longer incapacitated by dysfunctional feelings, they are free to choose behaviors that eliminate the problem or at least lessen its disappointing impact.

Rational emotive therapy is often referred to as the A, B, C, D, and E approach to counseling.

A   is the activating event: "I failed my math test."
B   is how I evaluate the event.
B_1—irrational message. I failed the test; therefore, I'm a total failure as a person.
B_2—rational message. I failed the test; this is unpleasant and inconvenient, but that is all it is. I need to study more efficiently for the next exam.
C   represents the consequences or feelings resulting from my self-message at the B stage.
The B_1 message will cause you to feel very depressed. The B_2 message won't make you feel great, but it will not be so overwhelming as to inhibit your performance on your next test.
D   represents the disputing arguments you use to attack the irrational self-messages expressed in B_1. The counselor's function is to help you question these irrational self-messages once they have been identified.
E   represents the answers you have developed to the questions regarding the rationality of your B_1 self-messages.

For example, counseling would proceed through the following steps:

A—something unpleasant happens to you.
B—you evaluate the event as something awful, something that should not be allowed to happen.
C—you get upset and nervous.
D—you question your B self-message:
    1. Why is it awful?
    2. Why shouldn't it be allowed to happen?
E—you answer:
    1. It's a disappointment.
    2. It's a setback, but not a disaster.
    3. I can handle it.
    4. I would like things to be better, but that doesn't mean I'm always supposed to get things done my way.

Ellis (1969b) provides another example of RET in action in an article entitled "Teaching Emotional Education in the Classroom." He writes that, if Robert is so anxious that he cannot recite well in class, even though he knows the material, he anticipates the event (A) and is already feeling the blocking and nervousness (C) just by anticipating the event (A). At point (B_2), he is telling himself: "It would be unfortunate if I did not recite well because the other children would think I did not know my lesson. They might even think I am a dummy and I would not want that."

At (B_1), however, Robert is usually adding another statement to his rational message: "It would be awful if I failed, no one would like me, and I would be a bum." The great anxiety felt at (C) caused by the (B_1) message would sabotage Robert's efforts to recite in class the next time the teacher called on him.

Rational emotive therapy is direct, didactic, confrontational, and verbally active counseling. Initially, the counselor seeks to detect the irrational beliefs that are creating the disturbances. Four factors are helpful in detecting irrational thinking:

1. Look for "awfulizing."
2. Look for something you think you cannot stand.
3. Look for absolute uses of *should, must, ought, always,* and *never.*
4. Look for damning of yourself and others.

Once the irrational beliefs are recognized, the counselor disputes and challenges them. Ultimately, the goal is for children to recognize irrational beliefs, think them through, and relinquish them. As a result of this process and therapy, children will hopefully reach three insights: First, the present neurotic behavior has antecedent causes. Second, the reason that original beliefs keep upsetting them is that they keep repeating them. Third, they can overcome emotional disturbances by consistently observing, questioning, and challenging their own belief system.

People hold quite tenaciously to their beliefs, rational or not; consequently, the counselor vigorously attacks the irrational beliefs in an attempt to show the children how illogically they think. Using the Socratic method of questioning and disputing, the counselor takes a verbally active part in the early stages of counseling by identifying and explaining the child's problem. If counselors guess correctly, which often happens, they argue with and persuade the child to give up the old philosophical view and replace it with a new, essentially existentially oriented, philosophy.

Ellis (1962) believes that to the usual psychotherapeutic techniques of exploration, ventilation, excoriation, and interpretation, the rational therapist adds techniques of confrontation, indoctrination, and reeducation. Counselors are didactic in that they explain how children's beliefs (which intervene between an event and the resultant feelings), rather than events themselves, are the cause of emotional disturbances.

Because the counselor honestly believes that the children do not understand the reason for their disturbance, the counselor enlightens and teaches. Counselors frequently assign homework for the child as an integral part of therapy. The homework may consist of reading, performing specific tasks, and taking risks.

There is little transference in RET. Contrary to classical psychoanalysis, the counselor serves as a model of rational thinking and behavior. The children are urged to resolve problems with significant people in their lives.

In addition, the counselor sometimes makes use of conventional methods such as dream analysis, reflection of feeling, and reassurance. All these methods are employed together, with the end result being that the child's irrational thinking—which has resulted in irrational behavior—is destroyed and replaced with a more sane belief system.

Rational emotive counselors believe that a person's belief system (which is defined as the meaning of facts) is analogous to the acquisition of speech. Just as language is learned by imitation and modeling, so is the belief system. Therefore, the belief system and attitudes children acquire are largely a reflection of the significant persons in their lives. Furthermore, the belief systems incorporated into children's minds will determine whether they think rationally about facts. Continuing the analogy, it is suggested that, just as one continues to add vocabulary and modify one's speech, one can also change or replace one's belief system.

RET is modified when used with children because its style depends so much on verbal and abstract conceptualization skills. Working on the premise that people feel the way they think, the therapist attempts to change overt behavior by altering internal verbalization. A major disadvantage in using RET with children is that studies have shown that children do not generalize well to other situations; that is, the improved behavior is limited to the specific circumstances. Furthermore, Piaget's research would indicate that children in the preformal stages of cognitive development (see Chapter 2) might have difficulty in relating to the rational emotive counseling method.

One very effective technique used with children is role reversal. In this technique, the child describes the activating event and the emotional consequences. Next, the counselor explains that it is the thoughts that are upsetting the child. Then they role play the activating event, with the counselor playing the child. While acting out the event, the counselor demonstrates the appropriate behavior while uttering rational self-statements aloud. The roles are reversed again, with the child trying on new thoughts and being rewarded, preferably with social approval as reinforcement for rational statements and behaviors. It may be that the child will need to be rewarded for successive approximations.

An offspring of RET is REE, rational emotive education. The objectives of REE are to teach how feelings develop, to teach how to discriminate between valid and invalid assumptions, to teach how to think rationally in antiawful and antiperfectionist ways.

One study reported by Knaus (1974) illustrates quite effectively the results of reinforcing rational verbal expressions with disturbed children. The children become more rational not only in their verbal expression and belief systems but also in their behaviors. Some examples of beliefs that were reinforced by writing the statements on the board are:

I don't like school, but I can stand it.
I did something bad, but I'm not a bad person.
I don't like being called insulting names, but being insulted is not awful.
Just because someone calls you a "dumb-dumb" does not mean you are one.

Some children in the experiment improved in their rational behaviors to the extent that they were recommended for dismissal from treatment.

Ellis believes that all children act neurotically simply because they are children. He states that childish behavior can be differentiated from neurosis until the age of five. At this point, many children have integrated into their belief system the irrational belief that one should be thoroughly competent, adequate, and achieving in all possible respects if one is to be considered worthwhile. Ellis, Moseley, and Wolfe (1972) list several strategies for undermining this philosophy in children.

1. Teach children the joy of engaging in various games that are worthwhile because they are fun. De-emphasize the importance of winning at all costs by teaching children that you do not have to win to have fun and to be a worthwhile person.
2. Teach children that significant achievements rarely come easily and that there is nothing wrong with working long and hard to achieve one's goals.
3. Teach children that they are not bad people when they do not meet their goals. It is important that children like themselves during periods of failure even when they may not be trying their best to achieve their goals. It is also important to teach children that there are important differences between wants and needs. When we want something we cannot get, it does not mean that we are not getting what we absolutely need.
4. Teach children that, while it is good to strive for perfectionism in performance, perfectionism is not required for one to be a worthwhile person. It is not only OK to make mistakes, but making mistakes is a good way to learn why certain things happen and how to prevent them from happening again.
5. Teach children that popularity and achievement are not necessarily related, that it is very difficult to be liked by all people at all times, and that 100% popularity is not required to be a worthwhile person.

6. In summary, teach children not to take themselves and situations too seriously by turning minor setbacks into catastrophes. Positive reinforcement is recommended to balance constructive criticism when evaluating children's performances.

CASE STUDY

Identification of the problem

Jeff Lusetk is a quiet, serious 12-year-old seventh grader at Smith County Middle School. He was referred to the counselor because he was very upset after receiving a failing grade on a language arts test. After the test, Jeff seemed to be firmly convinced he would fail the class.

Individual and background information

Academic.   School records indicate that Jeff is a high achiever. He has excellent grades ("B" and above) in all his classes for the first two grading periods of the year. Except for the "F" on the last test, he has also maintained an above-average grade in language arts this grading period.

Family.   Jeff is the youngest of three sons. His father is retired, and his mother works as a grocery store cashier. Both of Jeff's older brothers, one of whom is a high school senior and the other a college sophomore, are excellent students. The family expects (or appears to expect) Jeff to excel also.

Social.   Jeff seems to get along well with his peers. He participates in group efforts and is especially good friends with one other student, John Powers, also a good student and a quiet personality.

Counseling method

The school counselor used rational emotive therapy as a counseling method to help Jeff recognize and evaluate the erroneous messages he was giving himself (and which upset him) about his low grade in language arts. The counselor also taught Jeff to replace the erroneous messages with "sane" messages and to recognize "insane" messages when he encountered them again. The basic steps used by the counselor included having Jeff examine each step along the way to becoming very upset and to look at the real message he was telling himself at each step.

Transcript[1]

Counselor (Co): Jeff, why do you think you're going to fail language arts?

[1]This case study was written by Sharon Simpson for a counseling course at the University of Tennessee in 1980.

Jeff: Because I failed the last test.

Co: You mean if you fail one test, you're bound to fail the next one?

Jeff: Well, I failed that test, and I'm stupid!

Co: What are you telling yourself about your performance on that test?

Jeff: I remember thinking it was a really bad grade—not at all the kind I was used to getting. Then I thought how terrible it would be if I failed language arts and how my mom and dad and brothers would hate me and would think I was lazy and dumb!

Co: It would be unpleasant and inconvenient if you failed language arts, but would this make you a hateful and dumb person?

Jeff: It makes me really worried about passing the next test that's coming up . . .

Co: I can understand how you would be worried about the next test, but does a bad grade make someone a bad or hated person?

Jeff: No, but it's not the kind of grade I usually get.

Co: OK, so a bad grade is unpleasant, and you don't like it, but it does not make you a bad person.

Jeff: *My* grade was an "F" and most of the other kids made "A's," so it made me look dumb.

Co: OK, it *was* a bad grade compared to the rest of class, but does this mean you are the dumbest kid around?

Jeff: No, I make mostly "A's," a few "B's." One bad grade does not make me a dumb kid.

Co: So, compared to your usual grade and the class's grades, this *was* a bad grade, and that is all it is, right?

Jeff: Yeah.

Co: What else are you telling yourself about the low test grade?

Jeff: Well, like I said, I immediately thought how terrible it would be if I failed language arts, and . . .

Co: Stop there for just a minute, Jeff. Suppose you did fail language arts, even with your other high grades. It would be a bad experience, but would it be the end of the world?

Jeff: No, I guess I'd have to repeat the class, that's all.

Co: Right, it would be inconvenient and maybe embarrassing. It would not be pleasant, but you would go on living.

Jeff: Well, I guess that's right.

Co: Are you beginning to see what you told yourself about the consequences of *one* bad grade?

Jeff: Yeah, I guess I believed that one bad grade was awful—the end of the world—and that I shouldn't even try any more because I would fail the class anyway.

Co: Was that the correct information to give yourself about your grade?

Jeff: No!

Co: OK! Let's look at the rest of the message you gave yourself after you got that bad grade. Remember what was next?

Jeff: I think I thought my family would hate me and think I was dumb and lazy because I failed that test and would probably fail language arts.

Co: Do you think your family's love depends on your grades?

Jeff: No, Jimmy made an "F" on a chemistry test the first part of the school year, and nobody hated him.

Co: What did your parents do?

Jeff: Let's see. Oh, yeah, they got him a tutor—a friend of Dad's knew a UT student who was majoring in chemistry.

Co: What did your brother in college do when Jimmy failed the test?

Jeff: He offered to help Jim on weekends. He's a brain—a physics major!

Co: So when your brother failed a test, your family helped him out. They didn't say he was "dumb" or "lazy" or that they hated him for it!

Jeff: No, they didn't. And I guess they wouldn't say it to me, either; in fact, Dad and Jim ask every night if I need help with my homework. I can usually do it OK by myself.

Co: OK. Let's go back over some of these bad messages you've been giving yourself about your bad grade.

Jeff: I got a bad grade. I thought I would fail language arts no matter what I did. I decided my family would hate me and think I was dumb and lazy.

Co: Do you *still* believe those "crazy" messages you told yourself about failing and the way your family would react?

Jeff: No!

Co: Next time you mess up on something—maybe a ball game, maybe a test—what message will you give yourself?

Jeff: Well, I'm not exactly sure what I'll say, but I *won't* tell myself that it's a disaster and I'll never be able to do anything else. I'll probably say that I don't like what happened and that I'm not happy about it. That's all. Now I guess I'll go study and try to ace that next language arts test. Thanks a lot!

SUMMARY: RESEARCH AND REACTIONS

Research relating to rational emotive therapy began with Ellis's (1957) review of his own casework employing three different methods of psychotherapy. Ellis found that, with orthodox psychoanalysis, 13% of his patients improved considerably, 37% showed distinct improvement, and 50% showed little or no improvement. With analytically oriented therapy, the figures were 18%, 45%, and 37%, respectively. Ellis found his system (then called *rational therapy*) to be the most successful, with figures of 44%, 46%, and 10%. In addition, Ellis found his system to be effective in one to five sessions as compared to the longer periods of therapy required for the other two approaches.

Maultsby (1971) has made significant modifications of Ellis's basic system by focusing on homework assignments for clients. He refers to his system as *rational behavior therapy*. In a study of 87 psychiatric outpatients receiving homework therapy for a period of ten weeks, Maultsby found that 85% of the patients who were judged most improved rated the homework as effective in their treatment.

Maultsby, Knipping, and Carpenter (1974) investigated the effectiveness of a rational emotive educational program as a preventive mental-health tool for high school and college students. The program was designed to teach students to utilize RET methods in analyzing their bad feelings and in developing strategies for solving their problems. The study was conducted with high school students already suffering from emotional upset. Following participation in the RET program, the experimental group improved significantly on several measures of personality assessment.

Rational emotive education for children in the elementary school setting is of interest to those who believe that it is important to teach children to think rationally about events before they are programmed to react irrationally. Several anecdotal studies have supported the view that the principles of RET can be effective in working with both disturbed and "normal" children (Ellis, 1969b, 1972; Ellis, Wolfe, & Moseley, 1966; Glicken, 1968; Hauck, 1967; Knaus, 1974). However, studies are needed to show that RET results in a generalized improvement in mental health. According to a survey of RET research by DiGiuseppe, Miller, and Trexler (1977), there is no evidence to support the idea that all children are able to acquire the principles of RET. As we have suggested earlier, many approaches to counseling will need to be adapted for those children functioning in the concrete cognitive stage.

Knaus and Boker (1975) and Albert (1972) investigated the effectiveness of RET education programs with elementary school children. Both studies showed lower scores for the experimental groups on the Anxiety Scale for Children, with the Knaus and Boker study showing an increase in self-esteem for the experimental group.

Carmody's (1977) study on "A Comparative Analysis of Rational-Emotive, Self-Instructional, and Behavioral Assertion Training" employed 63 subassertive adult outpatients who participated in four 90-minute sessions of group assertion training. Treatment effects were assessed by using self-report measures of social anxiety, assertiveness, and unproductive self-statements, and behavioral measures of assertiveness. Maintenance of treatment gains was measured on self-report and behavioral tests at a three-month follow-up assessment. The results indicated that: (1) the three groups were not significantly different over the short term period; (2) the RET group showed significantly more improvements on the self-report measure of unproductive cognitions than the other two training groups at posttest; and (3) the generalization of treatment gains was successfully demonstrated for all three training groups on role-played "generalization" assertive scenes. However, on a test of transfer of training at posttest, only the RET group evidenced significant generalization of treatment gains.

In the development of RET, Ellis has postulated, among other things, a system of beliefs or philosophies common to our culture that are inherently irrational and conducive to maladjustment. Jones (1968) constructed an instrument to measure these beliefs. He was able to conclude on the basis of his data that his Irrational Beliefs Test was sufficiently reliable and valid as a measure of irrational beliefs for use in both research and specific clinical situations. Ellis's theoretical position with respect to irrational beliefs was substantially confirmed by the results of the study.

Glass and Smith (1976) reviewed 375 outcome studies in psychotherapy, 35 of which were conducted with RET. In a ranking of ten types of therapy, RET placed second to systematic desensitization in outcome success, with behavior modification a close third. The other theories included Gestalt, psychodynamic, transactional analysis, Adlerian, client-centered, implosion, and eclectic.

In summary, RET is receiving considerable recognition in the literature. The study of Berkowitz and Alioto (1973) has demonstrated that activating events are not necessarily the causes of aggressive consequences. Rather, anger has been found to originate in human cognitions. However, an article by Zajonc (1980) challenges this assumption by presenting evidence for emotion occurring without cognition.

A comprehensive review of the literature on aggression by Berkowitz (1970) points out the futility and danger of "acting out" aggressive impulses as a way of relieving these emotions. Aggression apparently begets more aggression; therefore, a more productive system for treating aggression is needed. Ellis believes his RET is the answer.

REFERENCES

Albert, S. *A study to determine the effectiveness of affective education with fifth grade students.* Unpublished master's thesis, Queens College, 1972.

Berkowitz, C. Experimental investigations of hostility catharsis. *Journal of Consulting and Clinical Psychology*, 1970, *35*, 1–7.

Berkowitz, L., and Alioto, J. The meaning of an observed event as a determinant of its aggressive consequences. *Journal of Personality and Social Psychology*, 1973, *28*, 206–217.

Carmody, T. A comparative analysis of rational-emotive, self-instructional and behavioral assertion training. *Dissertation Abstracts International*, 1977, *38*, 1394–B.

Di Giuseppe, R., Miller, N., and Trexler, L. A review of rational-emotive psychotherapy outcome studies. *The Counseling Psychologist*, 1977, 7, 64–72.

Ellis, A. *The American sexual tragedy*. New York: Twayne, 1954.

Ellis, A. Outcome of employing three techniques of psychotherapy. *Journal of Clinical Psychology*, 1957, *13*, 334–350.

Ellis, A. *Reason and emotion in psychotherapy*. New York: Lyle Stuart, 1962.

Ellis, A. *The case for sexual liberty*. Tucson, Ariz.: Seymour Press, 1965.

Ellis, A. *The art and science of love* (rev. ed.). New York: Lyle Stuart and Bantam, 1969 (originally published, 1960). (a)

Ellis, A. Teaching emotional education in the classroom. *School Health Review*, 1969, *1*, 10–13. (b)

Ellis, A. Emotional education in the classroom. *Journal of Clinical Child Psychology*, 1972, *1*, 19–22.

Ellis, A. What rational-emotive therapy is and is not. *Counselor Education and Supervision*, 1974, *14*, 140–144.

Ellis, A. *How to live with a "neurotic"* (rev. ed.). New York: Crown Publishers, 1975 (originally published, 1957).

Ellis, A. *How to live with—and without—anger*. New York: Reader's Digest Press, 1977.

Ellis, A., and Harper, R. *A new guide to rational living*. Englewood Cliffs, N. J.: Prentice-Hall, 1975.

Ellis, A., Moseley, S., and Wolfe, J. *How to raise an emotionally healthy, happy child*. North Hollywood, Calif.: Wilshire Books, 1972.

Ellis, A., Wolfe, J., and Moseley, S. *How to prevent your child from becoming a neurotic adult*. New York: Crown, 1966.

Glass, G., and Smith, M. *Meta-analysis of psychotherapy outcome studies*. Paper presented at the annual meeting of the Society for Psychotherapy Research, Boston, June 1976.

Glicken, M. Rational counseling: A new approach to children. *Journal of Elementary School Guidance and Counseling*, 1968, *2*, 261–267.

Goodman, D., and Maultsby, M. *Emotional well-being through rational behavior training*. Springfield, Ill.: Charles C Thomas, 1974.

Hauck, P. *The rational management of children*. New York: Libra, 1967.

Jones, R. *A factored measure of Ellis' irrational belief systems with personality and maladjustment correlates*. Doctoral dissertation, Texas Technological College, 1968.

Knaus, W. *Rational emotive education, a manual for elementary school teachers*. New York: Institute for Rational Living, 1974.

Knaus, W., and Boker, S. The effect of rational-emotive education on anxiety and self-concept. *Rational Living*, 1975, *10*, 7–10.

Maultsby, M. Systematic written homework in psychotherapy. *Psychotherapy*, 1971, *8*, 195–198.

Maultsby, M., Knipping, P., and Carpenter, L. Teaching self-help in the classroom with rational self-counseling. *Journal of School Health*, 1974, *44*, 445–448.

Zajonc, R. Feeling and thinking: Preferences need no inferences. *American Psychologist*, 1980, *35*, 151–175.

CHAPTER

7

INDIVIDUAL PSYCHOLOGY

ALFRED ADLER

Alfred Adler, the founder of individual psychology, was born in Vienna, Austria, on February 7, 1870, the second oldest of six children. When Adler was 10 years old, he was found to be doing very poorly in mathematics. His teachers suggested to Adler's father that Alfred be removed from school and assigned as an apprentice to a cobbler. As is often true with paradoxical counseling strategies, Alfred became angry, studied harder, and placed first in his class. As a child, Adler suffered from rickets, pneumonia, and several accidents. Such frequent contact with doctors and illness influenced Adler to study medicine.

Adler spent his entire youth in Vienna and received his medical degree from its university in 1895. In addition to medicine, Adler was also knowledgeable in psychology and philosophy as well as the Bible and Shakespeare. Two years after his graduation, Adler married Raisa Timofeyewna Epstein, an intellectual and friend of Freud's, who had come from Russia to study at the University of Vienna (Alexander, Eisenstein, & Grotjahn, 1966).

In the fall of 1902, Adler joined Sigmund Freud's discussion group that was to become the first psychoanalytic society. Adler was not a proponent of Freud's psychosexual theory, and his writings about "feelings of inferiority" in 1910 and 1911 initiated a break with Freud. In 1910, Freud attempted to reconcile the gap between himself and the Adlerians and named Adler president of the Viennese Analytic Society as well as appointing him coeditor of a journal published by Freud.

Nevertheless, Adler continued to disagree with Freud's psychosexual theory. Adler was the first psychoanalyst to emphasize human nature as being fundamentally social. Upon Freud's demand that his entire staff accept his theory without any conditions, Adler resigned, along with seven others, and founded the Society for Free Psychoanalysis. In 1912, Dr. Adler changed the name to the Society for Individual Psychology (Orgler, 1965).

After World War I broke out, Adler served for two years as a military doctor and later was appointed the head of a large hospital for wounded and shell-shocked cases. In 1926, Adler accepted a visiting professorship at Columbia University in New York, and in 1935 he moved his family to the United States. His children, one son and one daughter, became psychiatrists and worked with the principles of individual psychology. On May 28, 1937, while giving a series of lectures in Scotland, Adler suddenly collapsed on the street and died of heart failure.

Adler had many accomplishments in his lifetime. In 1912, he founded the *Journal for Individual Psychology*, which was first published in America in 1935. In 1919, he organized the first child guidance clinics in Vienna. The staff of these clinics included physicians, psychologists, and social workers. Adler introduced the term *inferiority feelings*, and he developed a flexible, supportive psychotherapy to direct those emotionally disabled by inferiority feelings toward maturity, common sense, and social usefulness.

Adler originated the network of child guidance clinics, called *Erzie-bungs-bera-tungstelle*, which means literally "a place to come for questions about education"—a parent education center. Group discussions with families were originated by Adler. Many regard Adler to have been 50 years ahead of his time; present-day emphasis on group counseling and parent education would support this claim.

Perhaps the most helpful adaptations and development of Adler's work were made by Rudolf Dreikurs, a leading proponent and contributor to individual psychology until his death in 1972. Dreikurs was professor emeritus of psychiatry at the Chicago Medical School, director of the Alfred Adler Institute in Tel Aviv, and visiting professor at many universities in America and abroad.

Dreikurs was a pioneer in music therapy and group psychotherapy, which he introduced into private psychiatric practice in 1929. A former student and collaborator of Alfred Adler, Dreikurs developed specific technical procedures, based on Adlerian principles, in many fields of human relations. His literary works included nine books and numerous papers (Mosak, 1973). Dreikurs's most significant contribution to the field of counseling children was his ability to translate theory into practice. Many of Adler's complex ideas were developed by Dreikurs into a relatively simple, applied method for understanding and working with the behavior of children in both the family and school setting.

THE NATURE OF PEOPLE

If Freud had done nothing more than stimulate thinking and reactions in other theorists, he would have made a significant contribution to the field of counseling and psychotherapy. Like so many others, Adler reacted against Freud's ideas and developed a new theory. Freud attempted to interpret all behaviors and problems as extensions of sex, pleasure, and the death instinct. Adler, on the other hand, believed that all people develop some sense of inferiority because they are born completely helpless and remain that way for a rather long childhood. Such feelings of inferiority may be exaggerated by body or organ defects (real or imaginary), by having older and more powerful siblings, or by parent neglect or rejection. One way to cope with feelings of inferiority is through compensation or by gaining power to handle the sense of weakness. The effects of organ inferiority are reduced through development of skills, behaviors, traits, and strengths that tend to replace or compensate for these thoughts of weakness and powerlessness.

Adler viewed human behavior as falling on a continuum between masculinity—representing strength and power—and femininity—symbolizing weakness and inferiority. What he called *masculine protest*, a striving for power, was common to both sexes, especially women. Adler replaced Freud's concept of sexual pleasure as the prime motivator of behavior with the search for power.

According to Adler, personality development progresses along a road paved with evidences of either personal superiority or inferiority. As infants—small, helpless, inexperienced—we are especially subject to the whims of others and vulnerable to inferiority feelings. As we grow older, both family and society emphasize the advantages of size, beauty, and strength. Therefore, there develops within us a continual conflict between our wishes and dreams for superiority, our attempts to achieve it, and the social realities that may make us feel inferior. This striving for power (masculine protest) occupies a place in his theory similar to that of the Oedipus situation in Freudian theory. A person develops into a normal adult or a neurotic or psychotic personality as the result of this struggle between the masculine protest and social reality.

The need for success

Adler was struck by the importance of the hunger for success in human life—the ways by which people seek power and prestige and strive for goals associated with social approval. He was very concerned with the problems of competition, blocked ambition, feelings of resentment and hostility, and impulses to struggle and resist or to surrender and give in. Adler shifted his clinical attention from a primary focus on patients' psychosexual history to an examination of their success/failure pattern, their style of life. Adler's term *style of life* emphasizes the direction in which the individual is moving. Style of life analysis involves an assessment of children in terms of their habitual responses to frustration, to the assumption of responsibility, and to situations requiring the exercise of initiative.

Goals of behavior

Adler's individual psychology emphasizes the purposive nature of human strivings. All behavior, including emotions, is purposive, or goal directed. According to Adlerian theory, the cause of behavior is not the issue; the important thing is to determine what children want to accomplish, in either the real world or in their own minds. Behaviors will not be continued over time unless they "work" for the children. By looking at the consequences of their behavior, adults can determine their goals. Adler's conception was that people are guided by a striving for ideal masculinity. Adler described what he termed the *neurotic search for glory;* neurotics are characterized by an unrealistic goal of masculinity and mastery that they strive to overcome or attain. He also anticipated later psychoanalytic groups in his emphasis upon the social as well as the constitutional determinants of one's style of life. In fact, the term *individual psychology* is based on Adler's emphasis on the uniqueness of the individual and the creation of a personal lifestyle as opposed to Freud's emphasis on instincts common to all people. The individual's style of life is built from an interaction between heredity and environment; these lifestyle building blocks are used to fit oneself into life as the individual perceives it.

Lifestyle

Behavior is holistic, according to Adler. Usually by the age of four or five, children have drawn general conclusions about life, and the "best" way to meet the problems life offers. These conclusions are based on their biased perceptions of the events and interactions that go on around them and form the basis for their lifestyle. The style of life, unique for each individual, is the pattern of behavior that will predominate throughout that person's life. Only rarely will a person's lifestyle change without outside intervention. It is important that children understand their lifestyle—that is, the basic beliefs they have developed at an early age to help organize, understand, predict, and control their world.

The amount of social interest one possesses is, according to Adler, a good barometer of mental health. Social interest is a feeling for and cooperation with people—a sense of belonging and participating with others for the common good. Everyone has a need to belong to a group. Although social interest is inborn, it does not appear spontaneously but must be encouraged and trained, beginning with the relationship between the newborn infant and the mother. Children who feel that they are part of a group will do useful things that contribute to the well-being of that group, while those who feel left out, and therefore inferior, will do useless things in order to prove their own worth by gaining attention. From this concept comes the idea that misbehaving children are discouraged children—children who think that they can be known in only useless ways. Because children behave within the social context, their behavior cannot be studied in isolation. The study of human interaction is basic to individual psychology.

Many of life's problems center around conflicts with others. Solutions for these problems involve cooperating with people in the interest of making society a better place in which to live. A strong point in Adler's theory is his understanding of the implications of the social structure of life. Since every individual is dependent upon other people for birth and growth, for food and shelter and protection, for love and companionship, a great web of interdependence exists among people. Thus the individual, Adler points out, owes a constant debt to society. Each of us is responsible to our group, and those who do not learn to cooperate are destroyed. Adler believed that we cannot violate this love and logic that bind us together without dire consequences for the health of our personality. Pronounced egocentricity (the opposite of social interest) leads to neurosis, and the individual becomes healthy again only when this egocentricity is renounced in favor of a greater interest in the well-being of the total group. Critics of Adlerian theory who hold a less positive view of human nature point out that, even though people know they should cooperate, they ordinarily do not do so until forced. Cross-cultural research evidence is available to support this view.

Environment

Three environmental factors affect the development of a child's personality: family atmosphere, family constellation, and the prevalent methods of training. Through the family atmosphere, children learn about values and customs and try to fit themselves into the standards set by their parents. Children also learn about relationships by watching how their family interacts, and about sex roles by seeing the patterns adopted by their parents. The family constellation is important in that children formulate unique personalities based on how they interpret their position in the family relative to other siblings. One possible pattern is illustrated by the following examples. The first-born child, who is dethroned by the new baby, strives very hard to maintain the position of supremacy and seeks recognition by whatever means is possible. The second child feels inadequate because there is always someone ahead and seeks a place by becoming what the older child is not. This child may feel squeezed out when the third child comes and adopt the position that life is unfair. The youngest child may take advantage of being the youngest and become outstanding in some respect, be it good or bad. Youngest children may even seek a place by becoming openly rebellious or helpless.

In summary, Adler believed that the principal human motive, a striving for perfection, could become a striving for superiority and thus an overcompensation for a feeling of inferiority. Children are seen as self-determining persons, able to create a style of life in the context of their family constellation. By trial and error and observation, children form their own conclusions about life and their place in it.

THEORY OF COUNSELING

Adler (1964) held the point of view that four ties create reality and meaning in people's lives:

1. People are living on earth to help ensure the continuance of the human species.
2. Our survival depends on our need to cooperate with our fellow human beings.
3. Human beings are living in two sexes—the masculine, powerful side of our nature and the feminine, weak side of our nature.
4. Human problems can be grouped into three categories: social, occupational, and sexual.

Adler viewed the counselor's job as helping the child substitute realistic goals for unrealistic life goals and instilling social interest and concern for others.

As with most approaches to counseling, the goal of establishing a positive sense of self-esteem is primary. To accomplish this feeling of self-esteem, children need to feel good about finding a place in life and also about their progress in overcoming the unpleasant sense of inferiority associated with the dependence, smallness, and vulnerability introduced in early childhood. In the Adlerian view, the ideal or well-adjusted child would have the following qualities:

1. Respects the rights of others
2. Is tolerant of others
3. Is interested in others
4. Cooperates with others
5. Encourages others
6. Is courteous
7. Has a strong, positive self-concept
8. Has a feeling of belonging
9. Has socially acceptable goals
10. Exerts genuine effort
11. Is willing to share with others
12. Is concerned with how much "we" can get rather than how much "I" can get

In response to the specific pattern of inferiority feelings experienced by a child in a specific home situation, one unitary way of coping with the problem is discovered; one fundamental attitude is developed; one mode of compensation is achieved. Thus, a style of life is formed early in one's childhood—a style that is unitary, dependable, and predictable.

Adler recognized two fundamental styles of life: a direct and an indirect approach to the good things. We may choose to conquer through strength and power or to conquer through weakness. Power is usually tried first; if power is blocked, we choose another road to our goal. The second road is paved with gentleness and bids for sympathy. If both roads fail to take us to our goals, secondary feelings of inferiority arise. These secondary inferiority feelings, which Adler considered to be more serious than the primary universal inferiority feelings, may be seen as ego problems, which can be the most burning problem of all. The focus of counseling, therefore, is directed toward harnessing this drive to compensate for weakness so that positive, constructive behavior will be the result. Freud held that the backbone of civilization was sublimation. Adler thought that talent and capabilities arise from the stimulus of inadequacy.

Adlerians believed that, because children are pulled by their goals, adults need to know these goals. Knowledge of children's goals is a major key to understanding their behavior. We need to observe behaviors because movement tends to be more reliable than words. Adlerians work with priorities. For example, the need to belong has four possible priorities:

1. To be comfortable. The main objective of seeking comfort is to avoid stress. Such behavior may be irritating to others, and the price you pay for comfort may be reduced productivity.
2. To please others. The main objective for pleasing others is to avoid rejection. While other people may find it quite easy to accept a "me last" person, the price for this behavior is stunted growth.
3. To control. The main objective of trying to control others, yourself, and your environment is to avoid unexpected humiliation. Controlling others tends to make them feel challenged, with the resulting price for your priority being increased social distance between you and other people. Too much self-control results in a very structured life with little spontaneity.
4. To be superior. The main objective of trying to be superior is to avoid meaninglessness in your life. Such an attitude of superiority tends to make others feel inadequate. The price for superiority may be an overloaded lifestyle. The child may become overly responsible and perfectionistic, with all the resulting worry and anxiety when things are not perfect.

The family constellation

A goal of counseling would be to construct a picture of the child's lifestyle and how the style was developed. Such a lifestyle analysis would necessitate an examination of the family dynamics and the child's place in the family constellation. Ordinal position in the family constellation is a key to the lifestyle pattern developed by children and may have a significant effect on how they perceive reality. Although there are certain characteristics associated with each child's position in the family, we know that many exceptions exist; not all first borns are alike. However, we know that children, in an effort to find their special place in the family, do tend to select different roles, behaviors, and interests. In general, some stereotypic behaviors have been cataloged by Adlerians over the past 80 years. Some of these generalizations will be summarized below.

The only child.   The only child enjoys some intellectual advantages by not having to share mother and father with any siblings. Language development is usually accelerated because the child learns adult language patterns. However, the reverse is sometimes true in an extremely child-centered home where everybody talks baby talk. Frequently, only children may experience difficulties outside the home when peers and teachers do not pamper them in the manner to which they have become accustomed. Only children may be skillful in getting along with adults but experience difficulty in making friends with children of their own age. They enjoy being the center of attention. It is helpful in understanding these children to observe how they gain the approval and attention to maintain their center-stage position. Have they developed skills, do they elicit sympathy through being helpless, or do they act shy? Only children are more likely to have problems with the egocentrism block. They are usually interested only in themselves and may resort to tantrums and uncooperative behavior if their requests are not granted. Finally, only children may become overly dependent on adults because they are not taught to do things on their own. An exception to the rule are those only children who learn to play ball and other games by themselves when they have not had an opportunity to be around friends.

First-born and second-born children.   Often considered the special child, or "Christ Child," by the family, especially if they are male, first-borns enjoy their number 1 ranking but often fear dethronement by the birth of a second child. First-borns work hard at pleasing their parents. They are likely to be conforming, achievers, defenders of the faith, introverted, and well-behaved. Twenty-three out of the first twenty-five astronauts were first-born males. NASA was interested in recruiting high-achieving followers for the space program; there was no need for "creative astronauts" who might decide to take the scenic route home. First-borns often find themselves functioning as substitute parents in larger families.

Second-born children may be those extroverted, creative, free-thinking spirits that NASA was trying to avoid. More often than not, second-borns look at what is "left over" in the way of roles and behavior patterns that the first-born child has shunned; it may be easier to pick another role than to compete with the older sibling who has such a large head start. Second-borns may make lower grades in school even though they are brighter than number 1. Parents are often easier on second-born children, showing less concern with rules. In fact, second-borns may be the family rebels—with or without a cause! We can be sure that second-borns will usually be the opposite of the first child. It is easy for second-borns to become discouraged when trying to compete with successful, older, and bigger first-borns. The more successful first-borns are, the more likely second-borns are to feel unsure of themselves and their abilities. They may even feel squeezed-out, neglected, unloved, and abused when the third child arrives.

The youngest child.   Often referred to as Prince or Princess Charming, the youngest child could find a permanent lifestyle of being the baby in the family. Youngest children often get a lot of service from all the other family members. They may become very dependent or spoiled and experience a lag in development. It is easy for youngest children to develop real feelings of inferiority because they are smaller, less able to take care of themselves, and often not taken seriously. The really successful charmers may learn how to boss subtly or manipulate the entire family. They will make a decision either to challenge their older siblings or to evade any direct struggles for superiority.

When a five-year difference exists between the children in a family, the situation changes. With a five-year or longer gap, the next-born child often assumes characteristics of a first born; apparently, the five years remove the competitive barriers found among children who are closer together in age.

Extreme behavior patterns are often observed in children who find themselves the only boy or girl among siblings of the opposite sex. They may tend to develop toward extremes in either masculinity or femininity. Sex roles assumed by children often depend on roles perceived as most favored in our culture.

Large families appear to offer some advantages in child rearing by making it tough for parents to overparent each child. Children in large families frequently learn how to solve their problems, take care of themselves, and handle their conflicts because their parents cannot always give personal service and attention to each and every problem. Large families are probably good training grounds for learning how to be independent.

Many factors enter into the perceptions children have of their particular role in their family:

1. The parents may have a favorite child.
2. The family may be required to move.
3. Parents become more experienced and easygoing as they grow older.

4. Some homes are single-parent homes due to death or divorce.
5. The children may have a step-parent living in the home.
6. The family climate changes with each addition to the family.
7. Chronic illnesses or handicaps may be a problem in the family.
8. A grandparent may live in the home.

The family atmosphere

Dreikurs (1964), in his book *Children: The Challenge*, examined the importance of the family atmosphere on the development of the child. Whereas the family constellation is a description of how family members interact with one another, the family atmosphere is the style of coping with life that the family has modeled for the child.

The following 12 family atmospheres indicate how negative family atmosphere can affect children in an adverse manner.

1. Authoritarian. The authoritarian home requires unquestioned obedience from the children. Children have little or no voice in family decisions. While these children are often well behaved and well mannered, they also tend to be more anxious and outer directed. What was once a shy child may turn into a rebel with a cause in later life.

2. Suppressive. Right in tune with the authoritarian home is the suppressive family atmosphere in which children are not permitted to express their thoughts and feelings. Expression of opinion is limited to what the parents want to hear. Frequently children from such a family have a difficult time expressing feeling when it is allowed in situations outside the home, such as counseling. Close relationships are not encouraged in this type of family atmosphere.

3. Rejective. Children feel unloved and unaccepted in this family atmosphere. Some parents do not know how to show love and frequently have difficulty in separating the deed from the doer. Children and parents need to know and understand that love can be unconditional and not tied to unacceptable behavior. For example, "I love you, but I still am angered by your irresponsibility." It is easy for a child to become extremely discouraged in the rejective family.

4. Disparaging. Children criticized by everyone else in the family often turn out to be the "bad egg" everyone predicted they would be. Too much criticism generally leads to cynicism and an inability to form good interpersonal relationships.

5. High standards. Children living in the high standards atmosphere may think such things as "I am not loved unless I make all 'A's.' " Fear of failure leads to the considerable distress experienced by perfectionistic people. The tenseness and stress these children experience often prevents them from performing as well as they are able.

6. Inharmonious. In homes with considerable quarreling and fighting, children learn that it is important to try to control other people and keep others from controlling them. Power becomes a prime goal for these children. Discipline may be inconsistent in these homes, depending on the mood of the parents.

7. Inconsistent. Inconsistent methods of discipline and home routines are often sources of confusion and disharmony in the home. Lack of self-control, low motivation, self-centeredness, instability, and poor interpersonal relationships are often attributed to inconsistency in parenting practices.

8. Materialistic. In this type of home, children learn that feelings of self-worth depend on possessions and how much you own in relation to your peers. Interpersonal relationships take a back seat to accumulating wealth in the materialistic family.

9. Overprotective. Children are often prevented from growing up in these homes as parents do too much for them. They protect the children from the consequences of their behavior and, in doing so, deny the reality of the situation. This overindulgence by parents leads to feelings of helplessness and dependency in the child. Dependent children fall into the class of outer-directed people who rely on others for approval.

10. Pitying. Like overprotectiveness, pitying also prevents children from developing and using the resources they have for solving their problems. Such may be the case for handicapped children, especially. Children are encouraged to feel sorry for themselves and to expect favors from others to make up for their misfortunes.

11. Hopeless. Discouraged and "unsuccessful" parents may often pass these attitudes on to their children who make hopelessness a part of their lifestyle. A pessimistic home atmosphere may be due to economic factors, especially if the bread winners are lacking financial resources.

12. Martyr. Martyrdom is another pessimistic viewpoint of people suffering from low self-esteem, hopelessness, and discouragement. Once again, such children may learn that life is unfair and that people should treat them better. As with other types of negative family atmosphere, a breeding ground for dependency is formed.

When looking at the various types of family atmosphere, it is good to remember that atmosphere is not the total cause of behavior. Behavior is most influenced by the child's biased perceptions of the family climate.

Goals of misbehavior

As children grow and interact with their environment, they gradually develop methods for achieving their basic goal of belonging. Several factors, including the child's place in the family, the quality of interaction of parents with the child, and the child's creative reaction to the family atmosphere, are critical in the development of coherent patterns of behaviors and attitudes.

Dreikurs (1964) has made an especially insightful and useful analysis of the immediate goals by which children attempt to achieve their basic goal of belonging. Children who do not have a pattern of misbehavior have an immediate goal of cooperation and constructive collaboration. These children find their place and feel good about themselves through constructive cooperation. They generally approach life with the goal of being a collaborator, and their usual behavior is socially and personally effective. On the other hand, children who have a pattern of misbehavior are usually pursuing one of four mistaken goals: attention, power, revenge, and inadequacy or withdrawal. An understanding of the goal for which a misbehaving child is striving helps put the behavior in perspective and provides a basis for corrective action.

Attention.   All children seek attention, especially those of preschool age. However, excessive attention getting should diminish in the primary school years. Excessive attention-getting behavior that continues beyond the primary grades becomes a problem to teachers, parents, and peers. The child's goal is to keep you busy, and your natural reaction is to feel annoyed and provide the service and attention the child seeks. Attention getting appears in four forms:

1. Active constructive. This child may be the model child, but the goal is to elevate self, not to cooperate. This is the successful student whose industrious and reliable performance is for attention only.
2. Passive constructive. This is the charming child who is not as vigorous as the active constructive child about attention getting. This child is a conscientious performer and a prime candidate for teacher's pet.
3. Active destructive. This is the nuisance child—the prime candidate for the child most likely to ruin your day. This is the class clown, show-off, and mischief maker.
4. Passive destructive. This is the lazy child who gets your attention through demands for service and help. This child often does lack ability and motivation to complete work.

Power.   These children have an exaggerated need to exercise power and superiority. Every situation, debate, or issue is taken as a personal challenge from which it is necessary to emerge the winner; otherwise, these children think they have failed. The child's goal is to be the boss. Your reaction ranges between anger and feeling threatened or defeated. The child acts in a stubborn, argumentative way and may even throw tantrums. This child will likely lead the league in disobedience. Power struggling has two forms:

1. Active destructive. This child is the rebel who has the potential of leading a group rebellion.
2. Passive destructive. This child is stubborn, forgetful, and could also be the lazy one in the group.

Revenge.   These children feel hurt and mistreated by life. Their goal is to get even by hurting others. They do achieve social recognition even though they usually make themselves very unpopular with most other children. The child's goal, then, is to even up the score, and the adult's reaction is usually feeling hurt. Revenge has two forms:

1. Active destructive. This child is vicious and resorts to stealing, vandalism, and physical abuse to extract revenge. This child is a candidate to become a leader of a juvenile delinquent gang.
2. Passive destructive. This child is also violent, but in a passive way. This is the quiet, sullen, defiant child. Both of these revenge types believe their only hope lies in getting even.

Inadequacy or withdrawal.   These children often feel inferior and think they are incapable of handling life's problems. Their deficiencies may be either real or imagined. By giving up, they hope to hide their inferiority and to prevent others from making demands on them. The child's goal is to be left alone, and the adult's reaction is giving up because of a feeling of helplessness. Inadequacy has only one form:

Passive destructive. These children are usually described as hopeless. They often put on an act of being stupid just to discourage the teacher from asking them to recite and do work. They may have an unwritten contract with their teachers that says, in effect, "I'll leave you alone, if you leave me alone."

COUNSELING METHOD

The counseling methods pioneered by Adler were based on his experiences and philosophy about the nature of people. Many of Adler's original ideas have been used and modified by later Adlerians such as Rudolf Dreikurs, Heinz Ansbacher, Harold Mosak, and Don Dinkmeyer.

In Adlerian counseling, no distinction is made between conscious and unconscious material. The counselor uses dreams, for example, to discover the lifestyle of a child—that is, the type of defense utilized to establish superiority. The counselor tries to analyze the inferiority feelings that stem from real or fancied personal deficiencies, particularly so-called organ deficiencies (such as defective vision), or organic inferiority (weak heart), some form of which everyone is assumed to possess. Next, the counselor proceeds to examine the child's academic, extracurricular, and social adjustments. It is helpful to see how the child has maintained or achieved superiority in each of these major areas of life and to examine the inferiority feelings that may plague the child. A primary goal of Adlerian counseling is to point out to the child the overcompensation and defensive patterns being used to solve problems and to find better ways of succeeding in solving problems related to school, play, and other social concerns.

A summary of the main points in the Adlerian counseling method is presented below.

Main aspects

Counselor/client relationship. As is true with many counseling methods, the establishment of the counselor/client relationship is the key step to the process. The counselor's job is to reeducate children who have developed mistaken ideas about some concepts of their lives. The counseling relationship is based on the assumption that the counselor and child are equal partners in the process and that the child is a responsible person who is capable of learning better ways to meet personal needs. The positive view of human nature is indicated through the counselor's faith, hope, and caring attitude toward the child.

Life as holistic. Adlerians believe that lives are holistic. Dinkmeyer, Pew, and Dinkmeyer (1979) refer to the concept of *teleoanalytic holistic theory*, which regards any troubled or troublesome behavior as a reflection of one indivisible, unified, whole organism moving toward self-created goals. The foremost task of Adlerian counselors is to prove this unity in people, in their thinking, feeling, and behavior—in fact, in every expression of their personality (Ansbacher & Ansbacher, 1956). Adlerians believe that children are the artists of their own personalities and are constantly moving purposefully toward self-consistent goals. One technique that can be used with children is the lifestyle interview analysis, which is made up of present and past (early) recollections of the children themselves and their families, how they fit in, and how they perceive siblings and parents in relationship to themselves. Questions often used include:

1. What type of concern or problem would you like to discuss and how did this problem develop?
2. On a five-point scale, how are things going for you:

	Great	Medium	Poor
	1 2	3 4	5

   in school? _____
   with your friends? _____
   with your hobbies? _____
   with your parents? _____
   with your brothers and sisters? _____
   with your fun times? _____
3. Can you tell me about your mother and father? (Separate the answers for mother and father or for any other parent figures living at home.)
   What do they do?
   What do they want you to do?

How do you get along with them?

How are you like your parents?

How are you different from your parents?

4. Are there things in your family that you would like to be better? What? How?

5. Can you tell me about your brothers and sisters? (Make a list from the oldest to youngest child in the family and their ages.) Of all your brothers and sisters, who is:

a. most like you? How?

b. most different from you?* How?

6. What kind of child are you?

7. What kind of child did you used to be?

8. What scares you the most?

9. What used to scare you the most?

10. Have any of your brothers or sisters been sick or hurt?

11. What does each of the children in your family do best?

12. Who is the:

smartest?

best athlete?

mother's favorite?

father's favorite?

hardest worker?

best behaved?

funniest?

most spoiled?

best in mathematics?**

best in spelling?**

best in penmanship?**

most stubborn?

best looking?

friendliest?

strongest?

healthiest?

best musician?

best with tools?

These and other questions are used initially to explore the pictures children have painted of their lives. Later they are used to help children understand their lifestyles today.

*The sibling most different from your client usually has the greatest influence on your client's lifestyle.

**These three school subjects relate to the child's personality development. Good mathematics students are good personal problem solvers. Good spellers and good writers (good in penmanship) are generally well-behaved children who follow rules and cooperate with the social order.

Early recollections are also used to understand earliest impressions of life and how the child felt about them. Children are asked to remember as far back as they can. It is good to obtain recollections of specific incidents, as detailed as possible, including the child's reaction at the time. For example: "If we took a snapshot when that happened, what would we see? How did you feel?" It is also helpful to elicit four to six of those early recollections as a way of finding a pattern in the lifestyle. These tend to reflect a prototype that is apparent in the lifestyle analysis. Although the occurrences related by children may not be factually accurate, they are true insofar as they reflect the children's memories and feelings. This gives the counselor a clearer idea of the child's basic view of life and how some attitudes may have mistakenly crystallized. Examples of themes that may appear in these recollections and the child's mistaken beliefs include:

1. Early dangers—be aware of the many hostile aspects of life.
2. Happy times with adults around—life is great as long as many people praise and serve me.
3. Misdeeds recalled—be very careful that they do not happen again.

Understanding. Use a great deal of understanding with children. No matter what they are doing, they are probably doing the best they can at the moment. Ways of relieving some anxiousness and conflict include helping them interpret what is happening and giving the problem, child, or action a "handle." Use encouragement. Change negative situations to positive ones by telling fables where appropriate. "The Miller and the Donkey" is one story that helps children understand that they will never be able to please everyone, even by absurdly attempting the impossible. "The Frogs in the Milk" is another useful tale. It relates that two frogs who jumped into a barrel of milk simply paddled until they made butter; they were then able to jump out easily.

Confrontation. In some cases, confrontation is necessary when children are unable to change the mistaken ideas behind their behavior. Children can be confronted with educated guesses about the goals they are trying to achieve at others' expense. Be aware, also, of the child who is using depreciation. This often occurs when the counselor is viewed as an obstacle. Typically, the child is unwilling to move in a direction indicated by the counselor and attempts avoidance or wastes time. Counselors are advised to stay out of these power struggles.

Stages. Actual changes in children's perspectives occur in stages. First, they are limited to afterthoughts of insight. They can clearly see what they are doing to cause mistaken ideas or unhappiness to persist but only after they have misbehaved. In the second stage, children become able to catch themselves in the act of misbehaving. Added awareness enables them to sensitize themselves to inappropriate behavior. In the next stage, children have developed a heightened sense of awareness that enables them to anticipate the situation and plan a more appropriate behavior or response.

Practical methods

Methods developed by Dreikurs and Dinkmeyer from Adler's original ideas have been used by parents, counselors, and teachers in helping children. These methods were designed for practical application and use. The four goals of misbehaviors were designed to aid parents' and teachers' understanding that *how they feel* about what the child is doing will most clearly explain what the child's mistaken goal is.

Dreikurs's analysis and description of the four mistaken goals, the ways of identifying them, and the methods of correction have resulted in an impressive array of guidance and counseling approaches to help discouraged children and their often-discouraged families. The steps he outlines for determining a child's mistaken goals are both penetrating and simple. They involve answering the following questions in relation to a child's misbehavior: What is the adult's corrective response? What is the child's reaction to correction? When the child's goal is understood, it is possible through counseling with the child and parents to help the child develop a constructive goal and appropriate behavior.

In their description and analysis of specific immediate goals, Dreikurs and his colleagues have focused primarily on preadolescents. Dreikurs notes that, in early childhood, the status of children depends on the impression they make on adults. Later, they may develop different goals to gain social significance in their peer group and, later still, in adult society. These original goals can still be observed in people of every age. However, they are not all inclusive; teenagers and adults have other goals of misbehavior. Dreikurs reminds us that status and prestige can frequently be achieved more easily through useless and destructive means than through accomplishment.

Dreikurs advocates modifying the motivation rather than the behavior itself. When the motivation is changed, more constructive behavior follows automatically.

In order to use the "four-goal technique," the following steps must be taken:

1. Observe the child's behavior in detail.
2. Be psychologically sensitive to your own reaction.
3. Confront the child with the goal of the behavior.
4. Note the recognition reflex.
5. Apply appropriate corrective procedures.

It is important to remember that misbehaving children are discouraged children trying to find their place; they are acting on the faulty logic that their misbehavior will give them the social acceptance that they desire. Goal 1, attention getting, is a manifestation of minor discouragement, while Goal 4, display of inadequacy, is a manifestation of deep discouragement. Sometimes a child may switch from one kind of misbehavior to another. This is often a signal that the discouragement is growing worse.

In identifying young children's goals, it is most helpful to observe your own immediate response to their behavior. Your immediate response is in line with their expectations. The following four examples of behaviors show how you may feel, what the child may be thinking, what alternate behaviors exist, and what questions may come to mind about children's behavior.

Attention
You are annoyed, and begin coaxing, reminding.
Charlie thinks that he belongs only when he is noticed.
You can (1) attend to the child when he is behaving appropriately;
       (2) ignore misbehavior (scolding reinforces attention-getting behavior).
You ask: Could it be that you want me to notice you?

Power
You are angry, provoked, and threatened.
Linda thinks that she belongs only when she is in control or boss.
You can withdraw or "take your sail out of her wind" by leaving the room!
You ask: (1) Could it be that you want to be the boss?
       (2) Could it be that you want me to do what you want?

Revenge
You are deeply hurt and want to get even.
Sally thinks that her only hope is to get even.
You can (1) use group and individual encouragement;
       (2) try to convince her she is liked.
You ask: Could it be that you want to hurt me?

Inadequacy
You are feeling helpless and don't know what to do.
Tom thinks that he is unable to do anything, and that he belongs only when people expect nothing of him.
You can show genuine faith in the child, use encouragement.
You ask: Could it be that you feel stupid and do not want people to know?

A counseling interview that utilizes the four "could it be" questions might go as follows:

Counselor (Co): Alice, do you know why you did (the misbehavior)?
Alice: No. (This may be an honest response.)

Co: Would you like to work with me so that we can find out? I have some ideas that might help us explain what you are trying to get when you do _____. Will you help me figure this out?

Alice: OK.

Co: (Using one "could it be" question at a time and in a non-judgmental, unemotional tone of voice, asks:)
  1. Could it be that you want Mr. Jones to notice you more and give you some special attention?
  2. Could it be that you would like to be boss and have things your own way in Mr. Jones's class?
  3. Could it be that you have been hurt and you want to get even by hurting Mr. Jones and others in the class?
  4. Could it be that you want Mr. Jones to leave you alone and to stop asking you all those questions in math?

All four of these questions are always asked, sequentially, regardless of the child's answers or reflex because the child may be operating on more than one goal at a time. The counselor observes the body language as well as listening very carefully for the response in order to catch the "recognition reflex." An accurate disclosure of the child's present intentions produces a recognition reflex, such as a "guilty" facial expression, which is a reliable indication of his or her goal even though the child may say nothing or even say "no." Sometimes the confrontation itself helps the child to change. Another indication of the child's goal is the child's response to correction. If children are seeking attention and get it from the teacher, they will stop the misbehavior temporarily and then probably repeat it or do something similar. If children seek power, they will refuse to stop the disturbance, or even increase it. If they seek revenge, their response to the teacher's efforts to get them to stop will be to switch to some more violent action. A child with Goal 4 will not cooperate but will remain entirely passive and inactive.

Once the teacher suspects the goal of the child's misbehavior, it is most important to confront the child. The purpose of this confrontation is to disclose and confirm the mistaken goal to the child. The emphasis is on "for what purpose," not "why."

Corrective procedures

The next step is for the teacher to choose and use the suggested corrective procedures. They may include encouragement, logical consequences, or finding a friend for the child.

Encouragement.   Dreikurs (1964) wrote that encouragement implies faith in and respect for children as they are. Do not discourage children by having extremely high standards and being overly ambitious for them. Children misbehave only when they are discouraged and believe they cannot succeed by useful means. Children need encouragement as plants need water and sunshine. Telling children they can be better implies they are not good enough as they are.

Problems with Dreikurs's ideas on encouragement arise when parents ask how they are supposed to *not* expect their children to do better when they are performing below their ability levels. The answer seems to be in loving your children unconditionally and in spite of their behavior and performance. You do not have to love their misbehavior or pretend that you do.

Encouragement is advocated in place of praise and reinforcement. Praise is seen by Adlerians as a message that tells children that, under conditions determined by you, they are OK. It focuses on the product. Encouragement, however, tells children that you accept them where they are. It focuses on the process. It is often difficult to tell the difference:

Statements of Encouragement
I am proud of you.
That's a rough one, but I think you have what it takes to work
   it out.
Look at the progress you've made.

Statements of Praise
You certainly did a good job.
That was great work you did in math.
I like the way you handled that.
You played a good game!

Adlerian counselors believe that reward and punishment have detrimental effects on the development of the child, particularly in the democratic atmosphere that prevails today. Only in an autocratic society are they an effective and necessary means of obtaining conformity; they presuppose a certain person is endowed with superior authority. Children see rewards as one of their rights and soon demand a reward for everything they do if they are trained under this system. Punishment of children may be interpreted as their right to punish others. In fact, children often are hurt more by their retaliation than they are hurt by the punishment. They are experts in knowing how to hurt their parents, whether it is by getting into trouble or making low grades. Therefore, reward and punishment are rejected concepts in the Adlerian system.

Logical consequences.   Natural and logical consequences are Adlerian techniques favored over reward and punishment because they allow children to experience the actual consequences of their behavior. Natural consequences are a direct result of the children's behavior. If children are careless and touch the hot stove, they get burned. They will

be more careful of stoves in the future. Logical consequences are established through rules and family policy and are direct, consistent, and
logical results of a child's behavior. For example, if Frank comes home
late for dinner, he will find that his plate has been removed because it
has been assumed that, if he were hungry, he would have been there on
time to eat or would have called. Both types of consequences allow
children to experience the results of their behavior instead of arbitrary
punishment exercised through the personal authority of the parent.
These two techniques help to direct children's motivation toward proper
behavior through personal experience with the social order in which
they live. We are not recommending, however, that adults not protect
children in dangerous situations—we do not want to teach children
about the dangers of street traffic through personal experience!

Natural and logical consequences focus on the Adlerian belief that
people are responsible and capable of leading full and happy lives.
Consequences allow the child to understand an inner message that is
more likely to be remembered than punishment—which can harm our
relationships with children.

The use of natural and logical consequences gives children the message that you believe they are capable of making their own decisions.
It allows them an opportunity for growth through weighing the alternatives and arriving at a decision. When overly severe limits are set,
the child is deprived of making a decision that could foster self-respect
and responsibility. Allow children to do for themselves that which they
are capable of doing. Natural consequences are generally effective. Logical consequences, however, should be used only when there is no power
contest; otherwise they become punitive retaliation.

Family counseling.   Adlerian methods are well suited for counseling the entire family. The following interview guide is suggested.

1. Interview the parents on the following topics (while their children
   are observed in a playroom situation):
   a. Describe your children (use blackboard)—their respective
      ordinal positions, school work, hobbies, athletics, and so on.
   b. How does each child find his or her place in the family?
   c. What problems revolve around: getting up? meal time? TV?
      homework? chores? bedtime?
   d. Is there something in your family that needs to be better?
   e. Would you like to make a change?
   Before giving suggestions, it is preferable that the parents admit
   they are bankrupt in child-rearing ideas; that is, nothing has
   worked in improving the particular family concern.
2. Interview the children on the following topics (parents leave the
   conference room):
   a. Do you know why you are here today?

   b. Is there anything that bothers you in the family that you would like to change?
   c. How can we make things better at home?
   d. Who is the good child?
   e. Who is father's favorite?
   f. Who is mother's favorite?
   g. Who is best in sports?
   h. What do each of you do best?
   i. Which are your best school subjects?*
   j. Which are your worst school subjects?*
   Use "Could it be . . ." questions when appropriate. Ask who is in charge of discipline.
3. Interview the entire family. Summarize plans for the coming week, clarifying roles, behaviors, and expectations. Recommendations for each family generally include the following:
   a. Provide individual parent time for each child, each day.
   b. Have one family conference per week.
   c. Do one family activity per week.
   d. Each family member does chores.

SUMMARY: RESEARCH AND REACTIONS

Critics of the Adlerian system agree that, while it does explain much of our behavior, the theory tends to oversimplify some of the complex human behaviors brought to the counseling interview. Not everyone can be sorted into a birth-order category or a particular goal of misbehavior. Many of the Adlerian assumptions are nothing more than broad generalizations. Are not we all motivated by power and the drive to compensate for our inferiority as we seek to find a place in this world? Furthermore, there is a contradiction in the Adlerian system. On the one hand, it is noted that the basis of learning potential is the striving to compensate; on the other hand, the pessimist or the one who poses the greatest learning problem is characterized by deep feelings of inferiority. Adlerian counseling, like psychoanalytic counseling, puts the child on the spot—the child is wrong, and the counselor is right.

In spite of these critical remarks, the Adlerian counseling system offers a wealth of techniques for counseling children and families. Many of the other counseling theorists have borrowed both knowingly and unknowingly from Adler's work. Many of his common-sense ideas on effective counseling have been with us since the early 1900s.

---

*Once again, you may want to discuss with the family the three school subjects that relate to personality development (see p. 112). These assumptions about mathematics, spelling, and writing hold true for students who have the ability to do better and are not true for children handicapped by a particular learning or perceptual disability.

In a study conducted at the University of Tennessee, Mattice (1976) found that teachers and children considered the four goals of misbehavior a reasonable explanation of human behavior. She also found that children did better at formulating interpersonal goal statements about misbehavior than did teachers. School psychologists were found to have difficulty in categorizing the misbehavior goals. We might ask if it could be that our education interferes with our common sense.

The next five research reports are directed toward various tenets of Adlerian theory regarding birth order, social interest, and early recollections. Horn and Turner (1975) found a higher incidence of first-born women reporting premarital sexual intercourse—a finding that was interpreted to mean that first-born women are more likely than later-born women to model the wife–mother role. Hjelle's (1975) research supported the hypothesis that high social interest, internal locus of control, and high self-actualization are positively related. Reimanis's (1974) research found that young criminals showed higher levels of anomie and more childhood experience memories, which would suggest interference with development of social interest, than other youths. Nystul (1974) found no significant effect of birth order on self-concept as measured by the Tennessee Self-Concept Scale used on Oregon State University students. Fakouri (1974) found that a relationship between birth order and achievement existed, but that a relationship between birth order and dogmatism was not significant.

Weaver (1980) and Pelley (1980), in separate research studies at the University of Tennessee, have shown the effectiveness of the Adlerian method in training parents to parent more effectively. Both studies employed the STEP kit designed by Dinkmeyer and McKay (1976) for use with parent groups. Weaver found the method to be more effective with mothers from middle socioeconomic levels and somewhat less effective with mothers from lower socioeconomic levels. Pelley found the method to be effective in stimulating more group interaction in parent groups compared with groups not using the materials. Both studies supported the transferability of group learnings to the home setting.

REFERENCES

Adler, A. *Social interest: A challenge to mankind.* New York: Capricorn Books, 1964.

Alexander, F., Eisenstein, S., and Grotjahn, M. *Psychoanalytic pioneers.* New York: Basic Books, 1966.

Ansbacher, H., and Ansbacher, R. *The individual psychology of Alfred Adler: A systematic presentation in selections from his writings.* New York: Basic Books, 1956.

Dinkmeyer, D., and McKay, G. *Systematic training for effective parenting.* Circle Pines, Minn.: American Guidance Service, 1976.

Dinkmeyer, D., Pew, W., and Dinkmeyer, D., Jr. *Adlerian counseling and psychotherapy.* Monterey, Calif.: Brooks/Cole, 1979.

Dreikurs, R. *Children: The challenge.* New York: Hawthorn Books, 1964.

Fakouri, M. Relationships of birth order, dogmatism, and achievement motivation. *Journal of Individual Psychology,* 1974, *30*, 216–220.

Hjelle, L. A. Relationship of social interest to internal–external control and self-actualization in young women. *Journal of Individual Psychology,* 1975 *31*, 171–182.

Horn, J. M., and Turner, R. G. Birth order effects among unwed mothers. *Journal of Individual Psychology,* 1975, *31*, 71–78.

Mattice, E. *Dreikurs' goals of misbehavior theory: Child and teacher generation of a neo-Adlerian construct.* Unpublished doctoral dissertation, University of Tennessee, Knoxville, 1976.

Mosak, H. *Alfred Adler: His influence on psychology today.* Park Ridge, N.J.: Noyes Press, 1973.

Nystul, M. S. The effects of birth order and sex on self concept. *Journal of Individual Psychology,* 1974, *30*, 211–215.

Orgler, H. *Alfred Adler: The man and his work.* New York: Capricorn Books, 1965.

Pelley, A. *Family involvement in guidance programs.* Paper presented at the American Personnel and Guidance Association Convention, Atlanta, March 1980.

Reimanis, G. Anomie, crime, childhood memories, and development of social interest. *Journal of Individual Psychology,* 1974, *30*, 53–58.

Weaver, C. *The STEP program: A comparison of its effectiveness with middle and lower socio-economic status mothers.* Paper presented at the American Personnel and Guidance Association Convention, Atlanta, March 1980.

CHAPTER

8

FAMILY THERAPY

VIRGINIA SATIR

When Virginia Satir was 5 years old, she made a decision to become a detective for children to help figure out parents. She was not sure what she would be looking for, but even at this young age she knew that a lot of strange things were going on in families that did not always meet the eye. In 1980, some 54 years later, Satir, after working with thousands of families, reports that she is still finding a lot of puzzles in families.

Satir views family life as being like an iceberg. Most people are aware of only one-tenth of what is happening in the family—the tenth they can see and hear. Like the fate of the ship that depends on the captain's awareness of the total iceberg, the family must depend on the total awareness of the family structure if it is to survive. Satir refers to the hidden 90% as the needs, motives, and communication patterns of the family. In three books, Satir shares some of the answers she has found to the puzzles over the years: *Conjoint Family Therapy* (1967), *Peoplemaking* (1972), and *Helping Families to Change* (Satir, Stachowiak, & Taschman, 1975). Some of the early concepts in *Conjoint Family Therapy* have been embellished, according to Satir, as a result of her work with the Gestalt concepts presented by Fritz Perls and the body awareness work of Bernard Gunther.

Virginia Satir's qualifications as a certified detective on parents are well founded. She received formal academic training in psychological social work at the University of Chicago. She has experience as a teacher, consultant, and practitioner in psychiatric clinics, mental hospitals, family service centers, growth centers, and private practice. In 1959 she joined with two psychiatrists to form the initial staff of the Mental Research Institute in Palo Alto, California. She also served as the first director of training at the Esalen Institute in Big Sur, California. Satir has lectured in most parts of the world. She is a visiting professor to at least ten universities and a consultant to the Veterans Administration and to several other agencies and schools. As is true with most theorists presented in this book, she is most effective in demonstrating her methods rather than lecturing about them.

THE NATURE OF PEOPLE

Satir has a positive view of human nature. She is convinced, after studying thousands of families in depth, that, at any point in time, whatever people are doing represents the best that they are aware of and that they can do. She believes that people are rational and have the freedom and ability to make decisions in their lives. While Satir views people as being basically free, she sees the extent of our knowledge as the biggest limitation on personal freedom. People can learn what they do not know and can change their way of interacting with others. People can also make themselves healthier by freeing themselves from the past. Satir believes, like Maslow, that people are geared to surviving, growing, and developing close relationships with others. Although some behavior may be labeled psychotic, sick, or bad, Satir sees it as an attempt to reach out for help.

Self-esteem plays a prominent role in Satir's system. She sees self-esteem, which she defines as the degree to which people accept both their good and their bad points, as the basic human drive. It is a changing variable that fluctuates up and down within a healthy range, depending on the amount of stress one is experiencing. Self-esteem is related to one's participation in the family interaction. When individual family members are experiencing stress, their ability to communicate openly, to give and receive feedback, and to solve problems will depend on the collective self-esteem of the family. Family members may try to block communication in order to protect their own self-esteem in times of stress or in crisis situations. Family members having low self-esteem are often likely to create disturbances to make the others feel as badly as they do. For example, parents guilty of child abuse often have a low sense of self-esteem and may internalize the following rationale: "One way to punish myself for my wasteful ways is to punish that same behavior in one of my children."

Behavior, according to Satir, is directly related to one's family position and view of that position. If we feel good or bad about ourselves, then we are probably communicating that feeling to others. Satir views people as mature and functional when they are behaving in acceptable and helpful ways and when they are taking responsibility for their actions. Failure to communicate effectively and to behave responsibly are seen by Satir—like Adler and Glasser—as symptoms of a low self-concept. Therefore, self-concept needs to receive a strong focus if a person's mental and physical assets are to be developed to their fullest. An examination of one's place in life relates closely to the self-concept.

Satir makes the point that a high degree of self-esteem is necessary for qualifying as a good marriage partner. People with a healthy self-concept view their partners as enhancing their self-esteem by the two complementing each other's personalities. If, however, people have low self-esteem, they look to their partners as extensions of themselves. A marital relationship will be dysfunctional if one partner reaches out to the other as one who will supply what is missing in the self. In this dysfunctional couple relationship, the marriage or partnership is seen as a place for getting and not giving. For example, marriage may be entered into as a type of therapy for strengthening one's inadequate personality. However, the general outcome of a "taking" relationship is disappointment and an even lower sense of self-esteem.

By the same token, the birth of a child to parents having low self-esteem may be another way of compensating for feelings of inferiority. The child may be used as a mechanism for demonstrating the parents' worth to the community and their self-worth as parents, and also as an extension of themselves. They seem to be thinking, "If I did not fulfill many of my life's aspirations, perhaps I can relive them through my child." In such situations, children are never viewed as individuals with separate worth, value, and identities. Children of parents deficient in self-esteem have a heavy and difficult burden to bear. They are expected to live out the fantasies of their parents. Success and failure are viewed from the vantage point of the parent. Children showing individuality and different points of view may be accused of not loving their parents. They receive such messages as, "After all I have done for you, how could you do this to me?" or "If you loved me, you would practice the piano more."

Satir (1967) holds the view that children are the third angle of the family triangle. As such, they may find themselves in an intolerable position similar to the persecutor, victim, rescuer triangle described in transactional analysis (see Chapter 12). When the parents are in conflict, any direction the child turns will be considered as being for or against one of the parents. Given this state of affairs, Satir writes, if children seem to side with one parent, they run the risk of seeming not to love the other parent. Since children need both parents, making such a choice inevitably hurts them. Both parents have interlocking roles to play in the process of educating children emotionally, and failure of one angle of the family triangle or one parent results in the disturbance of the entire system and frequently results in disturbed children.

A further complication in the triangle is the fact that the child has already established an identity with the same-sexed parent, and the hurt of taking sides is further compounded by the stunted or stifled psychosexual development that can occur. Children need the opposite-sex parent as a person to be admired, respected, and loved; the same-sex parent needs to be a good role model. When the parents are divided, arguing, and fighting, children cannot achieve these identity and inter-personal goals. If there is no parental coalition or cooperation between the father and mother to fulfill their respective roles as man and woman and husband and wife, the child may need counseling to fulfill unsatis-fied wishes. Satir conceptualizes the role of this child as the *identified patient*, even though the entire family will be counseled.

Satir does not believe in the concept of triangular relationships; that is, there is no such thing as a relationship "between" three people. There are only shifting two-person relationships with the third member in the role of observer. The building blocks of Satir's system are two-person, interacting relationships. The key to success or failure in this system depends on the relationship between the husband and the wife. If the system is dysfunctional, and they are not acting in parental coalition, then both mates may look to the child to satisfy their unmet needs in the marital relationship.

According to Satir, children who are triangled into a marital situ-ation in the role of "ersatz mate," an ally who is wooed seductively by the parent of the opposite sex, are not happy. The child has loyalties to and needs for both parents. Although a child may appear closer to one parent, such an alliance is illusionary. Children cannot unambivalently side with either parent.

Satir writes that one develops a sense of self-esteem in the early childhood years. Beside the obvious physical needs, the children have needs for a warm, ongoing, predictable mastery over their world, and a validation of themselves as distinct and worthwhile people. Finally, they require a sense of what it is to be male or female and acceptance of this role. If parents consistently show that they consider their children masterful, sexual people, and if they also demonstrate a gratifying, func-tional male/female relationship, their children acquire self-esteem and become increasingly independent. In every way, self-esteem, indepen-dence, and individuality go together.

Satir would view mature people as those who are fully in charge of their feelings and who make choices based on accurate perceptions of themselves and others. Once choices are made, the mature person takes full responsibility for them. In summary, Satir regards mature people as (1) being in touch with their feelings, (2) communicating clearly and effectively, and (3) accepting differences in others as a chance to learn.

THEORY OF COUNSELING

Satir believes there are four components in a family situation that are subject to change and correction: the members' feelings of self-worth, the communication abilities of the family, the system, and the rules of the family. The rules are the way things are accomplished in the family. They are the most difficult component to uncover during therapy sessions as they usually are not verbalized or consciously known to all members of the family. Satir's goal is to have all members of the family understand the rules that govern their emotional interchange. These rules include: (1) freedom to comment, (2) freedom to express what one is seeing or hearing, (3) freedom to agree or disapprove, and (4) freedom to ask questions when one does not understand. The family unit will become dysfunctional when the unwritten rules are not understood. Satir tells families that are having problems with one of the members that there are no bad family members that cause pain, only bad rules. She believes that what is currently going on is the natural consequence of the experience of one's own life; consequently, there is hope that anything can change.

In family systems theory, the main idea is that the family functions as a unit, with certain rules, expectations, and emotions. Members of the family unit are interdependent; therefore, when stress is applied to one part of the system or to one family member, it will be felt throughout the system by all the other members in varying degrees. The family system has the potential to share and deal with the stress in a healthy, open, and productive way and the potential to close the communication process by focusing blame for the stress on one family member (the identified client).

To bring about changes in the functioning of a family, analyzing the interaction processes between the family members and the family system is as important as analyzing the communications content. Questions of who is "right" and who is "wrong" border on value judgments and have no place in the process of family growth and further development. The focus becomes discovering how the individuals adjust to the various events occurring within the family in such ways as to achieve satisfaction for its members and to avoid withdrawing from problems openly.

Satir emphasizes the necessity of developing trust before any meaningful change process can begin. When there is a willingness to take a risk, trust can be assumed. The second step is the development of awareness, or knowing what one is doing. With awareness comes understanding and the application of this new understanding to effective decision making. At this point, the new decision-making behavior can be put to use. The underlying theme is the development of self-worth and the freedom to comment.

Satir believes whether a family grows or not is primarily the responsibility of counselors and their input. They must be able to put people in touch with themselves at a feeling level. Counselors assume the role of teacher to reeducate the family to new ways of thinking, feeling, and communicating. The challenge is to bring about in people a curiosity and willingness to change and explore.

Communication is the single most important factor in Satir's system. She views communication as the main determinant of the kinds of relationships people will have with one another and of how people will adjust to their environment. Communication is the tie that binds the family together. When the family is operating smoothly, communication among family members is open, authentic, assertive, and received. Conversely, when a family system is in trouble, communication is blocked or distorted in a futile attempt to ward off anxiety and tension.

Fear of rejection is a common source of anxiety, and, because people fear rejection, they resort to one or a combination of response patterns in communicating with others. These universal response roles are the placater, the blamer, the computer, the distractor, and the leveler. The last response, leveling, is the one that helps people to develop healthy personalities; all the others are used to hide real feelings for fear of rejection. In such situations, people are feeling and reacting to the threat of rejection, but because they do not want to reveal "weakness," they attempt to conceal it. Satir (1971) is in agreement with Gestalt theory on nonverbal behavior: the body expresses where you are in terms of your whole integration. Each of the response patterns is accompanied by a unique body posture and nonverbal behaviors. A brief description of each pattern follows.

Placater. These people placate so that others do not get angry. Their motto is peace at any price. They talk in ingratiating ways to try to please, or apologize. They never disagree and even take on the air of a "yes-person." They have a low sense of self-esteem. They are unable to negotiate solutions of mutual benefit because this process is too threatening. In other words, placaters negate self in the interest of serving others and staying within the context of the situation. Nonverbal messages of the placater include: "Whatever you want is okay with me; I am just here to make you happy."

Blamer. These people are the fault finders, directors, and bosses. They also do not feel very good about themselves. They may feel lonely and unsuccessful and attempt to compensate for these feelings by trying to coerce others into obeying them so they can feel that they amount to something. Blaming is also a good way to create distance and prevent others from getting too close. The blamers are good guilt inducers: "After all I have done for you, how could you do this to me?" Blamers negate others, while focusing on the context of the situation and on themselves. Nonverbal messages from the blamer include: "You never do anything right. What is the matter with you?"

Computer. These people are calm, very correct, show no feelings, and speak words like a recording. They pretend there is no conflict when there is. Computers are the "superreasonable" people. Their bodies reflect their very rigid personalities. They negate self and others in order to concentrate on context. They cover up their vulnerability by using big words to establish a sense of self-worth. Nonverbal messages from the computer include: "I am cool, calm, and collected."

Distractor.   These people make statements that are completely irrelevant to what is going on. They change the subject and never make a response to the point. Their strong point is evading the issue. They may even resort to withdrawing from the situation to avoid a crisis. Distractors negate all three elements of reality: self, others, and the context of the situation. Nonverbal messages from distractors include: "Maybe if I do this long enough, it will really go away."

Leveler.   These people communicate their honest thoughts and feelings in a straightforward manner that addresses self, others, and the context of the situation. Their verbal messages and nonverbal body posture are consistent. Leveling occurs when all aspects of communication are congruent: body, voice tone, context, and facial expression. Levelers do not cover up, nor do they put other people down in the name of being open and honest. They are not phonies. Their communication proceeds in a natural, healthy flow. Their relationships are free and honest, so there are few threats to self-esteem. The leveling response is the truthful message for a particular person at a given time. It is single and straight. There is an openness and a feeling of trust in interactions with a person who is leveling. This response allows people to live as complete persons who are really in touch with their heart, head, and feelings. Satir (1972) states that being a leveler allows a person to have integrity, commitment, honesty, intimacy, competency, creativity, and the ability to solve real problems in a real way. The other four forms of communicating result in doubtful integrity, commitment by bargain, dishonesty, loneliness, incompetence, strangulation by tradition (inability to change traditional patterns), and destructive ways of dealing with fantasy problems.

Our society does not encourage people to use leveling responses. Although people would like to be honest, they are afraid to and play many games instead. Satir has outlined a variety of experiences to help family members become aware that they can choose to change their responses and how they can do this. Levelers can choose to use one of the other four response patterns if they are willing to accept the consequences; but for them such responses would not be the automatic response of people locked into a particular pattern. Levelers can choose to placate, blame, compute, or distract; the difference is that they know what they are doing and are prepared to accept the result of their behavior.

The message of the leveler is consistent. If a leveler says, "I like you," the voice is warm and the eye contact and body speak the same message. If the leveler is angry, the voice is harsh, the face is tight, and the words are clear: "I am mad as hell at you!"

Satir points out that every person she has seen with a behavior or coping problem was a member of a family in which all significant communication was double level—that is, phony or hidden (Satir et al., 1975). If people can learn to recognize harmful communication patterns and learn to level with their family members, then the family has a chance to make their life better and to solve problems more efficiently. As mentioned previously, Satir's system is based on two-person, interacting relationships. However, there are three parts to every couple: you, me, and us. In order for the relationship to continue and for love to grow, each part has to be recognized without being dominated by the other two. Although love is the feeling that begins a marriage, the process is what makes it work. The process is the "how," and it is this "how" that Satir teaches to her clients.

Satir divides all families into two types: nurturing or troubled. There are varying degrees of each type. Her main objective is for her clients to recognize which type they are and either to change from troubled to nurturing or to become more nurturing. The nurturing family helps to develop feelings of self-worth in the members, whereas the troubled family diminishes these feelings. In every family, factors to be considered include feelings of self-worth, communication, rules, and links to society.

Nurturing families are marked by aliveness, honesty, genuineness, and love. These families have the following characteristics:

1. People are listened to and are interested in listening to others.
2. People are not afraid to take risks because the family understands mistakes are bound to happen when risking.
3. People's bodies are graceful, and their facial expressions are relaxed.
4. People look at one another and not through one another or at the floor.
5. The children are friendly and open, and the rest of the family treats them as people.
6. People seem comfortable about touching one another and showing their affection.
7. People show love by talking and listening with concern and by being straight and real with one another.
8. Members feel free to tell one another how they feel.
9. Anything can be discussed—fears, anger, hurt, criticism, joys, achievements, and so on.
10. Members plan, but if something does not work out, they can adjust.
11. Human life and feelings are more important than anything else.
12. Parents see themselves as leaders and not as bosses. They acknowledge to their children their poor as well as their good

judgment; their hurt, anger, or disappointment as well as their joy. Their behavior matches their teaching.

13. When nurturing, parents need to correct their children. They rely on listening, touching, understanding, and careful timing, being aware of children's feelings and their natural wish to learn.

14. Nurturing parents understand that children can only learn when they are valued, so they do not respond in a way to make the child feel devalued. (Satir, 1972, p. 14)

COUNSELING METHOD

The counseling method of conjoint family therapy involves the entire family and is based on communication, interaction, and general information. The approach taught by Satir to families is both physical and emotional. Those counselors who would prefer to work less with emotions and more with facts will find the Adlerian method more comfortable.

Satir leads the family in role playing family situations and each other's actions and reactions to the happenings in a typical day in the life of the family. She uses some Gestalt techniques of sculpting (see below) a family argument or interaction, believing that the body is often a more honest reflection than the verbal message. Satir uses videotape replay to teach the concepts of communication discussed in the previous section. She uses various props in her role-play dramas, such as rope and step ladders, to demonstrate and analyze the types of family interactions that exist. The same dramas are staged to help family members learn how to level with each other in expressing their emotions with honest, direct language. Satir examines the family history by drawing family trees to look at how past and immediate family styles are passed on from parent to child. She uses ropes to demonstrate the complicated process of communication between parents and children.

Even with a multitude of techniques, Satir proposes no formula for therapy because therapy involves human feelings and the ability to respond on a human level. The family is viewed by Satir as a "people-making factory," where people are made by a process that is crude at best and destructive at worst.

An example of Satir's method

The following family therapy scene is typical of Satir's work:

A 40-year-old woman sits in a fetal position on the floor, hiding behind a sofa. Her husband, sitting in a chair, points an accusing finger at her across the room. One daughter, with arms outstretched, tries to make peace. Two children sit with their backs to the group, and a fourth child rubs his mother's back. Satir breaks the silent role play, rests her hand on the father's shoulder, and asks how he feels right now. She has asked the family to act out silently how each person in the family feels during a family argument. This sculpting method is excellent in creating awareness of personal feelings as well as the feelings of other family members.

The importance of including children

Including children is imperative for the success of family counseling in Satir's system. Satir advocates the inclusion of all the children, not just the child who has a problem, because all are a part of the family homeostasis—a process by which the family balances forces within itself to achieve unity and working order. Satir operates from the assumption that, when there is dysfunction within the family, all members feel it in some way. Therefore, the counselor works with all members of the family to help them redefine their relationships. Family members have their own perceptions about what is going on in the family, and input from each member is vital in building a functional family. The counselor works with the interpersonal relationships of the family, discovering how the members interact so that they may strengthen their bonding.

Before bringing the children in, Satir suggests meeting with the marital pair. She makes them aware of themselves as individuals as well as mates and parents. She also suggests preparing the parents in the initial interview for bringing the children into the counseling sessions. After the parents agree that the role of the children in family counseling is important, the children are included.

When working with children, there are many things for the counselor to consider. The counselor needs to be fully aware of the children's capabilities and potentialities. The counselor can plan the length of counseling sessions to conform to the ages of the children. Children have short attention spans, and the counseling process must hold their interest. Counselors are confronted with these obstacles; however, they can work within them, making the counseling process beneficial, productive, and enjoyable for all.

The counselor should begin by recognizing all of the children, repeating their names, ages, and birth order to let the children know they are being listened to. The counselor will also want to set rules for the sessions—for example, no one may destroy the property within the room, no one may speak for the others, all must speak so they may be heard, everyone must make it possible for others to be heard, and so on. When the ground rules have been established, in-depth discussion can then begin.

The counselors should set the mood by asking questions in a warm, specific, matter-of-fact way. They should create a setting in which people can take the risk of looking clearly and objectively at themselves and their actions. Satir suggests that the counselor ask many questions;

however, these questions should be questions that the children are able to answer. During this time, the counselor must be sure that the children understand what is happening and what the family is striving to gain. They need to feel comfortable and to be aware of themselves as individuals and as different from one another. They need to be made aware of the importance of communicating with one another—for example, to feel free to agree or disagree with other family members, to say what they think, and to bring disagreements out in the open. The children need to know that they will be treated as people with perceptions and opinions.

The counselor should demonstrate the idea of individuality by speaking to each child separately, differentiating each child, restating and summarizing what each child says. Counselors need to convey their sincerity in honoring all questions from each child, demonstrating that questions are not trouble making and illegitimate, but that all should ask questions about what they do not know or are unsure about. Counselors should convey their expectations of the children to increase the likelihood of the children's rising to meet them. Children do hear, are interested, and are able to contribute to the discussions.

It is important for the counselor to ask the children their ideas about why they are in counseling. Counselors should repeat what each child says to make sure they are understanding what the child means. The counselor may proceed by asking the children where they got their ideas about why they are there, who told them, and what was said. From this exchange, the counselor can gain some insight into the methods of communication within the family. The counselor encourages the children to talk about themselves and their feelings in relation to each family member. The counselor helps children to express frustration and anger and has the children ask their family members for answers to any questions they may have. The counselor may use confronting questions to provoke thought in the child. As the counseling sessions advance, questions concerning family rules and roles will arise. After having established good rapport and a comfortable atmosphere, the counselor may begin to bring out underlying feelings and confront the family members concerning the elements causing the family's dysfunctioning. The basis for further probing and confronting must be established between counselor and parent, counselor and child, parent and child, and counselor, parent, and child in the initial interviews. From the initial interviews, the counselor must gain the child's confidence in order to move forward.

The counselor wants to see where each child fits into the family unit. In the beginning, to build self-esteem within the children, the counselor will focus on the children, not ignoring the parents, but having the parents respond intermittently. Counselors help children to understand their parents, as parents and people, and also themselves as children and people.

Three keys to Satir's system

Satir's approach to family counseling focuses on three key ingredients:

1. Increasing the self-esteem of each family member by facilitating ways in which the family as a whole might better understand its systems and learn to implement changes toward open systems and nurturing attitudes and behaviors
2. Assisting the family in discovering ways to improve and open communication patterns by helping the family members to better understand and analyze their encounters with each other and learn the leveling response
3. Utilizing experiential learning techniques in the counseling setting to help the family understand present interactions, encouraging personal responsibility for one's own actions and feelings

Satir views the counselor as a facilitator, a change agent, helping the process of moving toward a more open family system, and thereby a nurturing family. The counselor is not the "expert." The process should help the family members become the experts on its own problems and growth.

Satir's technique

A family therapist will employ a variety of techniques to assist the family in self-discovery. Satir's method is designed to help the members discover what patterns do not work and how to better understand and express their feelings in an open, level manner. Rather than have them rehash past hurts, Satir would have the family analyze their "systems" in a present interaction in the counseling setting. There are many ways the counselor might accomplish this analysis. Below are several examples:

1. The counselor will ask the family to describe a situation that causes the difficulties that brought them to counseling or have them describe a typical situation from their recent experience that usually results in the problem. Family members will enact the situation.
2. The counselor might have the family sitting in a circle in chairs to simulate a family decision, such as deciding together where to go on their next vacation.
3. The family participates in a family sculpture, as in the example presented earlier. The counselor asks for someone to describe a typical family argument and then has that person "sculpt" the argument by placing each family member in appropriate positions—complete with gestures, facial expressions, touching, and so on. Then the counselor might follow this by asking each other

member how he or she would change it and letting each make the changes. It is essential to follow the process by discussion aimed at leveling and participation by each family member.

4. Each family member takes a long rope, one for each other person in the family, and ties them all around his or her waist. Next, the counselor instructs them to tie one rope to each other family member. Discussion of this tension and mass of ropes can help the family to better understand the complexity of its relationships and crossed transactions.

5. Role playing and reverse role playing are useful for stimulating family discussion.

6. Use of videotaped family sessions and discussions assist family members to achieve a better understanding of the reactions and responses of all members.

7. Use of games includes: (a) the simulated family game, (b) the systems game, and (c) communication games.

Satir's games, which are used for counselor training as well as family therapy, are based upon her definition of a *growth model*. The growth model views an individual's behavior changes as a process that is represented by transactions with other people. People will function fully when they are removed from the maladaptive system, or if the system is changed to promote growth. The model differs greatly from the *sin model*, which assumes that the individual's thinking, values, and attitudes are wrong and therefore must be changed; and the *medical model*, which states that the cause of the problem is an illness located in the patient.

Satir has developed various games to deal with the family's behavior when they operate within these three models. It is again imperative to state that all family members are present in the family counseling process. Many of the major game types utilized are as follows:

The simulated family game.   In this game, the various family members simulate each other's behaviors; for example, the son plays the mother. The family members may also be asked to pretend that they are a different family. Following this enactment, the therapist and family discuss how they differ from or identify with the roles.

Systems games.   These games are based upon either open or closed family systems; learning and insight may be obtained from both family types. Satir believes that emotional and behavioral disturbances are a direct result of a member caught in a closed family system. The closed system does not allow any individual the right to honest self-expression. Differences are viewed as dangerous since the overriding "rule" is to have the same values, feelings, and opinions. In the open system family, honest expression and differences are received as natural occurrences, and open negotiation occurs to resolve such differences by "compromise," "agreeing to disagree," "taking turns," and so on.

One game entails the original family triad taking these roles revolving around the five interactional patterns of behavior discussed earlier—(1) the placater, (2) the blamer, (3) the distractor, (4) the computer, or (5) the leveler. On the basis of these interactional patterns, various games have been constructed.

1. Rescue game. Behaviors 1, 2, 3, and 4 are played. Who plays each role is variable, but each member must remain in this role throughout the session.
2. Coalition game. Behaviors 1 and 2 are played. Two people always disagree and gang up on the third person.
3. Lethal game. Behavior 1 is used. Everyone agrees.
4. Growth vitality game. Each person includes him- or herself and others by honest expression and by permitting others to express themselves (leveling).

These techniques can be broadened beyond the initial family triad by incorporating all family members into a prescribed family situation and assigning various roles to each member. These sessions are extremely vital for younger children who have been "ruled" by the adage "Children should be seen but not heard." These games aid families in understanding the nature of their own family system. They also allow the members to experience new interactional patterns through identification of where they are and insight into possible alternatives. By utilizing the growth vitality game and the leveling role, families can experience the movement from a pathological system of interaction to a growth-producing one.

Communication games. These games are aimed at establishing communication skills. Satir believes that it is almost impossible to deliver an insincere or phony message if individuals have skin and/or steady eye contact with the listener. One communication game involves two members sitting back to back while they talk. Next they are turned around and are instructed to stare into each other's eyes without talking or touching. Satir (1967) reports that this type of interaction leads to many insights concerning the assumptions that each makes about the other's thoughts and feelings. Next, the family members or trainees continue to stare and then touch each other without talking. This process continues in steps until each partner is talking, touching, and "eyeballing" the other. Assuming these positions, they are asked to disagree with each other. Satir finds that this is nearly impossible. People either enjoy the effort or are forced to pull back physically and divert their eyes to get angry.

One of the most important parts of these games is the counselor's role. Throughout and after each session, the counselor intervenes and discusses the family's responses, feelings, and gut reactions in relation to themselves and other family members.

The counselor's role

In Satir's approach to family counseling, the counselor is a facilitator who gives total commitment and attention to the process and interactions. The counselor does not take charge and must be careful not to manipulate the reactions and verbalizations of the participants. By careful and sensitive attention to the interactions, transactions, and response (or lack of response) of each family member, the counselor can intervene at certain points to ask questions about whether the messages are clear and correct and how a particular person is feeling, giving each person a chance to interact or make corrections. For example, the counselor might interrupt the dialogue when one person makes a statement about how another feels or thinks by asking the second person if the statement is accurate and how he or she feels at that moment.

In short, the counselor will intervene to assist leveling and taking responsibility for one's own actions and feelings. The counselor will intervene to give the more quiet members permission to talk and be heard. By helping the family focus on understanding and analyzing a present interaction in the counseling setting, the members should be better able to understand past hurts and problems. The members also should be better able to understand past hurts and problems by understanding what patterns have been producing the trouble. With experience in openness and leveling, communication between family members can change, and growth can occur. The family is then better able to continue the discussions, come to new insights, and implement appropriate changes.

CASE STUDIES

The ability of people to assume other roles in the family group situation supports the idea that people can change their response roles and that families can change their ways of interacting and solving problems. Family members need to learn how to share both positive and negative feedback in ways that do not hurt or belittle one another. The following is a family role-play transcript where the leveling response is omitted:

Don (father-husband; blaming): Why isn't our dinner ready?
Sandy (mother-wife; blaming): What are you yelling about?
You've got as much time as I have.
Bill (son; blaming): Aw, shut up. You two are always yelling.
I don't want any dinner, anyway.

Don (blaming): You keep your trap shut. I'm the one who makes the rules around here.

Sandy (blaming): Says who? Besides, young man, keep your nose out of this.

Or:

Don (placating): Maybe you'd like to go out to dinner for a change?

Sandy (computer): According to the last issue of *Woman's Day*, they say that eating out is cheaper than cooking some things at home.

Don (placating): Whatever you would like to do, dear.

Bill (placating): You always have good ideas, Mother.

Sandy (computer): That's right. I have a list of the restaurants offering specials this week.

Perhaps one good leveling response by any of the family members could have helped this short exchange. Perhaps Sandy could have said that she needed a rest from a long, hard day and would like to have dinner out. Don could have made a statement rather than asking a phony question. Perhaps a leveling remark by Don might have informed Sandy that he was wondering what she wanted to do about dinner tonight. Bill could have made a small change in his remark to, "I really worry when we argue and fight in this family, and I would like this to stop." The counselor's job would be to rehearse these leveling responses until the problem is solved in the role-playing setting. Then plans are made to try the leveling response in real life.

Let's examine a second family session with the counselor present. The Frazier family is seated clockwise around the counselor in the following order: Jody, the wife/mother, 43 years old; Frank, the 11-year-old son; Larry, the husband/father, 44 years old; Joyce, the 14-year-old daughter; and Kathy, the 16-year-old daughter.

Kathy: Mom, just say yes or no. Am I going to be allowed to go out on weekdays or not?

Jody: Why don't you do what you want? You always do anyway.

Counselor (to Kathy): How does this make you feel?

Kathy: Well, I'd like to be able to do what the rest of the kids are doing, but I know Mom and Dad don't approve.

Co: That sounds funny because I heard your mom say it was up to you. (To Jody): Is that what you said? Maybe it was the expression on your face and the way you spoke your message to Kathy that made her think you didn't really mean, "Do what you want to do."

Kathy: Yes, her stern face said "no."

Co: What did she do with her face to tip you off?

Kathy: Well, she squinted her eyes and wrinkled up her nose.

Co: It's hard to read your mom's mind, but I am guessing that she thinks nobody listens to her very much. We can check this with her later. But I'm wondering if you have ever felt this way.

Kathy: Sometimes.

Co (to Jody): Do you ever have this feeling?

Jody: I think maybe we've hit on something new.

Co: Do you think no one listens to you?

Jody: I have a rough day just keeping house for this family. Larry comes home from work too tired to talk, and all I ever talk to the children about are their fights and arguments. I have to handle all the family problems.

Larry: Well, my job is all I can handle.

Jody: See, no one listens to my side of the story.

Co (to Larry): Were you aware of what Jody was saying when she said that? What did it feel like, Larry?

Larry: That it's all my fault that things don't go better in our family.

Co: Hold it one minute. Frank is doing something over here.

Larry (to Frank): Settle down over there and shape up.

Co: Let's take some time out and find out what's going on with Frank. I haven't been paying much attention to Frank and Joyce. (To Frank): How did you feel about what was going on over here?

Frank: Well, I, uh . . .

Joyce (blaming Frank): You weren't even paying attention.

Kathy: Frank, if you move over here with me, we can get along better.

Kathy (to Larry): Can't you do anything to make him mind me? It's all your fault he acts like he does.

Co (to Kathy and Larry): An interesting thing happened when Frank started acting up. I was wondering, Kathy, how you felt when your father said to your mother, "You don't do the things I want," and she replied to him, "Well, it's . . .

In this short segment, the counselor attempts to look at present communication patterns and the feelings these patterns conceal. After achieving awareness of the communication blocks, the family can begin to practice leveling as an alternative way of communicating.

SUMMARY: RESEARCH AND REACTIONS

Keebler (1976) examined the complex area of family therapy and reached some of the following conclusions. In spite of a 30-year history, there is little research data to support family therapy in general as an effective method. In fact, it is difficult to define exactly what constitutes family therapy or family counseling; the definition varies with the practitioner.

Although there has been some difficulty in documenting its effectiveness, the service of family counseling seems to be in demand. Treatment times for family therapy range from weekly visits for one year to monthly visits for four years to brief, one- to ten-session programs. Therapists and counselors from all three extremes claim they are effective. From this we can conclude that human beings are too complex for any one counseling approach to be effective for all. In her three books, Satir writes about her successes with over 12,000 families. She has also reported some research data to show that blood pressure, GSR, and EEG were significantly affected when people changed their stance and body posture and held it for at least 10 seconds during role-play demonstrations with double-level communication. For example, assuming the blamer posture would cause a physiological as well as an emotional response after 10 seconds. In other words, people engaging in harmful role behavior over a period of time could make themselves sick.

According to Keebler, most family therapists agreed that family therapy is not effective with every individual or family. Families that are too rigid or have broken completely with reality will probably not benefit from family therapy. Like most counseling, it works best with those people capable of taking action.

The impact of the family systems approach on counseling has been steadily growing as a result of successful research with families that have produced children with emotional disorders. By focusing on the family as the source of pathology, this approach has also moved in the direction of the marital therapists, for it has been found rather consistently in family therapy that problem children came from homes where there were disturbed husband/wife relationships.

Satir cites several researchers who contributed ideas to the development of her system—for instance, Harry Stack Sullivan's interpersonal theory of the 1920s (the behavior of an individual is influenced by his or her interaction with another) and the growth of group therapy, whose major contributors were J. L. Moreno and S. R. Slavson, also during the 1920s. Gregory Bateson and Murray Bowen began to look at families to discover why individuals became "schizophrenic." They believed that a person possibly represented the family situation. Bateson, of the Mental Research Institute, contributed the idea of double-leveling. Much of Satir's current theories show roots not only in classic theories of clinical psychology and psychiatry, but also in her past research at the Mental Research Institute and the National Institute of Mental Health. Satir appears to be synthesizing older and newer theories while adding highly developed original techniques. Her eclectic approach is unique in the field of family counseling.

REFERENCES

Keebler, N. Family Therapy: A profusion of methods and meanings. *APA Monitor*, 1976, 7, 4–5, 17.

Satir, V. *Conjoint family therapy: A guide to theory and technique* (Rev. ed.). Palo Alto, Calif.: Science and Behavior Books, 1967.

Satir, V. *Conjoint Family Therapy: A symposium on family counseling and therapy.* Conference proceedings, University of Georgia, Athens, January 1971.

Satir, V. *Peoplemaking.* Palo Alto, Calif.: Science and Behavior Books, 1972.

Satir, V., Stachowiak, J., and Taschman, H. *Helping families to change.* New York: Tiffany, 1975.

CHAPTER

9

BEHAVIORAL COUNSELING

DEVELOPERS OF BEHAVIORAL COUNSELING

Several names emerge as contributors to behavioral counseling, including Ivan Pavlov, John B. Watson, Edward L. Thorndike, Edward C. Tolman, Clark L. Hull, John Dollard, Neal E. Miller, H. J. Eysenck, L. Krasner, L. P. Ullman, Joseph Wolpe, Arnold Lazarus, and John Krumboltz. However, the name that is most well known to the general public, as well as most controversial, is B. F. Skinner. Skinner, while not developing new principles of behaviorism, has done the most to translate the theories and ideas of other behaviorists into an applied and useful technology. Skinner's methods are in wide use today by psychotherapists, educators, counselors, and parents.

Burrhus Frederic Skinner was born in 1904 in Susquehanna, Pennsylvania. He majored in literature at Hamilton College in Clinton, New York. Skinner's goal was to become a writer. After a few years with little success, Skinner regarded himself a failure as a writer. Reflecting later on this time in his life, Skinner commented that the reason for failure was he had nothing to say. Giving up on writing, he entered Harvard University to study psychology. The behavior of humans and animals was of special interest to him. He received his master's degree in 1930 and a Ph.D. in experimental psychology in 1931. Following graduation, Skinner began his most productive career as a teacher and researcher at the University of Minnesota, followed by an appointment as chairman of the psychology department at Indiana University. He later returned to Harvard to accept a professorship, which he continues to hold.

As he began to generate things to say in the field of behaviorism, Skinner's flair for writing returned. His numerous publications include:

The Behavior of Organisms, 1938
Walden Two, 1948
Science and Human Behavior, 1953
Schedule of Reinforcement (coauthored by C. Fersten), 1957
The Technology of Teaching, 1968
Beyond Freedom and Dignity, 1971
About Behaviorism, 1974
Particulars of My Life, 1976

Skinner's contribution to knowledge is not strictly confined to the laboratory. He has made considerable contributions to solving educational problems. He developed and advanced the concepts of programmed instruction, operant conditioning in classroom management, behavioral counseling, and the teaching machine (first developed by Sidney Pressey in 1923). Perhaps the most controversial of Skinner's works is *Beyond Freedom and Dignity*, in which he pictures a society where behavior is shaped and controlled by a planned system of rewards.

THE NATURE OF PEOPLE

A broad statement of the behaviorist view of the nature of people is probably best summed up by Skinner's (1971) belief that children are influenced and changed as biological entities by things that happen to them. He finds the notion that somehow or other the child of our past is still contained within us a form of animism that serves no useful purpose in explaining present behavior. Behaviorists view human beings as neither good nor bad but merely as products of their environment. People are essentially neutral at birth (the blank slate or tabula rasa idea) with equal potential for good or evil and for rationality or irrationality.

Behaviorists view people as responders. Self-directing mentalistic concepts of people are not accepted; people are seen as capable of making only those responses they have learned, and they make them when the stimulus conditions are appropriate.

Individuals, then, are viewed by behavioral counselors as products of their conditioning. The stimulus/response paradigm is the basic pattern of all human learning. People react in predictable ways to any given stimulus according to what they have learned through experience. Humans react to stimuli in much the same way animals do, except that human responses are more complex and organized on a higher plane.

Skinner regarded the human being as an organism who learns patterns of behavior, which are catalogued within the individual's repertoire, to be repeated at a later date. To be more specific, the organism learns a specific response when a satisfying condition follows an action. The number of these responses mount as time passes and satisfying conditions repeat. The interest of the behaviorist is in the science of behavior as it relates to biology. Skinner believes that "a person is a member of a species shaped by evolutionary contingencies of survival, displaying behavioral processes which bring him under the control of the environment in which he lives, and largely under the control of a social environment which he and millions of others like him have constructed and maintained during the evolution of a culture. The direction of the controlling relation is reversed: a person does not act upon the world, the world acts upon him" (1971, p. 211).

Since human behavior is learned, any or all behavior can be unlearned and new behaviors learned in its place. The behaviorist is concerned with observable events. These observable events, when they become unacceptable behaviors, can be unlearned. It is this unlearning or reeducation process with which the behavioral counselor is concerned. Behavioral counseling procedures can be developed from social learning theory.

THEORY OF COUNSELING

Behavioral counseling is a reeducation or relearning process. Adaptive or helpful behavior is reinforced, while maladaptive or unhelpful behavior is extinguished. The counselor's role is, through reinforcement principles, to help children achieve the goals they have set for themselves.

Behavioral counseling includes several techniques based on principles of learning employed to manage maladaptive behavior. Today, behavioral counseling is used with covert processes (cognitions, emotions, obsessive ideation) as well as with traditional overt behavior problems. Behavioral counseling involves two types of behavior, respondent and operant.

Respondent behavior is associated with classical conditioning, where learning occurs when a stimulus that already elicits a response (an unconditioned stimulus) is presented along with a neutral stimulus that elicits no response or a different response. With repeated pairings of the two stimuli, the neutral stimulus begins to elicit the same response as does the unconditioned stimulus. In the case of Pavlov's dogs, for example, the unconditioned stimulus of food was paired with the neutral stimulus of a bell. The response to the unconditioned stimulus was salivating. The neutral stimulus (the bell) became the conditioned stimulus, and the response to the conditioned stimulus became the conditioned response (salivating).

In operant conditioning, operant behavior refers to behavior that operates on and changes the environment in some manner. It is also referred to as instrumental behavior because it is instrumental in goal achievement. People using operant conditioning wait until the desired behavior or an approximation of the desired behavior occurs and then reinforce it with a rewarding stimulus known as positive reinforcement (praise, money, candy, free time, and the like). Negative reinforcement (different from punishment) occurs when the operant behavior is reinforced by its capacity to stop the aversive stimulus. For example, rats will learn to press a bar to shut off an electric shock, and children will take their seats at school to shut off the aversive sound of their teacher's scolding. Punishment, like positive reinforcement, occurs after the behavior is emitted but tends to decrease its occurrence. Extinction is the process of eliminating a learned behavior by ignoring the behavior or by not reinforcing it through attention and other rewards. Figure 9-1 may help explain these four terms.

Classical conditioning techniques used in counseling include: desensitization, counterconditioning, internal inhibition (massing of trials), and aversive conditioning. Operant methods include shaping and behavioral practice. See pages 147–151 for a complete description of these terms.

As with most counseling, the ultimate goal of behavioral counseling is teaching children how to become their own counselors for changing their behavior to better meet their needs. Using a broad definition of behavior as including both internal and external behavior, all behavior change may be attempted through behavioral counseling. Specific techniques are available for reducing and eliminating anxiety, phobias, and obsessive thoughts, as well as for reducing inappropriate, observable behaviors.

The goals of a behavioral counselor can be organized into three main categories (Krumboltz & Hosford, 1967):

1. Altering maladaptive behavior
2. Learning the decision-making process
3. Preventing problems

	Present	Remove
Positive <u>stimuli</u> candy praise free time	Positive reinforcement	Extinction
Negative <u>stimuli</u> spanking loss of free time criticism	Punishment	Negative reinforcement

FIGURE 9-1   Examples of Operant Conditioning

A fourth goal of learning new behaviors and skills could be added. The criteria for any set of goals in counseling have been summarized by Krumboltz (1966):

1. The goals of counseling should be individualized for each child.
2. The counseling goals for each child should be compatible with, though not necessarily identical to, the values of the counselor.
3. The degree of goal attainment by each child should be observable and assessed.

After the problem has been identified and the desired behavior change agreed upon by the counselor and child, the behavioral counselor is apt to employ a variety of counseling procedures to help the children acquire the behaviors necessary for the solution of their problems. The ultimate outcome of behavioral counseling is to teach children to become their own behavior modification experts—in other words, to program their own reinforcement schedules. It would be even more desirable to encourage children to move from extrinsic to intrinsic reinforcement—to please themselves with their behavior rather than to constantly seek the approval of others.

Since behavioral counseling differs from traditional counseling principally in terms of specificity, the behavioral counselor prefers to state goals as overt changes in behavior rather than hypothetical constructs. The basic counseling function involved in behavioral counseling is defined as discrimination—the differential responding to different situations (individuals, groups, institutions, and environmental settings). In behavioral counseling, the effectiveness of the counselor is determined by continuous assessments of the effects of each counseling procedure upon outcomes, rather than upon predetermined theoretical biases and/or counseling styles.

COUNSELING METHODS

Operant techniques

Behavioral counseling methods cover a wide variety of techniques. One method, contingency contracting, can be broken down into six steps.

1. The counselor and the child identify the problem to be solved.
2. Data are collected to verify the baseline frequency rate for the occurrence of the undesired behavior.
3. The counselor and the child set goals that are mutually acceptable.
4. Specific counseling techniques and methods are selected for attaining the goals.
5. The counseling techniques are evaluated for observable and measurable change.

6. Step 4 is repeated if the selected counseling techniques are not effective. If the techniques do prove effective, a maintenance plan is developed for maintaining the new behavior changes.

For example, Jerry completes no assignments in any of his school subjects. His grades are being lowered because of his unwillingness to complete these assignments. He is referred to the counselor.

Step 1. The counselor talks with Jerry about the problem. He is not happy with his grades but still has trouble concentrating on completing his work. He would like to do better with these assignments and make better grades.

Step 2. A five-day period is set aside to determine the exact amount of work Jerry completes. The record verifies the teacher's report that Jerry does not complete any assignments even though he starts about one-half of them.

Step 3. Jerry and the counselor agree that a good goal for a start would be to complete one assignment each day.

Step 4. For each assignment completed, Jerry would receive 10 points to be applied toward a total of 100 points, which could be exchanged for 30 minutes of free time during the school day.

Step 5. Evaluation of the contingency contract indicated that Jerry completed four assignments the first week, earning 40 points, and six assignments the second week, to run his point total to 100. He received his 30 minutes of free time. The following week he earned 100 points and received a second 30 minutes of free time. He was also successful during week three.

Step 6. The counselor and Jerry agreed that it was not necessary to continue with the point system. Jerry's grades were getting better, and everybody seemed happier—the teacher, Jerry, and his parents. As a maintenance procedure, Jerry agreed to check in with the counselor each Friday afternoon for reports on his completed assignments for the week, which he recorded on a pocket-sized score card. Of course, a good teaching procedure would be to continue to allow Jerry and his classmates to earn free time when assigned work is completed.

Self-management.   An adaptation of the six-steps method, the self-management plan, is designed for those children who are able to take more responsibility for their behavior. These plans also follow a step-by-step process: defining a problem in behavioral terms, collecting data on the problem, introducing a treatment program based on behavior principles, evaluating the effectiveness of the program, and appropriately changing the program if the plan is not working. The major difference between self-management and other procedures is that children assume major responsibility for carrying out their programs, including arranging their own contingencies or reinforcement when they have the skills to do so.

Steps in developing a self-management plan:

1. Choose an observable and measurable behavior you wish to change.
2. Record for at least one week (a) your target behavior, (b) the setting in which it occurs, (c) the antecedent events leading to the behavior, and (d) the consequences resulting from the behavior.
3. Set a goal you can achieve.
4. Change the setting and the antecedent events leading up to the target behavior.
5. Change the consequences that reinforce the target behavior.
6. Keep accurate records of your target behavior—your successes and failures.
7. Arrange a plan to maintain the goals you have reached.

Shaping.   The basic operant technique of shaping is a general procedure designed to induce new behaviors by the reinforcement of behaviors that approximate the desired behavior. Each successive approximation of the behavior is reinforced until the desired behavior is obtained. In order to administer the technique, the counselor has to know how to skillfully use (1) looking, (2) waiting, and (3) reinforcing. The counselor looks for the desired behavior, waits until it occurs, and then reinforces it when it does occur. In essence, the counselor is catching the child in good behavior—a much more difficult task than catching the child in bad behavior. An interesting exercise in teaching children how to become reinforcing people is presented by Thompson and Poppen (1979).

Biofeedback.   Biofeedback uses a machine to accomplish the three behaviors of looking, waiting, and reinforcing. Brainwaves, muscle tension, body temperature, heart rate, and blood pressure can be monitored for small changes and feedback to the client by auditory and visual means. The more the child relaxes, the slower and lower the beeping sound on the monitor. Biofeedback methods have been successful, for example, in teaching hyperactive children how to relax. The equipment may provide feedback with electric trains and recorded music. Both stop when the child stops relaxing and restart when the child takes the first small step toward relaxing again.

Modeling.   Modeling consists of exposing the child to one or more individuals, either in real life or in film or tape presentations, who exhibit behaviors to be adopted by the child. Counselors may be the model to demonstrate certain behaviors to the child, or peers of the child may be used.

Token economies.   Token economies are used on a group basis, as in a school classroom where the children earn tokens or points for certain target behaviors. These behaviors are classified as being either on-task or socially appropriate. The tokens or points also may be lost for off-task and socially inappropriate behaviors. The tokens or points earned may be cashed in periodically for things rewarding to the children: free time, game time, trinkets, sugarless candy, and the like.

Behavior practice groups.   Behavior practice groups have some advantages in counseling children. They provide a relatively safe setting in which the child can practice new behaviors before trying them out in real-life situations. These groups are also useful in supporting and reinforcing the children as new behaviors are attempted and goals are reached. Behavior practice groups could focus on any of several behavior changes including:

Weight loss
Study habits
Assertiveness training
Communication skills
Negative addictions such as drugs, alcohol, and smoking

In working with behavior practice groups, the counselor needs to develop a lesson plan with behavioral objectives, instructional methods, reinforcement, and evaluation. A good lesson plan would maintain a balance among three teaching strategies: (1) tell me, (2) show me, and (3) let me try it. For example, a lesson plan in assertiveness training might have the following objective:

Following ten weekly group meetings each child in the group will have demonstrated in at least three real-life settings the ability to:
1. make an effective complaint,
2. give negative feedback,
3. give positive feedback,
4. make a reasonable request, and
5. say no to an unreasonable request.

Classical techniques

Systematic desensitization.   Systematic desensitization, developed by Wolpe (1958, 1969) from earlier work by Jacobsen (1938), is a procedure used to eliminate anxiety and fear. A response incompatible with anxiety, such as relaxation, is paired with first a weak, then progressively stronger anxiety-provoking stimuli. The approach is based on the principles of counterconditioning. That is, if all skeletal muscles are deeply relaxed, it is impossible to experience anxiety at the same time. A child may be experiencing anxiety related to specific stimulus situations such as taking tests, performing in front of a group, fear of high places, or fear of some animal. The first step is to develop a hierarchy of scenes related to the fear or phobia, with mildly aversive scenes at the bottom and progressively more aversive scenes at the top. The child is then taught the deep muscle relaxation process and, while relaxed, is asked to visualize the various scenes in the hierarchy.

The relaxation exercises consist of successively tensing and relaxing 19 different muscle groups at six-second intervals until a high level of relaxation is achieved. The process is usually done with the child in a recliner-type chair or stretched out on a soft rug. The child is asked to go as high as possible on the hierarchy without feeling anxiety. When anxiety is felt, the child signals the counselor by raising one finger, and the counselor reverts to a less anxiety-provoking scene. Behavior practice facilitates the process. A child may successively practice giving a short speech in front of a mirror, with an audio tape recorder, with a videotape recorder, in front of a best friend, in front of a small group, and so on, until the speech can be given in front of a class of 25 students. The child's stimulus hierarchy might look like this:

0. Lying in bed in room just before going to sleep—describe your room
1. Thinking about speeches alone in your room one week before you give your speech
2. Discussing coming speech a week before in class
3. Sitting in class while another student gives a speech one week before your speech
4. Writing your speech at home
5. Practicing speech alone in room or in front of your friend
6. Getting dressed the morning of speech
7. Eating breakfast and thinking about speech before going to school
8. Walking to school on the day of your speech
9. Entering the classroom on the day of the speech
10. Waiting while another student gives a speech on the day of your presentation
11. Walking up before the class and looking at their faces
12. Presenting your speech before the class

The technique consists of asking the child to relax, imagine, relax, stop imagining, relax, and so on until, after repeated practice, the child learns to relax while visualizing each stage of the stimulus hierarchy.

Several relaxation exercises may be used with children. Following are two types of exercises frequently used.

1. Consciously "let go" of the various muscle groups starting with your feet and moving to your legs, stomach, arms, neck, and head as you make yourself as comfortable as you can in the chair or lying down.

    a. Stop frowning; let forehead relax.
    b. Let hands, arms, and so on relax.
    c. Tighten six seconds, relax; tighten again six seconds, relax.
2. Form mental pictures
    a. Picture yourself stretched out on a soft bed. Your legs are like concrete, sinking down in the mattress from their heavy weight. Picture a friend coming into the room and trying to lift your concrete legs, but they are too heavy and your friend cannot do it. Repeat with arms, neck, and so on.
    b. Picture your body as a big puppet. Your hands are tied loosely to your wrists by strings. Your forearm is connected loosely by a string to your shoulder. Your feet and legs are also connected together with a string. Your chin has dropped loosely against your chest. All strings are loose, your body is limp and just sprawled across the bed.
    c. Picture your body as consisting of a bunch of rubber balloons. Two air holes open in your feet and the air begins to escape from your legs. Your legs begin to collapse until they are a flat rubber tube. Next a hole is opened in your chest, and the air begins to escape until your entire body is lying flat on the bed. Continue with heads, arms, neck, and so on.
    d. Imagine the most relaxing and pleasant scene you can remember—a time when you felt really good and peaceful. Remember fishing in a mountain stream or pay attention to the little things like the quiet ripples on the water, the leaves on the trees. What sounds were present? Did you hear the quiet rustling of the leaves? Is your relaxing place before an open fireplace with logs crackling, or is it the beach, with warm sun and breeze? Continued practice will facilitate achievement of these images.

In summary, the technique of desensitization is based on a principle of learning referred to as *reciprocal inhibition*. That is, an organism cannot make two contradictory responses at the same time. If we assume that all responses are learned, they may be extinguished by relearning or by reconditioning. Therefore, relaxation, being more rewarding than anxiety, may gradually replace anxiety as the response to the anxiety-evoking situation.

Reactive or internal inhibition.   Reactive or internal inhibition, also referred to as *flooding*, is a process by which an anxiety-evoking stimulus is presented continuously, leading to fatigue and eventual unlearning of the undesirable response. When you were told to get back on your bike after a crash, you were being exposed to the flooding technique. Another application might involve taking a child with a fear of riding in cars on a four-hour trip. The initial response would be high anxiety or panic, which would, after a while, wear itself out.

Counterconditioning. In counterconditioning, a stronger pleasant stimulus is paired with a weaker aversive stimulus as a procedure for overcoming the anxiety evoked by the aversive stimulus. For example, a child may be given his or her favorite candy while sitting in the classroom. If the candy is sufficiently rewarding to the child, the anxiety evoked by the classroom should be diminished.

Aversive conditioning. Aversive conditioning is the application of an aversive or noxious stimulus like a rubber-band snap on the wrist when a maladaptive response or behavior occurs. For example, children could wear rubber bands around their wrists and snap them each time they found themselves daydreaming instead of listening to the teacher. When using the technique, it is recommended that opportunity be provided for helpful behavior to occur and be reinforced.

The following diagrams represent each of the four classical conditioning methods presented.

Key: ⊕ pleasant stimulus; ⊖ aversive stimulus.

1. Desensitization

    ⊖ ⊖ ⊖ ⊖ ⊖ ⊖ ⊖ ⊖, where ⊖ is giving a speech.

    The aversive stimulus is handled in small steps by visualization-relaxation and by practice until increasing larger steps can be handled.

2. Internal inhibition (flooding)

    ⊖⊖⊖⊖⊖⊖⊖⊖⊖⊖, where ⊖ is falling off a bike.

    The aversive stimulus is continually repeated until the fear response wears itself out.

3. Counterconditioning

    ⊕ and ⊖, where ⊕ is a candy bar and ⊖ is going to school.

    The larger pleasant stimulus overcomes the anxiety or fear evoked by the smaller aversive stimulus.

4. Aversive conditioning

    ⊖ and ⊕, where ⊖ is a snap of a rubber band on the wrist and ⊕ is daydreaming during class.

    The more painful stimulus overcomes the smaller reward gained from daydreaming in class.

CASE STUDY[1]

Identification of the problem

Amy Turner is a 7-year-old in the second grade. She has exhibited some behavior problems in her classroom. She does not complete her classroom assignments, tells lies about her work and about things that she does at home and school, and is reported to be out of her seat constantly.

Individual and background information

Academic.   Amy has an above-average IQ. She is an excellent reader and has the ability to do any second-grade assignment.

Family.   Amy is the only child of older parents, who have grown children from other marriages where their mates died. Amy's parents are in their fifties. Amy comes from an upper-middle-class family; her father has a large farm and works for TVA; her mother does not work outside the home.

Social.   Amy seems to get along relatively well with the other children but has only one close friend, Wendy. Amy has been caught telling lies by the other children, and they tell her they do not like her lies. She brings money and trinkets to share with Wendy and even lets her wear her nice coats, sweaters, and jewelry. Amy has no young children to play with and is mostly around adults who have let her pretty much have her way.

Counseling method

The counselor in this case used the behavioral counseling method to help Amy evaluate her behavior problems and to teach her to counsel herself. Using this method, a counselor has to carefully determine just how much right one has to influence the client's choices in modifying behavior. The criteria for determining when to use behavioral counseling would be based on (1) the frequency of the maladaptive behavior, and (2) the degree to which the behavior hindered her healthy development and that of the others in the class.

In this case the counselor used the following steps:

1. Established a warm, talking relationship
2. Wrote out the problems on paper
3. Listed rewards and consequences of the plans
4. Got a commitment from client on the plan of action that would most likely help
5. Used a behavior contract with positive reinforcement in the form

---

[1]The Amy Turner case was contributed by Mrs. Pat Atchley for a class in Counseling Theories and Techniques at the University of Tennessee, March 1980.

of a social reward (praise) for desirable behavior and token reinforcement (points to exchange for fun-time activities). Positive reinforcers were withdrawn (by loss of points) when undesirable behavior occurred.

6. Plans for a behavior contract were discussed with, agreed upon, and signed by the client, counselor, teacher, and parents because the child was exhibiting some of the undesirable behavior at home by not completing assigned tasks and telling her parents lies.

Transcript

Counselor (Co): Amy, your teacher sent you to me because you seem to be having some problems in class. Would you like to tell me what kind of problems you seem to be having? I'll write them down in a list so we can see what could be done to help you here and at home.

Amy: I just can't seem to get my work done or turned in on time.

Co: How do you stop yourself from doing this?

Amy: I just can't seem to be able to sit still long enough to finish, and then time is always up before I finish.

Co: Who else is affected by your getting out of your seat?

Amy: I guess I'm keeping the others from working when I go to their seats, and it bothers my teacher because she stops what she is doing and tells me to sit down and get busy.

Co: What happens when you don't finish your work?

Amy: Well, nothing really happens, except I try to get out of being fussed at and being kept in during play period for not doing my work.

Co: What do you mean, Amy?

Amy: I make up stories about I can't find my paper or somebody got it and I really hadn't even started it, or I hide what I have started in my desk or notebook and take it home and do it and then turn it in the next day and say I found it.

Co: What do you tell your mom and dad about your work for the day when they ask you?

Amy: Well, I tell a story to them, too. I tell them I did all my work, and usually the same things I tell the teacher I tell them too.

Co: How do you feel about telling stories?

Amy: I don't really feel good about it, but I want Mom and Dad to be proud of me and I really do want to do my work, but I just can't seem to do it, so I just tell a story.

Co: OK, Amy, you say you want to change, so let's look at the list of things you want to change and see what you and I can work out together.

Amy: OK, I'd like that.

Co: Let me read your contract terms to you. If you think there is anything you can't live with, we'll change it until we get it the way we think will help you the most. This contract tells you what will happen when you are able to finish your work. Your teacher, your mom and dad, myself, and you will all sign it to show you we are all willing to help you live up to the terms. Will you go over it with your mother and father and see if there is anything that needs to be changed?

Amy: I think it's OK just like it is.

Co: OK, you and I will sign first, and I will send a copy to your teacher and your parents to sign. We will try this for a week, and then you and I will meet at this same time next week to see how you are doing and see if there need to be any changes made.

Amy: OK.

Contract for Behavior and Learning

Positive Behaviors	*Points Earned*
1. Bringing needed materials to class	5
2. Working on class or home assignment until finished	5
3. Staying in seat	5
4. Extra credit (reading S-R-A or laminated task sheets)	1, 2, 3, 4, 5

You may exchange points earned for positive behavior for time to do "fun" activities:

	Total Points Earned
1. Writing on the small chalk boards	15
2. Playing Phonic Rummy	15
3. Playing with the tray puzzles	15
4. Getting to be the library aide for a day	15
5. Getting to use the cyclo-teacher	15
6. Playing "Old Maid" with classmates	10
7. Using the headphone and tape recorder to hear a story from tapes	15
8. Using clay, finger paints, and other art supplies	10

I, _____, agree to abide by the terms set forth in this contract. It is my understanding that my points earned will depend on my classroom work and behavior.

_____
Signature

We, your teacher, your parents, and your counselor, agree to abide by the conditions specified in the contract. It is our understanding that we will assist you in any way we can with your tasks and behavior problems.

_____

Teacher

_____

Parents

_____

Counselor

Behavioral counseling helps individuals to look at what they are doing and what happens when they do it. The contract helps children try different behaviors to see which one will work for them. Parents are encouraged to adhere to the terms of the contract and to positively reinforce all desirable behaviors at home. If the child continues to receive positive reinforcement for socially desirable and classroom adaptive behavior, a self-reinforcement system will be implemented gradually to help the child develop a sense of intrinsic reinforcement.

SUMMARY: RESEARCH AND REACTIONS

Behavioral counselors have more supporting data available than any other school of counseling. As noted previously, behavioral counselors must collect accurate data if their procedures are to operate with maximum efficiency. Therefore, behavioral counselors have done a thorough job of validating their claims of success.

The purpose of behavioral counseling is to change the client's overt and covert (cognitions, emotions, physiological states) responses. Bandura reacted to the oft-repeated dictum, "Change contingencies and you change behavior," by adding the reciprocal side, "change behavior and you change the contingencies ... since in everyday life this two-way control operates concurrently" (1974, p. 866). Behavioral counselors work with behavior that is objective and measurable. Behavioral counseling methods, not confined to one stimulus/response theory of learning, are derived from a variety of learning principles.

London (1972) declared that the distinguishing features of behavior counseling include the functional analysis of behavior and the development of the necessary technology to bring about change. Thus behavioral counseling is the application of specified procedures derived from experimental research to benefit an individual, a group, an institution, or an environmental setting.

Supporting research includes studies emphasizing the following behavioral counseling methods.

Contingency management.   Ayllon and Azrin (1965) demonstrated that tokens, when delivered contingent on specific behaviors, could have profound effects on the behavior of institutionalized psychotics. Many other applications have also been demonstrated (see Rimm & Masters, 1974).

Systematic desensitization.   Lang and Lazovik (1963) published the first controlled experiment that found greater reduction in the behavioral measure of snake avoidance for a desensitization group than for the no-treatment controls, who showed almost no change. Moreover, there was no evidence of symptom substitution in a six-month follow-up.

Self-control.   Goldiamond (1965) demonstrated the effectiveness of several self-control strategies for studying and marital difficulties among others.

Aversive control.   Blakemore, Thorpe, Barker, Conway, and Lavin (1963) reduced transvestism by applying electric shock, which was administered while the patient was putting on women's clothing.

Extinction.   Williams (1959) demonstrated that several disruptive behaviors could be reduced with extinction. These behaviors included crying, tantrums, food throwing, and food spilling.

Assertiveness training.   Lazarus (1966) compared behavior rehearsals, reflection-interpretation, and advice giving. Behavior rehearsal included modeling by the therapist, practice by the patient, and relaxation induction at the first sign of anxiety. Ninety-two percent of the behavior rehearsal subjects showed improvement, compared with 44% and 32% improvement, respectively, for the other two groups.

A balanced view of behavioral counseling can be found in Lazarus's (1977) article, "Has Behavior Therapy Outlived Its Usefulness?" Lazarus suggests that behavioral counseling methods by themselves are inadequate to treat the full range of human problems. He prefers a more eclectic approach such as his multimodal counseling discussed elsewhere in this book. He does, however, see behavioral methods as valuable tools in the counselor's repertoire of methods.

Levine and Fasnacht's (1974) article "Token Rewards May Lead to Token Learning" makes the point that reinforcement methods may serve to extinguish desired behavior when the reward or token replaces any intrinsic reward a person might receive from engaging in the desired behavior. For example, parents may reward or reinforce a child's piano practicing. The message to the child could be that piano playing is not worth doing without pay and therefore is not worthwhile in itself.

REFERENCES

Ayllon, T., and Azrin, N. The measurement and reinforcement of behavior of psychotics. *Journal of the Experimental Analysis of Behavior*, 1965, *8*, 357–383.

Bandura, A. Behavior therapy and the models of man. *American Psychologist,* 1974, *29,* 859–869.

Blakemore, C., Thorpe, J., Barker, J., Conway, C., and Lavin, N. The application of paradic aversion conditioning in a case of transvestism. *Behavior Research and Therapy,* 1963, *1,* 29–34.

Goldiamond, I. Self-control procedures in personal behavior patterns. *Psychological Reports,* 1965, *17,* 851–868.

Jacobsen, E. *Progressive relaxation.* Chicago: University of Chicago Press, 1938.

Krumboltz, J. Behavioral goals for counseling. *Journal of Counseling Psychology,* 1966, *13,* 153–159.

Krumboltz, J., and Hosford, R. Behavioral counseling in the elementary school. *Elementary School Guidance and Counseling,* 1967, *1,* 27–40.

Lang, P., and Lazovik, A. Experimental desensitization of a phobia. *Journal of Abnormal and Social Psychology,* 1963, *66,* 519–525.

Lazarus, A. Behavioral rehearsal vs. nondirective therapy vs. advice in effecting behavior change. *Behavior Research and Therapy,* 1966, *4,* 209–212.

Lazarus, A. Has behavior therapy outlived its usefulness? *American Psychologist,* 1977, *32,* 550–554.

Levine, F., and Fasnacht, G. Token rewards may lead to token learning. *American Psychologist,* 1974, *29,* 816–820.

London, P. The end of ideology in behavior modification. *American Psychologist,* 1972, *27,* 913–926.

Rimm, D., and Masters, J. *Behavior therapy: Techniques and empirical findings.* New York: Academic Press, 1974.

Skinner, B. F. *Beyond freedom and dignity.* New York: Knopf, 1971.

Thompson, C., and Poppen, W. *Guidance activities for counselors and teachers.* Monterey, Calif.: Brooks/Cole, 1979.

Williams, C. The elimination of tantrum behavior by extinction procedures. *Journal of Abnormal and Social Psychology,* 1959, *59,* 269.

Wolpe, J. *Psychotherapy by reciprocal inhibition.* Stanford, Calif.: Stanford University Press, 1958.

Wolpe, J. *The practice of behavior therapy.* New York: Pergamon Press, 1969.

10

PSYCHODYNAMIC COUNSELING

SIGMUND FREUD

Sigmund Freud was born in Freiberg, Moravia, in 1856 and died in London in 1939. However, he is considered to have belonged to Vienna, where he lived and worked for nearly 80 years. Freud was the first-born of eight children by his father's second wife. There were two sons, 20-odd years older than Freud, by his father's first wife.

Freud graduated from the gymnasium at 17 years of age and, in 1873, entered the medical school at the University of Vienna. He became deeply involved in neurological research and did not finish his M.D. degree for eight years. Never intending to practice medicine because he wanted to be a scientist, Freud devoted his next 15 years to investigations of the nervous system (Hall, 1954). However, the salary of a scientific researcher was inadequate to support a wife and six children. In addition, the anti-Semitism prevalent in Vienna during this period prevented Freud from receiving university advancement. Consequently, Freud was forced to take up the practice of medicine.

Freud decided to specialize in the treatment of nervous disorders. At the time, not too much was known about this particular branch of medicine. So Freud spent considerable time learning the techniques associated with treatment of "aberrations of the mind." First, he spent a year in France learning about Jean Charcot's use of hypnosis in the treatment of hysteria (Stone, 1972). Freud (1963) was dissatisfied with hypnosis because he thought that its effects were only temporary and did not get at the center of the problem. Freud then studied with Joseph Breuer, learning the benefits of the catharsis or "talking-out-your-problems" form of therapy.

Noticing that the physical symptoms of his patients seemed to have a mental base, Freud began to probe deeper and deeper into the minds of his patients. "His probing revealed dynamic forces at work which were responsible for creating the abnormal symptoms that he was called upon to treat. Gradually there began to take shape in Freud's mind the idea that most of these forces were unconscious" (Hall, 1954, p. 15). According to Stone (1972), this finding was probably the turning point in Freud's career. To substantiate some of his ideas, Freud decided to undertake an intensive self-analysis of his own unconscious forces in order to check on the material gathered from his patients. "On the basis of the knowledge he gained from his patients and from himself he began to lay the foundations for a theory of personality" (Hall, 1954, p. 17).

After a period of being shunned by most doctors and scholars, as is the case with most new and revolutionary ideas, Freud was accepted as a genius in the field of counseling. Many influential scientists such as Carl Jung, Alfred Adler, Ernest Jones, and Wilhelm Stekel recognized Freud's theory as a major breakthrough in the field of psychology. However, though Freud's academic career with the University of Vienna began in 1883, it was not until 1920 that this institution saw fit to confer on him the rank of full professor. Freud's recognition by academic psychology came in 1909, when he was invited by G. Stanley Hall to give a series of lectures at Clark University in Worcester, Massachusetts.

Freud's writing career spanned 63 years, during which time he produced over 600 publications. His collected works have been published in 24 volumes under the title, *The Standard Edition of the Complete Psychological Works of Sigmund Freud (1953–1964)*. Among his more famous works are *The Interpretation of Dreams* (1900) and *The Psychopathology of Everyday Life* (1901).

Freud seemed never to think that his work was finished. "As new evidence came to him from his patients and his colleagues, he expanded and revised his basic theories" (Hall, 1954, p. 17). As an example of his flexibility and capability, at the age of 70 Freud completely altered a number of his fundamental views—revamped motivation theory, reversed the theory of anxiety, and developed a new model of personality based on id, ego, and superego.

Freud developed his psychoanalytic model of people over a period of five decades of observing and writing. The major principles were based on the clinical study of individual patients undergoing treatment for their problems. Free association became Freud's preferred procedure after he discarded hypnosis.

Psychoanalysis includes theories about the development and organization of the mind, the instinctual drives, the influences of the external environment, the importance of the family, and the attitudes of society. As useful as psychoanalysis is as a therapeutic tool, its impact and value reach far beyond its medical application. It is the only comprehensive theory of human psychology. It has proven itself increasingly helpful to parents and teachers in the upbringing and education of children.

Although it has been changed in some areas down through the years, the basic concepts of psychoanalysis still remain, and even today, it is recognized as very influential in counseling theory. Almost all counseling theories have extracted some of their basic premises from the psychoanalytic method. This alone shows the influence and durability of the theory.

THE NATURE OF PEOPLE

The concept of human nature in psychoanalytic theory found its basis in psychic determinism and unconscious mental processes. Psychic determinism implies that mental life is a continuous manifestation of cause-related relationships. Mental processes are considered the causative factors in the nature of human behavior. Mental activity and even physical activity may be kept below the conscious level. Freud (1965) noted that conflict, repression, and anxiety often go together, with the result that people often do not understand their feelings, thoughts, actions, or behaviors. Analysis on the basis of unconscious determinism is the base of psychoanalytic counseling. Counseling leading to catharsis will then lead to confronting the unconscious mind or to a way of learning to cope, understand, and grow in mental development.

Freud viewed people as basically evil and victims of instincts that must be balanced or reconciled with social forces in order to provide a structure in which human beings can function. To achieve balance, people need a deep understanding of the forces that motivate them to action. According to Freud, people operate like energy systems, distributing psychic energy to the id, ego, and superego. Human behavior is viewed as determined by this energy, by unconscious motives, and by instinctual and biological drives. Psychosexual events during the first five years of life are seen as critical to adult personality development.

Sugarman (1977), believing that Freud's concept of the nature of people is often misinterpreted, presents a contrasting view of Freudian theory in which a humanistic image of people is recognized in the following eight ideas:

1. People have a dual nature, biological and symbolic.
2. People are both individuals and related to others simultaneously.
3. People strive for goals and values.
4. One of the strongest human needs is to give meaning to life.
5. One's internal world, including the unconscious, is more important than overt behavior.
6. People are social creatures whose need for interpersonal relationships is supreme.
7. People are always evolving, always in process.

8. People have a certain amount of autonomy within the constraints of reality.

In summary, according to psychoanalytic theory, the basic concepts of human nature revolve around the notions of psychic determinism and unconscious mental processes. Psychic determinism simply implies that our mental function or mental life is a continuous logical manifestation of causative relationships. Nothing is random, nothing happens by chance. Though mental events may appear unrelated, they are actually closely interwoven and dependent upon preceding mental signals. Closely related to psychic determinism are unconscious mental processes, which exist as fundamental causative factors in the nature of human behavior. In essence, much of what goes on in our minds and hence our bodies is unknown, below the conscious level, so that we often do not understand our feelings and/or actions. The existence of unconscious mental processes is the basis for much of what is involved in psychoanalytic counseling. Analysis leading to catharsis is employed to dredge up unconscious elements contained within the recesses of the mind. By confronting these elements, the counselee can achieve growth and mental health.

THEORY OF COUNSELING

Freud's concepts of personality form the basis for a psychoanalytic counseling theory. The principal concepts in Freudian theory can be grouped under three topic headings: structural, dynamic, and developmental. The structural concepts include id, ego, and superego. The dynamic concepts are instinct, cathexsis, anticathexsis, and anxiety. The developmental concepts are identification, displacement, defense mechanisms, and psychosexual stages.

Structural concepts

Id.   The id exists to stimulate the organism's basic needs and drives (instinct) and to provide for the discharge of energy produced by contact between the organism and the external or internal environment (pleasure principle). Through this mechanism, tensions can be released via impulsive motor activity and image formation (wish fulfillment). The id is not capable of thought but can form, for example, mental pictures of hamburgers for a hungry person.

Ego.   Often called the executive of the personality, the ego strives to strike a balance between the needs of the id and the superego in conjunction with the reality of the external world and bring the mental images formed by the id (the hamburgers, for example) into reality.

Superego.   Composed of two parts—the ego ideal (the ideal rather than the real) and the conscience (developed from the child's concepts of parents' and/or other influential individuals' moral inclination)—the superego is, in essence, a person's moral standard. Often thought of as the judicial branch of the personality, the superego can act to restrict, prohibit, and judge conscious actions. Unconsciously, the superego can also act, and the unconscious process of the superego will often lead to detrimental forms of human behavior.

Ideally the ego, superego, and id systems work together as a cooperative unit, helping people fulfill their basic needs and desires and carry on satisfying relationships with others and efficient transactions with the environment. When the three systems are at odds, the individual is dissatisfied with self and the environment, and efficiency is reduced. Extreme disunity may be labeled as maladjustment.

Dynamic concepts

Instinct.   An instinct is an inborn psychological representation, referred to as a *wish*, which stems from a physiological condition referred to as a *need*. For example, the need for hunger leads to a wish for food. The wish becomes a motive for behavior. Life instincts serve to maintain the survival of the species. Hunger, thirst, and sex needs are served by life instincts. *Libido* is the term Freud used to describe the energy that permits life instincts to work. Freud also coined the term *death* (or destructive) *instincts,* which referred to a wish to die or a wish to commit aggressive acts.

Cathexis.   Cathexis refers to directing one's energy toward an object that will satisfy a need.

Anticathexis.   Anticathexis refers to the force exerted by the ego to block or restrain impulses of the id. The reality principle or superego directs this action of the ego against the pleasure principle emanating from the id.

Anxiety.   Anxiety can be seen as a conscious state where a painful emotional experience is produced by external or internal excitation— a welling-up of autonomic nervous energy. Closely akin to fear but more encompassing is the anxiety that originates from internal as well as external causes. Freud believed there were three types of anxiety: reality, neurotic, and moral. Reality anxiety results from real threats from the environment. Neurotic anxiety results from the fear that our instinctual impulses from the id will overpower our ego controls and get us into trouble. Moral anxiety results from the guilt we feel when we fail to live up to our standards.

Developmental concepts

Identification.   Identification refers to the development of role models people identify with or imitate. They may choose to imitate a few traits of the model or the total person.

Displacement.   Displacement refers to redirecting energy from a primary object to a substitute when an instinct is blocked. For example, anger toward a parent may be directed toward a sibling or another object because of the fear of reprisal from the parent. Freud believed that human behavior is motivated by basic instincts. He thought that rechanneling of energy from the sexual instinct into productive activity, which he called *sublimation,* was the major reason for the advancement of civilization. Aggressive sports are sublimations of destructive impulses, while creative activities are sublimations of sexual impulses.

Defense mechanisms.   Defense mechanisms are the measures taken by the ego to protect itself against heavy pressure and anxiety. Repression, projection, and reaction formation are the main ego defenses.

Repression forces a dangerous memory, conflict, idea, or perception out of the conscious into the unconscious and places a lid on it to prevent resurfacing of the repressed material. In the discussion of repression we need to consider the concepts of unconscious, preconscious, and conscious. *Conscious* refers to that part of mental activity that we are fully aware of at any given time. *Preconscious* refers to thoughts and feelings that are not immediately available but which can be brought back to consciousness with effort. The concept of the *unconscious* is the foundation of psychoanalytic theory and practice. This concept holds that there are drives, desires, attitudes, motivations, and fantasies in one part of the mind we are not aware of. They are very important because they are responsible for many of our conscious feelings, thoughts, attitudes, and actions. They also influence our relationships with others.

Projection consists of attributing characteristics in oneself to others and things in the external world. For instance, a teacher may find it uncomfortable to admit that he doesn't like the children in his class, so instead he says that the children don't like him. He projects his dislike for his students on to the students.

Reaction formation refers to the development of attitudes or character traits exactly opposite to ones that have been repressed. Anxiety-producing impulses are replaced in the conscious by their opposites. For example, "I love booze" is replaced by "Liquor should be declared illegal."

Other ego defense mechanisms include the following:

Rationalization—attempting to prove that one's behavior is justified and rational and thus worthy of approval by oneself and others. When asked why they behaved in a certain manner, children may feel forced to think up logical excuses or reasons.

Denial—refusing to face unpleasant aspects of reality or the refusal to perceive anxiety-provoking stimuli. Children may deny the possibility of falling while climbing high trees.

Fantasy—seeking gratification of needs and frustrated desires through the imagination. A fantasy or imagined world may be a more pleasant place than the real world of a child.

Withdrawal—reducing ego involvement by becoming passive or learning to avoid being hurt; for example, the shy child or school-phobic child.

Intellectualization—separating the normal affect, or feeling, from an unpleasant or hurtful situation. For example, the grief of a child whose dog has been hit by a car might be softened by saying, "Our dog is really better off dead; he was feeble and going blind."

Regression—retreating to earlier developmental stages that were less demanding than the present level. An older child may revert to a babyish behavior when a new baby arrives in the family.

Compensation—covering up a weakness by emphasizing some desirable trait or reducing frustration in one area by overgratification in another area of life. For example, the class clown may compensate for poor academic performance by attention-getting behavior.

Undoing—engaging in some form of atonement for immoral or bad behavior or the desires to participate in same. For instance, after breaking a lamp, a child may try to glue it back together.

Acting out—reducing the anxiety aroused by forbidden desires by expressing them. The behavior of a revenge-seeking child is an example.

Psychosexual stages

Freud (1949) viewed personality development as a succession of stages, each characterized by a dominant mode of achieving libidinal pleasure and by specific developmental tasks. How well the adjustment is made in each stage is the critical factor in development. Freud believed that personality characteristics are fairly well established by the age of six. Gratification during each stage is important if the individual is not to become fixated at that level of development. The key to each stage is how well parents help their child adjust to the stage and make the transition to the next stage. The difficulty with Freud's system comes when counselors emphasize the extremes rather than the normal range of behaviors. The trick seems to be in maintaining a balance between the extremes. The five developmental stages are oral, anal, phallic, latency, and genital.

Oral stage (birth–1 year).   This stage is characterized by two substages: oral erotic and oral sadistic. The oral erotic substage is characterized by the sucking reflex, which is necessary for survival. The main task for the child is to adjust to the weaning process and learn to chew food in the oral sadistic substage. The mouth is characterized as an erogenous zone because pleasure is obtained from sucking, eating, and biting. Adult behaviors such as smoking, eating, and drinking and personality traits of gullibility, dependency (erotic), and sarcasm (sadistic) originate in the oral period.

Anal stage (1–3 years).   During this time, the membrane of the anal region presumably provides the major source of pleasurable stimulation. Two substages are also evident in this stage: anal expulsive and anal retentive. The major hurdle in this stage is the regulation of a natural function (bowel control). Toilet training requires that the child learn how to deal with postponing immediate gratification. Again, the manner in which the parents facilitate or impede the process will form the basis for a number of adult personality traits. Stubbornness, stinginess, and orderliness (anal retentive) and generosity and messiness (anal expulsive) are among adult traits associated with the anal stage.

Phallic stage (3–6 years). Self-manipulation of the genitals provides the major source of pleasurable sensation. The Oedipal Complex occurs during this stage. The female version is sometimes referred to as the Electra Complex. Sexual and aggressive feelings and fantasies are associated with the genitals. Boys have sexual desires for their mothers and aggressive feelings toward their fathers; girls develop hostility toward their mothers and become sexually attracted to their fathers. Attitudes toward persons of the same and opposite sex are beginning to take shape during this period. Freud has been attacked for his ideas about castration complexes. Criticisms range from labeling his castration ideas as ridiculous to calling them projections of his own fears. In any case, Freud believed that boys are afraid that their fathers will castrate them for loving their mothers. Girls' castration complexes take the form of penis envy; compensation for lacking a penis comes with having a baby.

Latency stage (7–13 years). Sexual motivations presumably recede in importance during the latency period as the child becomes preoccupied with developmental skills and activities. Children generally concentrate on developing their friendships with people of the same sex. Sexual and aggressive impulses are relatively quiet during this phase. As for aggression, Freud obviously never taught a group of children in this age group.

Genital stage (12–14 years). After puberty, the deepest feeling of pleasure presumably comes from heterosexual relations. The major task of this period is the development of relationships with members of the opposite sex. This can be a risky task involving rejection and fear of rejection. Once again, the ease with which this task can be accomplished will have tremendous impact on future heterosexual relationships.

Oral, anal, and phallic stages are classified as narcissistic because children derive pleasure from their own erogenous zones. During the genital stage, the focus of activity shifts to developing genuine relationships with others. The goal would be that the young person would move from a pleasure-seeking, pain-avoiding, narcissistic child to a reality-oriented, socialized adult.

COUNSELING METHODS

The primary goal of counseling from a psychoanalytic frame of reference is to make the unconscious conscious. The techniques used are directed toward discovering repressed conflicts and bringing them into the client's conscious awareness. Once repressed material is brought to the conscious level, it can be dealt with in rational ways with any number of methods discussed in this book. Several methods are used to uncover the unconscious. Detailed case histories are taken with special attention given to the handling of conflict areas. Hypnosis, though rejected by Freud, is still used to assist in plumbing the unconscious. Analysis of resistance, transference, and dreams are frequently used methods, as are catharsis, free association, and interpretation. All of these methods have the long-term goal of strengthening the ego. The three principal counseling methods that will be discussed are catharsis, free association, and interpretation.

Catharsis

Freud, along with Breuer, first discovered the benefits of catharsis through hypnosis. Freud found that if, under hypnosis, hysterical patients were able to verbalize an early precipitating causal event, the hysterical symptoms would disappear. Freud soon discarded hypnosis because he was not able to induce in everyone the deep hypnotic sleep that enabled the patient to regress to an early enough period to disclose the repressed event. Freud discovered that for many people the mere command to remember the origin of some hysterical symptom worked quite well. Unfortunately, many of his patients could not remember the origin of their symptoms even upon command. Freud thus decided that all people were aware of the cause of their illness, but for some reason certain people blocked this knowledge. It was Freud's belief that unless this repressed traumatic infantile experience could be dredged up from the subconscious to the conscious and verbalized and relived emotionally, the patient would not recover. Since not everyone had the ability to find this subconscious material, the analyst had to use more indirect means to gain access to the subconscious mind. Freud developed the methods of free association and interpretation to bring everyone to the emotional state of catharsis that was so necessary for cure.

Free association

In traditional psychoanalysis, the patient lies on a couch with the analyst at his or her head, so that the patient is not looking at the analyst. The patient is then given the order to say whatever comes to mind. It is hoped that through this means the subconscious thoughts and conflicts will be given freedom to reach the conscious mind. There is a great struggle within the patient to keep from telling the analyst his or her innermost thoughts. This resistance, as it is termed by psychoanalysts, is something that the analyst must constantly struggle against.

During the time the patient is trying to associate freely, the analyst must remain patient, nonjudgmental, and insistent that the patient continue. The analyst must also look for continuity of thoughts and feelings. Even though it might appear at first glance that the patient is idly rambling on, psychoanalysts believe that there is a rational pattern to this rambling. In order to correctly interpret what the patient is saying, the analyst must pay attention to the affect, or feeling, behind the patient's verbalization, noting the patient's gestures, tone of voice, and general body language during free association. The analyst, at this point, makes some interpretations about the client's statements. It is hoped that doing this will open another door for free association.

Free association, in turn, leads to another very important technique for the analyst—interpretation. Three major areas of interpretation will be described: dreams, parapraxia, and humor.

Interpretation of dreams.   To Freud, dreams are a means of expressing a wish fulfillment. In order to correctly interpret the power of the id, the analyst must learn about and interpret the client's dreams. According to Freud, there are three major types of dreams: those with meaningful and rational content (almost invariably found in children), those with material very different from waking events, and those with illogical and senseless episodes. According to Freud, all dreams are centered around a person's life and are under the person's psychic control. Every dream is a revelation of an unfulfilled wish. In children's dreams, the wish is usually very obvious. As the individual matures, the wish, as exposed in the dream, becomes more distorted and disguised. Freud said that the initial conscious wish is fought by the ego and thus is pushed back to the unconscious mind; it brings itself back into the conscious mind by means of a dream.

Freud's method of dream interpretation was to allow the client to freely associate. Certain objects in dreams were universal symbols for Freud. For example, a car in someone's dreams usually represented analysis, the number 3 represented male genitals, jewel cases were vaginas, peaches were female breasts, woods were pubic hair, and dancing and riding were symbols for sexual intercourse.

Freud (1952) believed every dream to be a confession and a by-product of repressed, anxiety-producing thoughts. Freud thought that many dreams were representations of unfulfilled sexual desires. Many were also expressions of guilt and self-punishment from the superego. Nightmares, the most terrifying of all human experiences, result from the desire for self-punishment. Since we consciously and subconsciously are aware of those things that we fear most, these are the things that we put into our nightmares to punish ourselves.

Parapraxia. Parapraxia is what are popularly called Freudian slips. They are consciously excused as harmless mistakes, so they are one of the id's ways to get unconscious material through to the conscious. The analyst must be very aware of any slips of the tongue while dealing with a patient. The Freudians also believe that there are no such things as "mis"takes or items that are "mis"placed. According to psychoanalytic thinking, there is an unconscious motivation for everything that we do. If we cannot remember a person's name, there is a reason for it. If we cut a finger while peeling potatoes, there is a reason for it. The analyst must take all of these unconscious mistakes and put them into some kind of conscious pattern.

Humor.   Jokes, puns, and satire are all acceptable means for unconscious urges to gain access to the conscious. The things that we laugh about tell us something about our repressed thoughts. One of the fascinations of humor, according to psychoanalytic theory, is that it simultaneously disguises and reveals repressed thoughts. Repressed thoughts, released by humor, usually generate from the id or superego. Since sexual thoughts are usually repressed, many jokes are sexually oriented. Since aggressive thoughts are usually repressed, they are expressed in humor by way of satire and witticisms.

Again, the analyst must watch for patterns. What does the client think is funny? How does the client's sense of humor fit into a pattern from the unconscious? According to Freud, the dream guards against pain; humor, on the other hand, serves to acquire pleasure. From these two activities, all of our psychic activities meet.

Implications for counseling children

The greatest problems in applying psychoanalytic techniques to counseling children are their relatively undeveloped verbal skills and inadequate cognitive development. Traditionally, raising unresolved and unconscious conflicts from the past to consciousness is achieved by means of free association and dream analysis and interpretation. Children are relatively receptive to dream analysis as long as it is kept in the realm of metaphor. In that way it can remain in the child's realm of make-believe and thus be more under control and less threatening. Resolution of dreams involving conflict is a sign of therapeutic progress and emotional growth.

The problem of free association is more difficult. Children seem to be unable or unwilling to do this. It is now widely believed that nondirective free play, particularly that involving symbolic make-believe (using dolls as particular real people, a stick as a gun, and the like) is closely analogous to free association. The assumption is that children will translate their imagination into symbolic play action rather than words. Some counselors use play therapy as a necessary prelude to verbal psychodynamic counseling and not necessarily as therapy in itself.

CASE STUDY[1]

Identification of the problem

Dennis, age 9, was considered a disturbed, slow, resistant boy who had to be pushed into doing everything he was supposed to be doing. He rarely participated in any family activities and had no friends in the neighborhood. His school mentioned such problems as regression, playing with much younger children, thumbsucking, daydreaming, soiling, bullying, and tardiness. The first counseling session begins with Dennis entering the playroom.

Transcript

Dennis: Well, what are we going to do today?

Counselor (Co): Whatever you'd like. This is your time.

Dennis: Let's talk.

Co: All right.

Dennis: Let's go back in history. We're studying about it in school. I'm going to be studying about Italy next week. I can't think of anything to talk about. I can't think of one thing to say. Can you?

Co: I'd rather discuss something you suggest.

Dennis: I can't think of a thing.

Co: We can just sit here if you like.

Dennis: Good. Do you want to read?

Co: OK.

Dennis: You be the teacher, and I'll be the student. I'll read to you. Now you be ready to ask me some questions. I don't like spelling. I like social studies, and I like history more than any other subject. I'd like being the teacher for a change. (Dennis asks therapist questions from a reading text.)

Co: You like to ask questions you think I'll miss.

Dennis: That's right. I'm going to give you a test next week. A whole bunch of arithmetic problems, and social studies, and other questions. Now, I'm going to read like my friend does. . . . Notice how he reads?

Co: Seems to read fast without pausing.

Dennis: Yes.

Co: You'd like to be able to read like that.

Dennis: Not much. Let's name the ships in the books. (Counselor names each of the types of boat.) I have so much fun making up those names. That's what we'll do next week. (Counselor begins reading again.) Stop me when I make a mistake or do something wrong.

Co: I'd rather you stop yourself.

---

[1]Michael Gooch contributed the case of Dennis while completing a counseling course at the University of Tennessee.

Dennis: The teacher always stops me.

Co: I'm a listener, not a teacher.

Dennis: Be a teacher, all right? (Counselor begins reading again.) That reminds me I have three dogs at home. The set cost me three dollars. Two have been broke. (The session is about to end. Counselor examines some darts and a board.)

Dennis: Oh boy, darts. Maybe we can play with them next week.

Co: You're making lots of plans for next time.

Dennis: Yeah.

Several counseling sessions followed this one. Dennis showed marked improvement at school and at home. Dennis's mother and teacher spoke more positively of him.

Comments

The counselor gave Dennis his complete undivided attention, participating in his games, tasks, projects, and plans. Here was someone with whom Dennis could talk and share his interests and ideas at a time when no one else would understand and accept him. He needed someone who would let him lead the way and let him be important in making decisions and plans. Dennis played the role of the initiator, the director, the teacher. He needed to have someone else know how it felt to be the follower, the one who is told what to do, the one ordered into activity and made to meet expectations. He needed to gain respect and confidence in his ability to face tasks and problems and to see them through successfully. In short, he used the therapy experience to improve his relationships and his skills. He became a competent, self-dependent person by practicing behavior, which gave him a sense of self-adequacy and self-fulfillment.

SUMMARY: RESEARCH AND REACTIONS

Just as Sigmund Freud was the father of psychoanalysis, he was the grandfather of child psychoanalysis. His therapy with adults conducted at the Vienna Psychoanalytic Institute was continuous and lengthy, often requiring several years to complete. A school for children was established adjacent to the Institute. Anna Freud, Freud's daughter, began to take a great interest in these children and eventually devoted herself almost exclusively to the study of children. She stands today as the outstanding pioneer in the field. The Institute also trained other prominent child analysts, most notable among them Peter Blos, Marianne Kris, and Erik Erikson, the last best known for his theory of sequenced tasks as the means to development of one's identity.

Melanie Klein (1932) contributed to and enlarged upon the work done earlier at the Institute. She wrote of ways that free-play activity could be utilized in a similar manner that traditional free association was utilized with adults. She also added to existing knowledge in the areas of working through displacements and transference verbally.

Virginia Axline (1947, 1964) did much to popularize the term *play therapy*. She developed the idea of helping the child develop the trust necessary for a therapeutic alliance by following the child's lead in free-play activities, not intruding into the process, and withholding interpretation. She felt that in this way the child would give symbolic messages that could later be expressed verbally and interpreted as the relationship developed. Ekstein (1966) expanded upon this concept somewhat. He too believed that verbal communication must often be by-passed for the sake of symbolic action, but he was not so opposed to taking an active part in the child's play or acting out of fantasy. He believed that "playing" a make-believe situation with children encouraged them to act out and then later talk about real-life situations that were bothering them. There is less threat in make-believe than in direct talk with adults, the source of much of a child's anxieties.

According to Maenchen (1970), the differences in technique between adult and child analytic psychotherapy are shrinking. She sees a lessening of reliance on play therapy, more emphasis on the therapist interpreting "the moment" with the child, and more use of verbal games to elicit free association. She also sees more emphasis placed on the relationship between child and counselor. Pothier (1976) agrees with Maenchen by designating a special category for relationship therapy in her listing of counseling methods.

Rutter (1975) points to four primary trends in analytic approaches to children: (1) a move to briefer treatment, which encourages clearer focus on problems, the setting of definite goals, and more definite strategies; (2) greater attention to conscious conflicts and current environmental stresses; (3) a shift away from treatment of the individual toward a focus on the family as a group; (4) less preoccupation with the interpretation of intrapsychic mechanisms and a greater reliance on the therapist/child relationship itself as the main treatment agent. This last trend seems to have a consensus of support of professionals in the field.

REFERENCES

Axline, V. *Play therapy*. Boston: Houghton Mifflin, 1947.
Axline, V. *Dibs: In search of self*. Boston: Houghton Mifflin, 1964.
Ekstein, R. *Children of time and space of action and impulse; clinical studies on psychoanalytic treatment of severely disturbed children*. New York: Appleton-Century-Crofts, 1966.
Freud, S. *An outline of psycho-analysis* (James Strachey, Trans.). New York: Norton, 1949 (originally published, 1940).
Freud, S. *On dreams* (James Strachey, Trans.). New York: Norton, 1952 (originally published, 1901).

Freud, S. *An autobiographical study* (James Strachey, Trans.). New York: Norton, 1963 (originally published, 1925).

Freud, S. *New introductory lectures in psychoanalysis* (James Strachey, Ed. and Trans.). New York: Norton, 1965 (originally published, 1933).

Hall, C. *A primer of Freudian psychology.* New York: Mentor, 1954.

Klein, M. *The psychoanalysis of children.* London: Hogarth Press, The Institute of Psychoanalysis, 1932.

Maenchen, A. On the technique of child analysis in relation to stages of development. *The Psychoanalytic Study of the Child*, 1970, *25*, 175–208.

Pothier, P. *Mental health counseling with children.* Boston: Little, Brown, 1976.

Rutter, M. *Helping troubled children.* New York: Plenum, 1975.

Stone, I. *Passions of the mind* (James Strachey, Trans.). New York: Norton, 1972.

Sugarman, A. Psychoanalysis as a humanistic psychology. *Psychotherapy: Theory, Research, and Practice*, 1977, *14*, 204–211.

CHAPTER
11

LOGOTHERAPY

VIKTOR FRANKL

Viktor E. Frankl was born in Vienna, Austria, in 1905 and was educated there. He received his M.D. in 1930 and his Ph.D. in 1949 from the University of Vienna. In 1928, Frankl founded the Youth Advisement Centers in Vienna. He was on the staff of the Neuropsychiatric University Clinic from 1930 to 1938. From 1936 to 1942, he was a specialist in neurology and psychiatry and then head of the Neurological Department at Rothschild Hospital, Vienna. He became head of the Neurological Policlinic Hospital (in Vienna) in 1946. In 1947, he was appointed associate professor of Neurology and Psychiatry at the University of Vienna, becoming a professor in 1955.

Frankl began his professional career with a psychoanalytical background, having been a student of Freud. However, he became influenced by the writings of existential philosophers such as Heidegger, Scheler, and Legan and developed his own existential philosophy. In 1938, he first used the terms *existenzanalysis* and *logotherapy* in his writings. In order to avoid confusion with others who were writing on existenzanalysis, he concentrated on logotherapy.

From 1942 to 1945 Frankl was imprisoned in German concentration camps, including Auschwitz and Dachau. His father, mother, brother, and wife were killed in the camps or gas chambers. Frankl's philosophy, which was developed by practice and teaching, was tested and strengthened in his concentration camp experiences. These experiences convinced him that there was one ultimate purpose to existence.

During the many months of camp life, some people fell victim to the degenerating influences; others reached within themselves and

173

found the faith to sustain themselves. Those who had no faith in themselves or the future gave up and ceased to live. Those who survived accepted the difficult task life set before them and found meaning in life. The circumstances set before each person were the same, and the way each accepted those circumstances determined his or her fate. The sort of person the prisoner became was the result of an inner decision rather than the camp influence alone.

Despite the inhumanity of the concentration camps, Frankl found that people could preserve within themselves an area of inner peace that no one could destroy. Under any circumstances people can decide what shall become of them mentally and spiritually. Frankl (1962) states that it is this spiritual freedom of independence of mind, even in such terrible conditions of psychic and physical stress, that makes life meaningful. If there is a meaning to life, there can also be meaning in suffering since suffering, like death, is an inescapable part of life. Frankl reasoned that without suffering and death life could not be complete.

Frankl wrote about his experiences as a prisoner in a book entitled *From Death-Camp to Existentialism* (1946). He was able to develop a philosophy of life that enabled him to find meaning in his life while a prisoner, as well as meaning in suffering and in death. His development of logotherapy emphasized that people are and always remain capable of resisting and braving even the worst conditions, seeking to find meaning in their lives. Frankl's primary lesson of existentialism is: to live is to suffer, to survive is to find meaning in suffering.

In 1962, Frankl wrote a revision of *From Death-Camp to Existentialism* entitled *Man's Search for Meaning*, that includes a section on the basic concepts of logotherapy. In 1967, Frankl published *Psychotherapy and Existentialism*, which consisted of selected papers he had written about logotherapy. *The Will to Meaning*, which deals with the foundations and applications of logotherapy, was published in 1969. Frankl's most recent book, *The Unconscious God* (1975a), is concerned with the interrelationship between psychotherapy and theology. Frankl has published over 20 books and numerous articles.

THE NATURE OF PEOPLE

Frankl believed that, in addition to their physical and psychological dimensions, people possess a spiritual dimension. All three areas must be explored if human beings are to be fully understood. It is through the spiritual dimension that people are able to reach beyond themselves and make their ideals part of reality. Logotherapy assumes that people primarily seek life tasks and that pleasure comes from accomplishing these tasks. It asserts that people are unique in the sense that they lead their own life, and that this life is irreplaceable. A further assumption states that people are free, within obvious limitations, to make choices regarding their lives. This freedom allows us to change, to decide who we are and what we would like to become.

Along with freedom comes responsibility, and we must use our freedom wisely or pay the consequences of irresponsibility. Because of changing values, people are forced more than ever to rely on their personal conscience. Frankl finds freedom in the face of three things: (1) the instincts, (2) inherited disposition, and (3) the environment. Although people are influenced by all of these, they still have freedom to accept or reject and to make decisions. People do not function primarily on the biological level. Since they can rise above this level and function on the psychological and spiritual levels, people are individually unpredictable.

It is important to keep in mind that Frankl does not see body, mind, and spirit as separate components. People are viewed as a unity, and, to emphasize this oneness, Frankl introduced the concept of dimensions. His theory holds that people are trapped in the dimension of their bodies and driven in the dimension of their psyches. But in the dimension of their *noos*—the dimension that is exclusively human—they are free. (The religious connotation of noos is misleading because the noetic dimension exists in everyone, including the nonreligious.) In the noetic dimension people decide what kind of person they are and what kind of person they are going to become. It is here that people make decisions and choices.

In using the term *spiritual* within the frame of logotherapy, Frankl again refers to the specifically human dimension, not the religious. Through this metaphysical aspect, people are able to transcend many of their problems. By incorporating this existentialist attitude, logotherapy is applicable for people of many ethnic backgrounds.

Frankl quotes the philosophy of Nietzsche to support the theory and practice of logotherapy:

"He who has a why to live can bear almost any how."
"That which does not defeat me makes me stronger."

Glasser's reality therapy would also be at home with these ideas, especially the one about gaining strength.

In summary, Frankl believes that people are free to exercise control over their lives. He takes issue with the idea that we are under the control of our environment.

THEORY OF COUNSELING

Logotherapy is the third school of Viennese psychotherapy. Freud's psychoanalysis, based on the will to find pleasure in life, is the first, and the individual psychology of Alfred Adler, based on the will to obtain power, is the second.

Logos, the will to find meaning in life, is based on a Greek word that denotes meaning. Logotherapy focuses on the meaning of human existence as well as on one's search for such a meaning. Our search for meaning is a primary force in life and not a secondary rationalization of instinctual drives. *Logos* means not only meaning but also spirit. Spiritual issues such as our aspiration for a meaningful existence, as well as the frustration of this aspiration, are confronted by logotherapy in spiritual terms. They are dealt with as being real issues instead of being traced back to unconscious roots and sources. The logotherapy philosophy is to help people become fully aware of their own responsibility for the essence of their existence. One of logotherapy's major functions is as a catalyst, giving us a foundation for our counseling.

People have the option to be responsible to whomever they may choose. The counselor practicing logotherapy does not impose value judgments on people. It is, therefore, up to us to decide whether we should interpret our life as responsible to society or to our own conscience. Logotherapy is neither teaching nor preaching. The role played by the counselor is like that of an eye specialist rather than that of a painter. A painter gives us a picture of the world as he sees it; an eye specialist tries to sharpen our perception of the world, widening and broadening the visual field of the client so that the whole field of meaning and values becomes conscious and visible. Logotherapy does away with the concept of self-actualization. Frankl (1962) writes that to strive for self-actualization would be a sure way to miss it. Self-actualization can never be an end in itself; it is a by-product of fulfilling life's meaning.

The philosophy of logotherapy includes the idea that people are haunted by the experience of inner emptiness, a void within themselves. People are caught in this situation, which Frankl has termed the *existential vacuum*. A statistical survey conducted in the Neurological Department at the Vienna Policlinic Hospital (Frankl, 1962) revealed that 55% of the persons questioned showed a more or less marked degree of the existential vacuum. More than half of them had experienced a loss of the feeling that life is meaningful. This existential vacuum manifests itself mainly in a state of boredom.

According to logotherapy, this emptiness can be filled and meaning restored by: (1) doing a deed, (2) experiencing a value, and (3) suffering. The first way refers to achievement and feeling a sense of accomplishment. The second way is by experiencing something of personal value, such as a work of art or music, or by experiencing someone through a love relationship. Frankl (1962) writes that love is the only way to grasp others in the innermost core of their personalities. By loving someone, one sees the person's potential, which is not yet actualized, but yet ought to be. Love helps people become aware of what they can be, thus making these potentialities come true.

The third way to find a purpose or meaning is through unavoidable suffering, such as an incurable disease or loss of a loved one. What matters above all is the attitude we take toward suffering; this attitude determines the amount of suffering we bring upon ourselves. According to Frankl, logotherapy cannot stop unavoidable suffering, but it can stop despair, which is suffering behind which the sufferer sees no meaning. Suffering itself has no meaning; but a person can assume meaningful attitudes toward events that themselves are meaningless. Suffering can have meaning if it changes the sufferer for the better.

COUNSELING METHOD

The counselor practicing logotherapy is concerned with existential, spiritual, and philosophical problems; therefore, our discussion is geared toward these problems. Frankl believed that the philosophy underlying a therapy is more important than the therapy itself. The concepts presented in logotherapy compose a total philosophy of life. Frankl (1969) emphasized the existential neurosis, which derives from the individual's inability to see meaning in life, and believed that counseling consists largely in helping the client to find an "authentic existential modality." The goal of logotherapy is to reveal the flaws in the client's world view, or system of values, and to help achieve a readjustment of that view.

Diametrically opposed to traditional Freudian analysis, Frankl believes the curative process in counseling is the fundamental being together of counselor and client. If the two are existentially attuned, the counselor is together with the client's way of existing (what Rogers has called *empathy*). The client begins to partake of the counselor's way of living and gradually, feeling understood and cared for by the counselor, gets the courage to emulate the counselor's healthy mode of existence. The client moves on to self-help by daring to be his or her own true self. In developing the relationship with the client, the counselor exerts considerable verbal persuasion and evangelizing in helping the client to find meaning in life. Frankl liked Hegel's thought that life is not something, but the opportunity for something. The meaning of life is not to be stated once and for all; rather, it changes with each situation, from moment to moment, day to day. The important thing to Frankl is that value and meaning be found in every situation. He agrees with Glasser that our answer to the meaning of life must consist of right action and right conduct, not talk and meditation. In summary, for Frankl, helping people to find meaning in life is helping them to learn how to solve life's problems and how to fulfill life's tasks. Agreeing with Freud, Glasser, Maslow, and Rogers, Frankl believes that love is the highest goal of humankind. It is logotherapy in full action. He views encounter as being necessary in all true personality change. In fact, he believes that love and religion are the two influences that can alter life patterns in any significant way.

Perhaps the most eclectic of any approach to counseling currently available, logotherapy has no steps, design, or rigid methodology. The counseling style will be geared to the individual client and the counselor. Arnold and Gasson (1954) point out that neither logotherapy nor psychotherapy is specific, or causal, therapy. Psychotherapy may be used successfully with people suffering from problems other than those having psychogenic causes, and logotherapy may be successful for problems other than those originating from a weak philosophy of life. A successful counselor following the logotherapy philosophy in counseling children will be required to be creative and inventive and be able to individualize counseling to fit the child.

Two such creative techniques were derived by Frankl to counsel people suffering from anxiety and obsessive-compulsive neuroses. Anxiety neuroses and phobic conditions create anticipatory anxiety, which produces the exact situation the client fears. This activity creates a vicious circle that the client will withdraw from or avoid. In cases involving anticipatory anxiety, paradoxical intention is used. In this approach the phobic person is invited to imagine, if only for a moment, precisely that which is feared. An example would be cases of sleeplessness. The fear of sleeplessness results in a hyperintention to fall asleep, which in turn causes the patient to stay awake. To overcome this, a logotherapist would advise the patient not to try to sleep, but rather to try to do just the opposite—that is, stay awake as long as possible. Once the anticipatory anxiety of not sleeping is replaced by the paradoxical intention not to fall asleep, sleep will follow.

A case report may serve to develop and clarify the method of paradoxical intention. Frankl (1962) once received a letter from a young medical student who had in the past listened to his clinical lectures on logotherapy. She reminded him of a demonstration of paradoxical intention that she had reported: She was having a problem of trembling while dissecting in the anatomy laboratory at the medical school she was attending. Her trembling would begin when the anatomy instructor entered the room. She told herself the following: "Oh here is the instructor! Now I'll show him how to tremble!" Whenever she deliberately tried to tremble, she was unable to do so.

In using paradoxical intention with children, the child is encouraged to do or wish to happen the very thing that is feared. The pathogenic fear is replaced by a paradoxical wish. Frankl (1978) describes how paradoxical intention was used with a junior high school girl, Vicki, who was failing her speech class. Although she was making "A's" in all of her other courses, she was too nervous to make a speech in front of her class. Each time Vicki stood up to make a speech, she became too afraid to talk or even stand up. Behavior modification and role-playing procedures were tried unsuccessfully. Finally, paradoxical intention was tried. The girl was instructed to show the whole class how fearful she was when she was going to give her speech. Vicki was told to cry, sob, shake, and perspire as much as possible. Frankl even demonstrated this new behavior to her. During her next speech, she attempted to follow Frankl's advice and could not. She received a grade of "A" for the speech.

Frankl (1975b) presents an example of how paradoxical strategies can be used in the classroom. An 11-year-old girl (Libby) was constantly staring at certain other children in the classroom. This created a lot of hostility in the other children, which was directed toward Libby. The teacher attempted various interventions to stop Libby's staring, including behavior modification, isolation, and counseling. The staring became worse. Frankl recommended that Libby be given an assignment to stare at various children for a period of 15 minutes for each child. She was also told that she would be excused from classwork for the entire day. The teacher said that, if Libby forgot her staring assignment, she would remind her to stare. The teacher said, "Doesn't that sound like fun?" Libby was not so sure and replied that it sounded like a goofy idea. The teacher explained that sometimes we can break a habit by forcing ourselves to do something we do not want to do. To make a long report short, Libby was unsuccessful in meeting her staring assignment for the next eight school days. The teacher began each school day by asking Libby if she wanted to try staring today. Libby's answer was always "no!" She never fell back in her old pattern of staring. Libby even developed a sense of pride about her achievement and increased her circle of friends.

De-reflection is another technique, which consists of ignoring the trouble. The degree to which this is achieved depends on the person's reorientation toward a more positive or worthwhile mission in life. The person must be de-reflected from anticipatory anxiety to do something else. Through this process, clients learn to ignore their neurosis by focusing their attention away from themselves. They are reoriented toward activities designed to help them realize their potential. For example, the counselor could ask children suffering test anxiety to try to fail the next several tests they take. If children have the capacity to pass, they will probably do much better because the anxiety or pressure is removed. The following accounts support this theory (Frankl, 1967).

Miss B compulsively observed the act of swallowing; she anxiously expected that the food would go down the wrong way and she would choke. Anticipatory anxiety and compulsive self-observation disturbed her eating to the extent that she became very thin. She was taught to trust her body and its automatically regulated functioning. The patient was therapeutically de-reflected by the following formula:

> I don't need to watch my swallowing, because I don't really need to swallow, for actually I don't swallow, but rather it does.

She was able to leave swallowing to the "it," the unconscious and unintentional act of swallowing.

Gerhardt B., 19 years old, suffered since he was 6 a disturbance that began during a storm in which a bolt of lightning struck near him. For eight days he could not speak at all. He was given psychoanalytic treatment for five months and took speech and breathing exercises for four additional months. Frankl attempted to make it clear to him that he would have to give up any ambition of becoming a good orator. Frankl further explained that, to the degree to which he became resigned to being a poor speaker, he would improve his speech. He began to pay less attention to the "how" and more to the "what" of his speech.

To sum up, Frankl (1962) would say that anticipatory anxiety must be counteracted by paradoxical intention; hyperintention as well as hyperreflection must be counteracted by de-reflection.

The question might be raised as to how Frankl would counsel children. From his written philosophy and case studies with older youth, one may conclude that Frankl's technique would be similar to Glasser's, with some of Ellis's method of using propaganda and counterpropaganda to appeal to the child's level of reasoning. Frankl and Ellis both believe that we get ourselves into trouble with faulty logic. Frankl would definitely support contracts and plans to build commitments to become involved in living, to begin accomplishing tasks, and to expand one's value system and view of life. Frankl would attack debilitating self-messages much as Ellis would with rational emotive therapy.

Logotherapy can be adapted to assist children in examining the meaning and purpose in their daily living through methods such as the following. We ask children to fill in the four squares presented in Figure 11-1 with information related to:

1. their high points from last week
2. how their week could have been better
3. things they need to do or plan for next week
4. high points they are looking forward to next week

The high points activity focuses on how to increase enjoyment and purpose in daily life. The connection between planning and high points is made; that is, life works better when we plan our work and play, and sometimes we might find that work tasks are actually fun to do. The counselor can take dictation for children who cannot write or understand all of the activity; some counselors may want to use pictures in the four squares. High points is also a good activity for group counseling, where sharing of high points works as a brainstorming mechanism in helping children to think of more ways to enjoy living and better ways to accomplish their work activities.

High Points Activity

My high points from last week	How my week could have been better
Things to do and plan for next week	High points for next week

FIGURE 11-1   High Points Activity

CASE STUDY

The following case is taken from Frankl's *The Will to Meaning: Foundations and Applications of Logotherapy* (1969, pp. 129–130). The following counseling dialog was taken from an interview Frankl conducted with a Jewish youth who had to be institutionalized in Israel for two and a-half years because of severe schizophrenic symptomatology.

Frankl: When did your doubts develop?

Client: I started doubting during my stay at the hospital in Israel ... I blamed God for having made me different from normal people.

Frankl: Is it not conceivable, however, that even this was purposeful, in one sense or another? What about Jonah, the prophet who was swallowed by the whale. Wasn't he also "confined"? And why was he?

Client: Because God had arranged it, of course.

Frankl: ... Anyway, you didn't have to stay in a whale but rather in an institution. Is it inconceivable that through the two and one-half years of confinement God wanted to confront you, too, with a task? Perhaps your confinement was your assignment for a specific period of your life. And didn't you eventually face it in the proper way?

Client (now becoming more emotionally involved, for the first time): You see, Doctor, that is why I still believe in God.

Frankl: Say more.

Client: Possibly God wanted all of that; possibly He wanted me to recover ...

Frankl: Not just recover ... What is demanded of you is more than recovery ...

SUMMARY: RESEARCH AND REACTIONS

Research related to logotherapy is largely limited to individual studies related to specific cases. The question of whether logotherapy includes what might be called a therapeutic technique has often been raised. To this charge, Frankl would point to the technique of paradoxical intention. In fact, Frankl reports several successful cases where he utilized paradoxical intention. Essentially he tells fainters to faint, sweaters to sweat ten quarts, blushers to blush, and neurotics to go crazy.

Paradoxical intention is carried out in as humorous a setting as possible. This enables people to put themselves at a distance from the symptoms, to detach themselves from their neurosis. Gordon Allport (1956) has stated that neurotics who learn to laugh at themselves may be on the way to self-management, perhaps to cure. Paradoxical intention may also be used therapeutically in cases that have an underlying somatic basis.

As mentioned previously, logotherapy includes the therapeutic device of de-reflection. Just as paradoxical intention is intended to counteract anticipatory anxiety, de-reflection is intended to counteract the compulsive inclination to self-observation. Through de-reflection, patients learn to ignore their symptoms. In a paper entitled "Frankl's Logotherapy," Kaczanowski (1960) said that de-reflection is less specific and more difficult than paradoxical intention, yet it is a more logotherapeutic procedure. Allport (1956) believes that de-reflection can only be attained to the degree to which the patient's awareness is directed toward positive aspects. The patient must be de-reflected from the disturbance to the task at hand and must be reoriented toward a specific vocation and mission in life. Allport believes that the focus of striving shifts from the conflict to selfless goals. Thus life as a whole becomes sounder even though the neurosis may never completely disappear.

It would be unfair to judge logotherapy solely on the basis of the techniques of paradoxical intention and de-reflection as these techniques are applicable to rather specific symptoms of neurotic conditions. Existential frustration and loss or lack of meaning in life represent concerns requiring more in-depth exploration than that afforded by paradoxical intention and de-reflection. However, logotherapy as a process is most helpful with philosophical or spiritual problems. Logotherapy has much in common with eclectic methods of counseling. According to the logotherapist, no preaching or teaching is involved, yet logotherapy appears to be a discussion with a didactic structure. Terms such as *reasoning, convincing, instructing, training*, and *leading* occur in the therapy sessions. Suggestion, persuasion, and reasoning appear to be part of the process.

The biggest problem facing logotherapy may be its oversimplification of the nature of the human personality and the fact that most people have not developed the capacity to experience a spiritual depth upon which they can truly depend.

What, then, is the value of logotherapy? Its major value is the discussion and acceptance of philosophical problems involved in making life meaningful. People are asking questions such as, Who am I? Where am I going? Why? Frankl acknowledges that these are real problems and asks us to evaluate them. Most therapies do not deal with the spiritual dimension of people. Because logotherapy does, its concepts are rather vague, with neither the theory nor the technique systematically developed. Logotherapy may serve as an indication of the growing concern with aspects of life that are not considered in most other approaches to counseling. Contemporary civilization may have changed the nature of our problems. If this is the case, counseling should reflect this changing climate.

Frankl (1975a) cites evidence to show that people of all ages do seek to establish meaning and purpose in their lives. He refers to a survey of 171,509 students published by the American Council on Education, in which 68.1% of the students selected developing a meaningful philosophy of life as their highest goal. A second survey, conducted by Johns Hopkins University staff, found that only 16% of 7948 students from 48 colleges selected making a lot of money as their top priority in life; 78% of the group checked "finding a purpose and meaning to my life" as their first goal. The findings with students are consistent with those cited by Frankl for 1533 workers who ranked "good pay" as a distant fifth in their list of job factors.

Frankl (1975a) also cites evidence to show that several young people suffer from the existential vacuum feeling. One report indicated that among 500 Viennese youngsters, the percentage of children suffering from the existential vacuum feeling rose from 30% to 80% in a two-year period. Frankl (1973) observes that the increase in suicide and drug abuse among the young is also an indication of the spreading human condition he calls the existential vacuum. This feeling was reported by 25% of a group of European university students and by 60% of a comparable group of American students (Frankl, 1975a).

Frankl does not believe logotherapy to be a panacea. He does believe that the philosophy of logotherapy is open to cooperation with other approaches to counseling as well as the counselor's personal style.

REFERENCES

Allport, G. *The individual and his religion.* New York: Macmillan, 1956.

Arnold, M., and Gasson, J. *The human person.* New York: Ronald Press, 1954.

Frankl, V. *Man's search for meaning: An introduction to logotherapy.* New York: Washington Square Press, 1962.

Frankl, V. *Psychotherapy and existentialism: Selected papers on logotherapy.* New York: Washington Square Press, 1967.

Frankl, V. *The will to meaning: Foundations and applications of logotherapy.* New York: New American Library, 1969.

Frankl, V. *The doctor and the soul: From psychotherapy to logotherapy* (2nd ed.). New York: Vintage, 1973.

Frankl, V. *The unconscious god.* New York: Simon & Schuster, 1975. (a)

Frankl, V. E. Paradoxical intention and de-reflection. *Psychotherapy: Theory, Research, and Practice,* 1975, *12,* 226–237. (b)

Frankl, V. E. *The unheard cry for meaning and psychotherapy and humanism.* New York: Simon & Schuster, 1978.

Kaczanowski, G. Frankl's logotherapy. *American Journal of Psychiatry,* 1960, *117,* 563.

chapter 12

TRANSACTIONAL ANALYSIS

ERIC BERNE

Eric Lennard Bernstein was born May 10, 1910, at his family home in Montreal, Canada. His family consisted of his father, who was a general practitioner, his mother, who was a professional writer and editor, and a sister five years younger than he. Eric respected his father a great deal, and up to the time of his father's death, he was permitted to make rounds with him, house to house. He was 10 years old when his father died from tuberculosis, at which time his mother assumed responsibility for supporting the two children.

After receiving his medical degree from McGill University at the age of 25, Berne moved to the United States and began a psychiatric residency at Yale University. He became a citizen around 1938 and shortly thereafter changed his name to Eric Berne. Following a tour of service with the armed forces from 1943 to 1946, he began working to earn the title of psychoanalyst. His first book, *Mind in Action*, was published in 1946. In 1947, Berne began analysis with Erik Erikson.

Berne encountered several frustrations during his adulthood. Each of his three marriages ended in divorce. However, he did gain seven children from his first two marriages; he found the role of parent to be very reinforcing and loved his children very much. It is said that he was overly permissive and more of a nurturing parent than an authoritarian, critical parent. One of the major rejections of his life occurred when, in 1956, his application for membership in the Psychoanalytic Institute was denied. It was recommended that he continue through four more years of personal analysis and then reapply later for the coveted title.

This action greatly discouraged Berne but at the same time motivated him, and he immediately began work on a new approach to psychotherapy.

Although Berne (1949) first published information on the three ego states in his article "The Nature of Intuition," the core of transactional analysis was formed in 1954. At that time, he was involved in the psychoanalysis of a successful middle-aged lawyer he was treating by classic Freudian principles. During a session, the patient suddenly said, "I'm not a lawyer, I'm just a little boy." After listening to his patients relating "games" for some 30 years, Berne decided to gather certain of these breezily named games into a catalogue. Three years after its publication, *Games People Play* (1964) had been on the nonfiction best-seller list for 111 weeks—longer than any other book that decade. Some reviewers called the book psychiatric gimmickry, emphatically denying that it would ever be regarded as a contribution to psychological or psychiatric theory. Other reviewers found the book a real contribution to psychology, suggesting that Berne had offered a thesaurus of social transactions with explanations and titles. In 1967, Berne attributed the book's success to the recognition factor—some of us recognize ourselves in it, and some recognize other people.

Poker was Berne's favorite game because people play it to win. He had little patience with losers and was noted as saying that you might as well play to win if you are going to play. He saw losers as spending a lot of time explaining why they lost. Berne saw his mission as turning frogs back into princesses and princes—just as they were born. He viewed parents, other adults, and the environment as being responsible for turning children into frogs. He was not satisfied in just making frogs from frogs. In the final years of his life, Berne shifted his emphasis from games to life scripts.

Berne published 8 books and 64 articles in psychiatric and other periodicals and was editor of *Transactional Analysis Bulletin*. In an article in the *New York Times* magazine in 1966, Berne renounced the therapeutic value of shock treatment, hypnosis, and medication in favor of his easy-to-understand approach to psychotherapy. Today TA is an international organization with over 10,000 members. Eric Berne died in 1970.

THE NATURE OF PEOPLE AND THEORY OF COUNSELING

The nature of people and the theory of counseling sections are covered together for transactional analysis because the TA theory of counseling is basically a statement describing the human personality.

Berne had a positive view of the nature of people. He believed that children were born as princes and princesses, and shortly thereafter their parents and the environment turned them into frogs. He believed that people had the potential to regain their royal status providing they learned and applied the lessons of transactional analysis to their personal lives. Berne believed that the early childhood years were critical to personal development. During these early years, before children enter school, they form their basic life script, and they develop a sense of being either OK or not OK. They also arrive at conclusions about the "OK-ness" of other people. In Berne's view, life is very simple to live. However, people upset themselves to the point where they invent religions, pastimes, and games. These same people complain about how complicated life is while persisting in making life even harder. Life is a series of decisions to be made and problems to be solved. Berne believes people have the rationality and freedom to make decisions and solve their problems.

The TA theory of human nature and human relationships derives from data collected via four types of analyses:

1. Structural analysis, in which an individual's personality is analyzed
2. Transactional analysis, which is concerned with what people do and say to each other
3. Script analysis, which deals with the specific life dramas people compulsively employ
4. Game analysis, in which ulterior transactions leading to a payoff are analyzed

Structural analysis

In explaining the TA view of human nature and the difficulties people encounter in their lives, we begin with the structural analysis of personality. The personality for each individual is divided into three separate and distinct ego states. These ego states, which are the sources of behavior, are called Parent, Adult, and Child, or P, A, and C for short. The ego states represent real persons who now exist or once existed and had their own identities. Therefore, the conflicts among them often cause inconsistencies as well as flexibility in people.

The Parent–Adult–Child ego states proposed by Berne are not concepts like the id, ego, and superego of Freud, but rather phenomena based on actual realities. They each represent skeletal-muscular and verbal patterns of behavior and feeling based on emotions and experiences perceived by people in their early years. The three ego states are defined as follows:

Parent.   This aspect of personality contains instructions, attitudes, and behavior handed down mostly by parents and significant authority figures. It resembles a recording of all the admonitions, orders, punishments, encouragement, and so on experienced in the first years of life. Parents can take two different attitudes, depending on the situation:

Nurturing Parent, which manifests itself in nurturing or helping
   behavior
Critical Parent, which provides criticism, control, and punishment

The Parent feels and behaves as the one who raised you did—both
critical and nurturing. The Parent admonishes "you should" or "you
should not," "you can't win," "boys will be boys," "a woman's place is
in the home." The Parent, wanting to be in control and to be right, acts
with superiority and authority. But the Parent is also responsible for
giving love, nurturing, and respect to the Child in you.

Adult.   This ego state operates logically and nonemotionally, and
mainly provides objective information using reality testing and a com-
puterlike approach. Your Adult uses facts as a computer does to make
decisions without emotion. The Adult says "This is how this works"
with mature, objective, logical, and rational thinking based on reality.
The Adult ego state is not related to age. A child is also capable of
dealing with reality by gathering facts and computing objectively.

Child.   Here we find all the childlike impulses common to everyone.
It is a very important part of personality because it contributes such
things as joy, creativity, spontaneity, intuition, pleasure, and enjoyment.
The Child has two parts:

Adaptive Child, which emerges as a result of demands from significant authority figures. It is marked by passivity.
Natural, or Free, Child, which represents the impulsive, untrained,
   self-loving, pleasure-seeking part of the Child

The Child part of us is an accumulation of impulses that come
naturally to a young person and of recorded internal events or responses
to what is seen and heard. There is an element of immaturity but also
a source of deep feeling, affection, adaptation, expression, and fun. Figure 12-1 presents the ego states and their divisions in graphic form.
   The well-adjusted person allows the situation to determine which
ego state is in control, striking an even balance among the three. A
common problem is seen in the person who allows one ego state the
predominant control. For example, the Constant Parent is seen as dictatorial or prejudiced; the Constant Adult is an analytical bore; the
Constant Child is immature or overreactive. No age is implied by any
of these states, as even the young child has Adult and Parent states, and
senior citizens can emit a Child response.

Transactional analysis

The second type of analysis is the heart of TA—the study of the
transaction. Any time a person acknowledges the presence of another
person either verbally or physically, a transaction has taken place.

Nurturing Parent		Critical Parent
Verbal		*Verbal*
"Let me help you"		"You should"
Nonverbal		*Nonverbal*
Extends hand		Pointing finger

		Adult
		Verbal
		"The facts are"
		Nonverbal
		Attentive posture

Free Child		Adaptive Child
Verbal		*Verbal*
"I want"		"I did my job"
Nonverbal		*Nonverbal*
Excited expression		Expectant expressions

FIGURE 12-1

Transactions are often defined as a unit of human communication or as a stimulus/response connection between ego states of two people.

Transactions are grouped into three categories.

1. Complementary transactions, which Berne describes as "the natural order of healthy human relationships," occur when a response comes from the ego state to which it was addressed (see Figure 12-2). Example:

Sue: "Billy, have you seen my bike?"
Billy: "Yes, it is in the backyard."

2. Crossed transactions break communications. They occur when a response comes from one of the other two ego states (Figure 12-3). Example:

Sue: "Billy, would you help me find my bike?"
Billy: "Can't you see I'm watching my favorite program???"

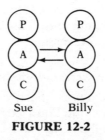

FIGURE 12-2

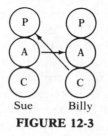

FIGURE 12-3

3. Covert, or ulterior, transactions involve more than one ego state of each person and are basically dishonest. On the surface, the transaction looks and sounds like number 1 or 2 above, but the actual message sent is not spoken (Figure 12-4). For example, the ulterior messages being sent in number 1 could be on a social or overt level.

Sue: "Billy, why don't you help me find my bike so we could go riding?"
Billy: "OK, it's a good day for a ride!"

Or the ulterior messages could be on a psychological, covert, or ulterior level.

Sue: "I wish you would be my boy friend."
Billy: "I hope you like me better than the other boys."

Script analysis

The nature of people can be further described by script analysis. A psychological script is a person's ongoing program for a life drama; it dictates where people are going with their lives and the paths that will lead there. The individual—consciously or unconsciously—acts compulsively according to that program. As mentioned before, people are born basically OK; their difficulties come from bad scripts they learned during their childhood.

The theory of scripts was developed by Berne (1961) as part of TA theory from its inception. A life script is that life plan your Child selected in your early years, based mostly on messages received from the Child in your parents. For example, at the request of her mother, a little girl takes it upon herself to save her alcoholic father. The same script may

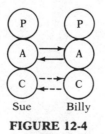

FIGURE 12-4

emerge once again later in life as she tries to save an alcoholic husband in an attempt to regain some of the pay-offs from the original experience. Although the Parent and Adult of your mother and father may have told you sensible things like "be successful," the unspoken injunction from the Child in your parents may communicate the message "You can't make it" (see Figure 12-5). Injunctions are prohibitions and negative commands usually delivered from the parent of the opposite sex. Injunctions are seldom discussed or verbalized out loud. Values we hold as guidelines for living may have come from injunctions. These injunctions determine how we think and feel about sex, work, money, marriage, family, play, and people.

The best way to learn about scripts is to follow Glasser's advice and examine how we spend our time and how we relate (transactions) with others. Scripts have main themes to them, such as: martyring, procrastinating, succeeding, failing, blaming, distracting, placating, and computing. Reviewing your life will help you to discover your theme. Basically there are three types of scripts: winner, loser, and nonwinner. A small percentage of our population seem to be naturally born as winners; everything they touch turns to gold. Conversely, a little larger percentage of our population seem to be natural losers; everything seems to turn out badly for them. The vast majority of the population, perhaps 80–85%, follow the nonwinners script. Nonwinners are identified by a phrase they often use: "but at least . . ." ("I went to school and made poor grades, *but at least* I did not flunk out").

TA borrows heavily from fairy tales for its terminology and analogies. For example, the Cinderella script is not an especially healthy plan because your prince or prize will not come if you sit around waiting for it. You have to make things happen. Even martyring yourself as Cinderella did for her stepmother and stepsisters won't help. The Santa Claus script is based on a similar myth. Again, you may have to be your own Santa. Since life scripts are formed in early childhood, considerable care needs to be given to the selection of children's stories. We have included a comprehensive list of books in this text that we believe to be helpful to children and their families (see Chapters 18 and 19).

In summary, Berne believed that scripts have five components: (1) directions from parents, (2) a corresponding personality development,

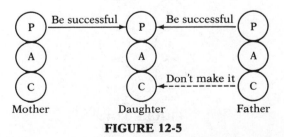

FIGURE 12-5

(3) a confirming childhood decision about oneself and life, (4) a penchant for either success or failure, and (5) a pattern for behavior.

Game analysis

Unfortunately, most of us in following our scripts learn how to use ulterior transactions. In other words, we play games. A game is an ongoing series of complementary ulterior transactions progressing to a well-defined, predictable outcome. Like every ulterior transaction, all games are basically dishonest, and they're by no means fun. One of the first games a child learns is "Mine is better than yours." The relatively benign outcome of Mine's better could range, in later years, to considerably more serious games. *Games People Play* offers a vastly entertaining and chilling overview of what the Not OK child can get into.

Life positions

On the basis of the transactions and scripts, children develop life positions that summarize their concepts of self-worth and the worth of others. The four life positions (described by Harris, 1969) are as follows:

1. I'm not OK–You're OK. This is the universal position of childhood. It represents the introjective position of those who feel powerless. In adults, withdrawal and depression are often experienced. The extreme of this position would be represented by a −5 on the x-axis and +5 on the y-axis in quadrant II of Figure 12-6.
2. I'm not OK–You're not OK. This is the arrival point of the child who cannot depend on parents for positive stroking (see page 192). Already not OK, the child perceives Mom and Dad as not OK, too. Adults in this category are losers who go through a series of helpless, disappointing experiences and may even become suicidal or homicidal. The extreme of this position would be represented by a −5 on both the x- and y-axes in quadrant III of Figure 12-6.
3. I'm OK–You're not OK. The individual feels victimized in this position. The brutalized, battered child will end up here. It is the position of the criminal, the psychopath. Whatever happens, it's someone else's fault. The extreme of this position would be represented by a +5 on the x-axis and a −5 on the y-axis in quadrant IV of Figure 12-6.
4. I'm OK–You're OK. This is the position of mentally healthy people. They possess realistic expectations, have good human relationships, and are capable of solving problems constructively. It is a "winner's" position. A winner is defined as an authentic being. The extreme of this position would be represented by a +5 on both the x- and y-axes in quadrant I of Figure 12-6.

The problem-solving stances taken by each of the four positions are depicted in Figure 12-6.

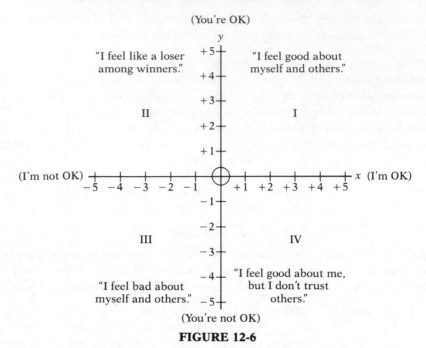

FIGURE 12-6

The pursuit of strokes

Human beings need recognition; in order to obtain it, they exchange what Berne calls *strokes*. When people acknowledge the presence of another, they give a stroke. The stroke can be either positive or negative. It is usually pretty obvious which is which, except in the case of ulterior transactions. Young children receive positive or negative physical strokes when they are cuddled or spanked, whereas adults attain primarily symbolic strokes in conversations or transactions with others. Positive strokes such as compliments, handshakes, open affection, or uninterrupted listening are the most desirable, but negative strokes such as hatred or disagreement are better than no recognition at all. A middle ground is maintenance strokes, which keep transactions going by giving recognition to the speaker but yet give neither positive nor negative feedback. All of these strokes can be either conditional or unconditional—given as a result of some specific action or given just for being yourself. Unconditional regard—"I like you"—has more positive stroke value than conditional acceptance—"I like you when you are nice to me."

The pattern of giving and receiving strokes most used by the individual is determined by the person's life position, as explained above. How people view themselves and others controls their ability to give and receive conditional and unconditional positive and negative strokes.

People engage in transactions to exchange strokes. According to Berne (1964), there is an inherent psychological hunger for stimulation

through human interactions and stroking, and any act implying recognition of another's presence is a means of satisfying these hungers.
Failure to fulfill these needs may cause a failure to thrive in infants
(James & Jongeward, 1971) and feelings of abandonment and not OK-
ness in both children and adults. Satisfied hunger yields feelings of OK-
ness and release of creative energy (Phillips & Cordell, 1975). Thus, it
is important to become aware of our psychological hungers and to
adequately satisfy them.

Negative strokes such as lack of attention, shin kicking, and hatred
send "You're not OK" messages. Diminishing, humiliating, and ridiculing strokes all treat people as though they were insignificant.

Positive strokes are usually complementary transactions. They may
be verbal expressions of affection and appreciation or they may give
compliments or positive feedback; they may be physical, as a touch; or
they may be silent gestures or looks. Listening is one of the finest strokes
one person can give another (James & Jongeward, 1971). All yield reinforcement to the I'm OK–You're OK position. Maintenance strokes,
although lacking in meaningful content, at least serve to give recognition
and keep communication open.

Structuring time

People have six options for structuring their time in their pursuit
of strokes:

1. Withdrawing, in which no transaction takes place. It involves
   few risks, and there is no stroking.
2. Rituals, which involve prescribed social transactions such as
   "Hello" and "How are you?" These are fairly impersonal transactions.
3. Pastimes, which provide mutually acceptable stroking. Pastimes
   are a means of self-expression but often involve only superficial
   transactions or conversations such as baseball, automobiles,
   shopping, or other safe topics for conversation.
4. Activities, in which time is structured around some task or career.
   Activities are a way to deal with external reality.
5. Games, in which the need is met in a crooked way. Intense stroking is often received, but it may be unpleasant. Games are considered to be destructive transactions.
6. Intimacy, which provides unconditional stroking. It is free of
   games and exploitation.

Obviously, some of these ways of structuring time are good and some
are bad, depending on the time and energy given to each. It is one of
the goals of TA therapy to help people learn productive ways of structuring their time.

Withdrawing may be the Adult's decision to relax or be alone, the
Parent's way of coping with conflict, or the Child's adaptation to protect

itself from pain or conflict. It is fairly harmless unless it happens all the time or when someone like your boss is talking to you. Withdrawing into fantasy may allow one to experience good stroking when the present setting does not appear to hold any.

Harris (1969) writes that a ritual is a socially programmed use of time where everybody agrees to do the same thing. Brief encounters, worship rituals, greeting rituals, cocktail party rituals, and bedroom rituals may allow maintenance strokes without commitment or involvement. The outcome is predictable and pleasant when you know you are doing the "in-step" thing, but most people need more intense stroking.

James and Jongeward (1971) believe that pastimes are, as they imply, ways to pass time. They are superficial exchanges without involvement that people use in order to size one another up. Conversations concerning relative gas mileage, the weather, or potty training may yield minimal stroking at the maintenance level while allowing one to decide whether to risk a more intimate relationship.

Doing work or activities, according to Phillips and Cordell (1975), is time spent dealing with realities of the world. It is getting something done that one may want to do, needs to do, or has to do. Activities allow for positive strokes befitting a winner.

Berne (1964) defines games as an ongoing series of complementary ulterior transactions progressing to a well-defined, predictable outcome. When your message to another person is ulterior, for some hidden purpose, you are playing a game. The Adult part of you is unaware that the Child or Parent has a secret reason for playing or wanting to play. Harris (1969) believes all games derive from the Child's "mine is better than yours" attempt to ease the not OK feeling, to feel superior while the other feels put down. A game may be recognized by the pay-off. When you think you've won, but part of you knows you took unfair advantage— that's a game. Games are differentiated from rituals and pastimes in two ways: (1) their ulterior quality and (2) the pay-off. Games are a way, too, of using time for people who cannot bear the stroking starvation of withdrawal and yet whose not OK position makes the ultimate form of relatedness—intimacy—impossible (Berne, 1964; Harris, 1969).

James and Jongeward (1971) write that intimacy is a deep human encounter stemming from genuine caring. Steiner (1974) views intimacy as the way of structuring time when there is no withdrawal, no rituals, no games, no pastimes, and no work. Conditions favorable for intimacy include a commitment to the position I'm OK–You're OK and a satisfying of psychological hungers through positive strokes.

Rackets

Some people find themselves involved in what is known in TA theory as a stamp-collecting enterprise, where they save up archaic, bad feelings until they have enough to cash in for some psychological prize. The bad-feelings racket, or stamp collecting, works in much the same way that supermarket stamp collecting works. People save brown stamps for all the bad things others have caused them to suffer and gold stamps for all the favors others owe them. Gray stamps refer to lowered self-esteem, red stamps symbolize anger, blue stamps mean depression, and white stamps connote purity (James & Jongeward, 1971). When the bad-feelings stamp books are filled, they may be cashed in for such things as a free divorce, custody of children, nervous breakdown, blow-up, drunken binge, depression, tantrum, runaway, or love affair. Good-feelings stamps are used to justify playtime, relaxation, and breaks from work. According to McCormick and Campos (1969), stamp collecting is a racket that we learn from our parents. The collector uses the stamps as excuses for behavior and feelings, and the suppliers may not even be aware they are giving them out. The I'm OK–You're OK people do not need stamps because they need no excuses.

COUNSELING METHOD

Transactional analysis is the ideal system for those who view the counseling process as teaching. As noted in the previous section, TA abounds with terms, diagrams, and models. Clients are taught the vocabulary of TA so that they can become proficient in identifying ego states, transactions, and scripts. The counselor's role includes teaching and providing a nurturing, supportive environment in which clients feel free to lift or eliminate restricting injunctions, attempt new behaviors, rewrite scripts, and move toward the I'm OK–You're OK life position. Contracting between counselor and client is a large part of the TA process.

Concepts in TA have been taught to all age and ability levels from the very young to the very old and from mentally retarded children to gifted children.

TA involves teaching the principles of transactional analysis to participants and then letting them use these principles to analyze and improve their own behavior. TA points that would be most useful in counseling children are:

1. Definition and explanation of ego states
2. Analysis of transactions between ego states
3. Positive and negative stroking (or warm fuzzies and cold pricklies)
4. I'm OK, You're OK
5. Games and rackets
6. Scripts

Put simply, the primary goal in transactional analysis is to help the person achieve the I'm OK–You're OK life position. A variety of methods and techniques can be used to accomplish this aim. Because the terms and concepts of TA can be easily learned and understood by children, the approach has become popular in helping school-age children.

The I'm OK–You're OK life position is one the child chooses to take. The other three positions more or less evolve of themselves; the child feels no sense of free choice in the matter. According to Harris (1969), the first three positions are based on feelings; the fourth position—I'm OK–You're OK—is based on thought, faith, and initiation of action. The first three have to do with "why"; the fourth has to do with "why not." We do not drift into a new position. It is a decision we must make. Utilizing the graph in Figure 12-6, we can plot a person's progress in moving from one quadrant to another, providing each step on the number axis is defined in observable terms. The x-axis would refer to gains and losses in self-esteem; the y-axis would indicate the same for our relationships with others.

Ideally, the role of a transactional analyst is that of a teacher. Once children are taught how to speak the language of TA, the counselor can help them to analyze their own transactions and to see how this behavior affects others and vice versa. Children learn to identify the source of the reasoning that goes into their decisions; that is, they learn how to use their Adult in dealing with the demands of their Parent and Child.

Probably the most important concept to remember when dealing with children is that we all grow up feeling not OK. Children function on the basis of the OK-ness they see in their parents. If Mommy frequently responds to the child with *her* not OK Child, the stage is set for the establishment of the I'm not OK–You're not OK position. In the case of the severely abused child, the extreme I'm OK–You're not OK position is a real possibility. One of the best ways for youngsters to develop strong Adult ego states is to observe their parents use their Adults in handling inappropriate responses from the demanding Parent or Child.

TA principles can be effectively taught to children with a variety of tools such as posters, pictures, humorous role playing, and so on. Alvyn Freed and Margaret Freed have given examples in their books *TA for Tots* (1974a) and *TA for Kids* (1974b). The kids learn how to be "prinzes" instead of "frozzes." They also learn how to give and get warm fuzzies (positive strokes) and how to avoid giving and getting cold pricklies (negative strokes). Of course, in getting strokes, one must not play games.

As mentioned before, the goal of TA counseling is to help children learn to control their responses with their Adult, thereby achieving the I'm OK–You're OK life position. It must be remembered, however, that strengthening a child's Adult will cause his or her role in the family to shift. Hopefully, the child will no longer be as active in playing the destructive games that dominate most families. Family members' roles will of necessity shift also. For this reason, the child's parents must be included in the counseling process in order to achieve lasting results.

Children can learn all about warm fuzzies and cold pricklies, but, because of the tremendous influence of their parents, it is next to impossible without effective intervention for them to reverse the "loser" life script their parents may have given them. Everything the parents do and say to children tells them that either they are OK or not OK, depending on what life position the parents themselves occupy. People attract not what they want but what they are. People also raise not the children they want but the children who reproduce what they, the parents, are.

Positive stroking and respect are two things we all need in building a winner's script. The child needs positive strokes, both conditional (We'll have some ice cream after you put away your toys) and unconditional (I love you no matter what). Children come to see themselves as OK because their parents treat them that way.

As a positive stroke, it's hard to beat respect. The conclusion the child reaches is this: If my OK parents think I'm OK, then I really must be OK. If you want the Adult in your youngster to grow, you must respect your child.

Another useful TA principle for both teachers and parents is to teach "do" and not "don't." It is baffling to children when parents and adults attempt to teach appropriate behavior by catching children doing inappropriate behavior. Since Mommy is OK, the child thinks, "It must be all my fault." Chalk up another not OK episode for the child.

A slightly different aspect of the same idea is that, in counseling and teaching children that they must "do more" or "do better," it is also important to let the child know *what*. The Parent in all of us admonishes "do better." It is our Adult who supplies the "do *what* better."

As children and their families become better acquainted with the whys of their relationship, they learn to avoid the undesirable ways of structuring time. Again, the goal of TA is to help the individual learn to lead a full, game-free life. And everyone does have that choice. The usefulness of the P–A–C model comes in creating awareness of how the Parent, Adult, and Child function in decision making.

As mentioned earlier, several techniques for teaching TA to children have been developed. The concepts of positive and negative stroking have been taught with smiling and frowning faces as well as with fuzzy yarn balls and sharp, prickly plastic objects to connote warm fuzzies and cold pricklies. The warm fuzzy–cold prickly fairy tale (Steiner, 1975) was written for the Child in all of us. A summary of the fairy tale follows.

> There once existed a town where people shared their warm fuzzies without fear of running out of their supply of fuzzies. One day a wicked witch appeared and planted the idea that people should hoard their fuzzies in case there happened to be a shortage of fuzzies. When the townspeople did this, their backbones began to shrivel up. The witch cured the shriveling backbones by giving everybody a bag of cold pricklies to share. The sharing of cold pricklies continued until a good witch arrived and put the townspeople back on the right track, sharing their warm fuzzies.

Counselors and teachers can follow the story by bringing a bowl of sugar-free candy to class and telling the children that the only way they can have a piece of candy is if someone gives them a piece. The counselor or teacher serves as a model in the exercise, making sure each child receives a piece of candy.

Posters can be made with representations of the various ideas of TA (stroking, ego states, I'm OK–You're OK, lists of games with appropriate illustrations, lists of scripting phrases, and so on). The use of puppets, dolls, and make-believe stories can be successful with younger children who cannot yet read.

A three-step process would be effective in teaching TA to any child. First, explain the principle, with a story, a poster, puppets, and the like. Second, ask the children to "read" back what they understand of the TA principle (correcting them as you go along). Third, ask the children to give examples of the principle from their own experience ("What positive strokes have you received today?") or to identify examples of the principle you gave them ("What ego state does 'You must always go to bed early' come from?").

Teach children who are having conflicts with others new stroking patterns. They first need to analyze others' behavior. What response does mother, teacher, friend give to the child's positive or negative strokes? What strokes does the other person like? Teach the child new ways of stroking from among these categories:

1. Self-stroking—doing nice things for yourself
2. Physical strokes—hugs, kisses, pats, backrubs, and so on
3. Silent strokes—winks, nods, waves, smiles, and the like
4. Verbal strokes—"I like you," "Good job," "Thanks"
5. Rewards or privileges—letting younger siblings go with you, playing with them, doing something for parents

Young children (5–7 years) may not be able to symbolize stroking and ego states as well as older ones, so less technical language may be necessary. Young children can understand warm fuzzy if a stroke feels good, and cold prickly if they feel bad after someone says or does something to them. They may need to get permission to ask for a warm fuzzy instead of manipulating for a cold prickly when they feel bad. Likewise, small children can understand "my bossy part," "my thinking part," "my angry part," or "my happy part" rather than the ego states, which they sometimes confuse with actual people.

Ego-grams (bar graphs showing children "how much" of each ego state they use; see Figure 12-7) can indicate to them where changes might be made. If they think that they want to make a change, work on strengthening low ego states by practicing appropriate behaviors. See if children think the ego-gram is different in various situations—at home, school, playing with friends.

Once children understand ego states, they can learn to distinguish

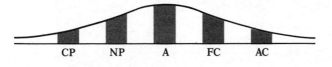

CP   NP   A   FC   AC

Key:

P   The Parent refers to a person's values, beliefs, and morals.

CP   The Critical Parent finds fault, directs, orders, sets limits, makes rules, and enforces one's value system. Too much CP results in dictatorial or bossy behavior.

NP   The Nurturing Parent is empathic and promotes growth. The NP is warm and kind, but too much NP becomes smothering, and children will not be able to learn how to take care of themselves.

A   The Adult acts like a computer. It takes in, stores, retrieves, and processes information. The A is a storehouse of facts and helps you think when you solve problems, but too much adult is boring.

C   The Child can be fun, expressive, and spontaneous, and sometimes it can be compliant and a follower of rules.

FC   The Free Child is the fun and spontaneous part of the child. When you cheer at a ball game, you are in the Free Child part of your personality. However, too much FC might mean that you have lost control of yourself.

AC   The Adapting Child is the conforming, easy to get along with part of your personality. Too much AC results in guilt feelings, depression, other bad feelings, and robot-like behavior.

FIGURE 12-7 Ego-gram

complementary, crossed, and ulterior transactions. If they bring in a situation that illustrates one of these, have them diagram it. In the case of crossed or ulterior transactions, encourage children to use their Adult to figure out ways to obtain a more successful result.

Some other methods for teaching the various TA techniques are described below.

1. Talk about the feelings and behaviors that go with each ego state. Have children identify their own ego states and the ego states of others. This can easily be done by relating the ego states to what children tell you about their experiences.

Child: My brother always tells me what to do. He's not my father.

Counselor: You feel rebellious when your brother acts like a bossy parent.

As children become aware of their ego states and can discriminate them, their Adult can gain control of which ego state is expressed and give them permission to replace destructive ideas with constructive ones.

2. The OK Corral diagram below is useful in helping children to identify how they feel and think about themselves and other people. Children are able to discuss what OK-ness and not OK-ness mean to them in terms of specific behaviors.

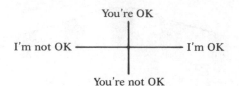

3. Games are intriguing to children. They can readily pick up on games in themselves and others, and describe them, once they have the concept. Any time children describe a pattern of games or recognize that "this always happens to me," the counselor can introduce games as a way of getting negative strokes to replace the positive strokes children think they cannot get. You can use such interventions as "You seem to mess up a lot. How do you manage that?" "What does this mean about you?" "How did it feel after it happened?" "What do you really want? How could you get it better?" "What 'bad' (scary) thing does this game prevent?"

Children can also identify the three game roles of persecutor, rescuer, and victim and learn to stay out of them. The Persecutor role can be demonstrated by having the child try to "put someone down" by pressing straight down on his or her shoulders. It is very difficult to put people down by doing this unless they lean over or bend their knees. The Rescuer role can be demonstrated by trying to pick up a limp person (of about the same size). It is also very difficult to hold up a person who does not want to stand. The Victim role is demonstrated in relation to the other two by the partner "giving in" and going down or staying limp.

4. Racket feelings can be discussed in terms of stamp collecting (see p. 194). Children can usually identify the bad feelings they save up and the prize they get. Hypothetical situations such as the following create bad feelings: "Did you ever have a rotten day? Your Mom yells at you at breakfast, your teacher catches you talking, the other guys play keep-away with your hat, and you drop your books in the mud when your dog jumps on you 'cause he's so glad to see you home. All day long you have felt mistreated and hurt, and that is the last straw. So you pick a fight with your little sister." Talk about how it feels to cash stamps in and how it feels to get dumped on. As small people, children are often the target of stamp cashing. Being aware of this can help children stop collecting stamps when it happens to them. One of the main ways of not collecting stamps is learning to talk about bad feelings with someone you can trust, and asking for and receiving the positive strokes you need.

5. Questions useful in figuring out a child's script for those counselors working with script issues include many of the same questions used in the Adlerian lifestyle interview.

What are the "hurt" points in your family?
Who is in your family?

What are the people in your family like?
Has anyone else ever lived with you?
What were they like?
Who is boss in your family?
What is your mother's (father's) favorite saying?
Describe yourself in three words.
Would other people in your family use the same words?
What bad feeling do you have a lot?
What good feeling do you have a lot?
Who is your mother's favorite?
Who is your father's favorite?

6. What *not* to do: If you are not in a position to protect a child from negative consequences, do not interfere with script behavior that still serves a purpose in the family. Do not ask children to give up their games or rackets before they learn more appropriate ways to get strokes. Do not decide for children what they "should" do. Do not encourage children to play TA counselor with people who have power over them and may not appreciate it.

All of the above exercises can be used in group and family as well as individual counseling. Role playing and acting out of games are very effective group techniques. Families in TA counseling come to recognize where their transactions become crossed, how and when scripting occurs, and how stroking behavior can change family feelings.

CASE STUDIES[1]

Transcript I

Jim, age 5, is being seen by the school counselor because he has been fighting with other children in his kindergarten class. Jim has only recently started this.

Counselor (Co): Jim, remember when I came to your class and read the story about the warm fuzzies and cold pricklies? (Jim nods.) Well, everybody, kids and grown-ups, needs to get some of these to live. Sometimes people do things to get cold pricklies like slaps or frowns, or being yelled at. Would you like to find out how to give yourself and other people nice warm fuzzies like smiles and hugs, and get them back from others?

Jim: Yes. Everybody doesn't like me now.

Co: What do you do to get hugs and smiles from your Mommy?

[1]The case study transcripts and several teaching ideas in the method section were contributed by Mary Wells Holbrook (Transcript II) and Jean Wycoff (Transcript I) as part of their work in the counseling theories and techniques class offered at the University of Tennessee.

Jim: I don't do anything, she just gives them to me. Or sometimes I hug her first or say "I love you."

Co: Sometimes mommies are busy. What do you do to get her
attention then?

Jim: Well, I get a hug from Grandma. But if I can't get one, I
make my little sister yell. Then somebody comes to see what's
happening.

Co: If you can't get a warm fuzzy, you get them to give you a
cold prickly?

Jim: Yeah.

Co: What do kids in your class have to do to get a hug?

Jim: They hug you if you fall down. But I don't fall down, so
nobody hugs me.

Co: If you can't get a hug or other warm fuzzy when you want
one, what do you do to get attention?

Jim: I make one of the other kids yell.

Co: Sometimes getting yelled at is better than nothing, huh?

Jim: Yeah.

Co: Do you think any of your teachers would give you a warm
fuzzy?

Jim: Miss Sally has a nice face.

Co: So when you feel bad inside and need a warm fuzzy, you
could get one from Miss Sally?

Jim: Yeah, like when I miss my Mommy. I could tell Miss Sally
that and ask her to hug me.

Co: That sounds like a good plan, Jim. And if you feel bad, or
sad, or lonely, or angry, and need to talk about it, you can
come here and talk to me about it.

Jim: OK.

Co: (Gives Jim a hug.) I give warm fuzzies, too.

Counselor feedback to Jim's teacher should include talking about giving
Jim some strokes when he is being good and not making a bid for
negative feedback.

Transcript II—Interview with a 10-year-old

Counselor (Co): Christopher, you've read Dr. and Ms. Freed's
book about stroking. Can you explain to me what they mean
by strokes?

Christopher (C): Stroking is when somebody does some type of
action, physical or verbal, that makes you feel either good or
not so good.

Co: I think that's a very good definition. Can you give me some
examples of a positive stroke?

C: Patting somebody, or hugging them, or saying something
nice.

Co: Like what?

C: You really did well today.

Co: Can you think of a positive stroke you've given someone today?

C: Not really.

Co: How about when I came in, and you looked up and smiled?

C: I guess. I smiled at most everybody in the class today.

Co: You have to remember that they don't have to be verbal; just a smile is a positive stroke. Can you think of any negative strokes you've given anyone today?

C: No.

Co: That's good. Of course, the same holds true for negative strokes—if, without realizing it, you looked at someone and gave them a hard frown or something, that could be a negative stroke that you didn't realize you gave.

C: I don't see why I would have given any, even by accident. There wasn't any reason to give any.

Co: Well, good. Can you think of any positive strokes anyone gave you today?

C: When I got 100 on our test today. Mrs. Kincaid said that that was very good.

Co: I'm glad. Any negative strokes?

C: No.

Co: Well, I told you your hands and face were dirty and I didn't like you coming downtown like that, right? You think you've got the idea about strokes?

C: Yes.

Co: How would you use stroking?

C: Well, whenever I thought somebody did a good job on something, I could tell them.

Co: You know, there's such a thing as giving strokes that are not asked for, strokes that you just offer freely. Can you give an example of one of those, maybe?

C: Just saying something nice when they don't even really need it . . . well, they do need it. Just saying it, but just saying it even if they haven't done anything.

Co: Be more specific.

C: Well, if you meet somebody, you can say "I like your shoes," or "Your hair looks nice," or something like that.

Co: Yes, those would be nice to hear. Can you tell me how you might use nonverbal positive strokes?

C: By patting somebody, or smiling at them, or giving them a hug.

Co: How do you think you would feel if you started giving more positive strokes and getting more positive strokes?

C: All covered over with strokes.

Among the many games identified by Berne, some are to be especially avoided in the counseling interview. These include the following:

1. Why don't you; yes but . . .

The Adult of the counselor is tricked into working for the client's Child or Parent. You as the counselor give advice:

> Counselor: "Why don't you ask your teacher to give you some extra help with math?"
> Client: "Yes, but what if she says she doesn't have time?"

The pay-off comes to the client in spreading bad feelings, as is done in the misery loves company game. For example, "I am not OK, and you aren't either because you can't help me solve my problem."

2. I'm only trying to help you.

Counselors may play this game with their clients. The message to clients is, "You are not OK, and I know what is good for you." The pay-off is for the counselor, who holds the faulty belief that "If I straighten my client out, then maybe I can get my own life in order." A truly helpful counselor offers help when it is requested, but believes that help can be accepted or rejected. When help fails or is rejected, the helpful counselor does not respond derogatorily, "Well, I was only trying to help you."

3. Courtroom

The courtroom game may put the counselor in the position of judge and jury if two clients can manipulate the counselor into placing blame. The pay-off is bad feelings for all—persecutor, victim, and rescuer— because the rescuer (counselor) usually ends up being victimized by the other two players.

4. NIGYYSOB and Kick me.

Counselors may find that some clients enjoy playing the role of kick me with the counselor just as they do with their bosses, colleagues, and spouses. They seem to enjoy being victimized. These clients work at getting themselves rejected. They even work at getting themselves terminated from counseling before any gains have been made. Kick-me players manipulate others into playing NIGYYSOB (now I've got you, you son-of-a-bitch) when they react to the bids for the negative attention the kick-me players make.

NIGYYSOB can be played by itself when a person tries to trap others in a double bind—damned if you do and damned if you don't—situation. For example:

> Mother: "Johnny, do you love me?"
> Johnny: "Yes, I do."
> Mother: "How many times have I told you not to talk with your mouth full?!"

5. Gossiping

Gossiping refers to talking about people who are not present. In a counseling interview, the counselor may wish to have clients role play dialogue between themselves and the missing persons, as was suggested in the Gestalt chapter. For example, a child complaining about a teacher could role play a conversation between the two of them, with the child playing the role of the teacher and then responding as he or she would in the classroom. The technique uses an empty chair to represent the missing person. Role-playing and role-reversal methods have a way of limiting gossip while creating greater awareness of the problem situations as well as the proper assignment of responsibility for the problem.

6. Wooden leg

The wooden leg game is the display of inadequacy pattern described in the chapter on individual psychology. Clients doing wooden leg games work to increase their disabilities as a way of avoiding the responsibility for taking care of themselves. These clients are experts in making people give up on them. Children are adept at convincing parents that they cannot handle certain chores and school subjects.

Paradoxical strategies, effective at times with these clients, focus on harnessing their rebellion into productive activity. For example, "Frank, you've got me convinced that you really can't make it." The rebellious client (Frank) will often rise to the occasion once again to show that you (the counselor) are the total idiot he has always believed you to be and begin to succeed where you predicted he could not.

For the clients who are really defeated and not rebellious, we stick to our advice of offering large doses of unconditional encouragement. Counselors of welfare and rehabilitation clients often find themselves in the wooden leg game. The pay-off goes to the client, who justifies not getting better or even getting worse as a way of increasing welfare payments.

7. If it weren't for you . . .

Related to wooden leg, the If it weren't for you game is another way of avoiding the assumption of responsibility for one's life and its unsolved problems. For example, "If it weren't for you and your good cooking, I could lose ten pounds." The counselor may want to examine with the client the pay-offs of being overweight and even develop a rationale of how being fat may be the preferred and "best" lifestyle for the client.

SUMMARY: RESEARCH AND REACTIONS[2]

Summarized below is some of the research on transactional analysis published during the 1970s.

Erskine and Maisenbacher (1975) found that a one-semester TA course for "worst-problem" high school students resulted in an increase in overall grade average, fewer discipline referrals, and a marked decrease in truancy for each student.

[2]Connie O'Connell and Linda VanBeke summarized the 1970s research studies as part of their course work in the counseling theories and techniques course at the University of Tennessee.

Bloomfield and Goodman (1976) studied the effects of a "feelings" course designed to improve communications skills in emotionally disturbed preadolescent children. Informal chartings by teachers showed decreased incidence of maladaptive behaviors following the course. The greatest decrease was in verbally aggressive behaviors.

Amundson and Sawatsky (1976) studied elementary school teachers (grades three to six) who agreed to present basic transactional analysis with children's material in their classrooms. Several teachers indicated that the program had a significant effect on their lives, especially with regard to their relationship with the students. The program was very effective with poorly behaved children in the classes.

Windell and Woollams (1974) studied people who had been involved in TA training and therapy since 1971. Results of a questionnaire that dealt with perceived changes in relationships with spouse and other individuals showed that the participants perceived their relationships with other people, especially their spouses, to change markedly. Eighty-four percent believed that their marriages had improved.

Adams (1974) evaluated a TA program administered to adult male prison inmates in 1971. Ninety-five percent of the participants felt that they had gained control of the destructive aspects of their behavior and had attained a more positive feeling toward themselves and others. During the six months of therapy, the punishment incident rate for each person in the group dropped by about 50%.

Thweatt (1974) found that 78% of the students in a psychology course integrated with TA reported an increase in self-awareness, and over 50% reported improvement in personal or family relations (specific changes).

Jesness (1975) studied 983 adolescent delinquents assigned to two institutions. The program of one institution was based on TA and that of the other was based on the principles of behavior modification. Improvement on psychological measures favored the participants in the TA program; behavior ratings slightly favored the behavioral program. Follow-up showed both groups were doing significantly better than the comparison group of the same age assigned to other institutions.

Spencer (1977) studied employees who had received an introductory TA course. Overall morale, interpersonal relationships, and productivity all improved.

REFERENCES

Adams, L. Uses of TA with adult male prison inmates. *Transactional Analysis Journal*, 1974, *3*, 18–20.

Amundson, N., and Sawatsky, D. An educational program and TA. *Transactional Analysis Journal*, 1976, *6*, 217–220.

Berne, E. The nature of intuition. *Psychiatric Quarterly*, 1949, *23*, 203–226.

Berne, E. *Transactional analysis in psychotherapy.* New York: Grove Press, 1961.

Berne, E. *Games people play.* New York: Grove Press, 1964.

Bloomfield, B., and Goodman, G. A TA approach to children's feelings. *Transactional Analysis Journal*, 1976, *6*, 323–325.

Erskine, R., and Maisenbacher, J. The effects of a TA class on socially malad-
   justed high school students. *Transactional Analysis Journal*, 1975, *5*, 252–254.

Freed, A., and Freed, M. *TA for tots*. Sacramento, Calif.: Freed, 1974. (a)

Freed, A., and Freed, M. *TA for kids*. Sacramento, Calif.: Freed, 1974. (b)

Harris, T. *I'm OK, You're OK*. New York: Harper & Row, 1969.

James, M., and Jongeward, D. *Born to win*. Reading, Mass.: Addison-Wesley,
   1971.

Jesness, C. Comparative effectiveness of behavior modification and transactional
   programs for delinquents. *Journal of Consulting and Clinical Psychology*,
   1975, *43*, 759–779.

McCormick, P., and Campos, L. *Introduce yourself to transactional analysis*.
   Stockton, Calif.: San Joaquin Transactional Analysis Study Group, 1969.

Phillips, P., and Cordell, F. *Am I OK?* Niles, Ill.: Argus Communications, 1975.

Spencer, G. Effectiveness of an introductory course in TA. *Transactional Analysis
   Journal*, 1977, *7*, 346–349.

Steiner, C. *Scripts people live*. New York: Grove Press, 1974.

Steiner, C. *Readings in radical psychiatry*. New York: Grove Press, 1975.

Thweatt, W. Integrating transactional analysis with a university psychology
   course. *Transactional Analysis Journal*, 1974, *3*, 23–25.

Windell, J., and Woollams, S. The effects of training on marriage. *Transactional
   Analysis Journal*, 1974, *4*, 209–213.

METHODS FOR COUNSELING WITH CHILDREN

CHAPTER

13

WHAT DO I DO?
ANSWERS TO PRACTICAL
QUESTIONS

WHAT SHOULD BE DONE BEFORE THE INTERVIEW?

Before the client first enters your counseling environment, look around. The counseling environment should contribute to a client's feelings of comfort and ease. A very cluttered, highly stimulating, overly "busy" room may be especially distracting to children. Their attention is easily drawn to interesting objects in the room and away from the counseling interaction. Children who tend to be restless and highly distractible may be affected by brightly colored objects, mobiles, ticking clocks, outside noise, or even the darting fish in an aquarium. Inasmuch as counselors are part of the environment, they should check themselves for distracting jewelry such as necklaces or bracelets, highly colorful ties, or patterns in clothing that may affect children.

The furniture in the counseling room should be comfortable for both adults and children. We suggested earlier that counselors not sit behind a desk or table during an interview because furniture can act as a barrier between child and counselor. Children also tend to see people sitting behind desks as authority figures—teachers, principals, and so on.

Check your appointment book in order to be prompt for scheduled sessions. Children (and adult clients) dislike to be kept waiting for long periods of time. The counselor's tardiness may be interpreted as a lack of interest, or the delay may cause restlessness, fatigue, or irritability on the part of the child.

211

Just before time for your counseling interview, check yourself as a counselor. Are you free from distracting worries and thoughts and ready to devote your attention to the child? Children are extremely sensitive to adult moods and can recognize insincerity or lack of concern quickly. Many counselors call their clients and reschedule appointments when they do not feel well rather than chance hurting the counseling relationship. Counselors having colds, headaches, or other minor ailments might want to admit to the child that they are not feeling up to par rather than have the child misinterpret their behavior as a lack of interest. Finally, alert those around you that you should not be disturbed, and you are ready to greet your child client.

WHAT DOES THE COUNSELOR NEED TO KNOW ABOUT COUNSELING RECORDS?

Most counselors keep some type of record of interviews with their clients. Notes that summarize the content of sessions and observations made by the counselor can assist in recalling previous information. Before deciding on which method of note taking is appropriate, it is wise for counselors to become knowledgeable about their state laws regarding privileged communication and also the regulations contained in the Buckley Amendment (the federal Family Rights and Privacy Act of 1974). This amendment gives parents and young people of legal age the right to inspect records, letters, and recommendations about themselves. Personal notes do not fall under these regulations; however, counselors in institutional settings will want to become aware of the full requirements of the law for their protection. See Chapter 20 for further discussion of privacy.

It is also common practice to video or audio tape counseling sessions. This procedure not only provides a record of the interview but also aids counselors in gaining self-understanding and self-awareness. Counselors can listen to their tapes with another counselor and continue to grow and learn by evaluating their own work. In addition, it may aid in promoting growth to listen to and discuss some sessions with the client.

Permission to record should be obtained from the child and parents before the procedure is begun. If the material is to be used for instruction or if any individual(s) other than the counselor will hear the client, written permission should be obtained. Again, it would be advisable to read state laws pertaining to privileged communication and the Buckley Amendment before deciding on use and a storage system for this data.

When introducing a recording system to children, it is usually best to show them the recorder, perhaps allow them to listen to themselves for a minute, and then place the equipment in an out-of-the-way place. Occasionally, children are unable to talk when they are being recorded; most, however, quickly forget the equipment. Should a child resist being recorded, the counselor might wish to pursue the reasons for this resistance. If circumstances indicate that recording is inhibiting the counseling progress, the counselor may choose to remove the equipment. At the other extreme, some children become so excited and curious about the taping equipment that counseling becomes impossible. Again, the counselor may think it is best to remove the equipment, or a contract may be made with the child such as, "After 30 minutes of the counseling work, Mickey may listen to the tape for 5 minutes." It is usually best to give as little attention to the recorder as possible after a brief initial explanation of its purpose and uses.

WHAT ARE SOME THINGS TO CONSIDER DURING THE INITIAL CONTACT?

Seeing a new client can be rather unnerving for many counselors. Beginning counselors, facing child clients for the first time in a counseling situation, often have visions of ruining the children's lives during the first session—saying something horribly wrong and doing irreparable psychological damage to the children—or they have a horror of the children sitting silently and staring into space. Children are no longer like any other child the counselor has ever known; the children are *clients!* Nevertheless, these children are still people, with their own feelings, behaviors, problems, and expectations of counselors. They may come to counseling with fears of the unknown, just as the adult counselor may fear the new relationship. There are several methods counselors can use to allay these fears and to clarify what goes on in counseling for the child.

Children often have the idea that going for counseling means you are "sick in the head," "mentally ill," or "weird" in some way. They may have heard the counselor referred to as a shrink or head doctor. Many have erroneous ideas about counseling and the role of a counselor.

Some counselors prefer to ease the anxiety of the initial meeting by just talking in general conversation with the child for a few minutes. They may introduce themselves and then start to talk with the child about home, school, friends, hobbies, or other interests. For nonverbal clients or extremely anxious children, the first session or two may include only techniques of play therapy. The counselor can begin to build a good relationship with the child and can learn something about the child's world through these methods (see Play Therapy, Chapter 14). Other counselors prefer to go directly to the problem: "Would you like to tell me about why you have come to see me?"

During the initial interview, a counselor may want to explain the process of counseling to the child and the counselor's expectations for him- or herself and for the child. Following is a sample dialogue:

Counselor (Co): Do you know what counseling is?
Child: No. (If "yes," the counselor might say, "Tell me your ideas about what counseling is.")
Co: Well, at some time during our lives, most of us have things that worry or upset us—things that we would like to talk to

someone about. It could be something about school that concerns us, like another student in our class or our teacher; it
could be a problem at home with our brothers or sisters, or
perhaps we feel that our parents don't really understand how
we feel; it could be that we are having trouble with friendships; it could be that we have some thoughts or feelings that
it would be helpful to discuss with someone. A counselor listens and tries to help the other person work out things that
bother him, and to think with that person about ways to solve
these worries. Your job is to tell me whatever is bothering
you. My job is to listen carefully and try to help you find ways
to solve these problems.

For children who have been referred for counseling by others, the
counselor may want to begin with a statement such as, "Mrs. Jones told
me that you were very unhappy since you moved here and that you
might want to talk to me about it"; or "Mr. Clifford told me that you
would be coming by" (and wait for the client to respond and tell what
the trouble is).

In the first example, the counselor has informed the client that he
or she is aware of what the problem is and is ready to discuss it. In the
second example, the counselor is less directive and provides less structure, allowing the client to explain the problem, which may or may not
be the one for which the child was referred. The counselor will want to
consider the age and the cognitive, social, and emotional development
of the child, and the type of presenting problem before deciding which
opening statement to use. The younger the child developmentally and
chronologically and the more specific the problem, the greater is the
probability the child will respond more readily to a structured approach.
The above is only a sample of what might be said. It can be modified
to fit the situation, the age and maturity level of the child, and the
counselor's personality.

The counselor may or may not feel that it is necessary to structure
the initial counseling session by defining the role of the counselor and
the expectations of the child. Many children and counselors feel more
comfortable in a structured environment.

HOW MUCH SELF-DISCLOSURE
IS APPROPRIATE FOR THE COUNSELOR?

Children are very often interested in their counselors as people. They
may question counselors about their age, where they went to school,
where they live, and whether they have children. Counselors are faced
with the perplexing problem of how much personal information to share
with the child. If counselors refuse to answer any personal questions,
they run the risk of hurting the counseling relationship or being viewed
by the child as a mysterious figure, bringing forth more questions. How-

ever, if counselors answer all personal questions, the interview time may be spent centered around the counselor rather than the client. With seriously disturbed or acting-out clients, revealing your address or where your children go to school could be bothersome or even dangerous. A general guideline might be to share some bits of personal information (favorite sport or TV show, number of children). When the questions become too personal or continue for an extended period of time, the counselor can reflect to the child, "You seem to be very interested in me personally," and explore the child's curiosity and pursuit of the subject. An understanding of the child's curiosity about the counselor could promote understanding of the child as a person. Questioning the counselor can be a defense for some children who wish to avoid discussing their own problems.

A second problem concerning self-disclosure is related to the counselor's feelings and emotions. Counselor training programs are founded on the assumption that people are unique, capable of growth, and worthy of respect. These programs focus on listening and responding to clients with empathetic understanding and respect. Also emphasized is the idea that counselors should be genuine; however, genuineness is often interpreted as showing only genuine *positive* emotions and feelings. Counselor trainees are sometimes quite surprised when their supervisors encourage them to admit to the client their negative feelings, such as frustration or anger. Obviously, admitting emotions does not mean attacking and degrading the client; rather, it means admitting that the counselor is a person with feelings and is frustrated or angry over what is occurring ("I am really frustrated that we seem to be talking about everything but what occurred with your friend today").

The counselor's proper level of self-disclosure is a controversial issue in the profession. Some feel comfortable being completely open and honest about their feelings (high levels of self-disclosure); others think that such openness can interfere with the counselor/client relationships and prefer low levels of self-disclosure. Poppen and Thompson (1974) have summarized the arguments both for and against the issue. According to counselors favoring high levels of self-disclosure:

1. If counselors are open and honest about their thoughts and feelings, this will encourage similar behavior by their clients (Jourard, 1971).
2. Knowing that the counselor has had similar adjustment problems helps clients feel more at ease to discuss their own.
3. Children learn by imitation and can learn to solve their own problems through hearing about the experiences of others.
4. Counselors could be models for behavior.

On the other side of the argument, those opposing high levels of self-disclosure claim:

1. Clients are in the counselor's office for help with their problems, not to hear about the counselor's problems.

2. Counseling could become a time for sharing gripes or problems rather than a working session for personal growth.
3. Counselors can lose objectivity if they identify too strongly with the child's concerns.

Poppen and Thompson believe that:

> self-disclosure is more beneficial when it takes a here-and-now focus—that is, when self-disclosure becomes an open and authentic expression of the counselor's or student's (child's) thoughts and feelings experienced at a particular time. Self-disclosure, when examined in the here-and-now context means much more than dredging up the dark secrets of the past. (1974, p. 15)

WHAT TYPES OF COUNSELOR QUESTIONS SHOULD BE USED?

Lay people often feel that they must ask children multitudes of questions when listening to their stories or problems in order to get the "whole story." Usually, these questions are of the "who," "what," "when," "where," and "what did you do next" variety. They may or may not be asked for the purpose of helping the child or for clarification; too often they arise out of general curiosity. Some questions may even be totally irrelevant and interrupt or ignore the child's thoughts and expressions. Questions can also be used to judge, blame or criticize.

Child: The teacher called me a dummy in front of the whole class today!
Adult: (Sarcastically) What did you say this time to make him call you that?

At that particular moment, the important fact is not what the child said, but the fact that the child was embarrassed, hurt, and possibly angered. By listening and understanding feelings and expressions (see Active Listening, Chapter 4), rather than probing for the details of who said what and when it was said, the adult will still get the whole story eventually and will maintain a much friendlier relationship with the child. If counselors listen and respond with understanding, they will learn the child's important thoughts or problems.

As mentioned previously, some counselors do have the tendency to take over a counseling interview with children in their efforts to help. When counselors direct the interview, they run the serious risk of missing important feelings and thoughts. The counselor may guide the conversation in a totally meaningless direction.

Child: I hate my brother.
Counselor (Co): Why do you hate your brother?
Child: Because he's mean.
Co: How is he mean?
Child: He hits me.

Co: What do you do to make him hit you? (accusation)
Child: Nothing.
Co: Come on, now. Tell me about when he hits you—and what
your mother does when he hits you.

This example sounds more like an inquisition than a counseling session. The hitting and what mother does may or may not be what is really troubling the child. What could be more important is the feeling that exists between the child and her brother. Is it really "hate" because he hits her, or could there be other problems in the relationship that the counselor will miss by focusing on hitting rather than listening to the child tell about her relationship with her brother? It is also possible that "hating brother" could have been a test problem to see if the counselor really would listen and be understanding. The true problem could be overlooked entirely by a counselor who guides the interview by questions; it may be revealed later if the child decides the counselor is a friend and can be trusted.

You might have also noticed in the above example that the child answered the counselor's questions but offered no further information. Children easily fall into the role of answering adults' questions and then waiting for the next question; thus, the pattern of a question-and-answer session is set. Rather than being the listener and helper the counselor promised to be, suddenly the counselor is placed in a role of questioner. When the counselor runs out of questions, the interview may die if this pattern has been established.

Obviously, there are times in counseling when direct questions should be asked. The counselor may need factual information or clarification of what is being discussed. However, counselors will probably find that they get more information from children if they use open-ended questions. An open-ended question does not require a specific answer. It encourages the child to give the counselor more information about the topic but does not restrict replies or discourage further communication in the area. Suppose a counselor was interested in learning about a child's social relationships. Rather than asking the direct and closed question, "Do you have friends?" the counselor could possibly elicit more information about the child's social relationships by asking, "Tell me about what you like to do for fun—things that you enjoy doing in your free time." In this way, the counselor could learn not only about friends, but possibly also about the child's sports interests, hobbies, and other activities (or lack of activities). Another open-ended question that might help the counselor understand what is going on in the child's life is "Tell me about your family," out of which could come answers to such unasked questions as "Does your mother/father live in the home?" "How many people live in the household?" "What are your feelings about various members of the household?"

One further point might be made about questioning in counseling.

Both Glasser (1969) and Benjamin (1969) caution adults concerning the use of "why" questions with youth. "Why" questions are associated with blame—"Why did you do that?" is often interpreted in the mind of a child as "Why did you do a *stupid thing* like that?" "Why" questions put people on the defensive; when asked why we acted in a certain manner, we feel forced to think up some logical reason or excuse for our behavior. Glasser suggests that a better question might be a "what" question. Most of us are not really sure *why* we behaved in a certain manner, but we can tell *what* occurred. A "what" question does not deal with possible unconscious motives and desires but focuses on present behavior, allowing the client and counselor to look at what is happening now and what can be done.

In summary, counselors learn more by listening than by questioning. The habit of questioning is difficult to break. When tempted to question, counselors might first ask themselves whether the questions they ask (1) will contribute therapeutically to their understanding of children and their problems, or (2) will inhibit the further flow of expression.

HOW CAN SILENCES BE USED IN COUNSELING?

Think for a moment about the last time you were part of a group that suddenly became silent. What happens at a party when the conversation begins to die? Most of us are very uncomfortable with silences. We have been socially conditioned to keep the conversation going; when conversation begins to ebb, we search through our thoughts for a new topic of interest to introduce to the group. Though silences can be very productive in a counseling interview, counselors often find them difficult to bear.

Benjamin suggests several productive uses of silences. He states that the child may need a few moments of silence to sort out thoughts and feelings, and "respect for this silence is more beneficial than many words from the interviewer" (1969, p. 25). The child may have related some very emotional event or thought and may need a moment of silence to think about this revelation or regain composure. Benjamin further states that confusion can lead to a brief period of silence. The child or the counselor may have behaved or spoken in a confusing manner, and time may be required to sort things out.

On the other hand, silence may be a way of resisting counseling. The child may be reluctant to open up and talk with this stranger who promises acceptance, or simply be unwilling to admit and deal with the problem. Techniques such as play therapy, role playing, or confrontation may be necessary to help establish a better relationship and deal with the resistance.

Finally, Benjamin points out, silences can be used productively for problem solving. There are times when all of us need just a few moments to collect our thoughts so that we can work out problems that confront us or express our thoughts and feelings more clearly.

Silences can be productive, but how long does the counselor allow the silence to last? Obviously, an entire session of silence between child and counselor is not likely to be helpful. The child may begin spontaneously to speak again when ready. Children's nonverbal behavior may provide counselors with a clue that they are ready to begin. The counselor may "test the water" by making a quiet statement reflecting the possible cause of the silence: "You seem to be a little confused about what you just told me." The child's response to this reflection should give an indication of whether he or she is ready to proceed.

WHEN IS GIVING ADVICE HELPFUL?

The role of a counselor has often been interpreted as that of an advice giver, and some counseling theorists advocate giving advice to their clients. Their rationale is that the counselor is trained in helping and is more knowing and therefore should advise the less-knowing client.

We prefer to view the role of the counselor as one of using skills and knowledge to assist another person to solve his or her own problems or conflicts. Counselors who believe in the uniqueness, worth, dignity, and responsibility of the individual, and that, given the right conditions, individuals can make correct choices for themselves will be reluctant to give advice on solving life's problems. They will, instead, assist clients to make responsible choices through their counseling knowledge and skill.

An illustration of the difference between giving advice and assisting in problem solving might help to clarify the point. Consider the example of a 12-year-old girl who tells her counselor she is ten weeks pregnant. You may be sorting through ideas to conclude what would be her best solution. Should this 12-year-old, immature child have the baby and keep the child to bring up herself? Should she have the baby and place the child up for adoption? Should she have an abortion? Should she marry the father? Perhaps her parents or his parents will adopt the child. Taking this example to the extreme, let's hypothesize that you advise the child and her parents that she should have an abortion because of her young age, immature body, and a multitude of other factors. Ten years later she sees you and confesses to you that she has experienced severe guilt- and depression since the abortion because of her religious and moral beliefs. Abortion to her has been an unforgivable sin.

Using the same illustration, suppose you advise this 12-year-old and her parents that the best solution would be for the girl to have the baby and give the child up for adoption. Ten years later, she tells you she never sleeps at night without dreaming of her "lost" child and has spent the last three years diligently searching for the child.

Admittedly, this example is an extreme case; however, it is a very realistic counseling situation, especially as the rate of pregnancy among very young, unwed girls is rising rapidly. However extreme the example, the point is that each child client is an individual. Each has a different heredity, background, set of values, feelings, needs, and cultural mores. Because of these differences in lifestyle, temperament, and personality, only the individuals with the problem can make the best choices for themselves—with the counselor's guidance and assistance.

To emphasize this point further, a second example might be in order. Because most counselors believe in good communication between parents and child, they have the tendency to encourage young people to talk with their parents about their concerns, feeling confident that parents will be supportive and understanding. Recall Cliff in Chapter 1, who was threatened by neighborhood bullies who were going to beat him up on the way home from school. Cliff confides his fear of fighting to the counselor, who assures him that he should talk this over with his parents—they will understand and will probably talk to the neighborhood boys' parents, and everything will work out fine. Cliff is reluctant to talk to his parents, but the counselor persuades him they will understand and help. Cliff returns later to relate that his father lectured him for being a "sissy" and instructed him to "go out and fight like a man." Cliff is now more terrified than ever. He thinks that neither his parents nor the counselor understand his dilemma and cannot be counted on to support him. In this case, the counselor, not considering the home and culture of the client, gave advice that has intensified the problem. The counselor might have been more helpful in assisting Cliff to think of ways for solving the problem—ways that Cliff would choose.

A second possible disadvantage of counselors giving advice is the problem of dependency. Counselors want their child clients to become responsible individuals, capable of solving their own problems. Children have a multitude of adults telling them how and when to act, but only a few assist them to learn responsible problem-solving behavior. In counseling, children learn the problem-solving process; they learn that they do not have to depend on adults to make decisions for them. The process can develop confident, mature, and independent individuals moving toward self-actualization.

Excessive advice giving in counseling can foster dependency, over-conformity, and low self-esteem. Counselors who encourage excessive dependency in clients might investigate their own motivations and needs. Most counselors find it extremely frustrating for clients to depend upon them for decisions concerning their every move. A dependency relationship inevitably breeds hostility: the dependent person resents having to depend on the counselor; the counselor resents having to support the dependency of the client. This conflict is analogous to the typical adolescent struggle for independence. The attempt to resolve the dependence/independence crisis can result in poor parent/child communication and considerable conflict.

Since many people do see the role of a counselor as that of advice giver, some clients may become frustrated and angry when counselors will not give advice. When asked what they think they could do to work out the conflict or problem, children typically are unable to think of possible solutions. It is a new experience for many children to be involved in solving their own problems. When pressed to give advice, a counselor could reflect the feeling that the child is not sure what to do and would like to have an answer, and then again suggest that they explore possibilities together. If the child is persistent and demands an answer, the counselor may wish to explore the reasons for this demand.

AVOIDING GAB SESSIONS DURING COUNSELING

Children soon discover that the counselor is a good listener who gives them undivided attention. Because many children are not listened to by adults, they often take advantage of the counseling situation to talk about everything except the reason for coming to counseling. With the least suggestion, the counselor may find the child rambling off about a TV show, last night's ballgame, a current movie, tricks their pet dog can do, or any number of other irrelevant topics. Children can become very rambling when they wish to avoid the problem. Talkativeness then becomes a diversionary tactic either to avoid admitting what is troubling them or to avoid coping with the conflict. The conflict could be so traumatic or painful that the child does not want to face it.

Another possible reason for a counseling session becoming a gab session is that children do not understand their role in the counseling interview. If the purpose of counseling and expectations of the people involved are clearly defined in the initial interview, this will be less likely to occur.

Unfortunately, some counselors would prefer to chat with their child clients than to "work" during the counseling interview. Counselors sometimes find it easier to engage in a superficial relationship and general conversation for the time they are with the child rather than risk the involvement of caring and possibly uncovering and having to cope with intense feelings and emotions.

When counselors discover themselves being led into superficial or rambling conversations by their child clients, they may want to bring the conversation back to the problem at hand by reflecting to the child, "We seem to be getting away from the reason for our time together. I wonder if you could tell me more about . . ." If children consistently wander, it might be helpful to tell them you notice that they are wandering and then to explore possible reasons for the avoidance. A tape recorder could be an excellent means of determining when, how, and why the distractions occur. A contract might be drawn up, such as, "(*The counselor*) and I will work on *(the problem)* for 25 minutes. I am free to talk to *(the counselor)* about anything I choose for the last 5 minutes."

WHAT LIMITS SHOULD BE SET IN COUNSELING?

In training, most counselors are taught to be empathetic, respectful, genuine, accepting, and nonjudgmental—characteristics that writers such as Carl Rogers and Robert Carkhuff have defined as essential for a facilitative counseling relationship. Counselors may follow many other theories during the counseling process, but most believe that establishing a therapeutic relationship based on these ingredients is a necessary first step for effective counseling. The characteristics of empathy, respect, and genuineness have been operationally defined by Carkhuff (1969), and many training institutions teach counselors these behaviors according to his model. To define the counseling attitudes and behaviors involved in being accepting and nonjudgmental may not be quite so easy.

From the concepts of Rogers (1961), van Kaam (1965), and Frankl (1962), we may conclude that acceptance is born from genuine concern for people. Acceptance implies that counselors believe individuals have infinite worth and dignity, the right to make choices and decisions for their lives, and responsibility for their own lives. It is possible to accept an individual as a person of worth and potential without accepting the behavior of that person. Children should be viewed as unique and responsible individuals, capable of making wise choices; however, adults cannot be totally accepting of all child behaviors. Acceptance does not imply total permissiveness. Respect for the rights of all individuals involved must accompany acceptance, and counselors cannot allow children to infringe on their rights as people, nor on the rights of other family members, friends, or acquaintances.

To be accepting and nonjudgmental may be a difficult task for some counselors, especially when moral and ethical issues are involved in the counseling. Counselors are human beings with their own strong attitudes, values, and beliefs. Judgments are sometimes made very quickly, on the basis of little information, because of one's values and beliefs. It is difficult to remain open-minded enough to really hear the client's entire story if there is a strong conflict between the client's values and those of the counselor. See Chapter 20 for further discussion of this issue.

Being nonjudgmental does not imply total permissiveness. Being nonjudgmental involves withholding those judgments we ordinarily make to allow our clients to tell their whole story without being threatened by the counselor's condemnation. Counselors attempt to refrain from blaming, accusing, criticizing, and moralizing, but they also attempt to teach responsible and reality-oriented behavior to their child clients. The counselor does not tell children they are "wrong"; the counselor's job is to assist children to explore the consequences, advantages, and disadvantages of their choices, and perhaps better methods of resolving the conflict. For instance, rather than sermonizing to Cliff that fighting is wrong, the counselor might be more helpful by thinking with him about what would happen if he challenged the bully to a fight and whether there were other ways to gain his father's acceptance and respect.

In summary, being accepting and nonjudgmental are essential characteristics of good counseling, but they must be combined with respect for the rights of others, the reality of the situation, and responsibility for one's own behavior.

WHAT ABOUT THE ISSUE OF CONFIDENTIALITY?

Most counselors are taught in their training programs that whatever is said in a counseling interview should remain confidential unless there is danger to the client, another person, or property. Many explain the principle of confidentiality to their clients during the first interview; others discuss confidentiality only if the child questions whether what is said will be told to parents or teachers. Should information indicating that there is danger to a person or property be revealed during later interviews, counselors will want to remind the children of their obligation to report such danger to the proper authorities. Counselors do not have privileged communication in their counselor/client relationship unless they are licensed by a state regulatory board. Counselors' records can be subpoenaed, and counselors can be called to testify in court proceedings should the information they possess be necessary for a court decision. If counselors think that revealing the information required in their testimony could be harmful to the child, they may wish to request a private conference with the judge to share this information and their reasons for wanting to keep the information confidential.

Some counselors working with children do not think that confidentiality is an important concern of children. Counselors with this orientation maintain that children and adults should be encouraged to communicate more openly with one another and that the counselor can facilitate this process in the counseling interview. They further contend that parents and other adults can provide insight and needed information about the child; the significant adult in the child's life can become a co-counselor.

Careful evaluation of the child's presenting problem and the adults involved may help the counselor to decide whether strict confidentiality should be maintained or if others should be included. To avoid misunderstanding and maintain the trust necessary for the counseling relationship, the decision to include others or share information should always be discussed with the child. See Chapter 20 for further discussion of confidentiality.

IS THIS CHILD TELLING ME THE TRUTH?

A counseling problem that can arise out of being an accepting person and a good listener is the question of whether the child is telling the counselor the truth or enhancing or exaggerating in order to get attention or sympathy. Children will often tell their counselors of seeing people shoot one another, raging fires, robberies, or abuse by their parents. Unfortunately, many of these stories are true; however, children do have vivid imaginations, and it is difficult to know how much to believe. Counselors do not want to be gullible, nor do they want to deny the truth.

If counselors have some doubt about the truth of what they are hearing, questioning for more details of the incident may clarify truth and fiction. When asked to give specifics, children may admit they were "only kidding" or "making it up." Counselors might also admit their genuine opinion: "I am really having trouble with this because I have never heard of anything like it," or ". . . because it is hard for me to imagine that person doing this," and so on. An admission by counselors that they are having trouble expresses a genuine feeling and avoids labeling the child a liar or possibly denying a true story. It also provides the child with the opportunity to change a story while saving face. See Chapter 16 for further suggestions.

WHAT CAN BE DONE WHEN THE INTERVIEW BOGS DOWN?

There will be counseling sessions when the child does not feel like talking. It is possible that things have been going well for the past few days and the child really has nothing to discuss. There may be a lull before new material is introduced. One way to help avoid these unexpected empty periods is to be prepared for a session. Some counselors have general goals for their client (for instance, to increase assertiveness) and also define specific short-term goals for each session as counseling proceeds. Whether the counselor prefers to define objectives or not, notes of the previous session can be reviewed and a tentative plan made for the coming interview. Obviously, this plan is subject to change according to the content of the interview.

However, the best laid plans often go awry. When the child seems highly distracted, a short summary by the counselor or child of the past conversation may stimulate further communication. If the child does not seem to want to talk, the techniques of play therapy (drawing, clay, games) may be beneficial. There may be times (illness, extreme excitability, or apathy) when it is best to end the session short of the designated time. The length of the counseling sessions could vary from a few minutes to an hour depending on the client's age and presenting problem.

When sessions are bogging down, evaluate what is happening. Again, the tape recorder could be of assistance in assessing the lack of progress. Bogging down could be a sign that the child is ready for the counseling to conclude. It could be resistance on the part of the child client. It could come from the counselor's inadequate skills or lack of planning. Unproductive sessions will occur occasionally with all counselors, but frequent periods of nonproductivity should signal the counselor to investigate what is happening.

WHEN SHOULD COUNSELING BE TERMINATED?

How does a counselor decide when to end counseling? Does the counselor or the client decide? How does either party know when the client is ready to stand alone? If the counselor and client have clearly defined the problem brought to counseling and the goal to be accomplished, the termination time will be evident—when the goal is accomplished.

Termination may be difficult for children, for they usually find the sessions to be a time when a caring adult gives them undivided attention. Deep friendships are often formed between counselor and child, and the child (and possibly the counselor) does not wish to end this pleasant relationship. In order to ease the break, client and counselor can discuss a possible termination date several weeks ahead of time. Plans can be made and rehearsed about how the child will react should problems occur again. The child can be left with a feeling that the counselor still cares and will be available should trouble arise again. Counselors may even consider building in a follow-up time when they ask their child clients to drop them a note or call to let them know how things are going. The counselor may want to schedule a brief follow-up visit. Any informal method of showing the child that a counselor's caring does not end with the last interview can signal the continued interest of the counselor in the child's growth and development. Most successful counselors utilize a plan for maintaining the gains their child clients have achieved during counseling. Such maintenance plans require periodic follow-up contacts.

REFERENCES

Benjamin, A. *The helping interview.* Boston: Houghton Mifflin, 1969.
Carkhuff, R. R. *Helping and human relations* (2 vols.). New York: Holt, Rinehart and Winston, 1969.
Frankl, V. *Man's search for meaning: An introduction to logotherapy.* Boston: Beacon Press, 1962.

Glasser, W. *Schools without failure.* New York: Harper & Row, 1969.

Jourard, S. *The transparent self* (2nd ed.). New York: Van Nostrand Reinhold, 1971.

Poppen, W., and Thompson, C. *School counseling: Theories and concepts.* Lincoln, Nebr.: Professional Educators Pub., 1974.

Rogers, C. *On becoming a person.* Boston: Houghton Mifflin, 1961.

van Kaam, A. Counseling from the viewpoint of existential psychology. In R. Mosher, R. Carle, and C. Kehas (Eds.), *Guidance: An examination.* New York: Harcourt, Brace and World, 1965.

chapter 14

COUNSELING AND CONSULTING TECHNIQUES

Throughout the book, suggestions have been made for counselors working with children having specific learning, social, or behavioral problems. It has been emphasized that these techniques should be used only within a helping atmosphere. Counselors are cautioned that all children are unique and therefore respond differently. A counseling or consulting procedure that proved to be effective with one child may not be effective with another child. The success of most interventions depends on the relationship that has been established between the counselor and the child.

COUNSELING TECHNIQUES

Many children do not respond to "talking" therapy for a variety of reasons. Children may not have been encouraged or allowed to express their feelings and define their behaviors. They may not have the cognitive development to be able to express concerns. They may never have had the experience of an adult really listening to them and therefore may react with suspicion or resistance. For any number of reasons, many children prefer structure in counseling and require action-oriented approaches to facilitate the counseling process. Some techniques that may help counselors work with children are described below.

Role playing

Role playing can be a useful tool for counselors throughout the counseling process. Ohlsen (1977) reviewed the literature on role playing and points out some of its values: (1) It can facilitate communication when the client cannot verbalize the problem; (2) it often uncovers unrecognized feelings; (3) it is helpful in gaining feedback concerning behavior; (4) it increases sensitivity to another's needs; (5) it enables clients to see themselves as others see them; (6) it provides practice for decision making and exploring consequences; and (7) it provides an opportunity for the child to actually experience a situation, rather than just talking about it.

Negative role playing or rehearsal may be helpful in identifying what *not* to do. If children role play negative behaviors and their consequences, it may help them to evaluate objectively what is happening and the consequences of their behavior.

Role playing to define the problem.   Children often have trouble describing exactly what occurred in a particular situation, especially one involving interpersonal problems with parents, teachers, or peers. Moreover, they may be unable to see clearly how certain behaviors have evoked an unwanted response or consequence. For example, suppose young Jerome tells the counselor that he and his mother are in constant conflict. She is unfair and never allows him to do *anything* he asks. Role playing could provide some insight into what occurs when Jerome asks for permission.

> Counselor: I'll be your mother, and you show me exactly how you asked your mother to allow you to, for instance, have a birthday party. Talk to me exactly as you would to your mother if you were to ask her for the party.
>
> Jerome: Mom, you never let me do anything! You always say no to anything I want. I want a birthday party, and you'll be mean if you don't let me have one this year!

The counselor can now readily see that, if there is already a conflict between mother and child, this demand will increase the conflict and is unlikely to get Jerome his birthday party.

Children having trouble with peers might be asked to describe what happened and then to role play one or more persons in the incident. Verbal and nonverbal behaviors not adequately described in relating the incident often become more apparent when they are role played.

Role reversal.   Whenever conflicts occur between children, adults frequently ask one child "How would you feel if he hit you like that (said that to you, bit you, and so on)?" The purpose of this admonition is to have one child empathize with the other. However, many cognitive theorists, especially Piaget, emphasize that young children, especially up through the preoperational stage (11 years old), lack the cognitive development to be able to put themselves in another person's place. Since children understand better what they see, hear, or experience directly, role playing other children's positions could promote a better understanding than a verbal admonition.

> Counselor (Co): Barbara, I understand from your sister that you hit her on the head quite often. Would you agree that this is what happens?
>
> Barbara: Yeah, I can really make her move if I threaten to hit her good on the head!
>
> Co: Would the two of you describe to me what happened the last time you hit Judy?
>
> After the girls verbally describe the incident:
>
> Co: Now, Barbara, I wonder if you would mind playing Judy, and saying and doing exactly what Judy did. I would like Judy to say and do exactly what you did.

The purpose of this role reversal is to help Barbara experience Judy's feelings when she hit her. Hopefully, Barbara will then want to explore better methods of relating to Judy.

Role reversal can be an effective tool when communication breaks down between parents and children, between teachers and children, between peers, or between counselors and their clients. Each player can gain increased knowledge of the other's point of view.

Role playing used as behavior rehearsal. Most adults will rehearse a speech before presenting it to an audience in order to refine it and assure a smooth presentation. Children, too, may feel more comfortable about trying a new behavior if they can practice it before actually facing the real world.

Dave is a shy little boy who has no friends. In an effort to help Dave make friends, the counselor may want to help him decide exactly how he will approach another child and the things he will say to the child after the opening "hello." To build confidence, the counselor could first role play another child and allow Dave to practice his new behaviors in a safe atmosphere. When Dave feels secure in role playing meeting a new friend with the counselor, another child can be involved in the role-play situation to help Dave gain more realistic experiences in meeting other children.

The empty chair technique of role playing. The Gestalt technique of the empty chair is often used to role play a conflict between people or within the person. The child can sit in one chair and play his or her own part; then, sitting in the other chair, the child can play out a projection of what the other person is saying or doing in response. Similarly, a child may sit in one chair and discuss the pros of making a decision and then argue the cons of the decision while sitting in the opposite chair.

For example, Sharon was having trouble deciding whether to tell of her friend's involvement in a destruction of property. She thought her friend had behaved wrongly and that she should not let other children take the blame for the incident, yet she was reluctant to tattle on the friend and get her in trouble. The counselor suggested that Sharon sit in one chair and talk about what would happen if she did tell on her friend, and then move to the other chair to argue why she should tell. The technique helped Sharon to look at the consequences of both acts and make her decision.

A variation of the empty chair is suggested by Thompson and Poppen (1979). A problem can be explored in an individual or group situation by introducing the empty chair as a hypothetical person with characteristics and behaviors similar to those of the child and his or her particular problem. It is sometimes easier for children to discuss a hypothetical child and how this child feels or could change than to discuss their own feelings and behaviors. While discussing an imagined person, the children learn about themselves.

Three chairs.   Adults are often placed in the role of refereeing disagreements among children or between children and other adults. Usually the parties involved are blaming each other, and the counselor may be unable to fully understand what has occurred. In an attempt to clarify the situation, counselors may find it helpful to place three chairs in a semicircle and sit between the parties in conflict. The counselor listens closely to the first person and then turns to the other and repeats verbatim what has been said. When the second person responds, the counselor then turns to the first speaker and repeats verbatim what the second has said. The procedure allows each child to hear what has been said and to correct mistakes. The process is continued until the conflict is clarified. Usually both children will end up laughing.

Modeling

Peers are an important part of a child's world, and their influence can be used quite effectively to help children change. Children usually imitate the behaviors of people they like. A model may be presented to the child through the use of TV, films, videotapes, or books. Other models include friends, classmates, adults, and the counselor. An example is given below.

Charlene had mentioned a friend, Patty, a number of times during the counseling sessions. She indicated that she would like to be like Patty because Patty had a lot of friends, made good grades, and got along well with parents and teachers. The counselor asked Charlene to observe Patty's behaviors closely for one week, writing down on an index card those she particularly liked and wanted to imitate. The next week Charlene brought back her list of six behaviors. The counselor and Charlene selected the most important one for Charlene and began to work on that behavior. Role playing and behavior rehearsal were included in the counseling to help Charlene learn the new behaviors. The observed behaviors were practiced and modified until they were appropriate for Charlene. As the counseling progressed, Charlene continued to observe her model and to practice new behaviors until she became more like her idealized self.

Homework assignments

Homework assignments may be given to children in counseling for a variety of reasons. Homework can build continuity between sessions and facilitate counseling by encouraging "work" on the child's problems between sessions. A homework assignment could be a commitment by the child to keep a record of some particular feeling or behavior, to reduce or stop a present behavior, or to try a new behavior. Homework assignments provide the child with an opportunity to try out new or different behaviors and discuss the consequences with the counselor. For example, after Dave (in the example of Role Playing Used as Behavior Rehearsal) has rehearsed approaching a new person within the counseling session, the counselor might ask him to approach one new person during the coming week and try out this new behavior. Dave could evaluate whether the new behavior was effective for him and discuss the results with the counselor; if it wasn't, other methods could be explored.

Play therapy

Some counselors believe that play techniques should be a primary method for counseling with children younger than 12 years because of their limited cognitive development and ability to verbalize their thoughts and feelings, and because play is a natural mode of expression and communication for children. Play techniques can be of value to the counselor in many phases of the counseling process.

1. Play can be used as a means for establishing rapport. A child who is anxious, resistant, or suspicious of adults will usually relax and begin to talk more freely when the counselor utilizes play media.

2. Play can be used to help counselors understand children and their relationships and interactions. For example, puppets will often reveal the types of interactions that occur between adults and children or between children and their peers.

3. Play can be used to help children reveal feelings they are unable to verbalize. Children who are asked to draw a picture or build something with toys such as building blocks or clay may reveal their thoughts and feelings in their play. Children are often asked to draw pictures of themselves to determine how they perceive themselves or to draw their families to see how they perceive themselves in relation to other family members.

4. Play can be used for acting out feelings of anxiety or tension in a constructive manner. The child can be allowed to release anger or hostility through play media such as hammer and nails, soft foam bats, war toys, or physical activities such as football, baseball, volleyball, or running.

5. Play can be an effective method for teaching socialization skills. Children participating in a counselor-guided play session can test limits, gain insight about their behavior, explore alternatives, and learn about consequences in a protected environment.

Counselors may wish to carefully consider their objectives or goals for the use of play and structure the counseling session accordingly, or they may wish to allow the children to determine the structure of play sessions. Since each child is unique, counselors will want to consider each situation ,to decide if the objective of the play could be achieved more readily through counselor-directed play or if child-directed play would be more productive.

Proponents of play therapy differ on the question of limits. Some counselors think that no limits should be imposed on the child in a play room—that limits will hamper expression and understanding. Others propose that only limits to safeguard the welfare of the child and counselor and to protect property should be employed. Still other counselors would place limits on time, space, and certain behaviors. When limits are imposed, they should be clearly defined and discussed with the child before play is begun. If counselors include play techniques in regular talking counseling sessions without moving to a play room, there may be no need for a discussion of limits.

When selecting play media, counselors will want to consider the age and needs of the children, and the purposes for which play therapy will be used. Dolls, doll houses, puppets, clay, punching toys, blocks, planes, soldiers, tanks and trucks, hammers, soft balls, sand, magic markers, or crayons may be helpful for working with younger children. Games such as chess, checkers or backgammon, electronic games, published games (Life, Monopoly, Twister), paper-and-pencil games (tic-tac-toe), drawing supplies (paper and magic markers, blackboard drawing), or games that require the child to construct or solve problems may be more helpful for working with older children. Physical activities may be incorporated into counseling sessions or given as homework assignments.

The play media selected should meet the following objectives:

1. Facilitate the relationship between counselor and child
2. Encourage expression of feelings or thoughts
3. Aid the counselor in gaining insight into the child's world
4. Provide an opportunity for the child to test reality
5. Provide an acceptable means for expression of unacceptable thoughts or feelings

The counselor may choose to become involved in the play or simply to observe the child during the play. The counselor's skills of listening, observing, and detecting and reflecting feelings and thoughts are as important during play sessions as they are during regular counseling.

Strengths tests

Children with poor self-concepts may be helped to feel better about themselves by techniques that let them focus on their positive characteristics or behaviors. Counselors can have children make a list of all their strengths—for instance, honest, friendly, smile a lot, can throw a fast ball, and so forth. The counselor can then discuss with the children ways for utilizing each of these strengths in a positive manner.

Counselors working with children in groups can have each child tell something positive about each group member from time to time. An index card for each child can be passed around a group, and the counselor can ask each child to write a strength for every group member on his or her card. Each member can be asked to write a particular child a short letter pointing out his or her strengths.

Children sometimes have difficulty listing their own strengths or even those of others when the activity is initiated because their strengths have rarely been pointed out to them. Society seems to focus on children's mistakes and negative behaviors more often than their positive behaviors. Children usually find strengths testing very rewarding.

Diary

Most people have kept a diary or journal at some time during their lives in which they have recorded their innermost feelings and thoughts and other events. Children respond well to a homework assignment of keeping a diary. The log provides the counselor and child with a record of feelings, thoughts, and events to be explored. Keeping a journal or diary may also provide the child with a feeling of closeness to the counselor between sessions.

Incomplete sentences

Completing stimulus statements about likes, dislikes, family, friends, goals, wishes, and things that make the child happy or sad is a technique to help counselors understand children and find problem areas. This procedure may be especially helpful in assisting counselors to become acquainted with children and to establish better rapport with those who are anxious, fearful, or reluctant to talk.

Examples
The thing I like to do most is _____.
The person in my family who helps me most is _____.
My friends _____.
I feel happiest (or saddest) when _____.
My greatest wish is _____.
The greatest thing that ever happened to me was _____.

Cognitive restructuring

Cognitive restructuring (see Chapter 6) is directed toward changing or redirecting children's thoughts and feelings. Albert Ellis's rational emotive theory focuses on changing irrational ideas and the feelings that result from them. The theory stresses that an event is followed by thoughts about the event, and that our reactions to events occur as the result of what we tell ourselves ("It's terrible," "I cannot stand this," "They are laughing at me," and so on). The counselor's job is to confront the children with their self-defeating verbalizations and help them change their "internalized sentences," and thereby change their reactions.

For example, Bob takes great delight in bumping into Steve every time he sees him. Steve reacts violently and usually tries to slug him. Bob then "apologizes" and, when confronted with the behavior by adults, vows it was accidental and that he is so sorry. The counselor is working with Steve.

> Counselor (Co): So Bob is really getting you in trouble because you try to slug him when he bumps you.
> Steve: Yeah, but it's no accident that he bumps me. He does it to make me mad and get me in trouble.
> Co: How do you feel when he bumps you to get you in trouble?
> Steve: Bad . . . and mad!
> Co: Let me guess what you are telling yourself when this happens. He's trying to show how big and powerful he is, and he's trying to make me look like a fool—or maybe a chicken. It would be terrible if the kids thought I was a chicken.
> Steve: Yeah.
> Co: Would finding a better way to handle Bob than getting into trouble make you a chicken?
> Steve: No!
> Co: Would being smart enough to avoid a fight and stopping Bob's behavior make you a chicken?
> Steve: No!
> Co: OK, then we need to find a way to stop Bob that won't get you into trouble.

The counselor would then help Steve find better ways of thinking—for example, "I don't like the way Bob is treating me, but I know I'm not a chicken, and I'm not going to let him get me in trouble."

Cognitive restructuring teaches children to label their feelings. Counselors then help them to deal with these feelings appropriately. In the above example, Steve has identified his feelings when he is bumped, been told that he does not have to accept others' opinions as facts, and helped to find an alternative "internalized sentence."

Bibliocounseling

According to McKinney, bibliocounseling (or bibliotherapy) has been defined as "the dynamic interaction between the personality of the reader and literature, which can be used for personality adjustment and growth. . . . The important variables, then, are the reader and his or her characteristics, the story and its involvement properties, and the various individual reactions to the story" (1977, p. 550).

In an article citing the benefits of bibliocounseling for abused children, Watson (1980) suggests that children may become psychologically and emotionally involved with characters they have read about. Vicarious experiences through books can be similar to the child's thoughts, feelings, attitudes, behavior, or environment. Directed reading can lead to expression of feeling or problem solving. Watson quotes a 1972 article by Rongrone that lists the goals of bibliotherapy as: (1) teaching constructive and positive thinking; (2) encouraging free expression concerning problems; (3) assisting persons to analyze their attitudes and behaviors; (4) looking at alternative solutions; (5) encouraging the client to find an adjustment to the problem not in conflict with society; and (6) allowing clients to see the similarity of their problems to those of others.

When using bibliocounseling with children, counselors will want to discuss the stories with their client. Discussion focused around characters' behaviors, feelings, thoughts, relationships, cause and effect, and consequences will be more effective than just asking the child to relate the story. Counselors can guide children to see the relationships and application of the story to their own lives.

Bibliocounseling is another means of cognitive restructuring directed toward educating children about certain areas of concern such as sex, physical disabilities, divorce, death, and the like. It is assumed that, once children have enough information about a problem, their attitudes and behaviors will change. The ideas and facts presented in the books should be discussed with the children in order to clear up questions that arise from the reading. Suggested books for bibliocounseling with exceptional children or children with special concerns are given at the end of Chapters 18 and 19.

Storytelling

We have found storytelling an excellent counseling technique to help children deal with feelings or behaviors they are not ready to admit and also to help children see unrecognized consequences of their behavior. An example is given below.

Marcia was a very bright child and had a very vivid imagination. Her parents and teachers complained that they never knew when she was telling the truth, and her peers were beginning to reject her because of her stories. The counselor was also having trouble knowing when Marcia was telling the truth. She would tell the counselor of things that had happened that could be true, yet the counselor had doubts about their occurrence. During one session, the counselor related a story to Marcia about a girl named Mary who was about Marcia's age and very similar to Marcia. The counselor went on to tell how Mary told exaggerated stories to everyone to try to make friends and impress them;

however, no one who knew her believed anything she said. One day, Mary saw someone robbing the house down the street, but when she ran for help no one believed her. The counselor asked Marcia what she thought of Mary's situation and what she thought Mary could do to straighten it out. Before the discussion ended, Marcia stopped talking about Mary and substituted "I" in exploring alternatives and developing a new plan for making friends.

Assertiveness training

There are children whose typical response to everyday interactions is withdrawal. Some of these children may have poor self-concepts and feelings of inferiority that inhibit them; others may have experienced negative consequences as a result of speaking out, and therefore anxiety inhibits them. Children who are withdrawn and passive need to be encouraged to recognize their rights as people as well as accepting the rights of others. An example of assertiveness training follows.

Tim and Charles were very good friends. However, Tim always took from Charles whatever he wanted or needed—toys, pencils, food, and so on. Charles responded very passively, always allowing Tim to have his way. The counselor asked Charles to describe in detail the latest incident in which Tim had taken Charles's new bike, ridden it all afternoon, and brought it back scratched up. The counselor encouraged Charles to formulate an assertive statement such as, "I want to ride my new bike. Would you go and get your bike to ride?" Charles and the counselor took several incidents from the past, and Charles was encouraged to state (1) his needs, and (2) what he would like to have happen in each situation. They then used behavior rehearsal to give Charles an opportunity to practice his assertiveness.

After several sessions, Charles made a commitment to try out his new response. He reported that he told Tim, "I want to use my magic markers now. Would you get your own?" and that it had worked. The counselor worked for several months on helping Charles to learn how to become appropriately assertive. Each new situation was discussed and practiced in the counseling sessions before it was actually tried in daily living.

A word of caution is necessary to counselors teaching assertiveness to children. The adults in the child's life must be prepared for the child's new behavior. Parents who discipline children by very authoritarian methods may not tolerate assertiveness on the part of their child. In order to avoid unpleasant consequences, the counselor will want to determine the result of the child's behavioral change on the child's significant others or the environment before teaching the child this new skill.

Relaxation exercises and systematic desensitization

Many adults think that children have little anxiety and tension in their lives. Counselors working with children, however, will recognize that they often manifest their anxiety and tension through their behaviors even if they don't express it verbally. Teaching relaxation to children can be a highly effective method for helping them to cope with anxieties and tensions.

Some relatively simple relaxation exercises are described in Chapter 9. For children with deeper anxieties and tensions, deep muscle relaxation by Wolpe and Lazarus (1966) may be used. The procedure is also the first step for desensitization. Wolpe and Lazarus have published a very explicit set of exercises, and Lazarus (1971) has also recorded the relaxation exercises on a set of cassette tapes. Chapter 9 describes in some detail the use of relaxation and desensitization to remove anxieties.

Hypnotherapy

Hypnosis is a technique that has been controversial; however, recent research indicates that it can be a useful tool for working with children. Children seem to be fascinated with the procedure and therefore are usually hypnotized more easily than adults. Hypnotherapy has been used successfully with children experiencing anxiety, high blood pressure, asthma, and psychosomatic pain; and to overcome such habits as nailbiting, thumbsucking, tics, insomnia, or sleepwalking.

The danger of hypnotherapy, of course, comes when untrained persons attempt to use the procedure. Counselors may wish to investigate the possibility and availability of training in the area. Hypnotherapy appears to be a highly effective counseling tool for working with certain problems of children.

CONSULTING TECHNIQUES

In 1979, Kahnweiler reviewed the literature in four major journals published by the American Personnel and Guidance Association to examine the history of consultation. The first articles on the counselor as a consultant appeared in 1957 and focused on consultation as an alternative to direct-service counseling. These articles sought to present an acceptable rationale for the use of consultation. Models for consultation did not appear until several years later. Many of the early models were vague and abstract, but by the end of the 1960s, models for behavioral consultation, Adlerian consultation, teacher-consultation groups, in-service training, and classroom observation had appeared in the literature (Kahnweiler, 1979).

Tolbert states that "consultation provides a means to serve as a change agent, modify the environment, and build system-wide developmental programs" (1978, p. 206). Consultation can be an effective technique for many settings; for example, one-to-one interactions, small groups, psychological education in large groups, outreach programs, and preventive education. For the present purposes, consultation will refer to the one-to-one interaction between the counselor and a significant adult in the child's life, or a counselor-led small group of significant adults, with the purpose of finding ways to assist children toward functioning more effectively or becoming more self-actualizing persons.

We believe that counseling and consultation require essentially the same skills and techniques. Both processes have the goal of helping children help themselves. The essential difference in the process is that the interview is conducted with a third party, the client, rather than the child directly involved. The counseling process described in Chapter 2 can be utilized in both counseling and consulting situations.

Counseling	*Consultation*
1. Establish rapport by listening and communicating understanding and respect.	1. Establish rapport by listening and communicating understanding and respect.
2. Identify the problem. "What are you doing?"	2. Identify the problem. "What do you see as Jenny's main problem?"
3. Identify consequences. "How does this help (or hurt) you in reaching your goal of _____?"	3. Identify consequences. "What happens when Jenny does this?"
4. Evaluate past solutions. "What have you tried to solve this?"	4. Evaluate past solutions. "What have you (or Jenny) tried to solve this?"
5. List alternatives. "What could you be doing?"	5. List alternatives. "Can you think of other things that might help?"
6. Contract—make a plan. "Which alternative will you choose, and when will you do this?"	6. Contract—make a plan. "Which alternative will you choose, and when will you do this?"
7. Follow up to evaluate results of plan.	7. Follow up to evaluate results of plan.

In consultation, as in counseling, the counselor will want to listen, and reflect and clarify feelings throughout the interview. Similarly, counselors will want to avoid the use of labels and diagnoses. Information (not advice) may be provided to the counselee or the adult in consultation.

For significant adults in children's lives (parents or teachers), the small group meeting known as the case group or C-group might be helpful (Poppen & Thompson, 1975). The discussion in the group follows the guidelines listed below.

1. A brief description of the case is presented.
2. A discussion of the present situation follows.
   a. What is happening?
   b. What behavior is helpful or hurtful?

3. How does the child view him- or herself and the situation?
   a. View of self
   b. Goals
   c. Self-evaluation of behaviors
4. How are others involved? What are their reactions?
5. What are alternative or new behaviors?
6. What helpful resources are available?
7. Design a specific plan of action.

This is a sharing group; there is no expert advice, no diagnostic labels, no blame placed. Participants share feelings and experiences and help each other find new ways of coping with the presenting problem.

Consulting can help counselors reach more children by teaching adults (parents, teachers, and other significant persons in the children's lives) to behave in more helpful ways. Providing indirect services to children through consultation can be an important part of the counselor's role; unfortunately, few counselors are utilizing their skills in this area. Following are techniques counselors may wish to try in their consultative efforts with the adults in the child's world. Not every technique will work with every child. The uniqueness and the specific needs of each child must be considered before selecting any counseling or consulting procedure.

Role shift

Simply changing one's own behavior may elicit a behavior change in another person. Adults who change their response to children's behaviors may cease to reinforce them or present children with an unexpected response, which causes them to change.

Thompson and Poppen (1979) suggest that adults be asked to list *everything* they have tried with the child that has been ineffective. The adults are then asked to commit themselves to never again trying any one of these ineffective techniques with this child. The list should be kept as a reminder of "what not to do" with this child.

When the child has behaved inappropriately, the adults can stop and ask themselves, "What response does this child expect?" Does the child expect the adult to be shocked, outraged, or angry? For instance, Glen reacted to the scoldings of his mother by drawing grotesque pictures of her and placing them around the house. He took great delight in watching her reactions when she found the pictures. The mother decided that Glen enjoyed her outrage when he got back at her with the grotesque pictures. The next time she found a picture, she calmly commented to him, "I must have really made you angry when I scolded you for you to draw me like this." The mother left the picture up and went on with her work. Glen quietly removed his pictures later in the day. This technique seems to work best when the child's expectation is to get attention, to shock (as with curse words or dirty language), to frustrate, to anger, or to seek revenge.

Descriptive discussions of children

Many times adults have become so frustrated with children's problems that the child is perceived as "all bad." Counselors can gain some understanding of adults' perceptions and expectations of children by asking them to describe the children and their behaviors in some detail (Thompson & Poppen, 1972). If the entire description focuses on negative traits or behaviors, the counselor might ask the adult if there is *anything* good about the child. The adult can then be asked to make a list of any strengths the child may have. Hopefully, focusing attention on the positive side of the child will help the adult to decrease attention to the negative and increase awareness of the positive.

Listing of behaviors

A technique similar to the descriptive discussion to change perceptions of children is listing of behaviors. For instance, Mr. Jones told the counselor that Sherry was a cry-baby; she cried at *everything* that did not go her way. The counselor asked Mr. Jones to keep an exact count of the times that Sherry cried during the next week. The next week Mr. Jones admitted that, according to his count, Sherry had cried only three times that week—once when she fell, once when she was told to go to bed, and once when she was refused a request. Mr. Jones began to change his perception of Sherry as a cry-baby.

Listing the number of times a behavior occurs can also provide a baseline count to determine if an intervention has helped to reduce an inappropriate behavior or increase an appropriate one.

Logical consequences

Proponents of Adler's individual psychology advocate allowing children to experience the natural or logical consequences of their behavior, rather than punishment, as the preferred form of discipline (see Chapter 7). They suggest that adults who punish children become authority figures and lose the friendship of the child. They also point out that natural or logical consequences are reality oriented and teach the child the rules of society, whereas punishment may teach unwanted lessons such as power is authority.

Obviously, adults cannot allow children to experience the consequences of all their behavior; children cannot learn that busy streets are dangerous by being allowed to play in streets. However, a thoughtful adult can find ways to arrange for children to see the consequences of inappropriate behavior. When Peter colors on the walls instead of paper, for instance, Peter is handed the sponge and cleanser to remove the coloring. The logical consequence of being late is to miss an event or a meal, lose the privilege of going out again, or have to come home earlier next time. The logical consequence of breaking someone's property is to earn enough money to replace it. The logical consequence of behaving inappropriately in a group is usually rejection by the group or isolation. Discipline with logical consequences teaches children the order and rules of society very quickly.

ISOLATION TECHNIQUES

There may be times when children's behaviors become so unacceptable that they must be removed from the group (the classroom, family, or peer group). For many years, parents have sent children to their rooms when they acted out. Our society isolates adults who behave inappropriately by ostracization and in extreme cases by imprisonment. Isolation techniques are a form of logical consequences.

Four steps of isolation have been outlined by Thompson and Poppen (1979). For children with minor problems of maintaining attention, a second seat may be arranged away from the group, in a quiet place but not out of sight. When children are not directing attention toward the task of the group, they may be quietly reminded that their present seat, seat 1, is for working on science, participating in a group discussion, and the like, and that they will have to move to seat 2. Children are given the choice of returning to the group when they are ready to participate in the group activity. The success of this technique is based on the premise that children like to be part of a group and will change their behavior in order to remain within the group.

The second step of isolation is the quiet corner. Some children are highly distractible and highly distracting to their peers. They must be completely screened from the group in order to accomplish their work. A quiet corner can be constructed with screens, study carrels, bookshelves (books facing outward), or very large, decorated furniture cartons. The quiet corner should contain a desk and chair and books, puzzles, or other quiet materials. There should not be windows and doors in a quiet corner. When children misbehave, the adult can signal the child quietly that the behavior is not appropriate and ask the child to go to the quiet corner. Children should have the choice of returning to the group when they are ready to participate more acceptably. A short time limit of 10 to 15 minutes may have to be imposed before allowing the children this choice.

For problems of a more severe type, counselors may wish to suggest a time-out room. This procedure can be used when children need to be completely away from the group. Thompson and Poppen (1979) suggest that time-out be used not as a punishment but as a "cooling-off" time. Children can be instructed to make a plan for avoiding the trouble in the future while they are in the time-out room.

When children's problem behaviors are so severe that the first three isolation procedures have not worked, they may be asked quietly to leave the premises (school, church, club, recreational center) and come back tomorrow to try again. The children should be aware of what behaviors are acceptable and unacceptable and the conditions for remaining in the group. Since this procedure often requires the assistance of parents, school personnel, or other community workers, a written agreement between all parties is advisable. Many schools use "in-house suspension" in order to provide a place where children who cannot remain in the group can go for supervised study. Other community resources involved in youth services may cooperate in arranging for supervision.

There are times when adults may need a time-out. Dreikurs et al. (1971) have suggested that parents who find themselves as referees in children's conflicts with others take a time-out in the bathroom. It is their contention that, though children try to involve adults in their conflicts to get attention, unless there is danger of physical harm or property destruction, children will learn to settle their differences (and learn the consequences) more effectively without relying on adults.

Isolation techniques are designed to teach children the logical consequences of their behavior. Acceptable and unacceptable behaviors should be clearly defined for children. Adults are encouraged not to nag, lecture, or scold when using the procedures. Isolation techniques should be viewed not as a punishment but as a positive method of discipline.

Contracting

Contracting is a consulting, counseling, or teaching technique in which the adult(s) and child draw up a written agreement defining appropriate and/or inappropriate behaviors. The aim is to help children commit themselves to new behaviors or to help students improve their academic performance. Contracts may be one-sentence agreements such as, "Sally will speak to one new friend by Saturday"; or they may be quite detailed, defining unacceptable behavior and its consequences, and acceptable behaviors with specified rewards for accomplishing this behavior. Learning contracts also range from a one-sentence written promise—for example, to work three math problems—to very detailed contracts with points and grades for specific school work. Learning and behavior contracts may be drawn up separately, or the expected learning and behaviors can be included in one contract. All parties of the contract should be involved in discussing the terms of the contract, and all parties should sign the contract. Each party will want to keep a copy as a written reminder of the agreement.

Learning contracts may be used for students who want to complete an independent project or other study. The teacher and student can discuss the proposed work and write out a contract describing the project, how it will be completed and evaluated, and the points to be earned. For students who seem to have lost all motivation and become totally discouraged with learning, Thompson and Poppen (1972) suggest a D– contract. The teacher will give the student a grade of D– for mastering a series of basic skills. This contract could become a life-line for failing students. Below are some examples of different types of contracts.

Behavior Contract

When Jenny disrupts group activities by pinching or hitting other group members, Mr. Sawyer will point to the quiet corner. Jenny will take her book and herself to the quiet corner for a minimum time of 10 minutes. After that time, Jenny is free to return to group activities when she feels she can participate fully without disrupting others. Mr. Sawyer agrees not to nag, scold, or lecture Jenny about pinching and hitting.

_____

Jenny's signature

_____

Mr. Sawyer's signature

Behavior and Learning Contract

Behaviors	*Points*
1. Attending class	4
2. Bringing books, paper, and pencil	2
3. Giving correct answer	2
4. Working during assigned times	5
5. Worksheets completed (6)	10 each
6. Unit tests (2)	50 each
7. Extra credit: projects, reports	10

Grades   (to be assigned at the end of a four-week period based on accumulated points as follows):

167–185	A
148–166	B
130–147	C
111–129	D
0–110	F

*Free-time privileges**
90 points = 30 minutes free time

Alternative activities for free time
1. Reading books or magazines
2. Games in learning center
3. Going to the library

Student _____

Teacher _____

*Adults will want to ascertain what rewards are reinforcing to students.

Counselors might also want to teach parents to set up contracts for children in the home. Following is an example of how a parent/child contract might look.

Parent and Children Contract

	Points	M	T	W	T	F	S	S
1. Writes down school assignments	2							
2. Completes homework before 6:00 p.m.	3							
3. Receives an "A" paper	5							
4. Receives a "B" paper	3							
5. Picks up room and makes bed	3							
6. Gets bath and to bed by 9:00 p.m.	3							
7. Does weekly assigned household chores	5							

Extra points may be earned by:
1. Running errands   3
2. Doing extra chores   3–5

Points earned can be cashed in for:
1. 10 points: Stay up hour later
2. 20 points: Special treat with friend
3. 20 points: Movie treat
4. 50 points: $2.00 spending money
5. Other rewards are negotiable.

Adults will want to consider carefully the terms and rewards included in a contract with a child. Activities and rewards should be realistic and reasonable.

Reinforcement

The principles of behavior modification state that behavior followed by positive reinforcement will increase in frequency, and behavior followed by negative reinforcement will decrease in frequency. However, adults need to be aware that not everything they view as positive will be rewarding to all children. Candy may be a reward for one child, while another child may have access to a great amount of candy and not find it reinforcing. Most adults view being scolded or nagged as negative; for children who get little attention, scolding and nagging could be positive. Some behaviors can be extinguished by ignoring them.

Adults will want to talk with children and observe their behavior before suggesting rewards and using reinforcers.

Adults can reinforce negative behaviors or fail to reinforce positive behaviors without being aware of what they are doing. Observation of children's environments and interactions may help counselors to understand what is reinforcing to children and why certain behaviors are difficult to change. New reinforcements can be arranged when all the contingencies are recognized. Keat (1979) suggests using a reinforcement survey with children. Such a survey contains reinforcers in the areas of foods, beverages, dancing, music, reading, school activities, socializing, animals, games, play, material objects, television, movies, quiet time, allowance, praise, shopping, sports. Children are asked to respond to their favorites. Appropriate reinforcers for individual children can be selected from the list of activities and objects they have indicated are rewarding to them.

Reinforcers are more effective if they are administered immediately. For children trying new behaviors, a pat on the shoulder, verbal encouragement, or praise may be all that is necessary to reinforce the behavior. Other children, especially younger or less mature children, may need a tangible reinforcer immediately (token, candy, food). A card system may also be used to provide immediate reinforcement. Desired behaviors are listed on the card, and the adult can check the area of acceptable behavior on the card immediately when it is exhibited. In order to be highly effective, checks should be paired with verbal praise or encouragement for the acceptable behavior. A tangible reward can be collected later for the checks on the card.

Reinforcers should be varied so that they do not lose effectiveness. Similarly, the adult will want to consistently reinforce new behaviors during the initial learning period and then vary the time intervals between reinforcers or the number of times the behavior must occur before a reinforcer is given in order to maintain the behavior.

REFERENCES

Dreikurs, R., Grunwald, B., and Pepper, F. *Maintaining sanity in the classroom.* New York: Harper & Row, 1971.

Kahnweiler, W. M. The school counselor as consultant: A historical review. *Personnel and Guidance Journal,* 1979, 57, 374–379.

Keat, D. *Multimodal therapy with children.* New York: Pergamon Press, 1979.

Lazarus, A. A. *Relaxation exercises.* Chicago: Instructional Dynamics, 1971.

McKinney, F. Explorations in bibliotherapy. *Personnel and Guidance Journal,* 1977, 55, 550–552.

Ohlsen, M. *Group counseling* (2nd ed.). New York: Holt, Rinehart and Winston, 1977.

Poppen, W., and Thompson, C. *School counseling, theories and concepts.* Lincoln, Nebr.: Professional Educators Pub., 1975.

Thompson, C., and Poppen, W. *For those who care: Ways for relating to youth.* Columbus, Ohio: Charles E. Merrill, 1972.

Thompson, C., and Poppen, W. *Guidance activities for counselors and teachers.* Monterey, Calif.: Brooks/Cole, 1979.

Tolbert, E. L. *An introduction to guidance.* Boston: Little, Brown, 1978.

Watson, J. J. Bibliotherapy for abused children. *School Counselor*, 1980, *27*, 204–208.

Wolpe, J., and Lazarus, A. *Behavior therapy techniques.* New York: Pergamon Press, 1966.

CHAPTER
15

GROUP COUNSELING WITH CHILDREN

Many counselors suggest that groups are a more natural setting for working with people than individual counseling. Children and adults function as members of groups in their daily activities—in the family, the classroom, the work setting, or the peer group. Therefore, according to these writers, group counseling is more reality oriented than individual counseling. Different types of groups appear to be increasing in popularity as loneliness and separation from family and friends increase in our society. At one time, group counseling was considered an effective method of counseling because the counselor could help a number of children in a more economical manner. However, a more important reason is that children can unlearn inappropriate behaviors and learn new ways of relating more easily through the interaction and feedback in a safe, practice situation with their peers.

GROUP COUNSELING DEFINED

Dyer and Vriend (1980) have operationally defined group counseling as a model that includes the following elements.

1. Children identify thoughts or behaviors that are self-defeating and set goals for themselves with the help of the counselor-facilitator and other group members.
2. The counselor and the group assist children in setting specific and attainable goals.
3. Children try new behaviors in the safe atmosphere of the group

and make commitments to try the new behaviors in the real world.

4. Children report the results of the homework assignments during the next sessions and decide to continue the new ways of thinking and behaving or to reject them for further exploration of alternatives.

The model of group counseling as defined by Dyer and Vriend is similar to the process of individual counseling presented in this book.

In his description of group counseling as a helping process, Ohlsen (1977) points out that in groups children learn to help other people and to accept their help and learn to talk openly about themselves and give up facades. Groups encourage members to take risks and to accept responsibility for their growth and the growth of others. Ohlsen's definition of group counseling closely follows the Dyer and Vriend model. Ohlsen, too, views group counseling as providing a safe atmosphere for children to discuss their concerns, to define goals, and to try new behaviors.

As with individual counseling, many writers have attempted to differentiate group counseling from group psychotherapy. Group counseling is focused on the developmental or situational stresses of normal children, whereas group psychotherapy focuses on more severe behavioral or personality disturbances. Gazda (1973) views group procedures as falling on a continuum. At one end are the preventive group processes, such as group guidance, human relations training, and human development education; at the other end are remedial group processes, such as group psychotherapy. Group counseling is defined as developmental and preventive.

Preventive activities may be used with large groups to provide relevant cognitive understandings or accurate information about self and others. When children experience difficulty with developmental tasks, group counseling would be the appropriate preventive-remedial intervention. Gazda would refer children who are emotionally disturbed or who are experiencing severe behavioral problems for group psychotherapy—the remedial end of his continuum. Gazda's emphasis on recognizing the developmental tasks of children at various ages and implementing preventive counseling to help them cope with these tasks would seem to be of utmost importance to counselors working with children. With more importance placed on preventive or developmental counseling, there is likely to be less need for remedial counseling.

TYPES OF GROUP COUNSELING

The number of group counseling methods is equivalent to the number of counseling theories. Any particular approach or orientation to counseling can be adapted to a group counseling setting. We ask that our readers keep this fact in mind as they read about the different counseling approaches presented in this book. However, we will mention four basic categories of groups that are open to any theoretical orientation and are appropriate for children. These four are the common-problems group, the case-centered group, the human-potential group and the skill-development group.

1. *The common-problems group* consists of children working on the same difficulty—for example, weight problems, low school achievement, or family divorce problems.

2. *The case-centered group* consists of children working on different problems. Each child has the opportunity to receive the group's full attention to his or her problem. The case-centered group affords each child the opportunity to be counseled and to counsel others.

3. *The human-potential group* provides an opportunity for children to develop their positive traits and strengths. The focus is on developmental concerns rather than the remedial concerns of the common-problems and case-centered groups. The human-potential groups focus on building stronger self-concepts in children by recognizing achievements, skills, and helpful problem-solving behaviors.

4. *The skill-development group* is directed to specific behaviors and skills. For example, the children may improve their basic communication skills by practicing active listening, or they may learn how to be assertive, rather than passive, passive-aggressive, or aggressive. Giving and receiving positive feedback and studying effectively are other frequent focuses for skill-development groups. Practitioners of transactional analysis work in skill-development groups as they help children to understand the nature of their communication styles.

The counseling skills and techniques discussed in Chapter 2 also apply to the group counseling setting. However, the group counselor has the additional tasks of directing communication traffic, facilitating the group process, blocking harmful group behaviors, linking ideas, taking a consensus, moderating discussions, and supporting the children who need encouragement and reinforcement. According to Trotzer (1977), the leadership function of the group counselor includes the promotion, facilitation, initiation, and guidance of interaction among group members. He also discusses the group counselor's responsibility for intervening when an individual's rights to privacy and to be heard are endangered. Other interventions include helping the group to become unblocked and getting on track when things become bogged down. The counselor may have to intervene when hostility is misdirected and when individuals are forced to accept group decisions without sufficient consideration given to reaching a group consensus.

FORMING A GROUP

Information for potential group members

Because of reports of people being verbally attacked and hurt in groups using extreme methods, parents or children may have reservations about participating in a group. It is helpful for counselors to explain fully the purpose of the group and the experiences planned in order to allay fears and clarify possible misconceptions. By providing this information to children before starting the group, the counselor can inform the children of their roles and what is expected of them and explain the role and expectations of the counselor as well. Explaining the process will provide the structure needed to facilitate the interaction once the group is begun. Following is an example of an informative statement.

> We are forming a group made up of young people about your age in order to talk about things that bother or upset us. Many of us have similar concerns, and it is often helpful to share these worries and help each other try to find ways of solving them. Each member will be expected to talk about what bothers him or her and try to figure out what can be done about the situation. In addition, members will be expected to listen carefully to each other and try to understand the other members' worries and help them solve their problems. The counselor, too, tries to understand what all the members are saying or feeling, to help them explain and clarify their thoughts and feelings, and to find solutions to their concerns.
>
> Most group members learn that they can trust the others in the group and feel free to discuss things that worry them. Members are free to talk about anything or anyone that bothers or upsets them. However, the group will not be a gripe session, a gossip session, or a chatting session. We will be working together to find solutions to what is upsetting you. There may be very personal information or feelings that you would prefer not to discuss in the group. You should not feel pressured to disclose these feelings or thoughts to the group. Whatever is said in the group cannot be discussed with anyone except the counselor. If there is anyone you would rather not have in a group with you, discuss this with the counselor.

Intake interview

Many group leaders prefer to hold an individual conference or intake interview with prospective members before forming the group. Other group leaders think that anyone should be eligible to join a group and that the intake interview is unnecessary. An intake interview does allow the leader an opportunity to talk privately with prospective members, to learn a little about them and their concerns, and to define some possible goals. It also gives the leader an opportunity to determine if the child will benefit from a group experience or if individual counseling would be more helpful.

Membership of the group

Some counselors, such as those following the Adlerian method, hold that anyone who wishes to participate in a group should be allowed to do so with attention being given only to similar age-related levels of interests and intellectual abilities of members. Other counselors attempt to select members of a group to provide for either heterogeneity or homogeneity. Homogeneity may be desired for common-problems groups, such as children whose parents are divorced. However, a homogeneous group of underachievers or drug users probably would be counterproductive since no peer model and peer reinforcement for improved behaviors would be present. For children with problems of acting out or withdrawal, a heterogeneous group would be more helpful in order to provide for active discussion and role models. As to whether to include boys and girls in the same group, most counselors prefer to include a balance of both sexes unless the problem discussed is such that the presence of the opposite sex would hinder discussion—sex education topics, for example. Serious consideration of possible consequences should be given before including in groups children of highly dissimilar interests and maturity levels, and children who are highly dominating, manipulative, very gifted, or mentally retarded. Children with extreme behaviors may be better candidates for individual counseling, especially during the initial stages of counseling.

The number of children selected to participate in the group will depend on age, maturity, and attention span. Young children of 5 and 6 years have a very short attention span and are unable to give much attention to the concerns of others. Counselors may want to limit the size of this age group to three or four and work with the children for only short periods of time at frequent intervals—for example, 20 minutes two to three times a week. As age and maturity levels increase, counselors will be able to work with more children for longer periods of time—for example, six children, ages 10 and 11, for 30 minutes twice a week. The maximum number of children in a group that functions effectively seems to be eight. However, the classroom meeting concept developed by Glasser (1969) has proven to be effective with an entire class of 30 students for periods of 20 to 30 minutes.

The group setting

A room away from noise and traffic is best. In addition, children should not fear being overheard if they are expected to talk openly about their concerns. Groups should be conducted with all members sitting in a circle. We always ask our groups to arrange the circle in such a way that everybody can see everybody else's face. Some counselors prefer to have the children sitting around a circular table; other counselors think that tables may serve as a barrier to interaction. Many counselors prefer to counsel groups of children while sitting in a circle on a carpeted floor. A carpeted floor provides an easy access for counselors to move the group into play therapy.

The first session

Part of the first session of counseling will be devoted to establishing ground rules and agreeing on some guidelines for the group. The frequency of the meetings, the length of each meeting, the setting, and the duration of the group should be determined, either by consensus of the group or by the leader. Members will also want to discuss confidentiality and what might be done if confidentiality is broken by a member; what to do about members who do not attend regularly; and whether or not to allow new members to join should a member drop out. These concerns can be decided during the first session or delayed and discussed if the problem occurs.

The group leader will want to remind members that they are expected to listen carefully to each other, to try to understand each other's feelings and thoughts, and to help one another explore possible solutions to problems. The children can be encouraged to wait until members seem to have explored and discussed their concerns thoroughly before changing the subject. The group leader can provide the role model for listening and reflecting feelings and content, and can reinforce these behaviors in group members.

By establishing ground rules and structuring the group during the initial session, the group leader defines expected behaviors. When inappropriate behaviors occur, the leader can ask the group, "What was the ground rule?" or can present the problem to the group for their discussion and resolution. Groups are formed to help the members. The leader is the facilitator but should not take over as disciplinarian and authoritarian.

Counselees may be reluctant to begin by having a person bring up concerns or worries for discussion, especially if the group members are not acquainted with one another. The leader could reflect their feeling of reluctance and, if appropriate, try an "ice-breaker" counseling technique. Leaders can ask members of the group to introduce themselves and describe themselves with three adjectives. They can be asked to introduce themselves and to complete a statement such as: "If I had my wish . . ." Members can be asked to share three wishes. They can be asked to complete the statement "I am a _____, but I would like to be a _____," with an animal, vegetable, automobile, flower, and so on. (Example: "I am a dandelion, but I'd like to be a long-stemmed rose.") These activities can be done in the entire group or in dyads; either method will ease the tension of the first session and promote interaction.

THE GROUP COUNSELING PROCESS

Just as in individual counseling, the group leaders will want to establish a therapeutic counseling atmosphere by demonstrating the facilitative skills of empathetic understanding, genuineness, and respect for the group members. Counselors can demonstrate their caring by being nonjudgmental and accepting, and by providing encouragement, support, and guidance. Counselors will want to be very adept at identifying, labeling, clarifying, and reflecting the feelings and thoughts of group members. This process becomes difficult as the group size increases. The counselor-facilitator must be concerned about and aware of the reactions of each child in the group. As the leader models facilitative behaviors, group members begin to participate in the helping process and become more effective helpers for one another.

Also as within individual counseling, the counselor-facilitator is responsible for helping children to identify and define their problems and the accompanying feelings and thoughts. The process of defining what is happening in the child's life plus looking at alternatives for solving the conflict is enhanced in the group setting because of the other group members. Ideally, the child will have a number of counselors to listen, understand, and help search for solutions; and the acceptance, encouragement, support, and feedback of a number of helpers. The counselor must be skilled in facilitating these interactions and also must possess information about group dynamics and the counseling skills to intervene and facilitate progress through the various steps of the counseling process.

As with individual counseling, it can be very helpful to the counselor and to group members to audio or videotape the session. Such tapes provide the counselor with an opportunity to observe nearly all the dynamics of the group, they provide a record of what occurred in the session, and they allow the opportunity for counselors to evaluate their leadership skills.

The process and techniques used in individual counseling (role playing, role rehearsal, play therapy, homework assignments, contracting, and so on) are just as appropriate for use in group counseling. In fact, individual counseling is often done in groups. An example follows:

Karen, Susan, Peggy, Mark, Ken, and Mike are 11-year-olds participating in a counseling group. This is their fourth session with the counselor.

Counselor (Co): Last time we met together, Susan told us about the misunderstanding she was having with her neighbor, Mrs. Jackson. As I remember, Susan, you were going to offer to use your allowance to replace the storm window you broke playing baseball or offer to babysit free of charge for her until the bill was paid. Can you bring us up to date on what's happened?

Susan: Well, she decided she would rather have me babysit for her to pay for the window. I babysat one hour last week. We are keeping a list of the times I sit and how much will go toward the cost of the window.

Co: It sounds like you and Mrs. Jackson have worked things out to the satisfaction of both of you.

Susan: Yeah, she really liked the idea of my babysitting to pay for the window.

Co: Good. Is there anyone else that has something they would like to discuss today?

All six children: Mr. Havens!

Co: You all sound pretty angry at Mr. Havens. Could one of you tell me what's happened?

Ken: We were all going on a trip to the ice skating rink next week. Yesterday, somebody broke some equipment that belonged to Mr. Havens. No one would tell who did it, so he is punishing us all by not letting us go ice skating.

Co: You think Mr. Havens is being unfair to punish everyone because of something one person did. You'd like to find out who broke the equipment.

Karen: That's right. We didn't break his equipment, so why should we have to miss the trip.

Co: Have you thought of anything you could do to work this out?

Mike: Yeah, break the rest of his old equipment!

Co: How would that help you get to go skating?

Mark: It wouldn't. It would just make him madder.

Peggy (timidly): We could tell him who did it.

Other five children: You know who did it? Who?

Peggy (very upset): If I tell, I'll be called a tattler, and no one will like me. Besides, I don't want to get anyone in trouble.

Co: Peggy, sounds like you are really feeling torn apart by this. You just don't know what to do. If you don't tell, the whole group will miss the skating outing. If you do tell, you'll get someone in trouble, and your friends might think you're a tattler and not want you around.

Peggy: Yeah, I don't know what to do!

Co: What do you think you could do?

Peggy: Well, I could tell who did it.

Co: What would happen if you told? (Silence) Let's help Peggy think of all the things that could happen if she told who broke Mr. Havens's equipment.

The group thinks up all the positive and negative results of Peggy's telling who broke the equipment: the group might still get to go skating; the person might beat up Peggy or try to get back at her in some other way; she might not be believed; the person could deny it and say Peggy broke the equipment; and so on.

Co: We've listed all the things that could happen if Peggy told. What will happen if Peggy does *not* reveal who broke the equipment?

Karen: We won't get to go skating, and the person will get away with it!

Other possibilities such as Mr. Havens's distrust of the whole group and the person thinking he or she "can get away with anything" are brought out and discussed.

Co: Can anyone think of any alternatives to solve this other than Peggy telling or not telling Mr. Havens?

Ken: She could write him an anonymous letter telling him who did it.

Co: What would happen if she did?

Mike: He probably wouldn't believe an anonymous letter.

Co: What do the rest of you think about that?

They all agree by shaking their heads that Mike is probably right.

Co: Is there anything else you could do to straighten this out?

Susan: Peggy could tell you (the counselor), and you could tell Mr. Havens.

Co: How will my telling Mr. Havens help you all to solve your problem?

Mark: Mr. Havens will believe you, and we'd get to go skating!

Co: I would have to tell Mr. Havens how I knew and give him some details to assure him that I was right. I really think this is the group's problem. What can you do to work it out?

Karen: Seems like it's up to Peggy, then.

Co: You all think it's up to Peggy to decide whether or not to tell.

The group agrees it is Peggy's decision.

Co: Peggy, we have looked at the consequences of your telling on the other person and not telling, and tried to think of other alternatives. Have you made any decision about what to do?

Peggy: No, I still don't know.

Co: So far, it seems that we have come up with two possible alternatives—to tell on the person or not to tell. I wonder if there are any other alternatives you can think of that might help Peggy. (Silence) Well, our time is about up for today, but this is really important. Let's meet together tomorrow and try to help Peggy come to some decision at that time. Peggy, I wonder if you would go over the list of alternatives and think about them before tomorrow. (Peggy agrees.) How would the rest of you feel about trying to put yourself in Peggy's place and think of what you would do if you knew who broke Mr. Havens's equipment. Also, you might think about how you would feel if you were the person who broke the equipment. What would you want Peggy to do?

The group agrees and adjourns.

The counselor has checked on the results of the last homework assignment for the group, listened, and reflected the group's anger and feelings that Mr. Havens is unfair. The counselor has then helped them to clarify and define the problem, and looked at possible alternatives and the consequences of these alternatives. No decision was reached, but the group agreed to a homework assignment of thinking further about the problem. Possibly the next session will bring new ideas and a resolution.

TERMINATION

Some group leaders prefer to set a specified number of group sessions and terminate the group at the end of this number; other leaders suggest that groups terminate when the members' goals have been achieved. Those counselors focusing primarily on meeting the developmental needs of youths would contend that group counseling should be an ongoing process. Before termination, the children should be helped to recognize the goals they have met or to explore other resources for meeting the goals not achieved. Group members should not be left feeling discouraged, that they have not been helped, and that they cannot be helped. Members may need to be referred for individual counseling or to other sources for further assistance.

GROUP GUIDANCE

Gazda (1973) has emphasized the preventive orientation of groups, suggesting that information giving and human development education be utilized through group processes. Through group guidance procedures, counselors can help children become more involved in school and with classmates, understand themselves and their feelings, learn to share ideas and feelings, and develop decision-making and problem-solving skills. The development of such skills will promote self-confidence in the child and build competencies for more effective functioning in daily living.

Group guidance units can present information about study skills, making friends, drugs, or any other area about which children need data to grow and develop in a healthy manner. Guidance activities designed to help children with self-concept development, peer relationships, improved adult/youth relationships, academic achievement, and career development may be found in *Guidance Activities for Counselors and Teachers* by Thompson and Poppen (1979).

Glasser (1969) contends that children's needs for love and self-worth are not being met in our society and suggests the need for classroom meetings and discussions in the schools to help meet these needs. Glasser has suggested three types of classroom meetings: the open-ended meeting, the problem-solving meeting, and the educational-diagnostic meeting. He advocates that counselors or teachers use all three types of meetings to help children feel loved and worthwhile.

Open-ended meetings are for discussing anything that is relevant to the children's lives in order to stimulate understanding and thinking. Discussion can include topics like "What is a friend?" "What would you do if all schools closed tomorrow and you never had to go again?" "What would you do if you inherited a million dollars today?" Open-ended meetings can discuss situations involving moral decisions and values — "What would you do if you saw your best friend cheating on a test?"— or social issues such as prejudice. The leader's job is to remain non-judgmental and to direct the discussion to stimulate thinking, help the children set goals, look at consequences, and make plans. The leader uses lots of "what," "where," "when," "who," and "how" questions and encourages members to think of what they would do in the situation under discussion. All the children's opinions are encouraged. The leader's opinions, judgments, and criticisms are *not* encouraged.

A behavior problem-solving meeting can be used to encourage the group to help one of its members solve a behavior problem or a group problem. The leader-counselor can present the problem and ask the group to think of ways to handle the conflict. Children often can decide on better methods for handling conflicts than adults can. Again, it is the leader's responsibility to facilitate an understanding and clarification of the problem, stimulate the children to think of alternative solutions and their consequences, and encourage commitment to a plan of action. Glasser cautions teachers and counselors not to use the behavior problem-solving meeting too frequently because the attention the child receives from being the focus of the discussion could reinforce the unwanted behavior.

Educational-diagnostic meetings are a method for teachers to quickly evaluate a unit of learning to determine if the children have understood what has been taught and the relevance of the material for their lives. Glasser criticizes schools for emphasizing memorization of facts rather than understanding and relevance. Educational-diagnostic meetings allow the teacher to assess how well the concepts of a unit are understood before and after the unit is taught. For example, before beginning a unit of study on photosynthesis, the teacher would ask how many of the children could define photosynthesis and could give examples of how it works. Following the unit, a second meeting could be held to see what the children now understand about photosynthesis.

Poppen (see Thompson & Poppen, 1979) has suggested that groups with children work well with structured activities, providing the activities are presented in a developmental fashion that allows children to move from easy to more difficult tasks. He proposes seven levels of group meetings:

1. *Involvement meetings.* These meetings are designed to help children participate freely in the group and to build a sense of belonging to the group. Children can, for example, construct name tags

that describe some of their favorite things and share these name tags with the group.

2. *Rules meetings.* These meetings are used to discuss what ground rules the group needs. The meaning of rules and why these are necessary or not necessary may also be discussed.

3. *Thinking meetings.* These group sessions are directed toward helping children to develop their cognitive skills. "What if" topics are often used. An example would be asking children to discuss the question, "What if you had one pill that would allow you to live for 200 years? Would you take the pill? Why? Why not? What information would you need before making your decision?" Educational-diagnostic meetings would be included on this level.

4. *Values-clarification meetings.* These meetings are designed to help children examine and understand their system of values, not to destroy or build new value systems. Children may be asked to write a newspaper ad for themselves describing the kind of people they are or to vote on how they like school and discuss why they answered the way they did.

5. *Hypothetical problem-solving meetings.* These meetings are designed to give children some group experience in solving practice problems. The primary aim in teaching group problem solving is to help children learn how to generate alternative solutions to problems. Too often children tend to cling to one problem-solving idea even if it is not working. A sample activity at this level is to ask three children to simultaneously play the role of a child in their age group who is having problems with her parents. Six other students could play the child's father and mother while the family tries to work out their difficulties. The rest of the children in the group evaluate the interaction and make suggestions on how to play their roles better.

6. *Actual problem solving.* When children are ready for this sixth level of group interaction, the counselor lets the children work with actual problems. Perhaps one child has a real family or school-related problem for the group's consideration.

7. *Group council.* The highest level for children to attain in this seven-stage sequence is the group council procedure recommended by Adlerian psychologists. The group is essentially governed on a democratic basis by a rotating, three-member council that represents the entire group. This type of group uses all of the skills developed in the preceding six levels of group interaction. All group problems from discipline to next week's picnic are brought before the council for discussion. We need to add that the counselor does retain veto power for solutions that might endanger self or others.

In conclusion, group counseling can be a highly effective method for changing children's lives or, better still, for helping to prevent excess stress and conflict in their lives. It is rewarding for children to find their place in a group and to help one another. It is rewarding to the group counselor to watch children grow and develop into caring, functioning group members.

REFERENCES

Dyer, W., and Vriend, J. *Group counseling for personal mastery.* New York: Sovereign Books, 1980.

Gazda, G. M. Group procedures with children: A developmental approach. In M. M. Ohlsen (Ed.), *Counseling children in groups: A forum.* New York: Holt, Rinehart and Winston, 1973.

Glasser, W. *Schools without failure.* New York: Harper & Row, 1969.

Ohlsen, M. M. *Group counseling* (2nd ed.). New York: Holt, Rinehart and Winston, 1977.

Thompson, C., and Poppen, W. *Guidance activities for counselors and teachers.* Monterey, Calif.: Brooks/Cole, 1979.

Trotzer, J. *The counselor and the group: Integrating theory, training, and practice.* Monterey, Calif.: Brooks/Cole, 1977.

16

CHILDREN'S CONFLICTS WITH OTHERS: ALTERNATIVES FOR INTERVENTION

The suggestions in this chapter are techniques collected from a variety of resources on counseling children with learning and social problems. Some suggestions are to be used in working directly with the child; others are consultation techniques for parents and teachers. In each case, it is essential that the procedures be incorporated into a therapeutic counseling or consulting atmosphere that includes caring, respect, empathetic understanding, acceptance, and so on. The techniques presented can be preventive and developmental as well as remedial; it is nearly impossible to say that any given technique has one application to the exclusion of the others. In any case, the techniques should be adapted to meet the unique needs of children and their behaviors.

FIGHTING

Fighting is one of the most common behavioral problems of children today. Many children have not learned to settle their misunderstandings other than by physical means. Fighting may be a way of gaining attention; a learned behavior from parents, peers, or other significant people in the children's lives; or a way of striking back at a world perceived as cruel and hostile. Resolution of disagreements and conflicts by means other than fighting is a viable goal of school personnel and parents;

however, fighting will occur despite the best efforts of adults. Following are various suggestions for working with fighting behavior. (See also Destructiveness.)

1. Examine the situation that brought on the encounter. Determine the sequence of events and if there is a particular time, place, or situation in which fights are likely to occur. Become an environmental engineer; rearrange the time schedule or the physical environment. Intervene in the sequence of events to prevent or circumvent fight-arousing conditions.

2. Fighting can be a compensation for feelings of inadequacy, ignorance of social skills, learned behavior from the home, or a means of covering up emotional or learning problems. Investigate these possibilities by becoming a "child watcher" and listening actively to the child (see Chapter 4).

3. Use group or family discussions to focus on how fighting helps or hurts the fighter, how others feel about fighting, the consequences of fighting, and ways in which the fighter could solve conflicts more effectively. Children should also be encouraged to practice new behaviors before the group and use their feedback to improve relationships.

4. Determine the goal of the fighter (see Goals of Misbehavior, Chapter 7). Is the child seeking attention, power, revenge, or free time? Is the fighting a learned behavior? Could the fighting be due to a lack of social skills?

5. Contract with the fighter to not fight for a short period of time (two hours, four hours, one day). Continue to renegotiate the contract until the behavior decreases significantly. Rewards for not fighting and consequences for fighting behavior may be included (see Chapter 14).

6. Allow two evenly matched students to fight it out under supervision with pillows, styrofoam bats, or socker-boppers. In an extreme case cited by Stradley and Aspinall (1975), a school administrator set aside one night a month for chronic fighters to meet, with parents required to be present.

7. Arrange with the physical education teacher for students to work out their emotions with punching bags or other equipment, under supervision. Each time students are found fighting, encourage them to go to the gym and work out for a certain period of time (for example, 15 minutes). After a cooling-off period, the fighters are required to write a plan for avoiding future fighting. Nonwriters may dictate or tape their contracts.

8. Have the fighters write out their side of the story or tell it to a tape recorder. Ask the children to read their stories to you or listen to the tape with them. Discussion of the stories provides a release for emotion, and a stimulus for evaluating the behavior and its consequences and for planning other ways to solve such situations in the future (Collins & Collins, 1975).

9. Films, television, or stories can stimulate the children to think

more objectively about fighting and its consequences. Follow the film or story with a family or group discussion examining the causes and consequences of fighting and other ways the situation could have been solved.

10. Children and parents or teacher may cooperatively draw up a list of ground rules concerning fighting. Each time the adult notices the child about to become involved in a fight, the adult asks, "What is the ground rule?" Have the child repeat the rule. Early and consistent intervention is necessary. A variation of this technique is to clearly define the consequences of fighting, and when fighting is about to occur, ask, "What happens when someone fights?"

11. Encouragement from friends or peers (or other kinds of peer pressure) will help the child to control fighting behavior. Find the fighters a good model with whom they can work or play. Ask them to describe or list the model's behavior. Rehearse and practice liked behaviors.

12. Have the fighting children clean a window, one on each side of the window, facing one another. Encourage them to look *really mean* and glare at each other. The first child to smile loses the game of "looking mean" but wins a big hug or other reinforcement (Blanco, 1972).

13. Isolation techniques such as seat 2, the quiet corner, and time-out rooms are effective for helping children cool off. When the children feel ready to return to the family group or classroom, they are allowed to do so without lectures or blame, provided they have a plan for staying out of fights (see Isolation Techniques, Chapter 14).

14. The adult may quietly ask the fighters to leave the room and develop a plan for solving their conflict. Since they are disturbing the other activities in the room, the adult may ask them to reschedule their fight for another time and place. Usually the children react in shock and quietly join in the group or family activities.

15. Three chairs are placed in a semicircle. The adult sits between the two fighters and asks them to describe what happened. The adult repeats verbatim to Child A what Child B says, and then to B what A says. This continues until usually everyone ends up laughing. The adults limit themselves to conveying messages between A and B, refraining from making judgments or placing blame (see Chapter 5). A discussion of a plan for avoiding future conflicts may follow.

16. Dreikurs, Grunwald, and Pepper (1971) suggest that parents who have trouble with their children fighting withdraw to the bedroom or bathroom until the fighting ceases. Precautions should be taken to prevent one child from harming the other.

17. Peer pressure, especially in small groups, is often effective in helping fighting children change their behavior. Carlin and Armstrong (1968) suggest a technique for reducing aggressiveness and rewarding cooperative group play. The adult may arrange rewards to be given to the group when they are playing or working cooperatively. They should be presented the reward and told the reason for it. Fines for the mis-

behavior of a member may also be levied on the group. The amount of reward less the fines is divided among group members at the end of the day. For the child who continually misbehaves and causes the group to be fined, isolation techniques are suggested. The misbehaving child would neither receive a portion of the reward for the time spent in isolation nor be the cause of excessive fining when in isolation.

18. Have the fighting children carry index cards and keep a record of the number of fights that occur each day. Have them role play exactly what happened and the consequences. Discuss alternatives for fighting, rehearse how the situation could have been handled more appropriately, and develop a plan for not fighting in future situations.

19. Use methods for building self-esteem so that fighting will not be necessary in order for the child to feel good about self (see Poor Self-Concept, Chapter 17). Responsibility and praise for a job well done will add to a positive self-concept; for example, "I appreciate your helping put up the games we used during this activity."

20. If excessive punishment or brutality seems to be a factor, counsel with the parents to help them learn more effective ways of relating to the child. Books such as Ginott's *Between Parent and Child* (1965) or Gordon's *Parent Effectiveness Training* (1970) may be a help.

VERBAL ABUSIVENESS

Most verbal abusiveness, such as rudeness, sarcasm, impoliteness, and name calling, is a cover for feelings of inadequacy, learned behavior from adults or other models, a call for attention, or a way of striking back at an unfriendly world. In this instance, the child needs interactions with adults who are calm, rational, consistent, and who behave in a mature manner. Adults need to be on guard and not allow the child's verbal abusiveness to provoke the same behavior from them. When adults resort to criticism, belittling, and name calling, they have little chance of changing children's behaviors.

1. Determine the goal of the verbal abusiveness. Could it be that the child is seeking attention, revenge, or power (see Goals of Misbehavior, Chapter 7)? Become a "child watcher" and listen attentively to help determine these needs and goals. Once the goal has been defined, the adult can help the child find a more constructive means of meeting this need.

2. Meet privately with rude, sarcastic, impolite, or name-calling children. Interpret their behavior to them as a cry for help. Then discuss the reasons they feel it necessary to use verbal abusiveness. Plan with the children ways to avoid the behavior in the future.

3. Meet with the "victims" of the abuser. Explain to these victims that, if they do not respond to the abuse, it is not as satisfying to the abuser and the behavior will decrease (Collins & Collins, 1975). Plan and rehearse their behavior when the abuser "attacks."

4. Contract with abusing children to reduce verbal abrasiveness. Clearly define unacceptable behaviors and their consequences. Rewards may also be included in the contract for appropriate responses (see Contracting, Chapter 14).

5. Provide opportunities for success. Praise and reinforce nonabusive behavior. Example: "I noticed how understanding you were when Tom had his accident today. That was a nice thing to say to him."

6. Role play or use films, filmstrips, or books to demonstrate and provide stimuli for group or family discussions. Examine what has occurred and the consequences. Discuss new and better methods of interacting. Behavior rehearsal may help the children practice the new behaviors.

7. Call together the parties engaged in the verbal battle and have them write out or tell their story to a tape recorder. Read the story aloud with them or play the tape and allow the children to discuss and evaluate what has happened. Ask them to make a plan for avoiding future verbal battles.

8. Encourage the teacher, parents, or other children to learn to ignore the verbal abuser. If the behavior becomes so unacceptable that it cannot be ignored, use isolation techniques such as seat 2, quiet corner, or the time-out room (see Isolation Techniques, Chapter 14).

9. Use role reversal. Have someone else play the verbal abuser and the abuser play the receiver of the verbal attack. Discuss how it feels to be in each position. Plan for better ways of handling conflicts. Role play the alternatives and consequences that will accompany the new behaviors.

10. Use techniques for building self-esteem so that the child will not have to resort to verbal abuse (see Poor Self-Concept, Chapter 17). Avoid criticism, name calling, and belittling remarks. Praise and reinforce cooperative behavior.

11. Give reprimands in a quiet, firm, and calm manner. Do not attack the child as a person. Focus on the behavior and admit how the behavior makes you feel; for example, "I get really angry when I hear students talking like that, and I would like you to stop now!" Avoid modeling the behaviors for which the reprimand is given.

12. Pair the children with good role models for work and other activities. Discuss with the children the behaviors they see in the models and the positive and negative consequences of these behaviors. Encourage the child to rehearse and practice these behaviors.

13. Try the "satiation principle" (Krumboltz & Krumboltz, 1972). Every time children use abusive language have them go into a room alone and practice being abusive. Ask them to talk to a tape recorder in an abusive manner for a period of time (for example, five minutes). Children soon tire of this procedure and begin to speak more carefully.

14. Put up a "graffiti sheet" in the child's room or private area for writing out feelings. Emphasize to the child that, if vulgar or derogatory

language is to be used, it must be used in private (Stradley & Aspinall, 1975).

15. Every time a child is verbally abusive, quietly place a check on a chart or card. Contract with the child so that, if a certain number of points are accumulated, privileges will be lost or other consequences previously agreed on will be imposed. If the points are less than the agreed number, the child is rewarded with special privileges chosen by the child. Avoid lecturing, reminding, scolding, or nagging when recording points; this is attention and thus reinforcing to the child.

PHYSICAL ABUSIVENESS

Physical abusiveness or bullying can be a compensation for poor self-concept. Children often hide fears and feelings of inadequacy with a bully act. Verville (1968) suggests that bullies generally feel inferior. Children may also be responding to or modeling adult behavior they have observed. Bullying may be an attempt to strike back at an unfriendly world or seek power and attention the child cannot gain otherwise. Bullying children need calm and consistent adult/child interactions. However, since bullying behavior usually provokes anger in the adult, the children may only receive criticism and punishment—increasing feelings of worthlessness and hostility.

1. Give reprimands in a quiet, adult manner without devaluing the child as a person. Focus the reprimand on the behavior. Instead of calling the child a name like *bully*, admit your feelings to the child: "I get angry when I see you hit the other children like that, and I would like you to stop."

2. Sociograms are helpful in learning who the bully likes or dislikes. Activities may be grouped with liked children and appropriate role models. Discuss with the children the behaviors they see in the model and the positive and negative consequences of these behaviors. Encourage the child to rehearse and practice these behaviors.

3. Have a family or group discussion. Present a hypothetical but similar example to the group. Films, filmstrips, or stories may be used to stimulate discussion. Guide the discussion to explore why children bully, how bullies feel about themselves, how other children feel about bullies, and more appropriate behaviors. Role play and rehearse the new behaviors. Utilize feedback and group encouragement to promote a change in behavior.

4. Praise and reinforce incidents of friendly and cooperative behavior. For example, if the child is helpful to another, verbally or physically, during play activities or during any social interaction, comment on the appropriate behavior. Catching children in good behavior is an effective intervention for most behavior problems.

5. Contract with the child to reduce specific acts of bullying. Clearly define unacceptable behaviors. Rewards for success may be included in

the contract as well as negative consequences such as isolation for breaking the terms of the contract (see Contracting and Isolation Techniques,
Chapter 14).

6. Provide outlets for the child's emotions in supervised activities
such as running, hammering, writing out feelings, blackboard and other
drawing, games, or talking out feelings.

7. Encourage responsibility by giving children responsible jobs at
which they can feel successful—for example, delivering materials or
messages, watering plants, feeding the fish. Avoid drudgery job assignments.

8. Encourage cooperation by finding an interest or ability in the
bully. Have the child pursue this interest or ability by helping others
or sharing it with others (for instance, sharing a stamp or rock collection,
building a science project).

9. Observe the child's environment to determine situations that
provoke bullying behavior. Try to engineer the child's activities to
reduce opportunities for bullying. Rearrange time schedules or the physical environment if possible. Intervene before the opportunity for bullying occurs.

10. Determine the goal of the bullying behavior. Could the child be
attempting to gain attention, power, or revenge, or to strike back at
what he or she perceives to be a hostile world (see Goals of Misbehavior,
Chapter 7)? Could the bullying be a learned behavior or the lack of
social skills?

11. Use ideas for building good self-concept (see Poor Self-Concept,
Chapter 17) so that the child will not have to resort to bullying to cover
feelings of inadequacy. Reinforce and praise cooperative behaviors.

12. Use role reversal. Have someone else play the bully and the
bully play the person being attacked. Discuss the feelings of each player.
Allow the children to suggest more appropriate methods of behaving
and to practice the new behaviors.

CRUELTY TO PEERS, ANIMALS, AND OTHERS

Cruelty to other people or animals is usually a sign of other problems. Extended counseling may be necessary to uncover the underlying
reasons for the cruelty. Children who are cruel to peers or animals may
be responding to punitive adults in their own life. Severe cases may
require intensive psychotherapy or even residential treatment. (See also
suggestions from Fighting and Destructiveness.)

1. Closely supervise the children in all activities.

2. Give the children releases for emotional tension—for example,
varying quiet with physical activities frequently. Encourage constructive physical releases such as running, playing ball, or cycling. Writing,
music, art, and talking may also be of help. Schedule times for releases
regularly during the day's activities.

3. Employ group or family discussions emphasizing cooperation with others. Discuss the feelings and events that provoked the cruel acts and plan ways for coping with these feelings.

4. Encourage cooperation, responsibility, and pursuit of interests by giving the children responsible jobs in which they can feel success— for example, delivering messages or filing materials. Caution should be taken not to place more responsibility on the child than can be tolerated. Find areas of interest and structure activities and jobs around these interests.

5. Contracting and isolation techniques may be used to control behavior to some extent (see Contracting and Isolation Techniques, Chapter 14). Clearly define and explain acceptable and unacceptable behaviors and the rewards and penalties for each.

6. Carefully structure the child's environment and the daily activities of the child so that there is little or no opportunity for unacceptable behavior. Plan each hour's activity in cooperation with the child, if possible. A daily schedule of work, play, study time, and planned leisure time can be posted in the child's room or school desk.

7. Avoid the use of physical punishment. Strong punishment produces further anger and the likelihood of aggression. It also provides a model for cruel and aggressive behavior. Limit TV viewing to nonaggressive programs. Remove as many models of aggression and cruelty as possible. Focus on and reinforce strengths and cooperative behaviors.

8. Determine the goal of the cruel behavior. Does the child see the world as cruel? Could the child be seeking revenge or power? What needs are not being met? (See also Goals of Misbehavior, Chapter 7.)

9. Diaries, play therapy, fantasy games, sentence completion, and active listening may be used as an aid to understanding cruel children. Diaries and play therapy also allow children to vent their thoughts and feelings in a nondestructive manner.

10. Interpret the child's cruel behavior as a cry for help and as an expression of loneliness and rejection. Ask the child to write out feelings of contempt and cruelty. Discuss the feelings and make a plan for more constructive ways of handling them.

11. Ask the cruel child to find an admired model and keep a list of the behaviors of the model for a short period of time. Discuss the behaviors with the child, rehearse new behaviors, and encourage the child to try out new ways of behaving.

12. With the child, draw up a behavioral contract, setting out rewards for appropriate behaviors and the consequences of cruel behavior. Clearly define acceptable and unacceptable behaviors (see Contracting, Chapter 14).

13. The child who has a tendency toward cruelty will need love, attention, acceptance, encouragement, patience, active listening, clearly defined limits, and structure in the environment (Dinkmeyer & McKay, 1973).

DESTRUCTIVENESS

Destructiveness or vandalism are problems of increasing severity in our society. (See also Fighting.) One of the counselor's first concerns is to find what is happening in the child's environment to cause such intense feelings and behavior. Is the child so angry at someone or something (school, for instance) that there is an intense need to strike out and hurt that person or place? Could the destructiveness be caused by frustration, feelings of failure, or feelings of revenge because the child feels no one cares? A second concern is gaining the child's trust in order to change this self-defeating behavior—a task that requires time and patience.

1. Determine the goal of the child's destructiveness. Could the motive be attention, feelings of rejection, anger, a need for power, or revenge (see Goals of Misbehavior, Chapter 7)?

2. Examine the situation that brought on the destructiveness or preceded the act. Is there a particular place, situation, or time in which destructiveness occurs most often? If so, become an environmental engineer, arranging the circumstances or schedule to avoid the situations.

3. Use logical consequences (see Dreikurs, Grunwald, & Pepper, 1971) as punishment or penalty for destructive behavior. Whatever the child destroys must be paid for or the cost worked off in some manner. Refrain from harsh punishments; they may reinforce the child's idea that the world is cruel and hostile and that destructiveness is the only way of getting back at this world.

4. Have the child write out a description of the destructive act and a plan for avoiding such behavior in the future. If the act occurs in school, tell the child you will place the description in his or her school file and remove it at the end of a specified length of time if the act has not been repeated. If the destructiveness occurs in the home or some other environment, arrange to file the description of the act in a safe place with the understanding that it will be removed and destroyed at the end of a specified length of time if the act has not been repeated (Collins & Collins, 1975). A reward might be arranged to accompany the removal of the description from the file.

5. Confront the child in a nonjudgmental manner by interpreting the destructive behavior as a distress signal. Offer to listen and help. An attitude of genuine caring and interest is necessary to building a helping relationship (Collins & Collins, 1975). Help the child make a plan to avoid destructive behaviors in the future.

6. Start a campaign of "Keep our school (home) clean!" Working together to build pride in personal areas is often helpful in preventing vandalism or destructiveness, especially if the children are involved and consulted during the planning and are given some responsibilities (Collins & Collins, 1975). "We" feelings build cooperativeness and responsibility.

7. Determine the child's areas of interest and involve the destructive child in working with these interests—not busy work but productive tasks. Peer teaching, peer tutoring, or sharing the interest in another way may be helpful. Guiding the child in pursuing interests and special abilities may be a productive way of diverting the child's behavior toward more constructive actions and building feelings of success.

8. To handle the negative feelings that often accompany vandalism and destructiveness, many parents or teachers have put up a large sheet of paper in the child's area or room—a "graffiti sheet." The child is allowed to write out feelings on the sheet (Stradley & Aspinall, 1975). Emphasize to the child that it is destructive to write out these feelings on other people's property.

9. Children can be encouraged to keep a diary of their feelings and thoughts or tell them to a tape recorder. Writing or talking provides a means of catharsis and gives the adult some insight into the child's world. The adult and child can then discuss these feelings and develop a plan for coping with them.

10. Play therapy with toys, play dough, music, or drawing may be used in an effort to understand the feelings underlying the child's destructiveness and as a means of catharsis (see Play Therapy, Chapter 14).

11. Hold group or family discussions focusing on the consequences of vandalism and destructiveness. Help the children look at what they are doing, the consequences, and alternative ways of behaving. Use behavior rehearsal to practice new methods of handling situations.

12. Help the destructive child find a friend and model. Encouragement and peer pressure are effective in helping vandalizing children redirect their behavior into more constructive paths. Pair destructive children with more mature role models to teach them effective ways of behaving. Discuss the behaviors of the model and allow the children to practice and rehearse these behaviors.

13. Refrain from punishing, scolding, lecturing, moralizing, preaching, or degrading destructive children. These methods reinforce the children's thinking that the world and people are cruel and uncaring.

14. Use contracting with rewards to help the child change destructive behaviors (see Contracting, Chapter 14). Be certain that the child understands the rules. Define appropriate and inappropriate behaviors clearly, with the rewards and consequences of each.

15. A resource person from a local law-enforcement agency may be asked to discuss laws and penalties for destructiveness and vandalism with the children, but scare techniques and threats should be avoided.

16. Arrange the child's schedule so that there is time during the day to work off energy. Vary the day's activities from quiet to physical. Encourage physical activities such as running, football or basketball, and bicycling, and quiet releases such as writing, music, art, or talking.

17. Work out a plan with the child and adult authority so that, when intense feelings are overwhelming, the child can signal the adult

and report to some agreed-on place to work out these feelings. For example, helping the custodians with maintenance and cleaning might aid in three ways: (1) to dissipate bad feelings, (2) to develop appreciation for the building, and (3) to create empathy for the custodian who has to take care of damage to the building.

TANTRUMS

Temper tantrums may create feelings of anger, frustration, and helplessness within the parents or other adults. Adults often feel they have lost complete control of the child and the situation when children throw temper tantrums. For some children, tantrums are a learned behavior for getting attention or for getting their way. Some children have learned to manipulate adults by throwing tantrums; some seek revenge.

1. Determine the motive for the tantrum. Is the tantrum an effort to gain attention, to cover feelings of inadequacy, to manipulate, or to embarrass or strike out at adults (see Goals of Misbehavior, Chapter 7)?

2. Children throw tantrums because it is a learned behavior that works for them. They get their way or what they want. The adult can stop the behavior by not allowing it to work. Ignore the behavior whenever possible; refuse to give in. The tantrum will become an unrewarding behavior.

3. If ignoring the tantrum becomes impossible, quietly ask the child to leave the room and write out a plan for avoiding tantrums in the future. The child should have the option of returning and behaving appropriately after a cooling-off period. It may be necessary to physically remove the child from the room. It is not as much fun for the child to put on the act if there is not an audience (see also Isolation Techniques, Chapter 14).

4. Alternative methods of venting feelings can be provided. Ask the children to keep a diary of their feelings, write them out on paper, or talk to a tape recorder. Play therapy can be utilized; fantasy games or storytelling may provide some catharsis and insight (see Play Therapy and Storytelling, Chapter 14).

5. Use active listening to help understand the child's feelings and the motives behind the tantrums (see Chapter 4).

6. The possibility of the tantrums being related to a physical problem should be investigated if the behavior continues over a period of time. Refer the child to a pediatrician for an examination.

7. Try to determine the sequence of events that brings on a tantrum or if there is a particular time, place, or situation in which tantrums are most likely to occur. Rearrange the environment or schedule to reduce the child's frustrations if possible.

8. Avoid threats, lectures, scolding, and nagging. These can be rein-

forcing because they are forms of attention. Define the behavior that is unacceptable and the consequences for such behavior (see Contracting, Chapter 14) and consistently carry out the terms of the contract.

9. Kaufman and Wagner (1972) present a "barb" technique for coping with tantrums in a male adolescent. They report a case study in which they (1) built rapport with the adolescent; (2) identified the situation(s) provoking the tantrum; (3) defined the adolescent's actual behaviors; and (4) defined the consequences of these behaviors. Role reversal was used to demonstrate his behavior to him. The counselor then gave the adolescent a cue that a put-down or insult was coming, and he was rewarded for appropriate responses to the "barb." In later sessions, barbs were given by other people and became more subtle in order to help the adolescent generalize his newly learned responses. The authors caution that the technique must be used systematically; that unplanned barbs must never be used in anger; that when the tantrum is unrelated to a barb, nothing should be mentioned concerning the technique or its rewards; and that moving too slowly or quickly through the program will hamper its effectiveness.

10. Severely disturbed children often have temper tantrums because they feel insecure. Using techniques of isolation and other forms of strictness may tend to intensify these feelings. In such cases, some tantrum-throwing children will become quiet when held affectionately and reassured.

11. Hare-Mustin (1975) found paradoxical intention a method for helping one 4-year-old boy. The child's tantrums were unpredictable and occurred anywhere. It was decided with the child that he should continue to have the tantrums, but only in a specified place. A room was selected, and each time the child began to have a tantrum he was immediately taken to this room. If he was not at home, he agreed to wait until he could return home and go to his "tantrum room." The next step was to decide on a time of day for tantrums to occur. A two-hour period was selected by the family. If the child started to have a tantrum at any other time, he was reminded to wait until the appropriate hour. The author reports a dramatic reduction and then disappearance of the problem behavior.

12. Peer pressure can be an effective tool for modifying children's behaviors. Group or family discussions of temper tantrums and their effects on others may help the tantrum-throwing child understand how others react to the behavior.

13. Have another child role play tantrum behavior. Discuss how the behavior helps or hurts the child and others and make a plan for alternative ways of behaving. Rehearse and practice the new behaviors.

14. Help the child find a mature model. Ask the child to keep a list of the liked behaviors of the model and ways the model handles frustrations. Rehearse and practice these ways of behaving.

15. Examine with children the self-messages that make them angry enough to throw tantrums and try to identify more rational and helpful self-messages (see Chapter 6).

CHRONIC COMPLAINING

Chronic complaining about feeling ill is a method of gaining attention or sympathy and of avoiding unpleasant situations. The behavior can be manifested as an exaggeration of symptoms or fantasies of diseases—"I think I have cancer." Other kinds of hypochondria are consistent headaches, stomach aches, and muscle aches.

1. Recommend to the parents and child that the complaining child be examined by a pediatrician to rule out the possibility of an actual physical illness.

2. Try to determine the motive or goal of the chronic complainer. Are the complaints a result of feelings of inadequacy, fear of failure, a need for attention or sympathy, or an attempt to avoid an unpleasant task? Help the child find ways of meeting this need in a more effective manner.

3. Enlist the cooperation of the pediatrician. Many pediatricians have required the children to come straight to their office whenever they feel a pain. Children (and parents) soon tire of repeated trips to the pediatrician.

4. Actively listen to the child's complaints (see Chapter 4). Do not overly sympathize but tell the child you will write a note or call the parents to suggest a trip to the doctor's office to check out the complaint.

5. Ask complaining children to write out their feelings or tell them to a tape recorder. A diary might be of help in determining the circumstances under which the feelings occur.

6. Excessive stress and tension can provoke chronic complaining. Check with parents, teachers, and other significant persons in the child's life. The child may be under pressure from school work, from problems within the home, or from peers.

7. Precautions should be taken to ensure that the child is not ill when complaints occur; parents and other adults can then firmly insist that the complainer attend to the task or return to class. Reassure the child that, should an illness occur, help will be provided (Blanco, 1972).

8. Chronic complaining may result from a lack of interest in the world around the child—school, friends, activities. Help these children to find an ability or activity in which they can feel successful. Encourage participation in groups, children's clubs or organizations, or neighborhood activities.

9. Enlist the aid of a "buddy" to encourage the complainer to become more involved in the world and to participate in friendships and activities.

10. Rutter (1975, pp. 238–239) suggests that "treatment consists of

dealing with the stresses which gave rise to the disorder and in helping the child find a better way of dealing with stress." Actively listen for clues to what these stresses are and plan with the child for more constructive means of coping with the tensions (relaxation techniques, physical activities, talking, writing, play therapy).

TATTLING

The tattler, like a gossiper, is attempting to gain attention and favor, usually with an adult authority figure. It is difficult to ignore tale bearers because many times they bring needed information to adults. However, the tattler is usually lonely and rejected by peers.

1. Determine the goal for tattling. Is the child attempting to gain attention or power or seek revenge (see Goals of Misbehavior, Chapter 7)? Confront the child with your hypothesis—for example, "Could it be that you are telling me this in order to get Warren in trouble?" (Dreikurs, Grunwald, & Pepper, 1971).

2. Meet privately with the tattler and interpret the behavior as a cry for help to gain acceptance and recognition in the group. Discuss the reasons the child may feel it necessary to tattle. Plan with the tattler for ways to avoid the behavior in the future and to gain attention and acceptance in other ways.

3. Help the tattler gain acceptance by capitalizing on special abilities and interests such as sports, hobbies, or special knowledge. Encourage the child to share these abilities and interests with others, or to peer teach or tutor another child.

4. The tattler may need help in learning social skills. Help the child to find a model. Have the child list the liked behaviors of the model and then rehearse and practice these new behaviors.

5. Turn your attention elsewhere when the tattler begins a tale. Say, "Rather than discussing that now, perhaps we should _____ ."

6. Use tattling as a topic for family or group discussions, guiding the group to look at motives for tattling and the reactions and feelings of others toward a tattler. Films, filmstrips, or stories may present a stimulus for these discussions. List alternatives for the tattling, and rehearse and practice them.

7. Use storytelling, choosing a hypothetical example similar to the child's problem, to show the consequences of tattling and the reactions of others to tattling (see Chapter 14). Ask the child questions about how the tattler must be feeling and how the other child, who is being tattled on, must feel.

8. Instead of listening to the tattler, ask the child to write out a brief note for you explaining what has happened.

9. Ignore the tattling behavior but praise and reinforce appropriate behaviors. Give attention to the child for cooperativeness.

10. When ignoring tattling becomes impossible, draw up a contract

with the child with rewards for not tattling. Penalties and rewards for appropriate and inappropriate behavior may be included (see Contracting, Chapter 14).

11. Use techniques for building self-esteem (see Poor Self-Concept, Chapter 17) so, that the child will not have to resort to tattling to gain attention and acceptance.

12. Pair tattlers with good role models for work and other activities. Discuss with the tattlers the behaviors they see in the model and the positive and negative consequences of these behaviors. Encourage the child to rehearse and practice these behaviors.

13. Krumboltz and Krumboltz (1972) suggest that it is helpful to teach a child the "discrimination principle"—to help children learn to identify clues that will help them to know when to report an incident to adults (such as danger to property or possible personal harm) as opposed to reports that are considered tattling.

SWEARING

Swearing can be a need for attention, an effort to shock others or to prove to peers that the child is "big," or modeling behavior. Swearing can also be a release for pent-up aggression or tension, or an expression of rebellion.

1. Determine the motive for the behavior (see Goals of Misbehavior, Chapter 7). Is the goal a need for attention or power, an effort to cover feelings of inadequacy, or an emotional release; or is the swearing a lack of social skills?

2. Confront the child, interpreting the swearing behavior as a need to shock or gain attention—for example, "Could it be that you want to shock me by talking in that manner?" (Dreikurs, Grunwald, & Pepper, 1971). Work with the child to make a plan to avoid swearing in the future.

3. Examine the child's world. Is there a certain time of day, a particular situation, or a certain event that provokes the swearing? If so, attempt to reduce the frustrations by rescheduling or rearranging the environment.

4. Ignore the behavior if possible. When this becomes impossible, contract with the child to decrease the swearing in a systematic manner (see Contracting, Chapter 14). Build in rewards for success and consequences for unacceptable behavior. Isolation techniques may or may not be used in the contract (see Isolation Techniques, Chapter 14), depending on the severity of the problem.

5. Try a type of implosive counseling or "flooding" with the swearing child (see Chapter 9). Place the swearer in an isolated room and ask the child to swear continually for a period of time, such as five minutes.

6. Small children may not be aware of the meaning of the words they use. Ask the child to define the word. Remind swearers that there

are certain words that are acceptable in certain places and at particular times and others that are not appropriate.

7. Work with the swearer to draw up a list of acceptable words to express feelings. Write out a contract with the child that, when frustrated, the child will say _____ instead of the usual swear words. The swearer might carry the list on an index card for easy reference.

8. Dreikurs, Grunwald, and Pepper (1971) suggest inviting the child to show how many bad words he knows. The authors further suggest that the counselor help swearing children to understand why they like to use these words and what they could do instead of swearing to feel important. Discuss alternative methods of expressing emotions (physical activities, art, games, music, new verbal responses). Rehearse these alternatives and contract with the child to try the new methods of responding to emotions.

9. Hold a family or group discussion focused on the motives for swearing and how others feel about the swearing person. Use role playing and role rehearsal to help children see the behavior and its effects on others. Discuss alternatives to swearing and role play these alternatives.

10. Use storytelling (see Chapter 14) with a hypothetical example similar to the child's problem. Ask the child for a reaction to the story.

11. If swearing seems to be a means for releasing tension or aggression, contract with the child to work off these emotions in more acceptable ways—running, writing, talking, physical exercises (see Chapter 14). Writing out feelings in a diary or talking into a tape recorder may also help the child to vent feelings.

12. A type of aversive conditioning may be used with a child who wants to stop swearing. For example, every time the child says a swear word, the punishment would be for the child to snap a rubber band worn on the wrist.

13. Help the child find a model. Have the swearer watch the model for several days and list the ways that the child reacts to frustrating situations. Rehearse and practice the new behaviors with the swearer.

LYING

During the period of normal development, young children often lie because of their inability to distinguish fact and fantasy or because of fear of disapproval and punishment. Habitual lying may be due to feelings of inadequacy, insecurity, and pressure from parents or other significant persons in the child's life. It could also be a learned behavior to escape responsibility or punishment.

1. Determine what needs of the child are not being met (see Goals of Misbehavior, Chapter 7). Is the child seeking attention or power? Is he or she attempting to evade reality or the consequences of misbehavior?

2. Arrange for successful experiences in learning and in daily inter-actions with peers. Use praise and other types of reinforcements for appropriate behaviors to build confidence and self-esteem. Lying may not be necessary if the child has confidence in him- or herself (see Poor Self-Concept, Chapter 17). Ignore the lying or fantasy behaviors while reinforcing positive behavior.

3. Avoid trying to trap the liar. If you have positive evidence that the child is lying, be quietly direct in your confrontation—for example, "Jeff, I know that you did not do your homework." If you do not have direct knowledge of the truth, admit to the child that you are having trouble understanding all the story and ask for more details. This response lets the child know you do not believe all that is being told and allows the child a chance to tell the truth.

4. When the child continues to tell stories that are obviously fan-tasies, the adult may confront the fantasizer in a nonjudgmental manner with statements such as, "You know, I have never seen or heard anything like that, and I'm really having trouble understanding what you are telling me. Could we begin again?" With this technique, you do not call the child a liar, but you do convey that you simply cannot accept all that is being said as the truth.

5. Note the areas in which lying seems to occur most often. Is the lying about school work, parents, money, clothes, or aggressive abilities? If the lying occurs most frequently in one area, examine the possibilities of changing the circumstances in this area to decrease the temptation or pressures to lie.

6. Talk with parents, teachers, and others close to the child. Are expectations and pressures placed on the child too great? Do parents expect perfect behavior and the highest school marks? Are teachers demanding too much work or work that is too difficult for the child? If so, counsel with these adults concerning ways of reducing pressures on the child.

7. Ignore fantasy tales that are meaningless or ask the child to write out the story and give it to you. Caution should be exercised not to ignore the child altogether. Respond to positive behaviors.

8. If the problem seems to stem from excessive pressure, decrease the push toward competition with others and emphasize competition with self: "You did six math problems yesterday. Let's see if you can do eight today."

9. Use the technique of storytelling (see Chapter 14). Choose a hypothetical example with behaviors similar to those exhibited by the lying child. Ask the child to react to the story and discuss these reactions.

10. Review the child's academic progress. Is lying a way to com-pensate for a learning difficulty or a cover for some other real or imag-ined failure?

11. Films, filmstrips, stories, and other materials may present stim-

uli for a good classroom or family discussion on lying and its consequences. Include in the discussion methods for avoiding lying and better ways of handling situations.

12. Dreikurs, Grunwald, and Pepper (1971) suggest that adults not pay attention or respond to lying behavior, fantastic stories, or something that seems exaggerated or incorrect.

13. A child feeling worthwhile, loved, and successful will not have to resort to lying (see also Poor Self-Concept, Chapter 17). Give the child responsible jobs such as carrying messages, watering plants, or feeding fish (not drudgery work) that will promote feelings of success. Use a sociogram to find admired classmates and pair the child with these children for group activities.

14. Enlist the aid of a buddy to involve the child in activities. Ask the child to keep a record of a model's behaviors to aid in learning behaviors for successful interpersonal relationships. Practice and rehearse these behaviors in a safe atmosphere. Encourage the child to try the new behavior.

15. Contract with the child not to lie. The contract should include acceptable behaviors and their rewards and clearly define unacceptable behavior and the consequences of the act (see Chapter 14).

TEASING

Teasing is a form of attention-getting behavior with several possible motives. Children may only get attention when they misbehave; they may be showing friendship for another; or they may have a hostile motivation. Teasing is sometimes the result of a lack of knowledge about how to make friends, how to be a friend, or other social skills.

1. Determine the goal of the teasing (see Chapter 7). Is the motive attention seeking, power, or revenge, or does the teasing come from lack of knowledge concerning social skills? Teasing can be a way of compensating for feelings of inadequacy or a means of covering up learning or emotional problems. Become a "child watcher," listening actively to investigate all possibilities (see Chapter 4).

2. Examine the circumstances under which the child seems to engage in teasing. What is the sequence of events? Is there a particular time, place, or situation in which teasing occurs most frequently? If so, rearrange the environment or schedule in order to reduce provoking circumstances.

3. Group or family discussions may help the child to see how teasing behavior affects others and can also produce suggestions and a plan for alternative ways of behaving. Peer pressure in group situations is an effective behavior modifier.

4. Ignore the teasing behavior as long as possible. When it is no longer possible to ignore the teasing, use an isolation technique such

as seat 2, quiet corner, or the time-out room (see Isolation Techniques, Chapter 14). The teaser should be free to return to the group when the child has worked out a plan for behaving more acceptably.

5. Cooperatively draw up a contract to decrease teasing behaviors. Clearly define unacceptable behavior and the consequences (see Chapter 14). Rewards for appropriate behaviors may be included.

6. Help the child find other ways to get the attention or acceptance desired. Encourage the child to pursue liked activities, interests, or hobbies and to share these with other children. Allow the child to peer teach or tutor another child. Assign responsible tasks to the child; avoid meaningless work or drudgery jobs.

7. Teasing is often modeling behavior. Check the child's environment to determine if the teaser is modeling an admired person. Help the child find a more appropriate model, observe the model's behaviors, and rehearse new and more acceptable ways of interacting with peers.

8. Have another child role play a teaser to allow the child to see the behavior more clearly and how others respond to teasing. Use role reversal to allow the teaser to see how teasing helps or hurts personal relationships. After the role playing, discuss the feelings of the person teasing and the person being teased.

9. Talk with the people being teased. Plan ways for these children not to reinforce the teasing behavior of the aggressor. Explain to the victim of the teaser that the behavior is not as much fun if the person being teased does not respond. Explain to them that the motivation of the teaser is to get attention even though it is negative attention. Role play situations, teaching the victims new methods of responding using techniques such as cognitive restructuring or ignoring the teasers.

10. Albert Ellis's ideas of irrational thinking may be incorporated into counseling with the person being teased (see Chapters 6 and 14 for an explanation of cognitive restructuring). Teach the victim to change internal thinking from "It is terrible to be teased" to "I don't like to be teased, but it is not the end of the world, and I can just ignore the teasing."

11. Children will have little need to tease if they feel they are a part of their environment and successful in the world. Find ways of providing successful experiences. Capitalize on the child's interests and abilities. Encourage participation in activities at school, at home, or in the community.

DISOBEDIENCE, NEGATIVISM, AND RESISTANT BEHAVIOR

Disobedience, negativism, and resistant behaviors are open displays of anger and antagonism toward authority figures. Children exhibiting these behaviors are often highly critical, easily irritated, and sometimes aggressive.

1. Determine the goals of the behavior. Actively listen to the child

to learn about the child's feelings toward self, family interactions, and the school (see Chapter 4). Children tend to strike out when their needs for love and respect are not met. Recognize the child's feelings. Admit that the child does have the power to disobey or resist (see Goals of Misbehavior, Chapter 7). Avoid threatening the child. Refuse to become involved in a conflict; tell the child you will discuss the matter at a later time (Dreikurs, Grunwald, & Pepper, 1971).

2. Dreikurs, Grunwald, and Pepper suggest that adults interpret the goal of the misbehavior to the child with "Could it be . . ." questions, but not at the time of the conflict. At a later time the adult could ask, "Could it be that you would like to show me that you are boss?" The question opens the door for a nonjudgmental discussion of the child's motive and for planning better methods for meeting these needs.

3. At a time when there is no conflict, discuss with the child the consequences of the negative behavior and plan alternative behaviors. Rehearse and practice alternative behaviors.

4. Avoid open confrontations with put-downs, threats, and name calling. Try active listening in an attempt to learn the reason for the negativism or disobedience (see Chapter 4).

5. Assess the environment in which the child is disobedient, negative, or resistant. Is the child receiving some reinforcement from peers or other significant persons? What are the circumstances provoking the behavior? Is there a time when negativism, resistance, and disobedience occur most often? Rearrangement of schedules or the environment may decrease the undesirable behavior.

6. Avoid possible conflict situations by allowing the child some choices—for example, "Do you want to complete the assignment now or after lunch?" Make a list of tasks to be done and cooperatively plan the day's schedule with the child.

7. Specify in advance consequences for disobedience, negativism, and resistant behavior. Hold a discussion with the child and draw up ground rules and the consequences for breaking the rules. Rules made in cooperation with children are carried out more readily.

8. When the child misbehaves, the inappropriate behavior should be clearly explained. Children often do not understand what they have done wrong. After defining the problem, work with the child to draw up a plan or contract to change behavior (see Contracting, Chapter 14). Rewards may be included for acceptable behavior and penalties for unacceptable behavior. Rehearse and practice new behaviors to help the child meet the terms of the contract.

9. Ignore the negativism, disobedience, and resistant behavior if possible. When ignoring the behavior becomes impossible, isolation techniques such as seat 2, quiet corner, or time-out room may be effective in changing the behavior (see Isolation Techniques, Chapter 14). Avoid physical punishment; it only provides a model of aggression for the child.

10. Disobedience, negativism, and resistant behaviors are often attempts to cover up lack of self-confidence, lack of social skills, or an inability to find success in school and other areas of life. Attempt to determine if the unacceptable behavior is compensatory behavior for a learning problem, a lack of self-esteem, or some other problem area. Look over the child's academic progress to determine if the behavior could be related to a learning problem. Carefully watch the child's interactions with others to determine if the problem is related to difficulties with social relationships. Listen for clues that may help you to understand the child's feelings about self and others (see discussion of active listening in Chapter 4).

11. Praise, telephone calls, or notes to the child's home about good behavior, and other positive reinforcers such as praise, privileges, or rewards may be effective in decreasing negative behavior.

12. Barcai and Rabkin (1972) report that they were successful in changing a 13-year-old girl's undesirable behavior by "excommunication." The girl had learned to control her family, behaving inappropriately to get their attention and manipulate their interactions. The family was instructed to define appropriate and inappropriate behavior, to totally ignore her when she behaved in an unacceptable manner, and to talk with and respond to her when she was behaving in an appropriate manner.

13. Suggest that parents or teachers leave the room for a few moments in order to remove themselves from the conflict. This arouses surprise and curiosity in the child about what the adult will do. The action also prevents the adult from entering into a conflict with the child (Dreikurs, Grunwald, & Pepper, 1971).

14. Encourage the child to use constructive methods for releasing negative feelings. Suggest techniques such as talking out or writing out feelings, drawing, music, or physical exercises. Arrange for periodic emotional outlets if necessary.

15. Find the negative, resistant, or disobedient child a model or liked friend. Ask the child to watch the model, record liked behaviors of the model, and then rehearse and practice these behaviors with the child.

16. Encourage negative children to pursue interests, hobbies, and abilities and to become involved in activities, clubs, or other organizations in which they can feel successful. Enlist the aid of a friend or buddy to involve the child in activities.

STEALING

Children may steal because of the high value society places on material wealth, because of ignorance of ownership rights, to impress others, or for the adventure of getting away with something. Although many children try stealing once or twice during their developmental years, persistent and repeated acts of stealing are indicative of other problems and require an understanding of the motives and needs behind the behavior.

1. Determine the motivation or goal of the behavior (see Goals of Misbehavior, Chapter 7). Is the behavior a need for attention, power, or revenge; or the result of a dare, an initiation, or peer pressure? Is this the first incidence of stealing, or is there a pattern of behavior? Actively listen to the child to try to understand the motive (see Chapter 4).

2. Temptation in all situations can be kept to a minimum to help the child control stealing. Adults can place too much temptation before even the most honest children.

3. Use logical consequences to cope with the stealing child. Have the child replace or make payment for stolen property through work if possible.

4. Give the child an opportunity to return the stolen property anonymously to an unpoliced area at a certain time without accusing anyone.

5. Have group or family discussions about stealing, its consequences, and the rights of ownership. Films, filmstrips, books, and newspapers can provide a stimulus for such a discussion. Discuss alternatives to stealing; plan and rehearse appropriate ways of handling situations that might be tempting to the child.

6. Make certain that children are aware of ownership rights. Comments such as, "This is school property, but it is our responsibility" remind the child of ownership rights.

7. If stealing occurs in a group, often the children can solve the problem themselves if allowed to do so. Present the situation to the group, ask them to draw up a plan for resolving the problem, and leave the room for a few moments. Upon returning, ask for a discussion of the plan, avoiding accusations and blame.

8. Avoid trying to trap the thief or making threats that cannot be carried out such as, "We are all going to stay here until the property is returned." Such threats inevitably end up with the adult having to withdraw the command.

9. If you have positive evidence that the child is stealing, be quietly direct in your confrontation and ask the child for a plan to pay for the stolen item and for avoiding stealing in the future.

10. Use behavior rehearsal to practice situations in which the child could be tempted to steal. Include incidences where peer pressure might occur. Discuss ways to handle these situations and practice the behaviors.

11. Adults can inform children when they are suspected of stealing. Discuss with the children the consequences should the behavior continue. Avoid scare tactics.

12. Use storytelling with a hypothetical example similar to the

child's problem (see Chapter 14). Ask the child for a reaction to the story. Discuss what might happen to the story character involved in stealing.

13. Help the stealing child find a model. Have the child watch the model for several days and list liked behaviors. Rehearse and practice these behaviors with the child.

14. Children may be stealing to feel more accepted by their peers. Most children who find some success in their lives and feel that they belong have no need to behave inappropriately. Find an interest, hobby, or ability (stamp or rock collection, knowledge of a particularly interesting area to children, sports ability) possessed by the child. Use this strength to help the child become involved in activities and find friendships.

15. If stealing is a prevalent or persistent behavior, ask a local law-enforcement person to talk with the children about the law and the consequences of stealing.

REFERENCES

Barcai, A., and Rabkin, L. Excommunication as a family therapy technique. *Archives of General Psychiatry*, 1972, 27, 804–808.

Blanco, R. *Prescription for children with learning and adjustment problems.* Springfield, Ill.: Charles C Thomas, 1972.

Carlin, A., and Armstrong, H. Rewarding social responsibility in disturbed children: A group play technique. *Psychotherapy: Theory, Research and Practice,* 1968, 5, 169–174.

Collins, M., and Collins, D. *Survival kit for teachers (and parents).* Pacific Palisades, Calif.: Goodyear, 1975.

Dinkmeyer, D., and McKay, G. *Raising a responsible child.* New York: Simon & Schuster, 1973.

Dreikurs, R., Grunwald, B., and Pepper, F. *Maintaining sanity in the classroom.* New York: Harper & Row, 1971.

Ginott, H. *Between parent and child.* New York: Macmillan, 1965.

Gordon, T. *Parent effectiveness training.* New York: Wyden, 1970.

Hare-Mustin, R. Treatment of temper tantrums by a paradoxical intention. *Family Process,* 1975, 14, 481–485.

Kaufman, L., and Wagner, B. Barb: A systematic treatment technology for temper control disorders. *Behavior Therapy,* 1972, 3, 84–90.

Krumboltz, J., and Krumboltz, H. *Changing children's behavior.* Englewood Cliffs, N.J.: Prentice-Hall, 1972.

Rutter, M. *Helping troubled children.* New York: Plenum, 1975.

Stradley, W., and Aspinall, R. *Discipline in the junior high/middle school.* New York: Center for Applied Research in Education, 1975.

Verville, E. *Behavior problems of children.* Philadelphia: W. B. Saunders, 1968.

CHAPTER
17

CHILDREN'S CONFLICTS WITH SELF: ALTERNATIVES FOR INTERVENTION

As in Chapter 16, the following techniques were derived from a variety of resources and methods for counseling with children. The reader is reminded that it is essential that the procedures be incorporated into a caring and accepting counseling or consulting atmosphere; and that the techniques should be modified to meet the individual needs of children and their particular social, learning, or behavioral problem.

SELF-DESTRUCTIVE OR SUICIDAL BEHAVIORS

Thoughts of or attempts to commit suicide often accompany a very poor self-concept and feelings of hopelessness, worthlessness, depression, or guilt. A depressed or suicidal child may be very quiet and withdrawn or highly active and agitated. Depression may be masked by overactivity, gaiety, or acting-out behavior. Feelings of depression leading to self-destructive attempts or acts frequently follow the death of loved ones, significant personal or material losses, events that profoundly affect self-esteem, or other traumatic life crises. Clues may include chronic sleeplessness, loss of appetite, withdrawal, or any extreme behavioral change.

The incidence of child suicide has increased dramatically during the past few years. No comment or sign indicating depression and thoughts of self-destruction should go unnoticed.

1. If you feel the child could be seriously contemplating suicide, suggest to the parents that they consult with a doctor or psychiatrist.

2. Never hesitate to consult with or refer suicidal children to someone thoroughly trained in suicide prevention—suicide-prevention centers, clinics, psychiatrists.

3. Refer to Poor Self-Concept later in this chapter for techniques to enhance self-concept.

4. Children with self-destructive or self-mutilating tendencies such as head banging, holding of breath, and hair pulling have responded to behavior modification techniques in which acceptable behaviors are rewarded and destructive tendencies punished by penalties such as the withdrawal of privileges or ignoring the behaviors. Children with severe tendencies usually require full-time supervision and psychotherapeutic intervention in a residential situation (Blanco, 1972).

5. Never ignore threats, hints, and continued comments about destroying oneself, "leaving this world," "you're going to miss me," and "life's not worth living." These comments may be attention-getting, but if children must use these techniques to get attention, they do need help. Follow up the "threat" immediately with active listening in an attempt to discover the feelings or events that brought on the self-destructive feelings (see Chapter 4).

6. At the time of crisis, listen to the child carefully and in a non-judgmental manner. Have the child tell you *everything* that has happened during the last few hours or days. You may gain some understanding or knowledge of factors contributing to the depression.

7. Suicidal children need the permission to call and the phone number of a person (the counselor or another close and understanding friend) they feel they can talk with in times of distress.

8. The parents of a suicidal child should be aware of the child's feelings and thoughts and helped to understand the situation without panic or guilt. Counsel with the parents about how to listen and talk with the child. Consult with them concerning danger signals and make a plan for handling crises should they arise.

9. If you suspect a child has suicidal tendencies, confront the child with your thoughts and feelings. You will not be placing the thought in the child's mind, but may provide an opening and opportunity for the child to discuss the troublesome thoughts and feelings.

10. Talk with suicidal children about what has happened in their lives recently. Losses of loved ones, pets, and other significant objects in the children's lives, feelings of personal failure, feelings of extreme shame or grief, or other traumatic events contribute to suicidal thoughts. Allow the children to express feelings without being judgmental, glossing over, or denying their right to these feelings.

11. If suicidal children admit to self-destructive thoughts, ask the children about their plan. A well-thought-out plan is a significant danger signal.

12. Ask suicidal children to tell you about their fantasies or dreams. Ask them to draw a picture or write out their thoughts. These techniques often give the adult some insight into the child's thoughts and feelings.

13. Often children do not understand death as final and irreversible; therefore, any child who is seriously disturbed or depressed needs careful attention. The months following the threat are also crucial, and careful attention should be continued until the conflict is completely resolved.

14. A sudden "recovery" after severe depression may be a warning signal. It often means a decision has been made to end one's life.

POOR SELF-CONCEPT

Unfortunately, most of children's negative feelings about themselves are formed from evaluations placed on them by adults. Adults lecture, scold, moralize, nag, belittle, label, and criticize. Sometimes children decide that they are really worthless, stupid, unlovable, and worthy of punishment because of the continued negative judgments placed on them by adults. Negative feelings about oneself can affect the child's motivation, work, interpersonal relationships, and future success. Once formed, a negative self-concept is difficult to reverse; however, these children can be helped.

1. Provide opportunities for success. Praise and reinforce the child's behavior whenever possible—for example, "You did a good job picking up the paper (straightening the books, throwing that ball, and so on)." Artificial and forced compliments are easily recognized by children and are ineffective.

2. Use strengths exercises with the children in a group situation. Give to each group member a list of the names of other group members. Each child should write a positive adjective or statement beside each name. Have each child read his or her list aloud (see Strengths Tests, Chapter 14).

3. Discuss with the children what they would like to do or accomplish. Working with the children, set up realistic goals and a step-by-step program to guide the children toward achieving their goals. Continue this guidance until the children feel they can work toward their goals alone.

4. Allow children with poor self-concepts to help someone else; arrange peer teaching or tutoring. Doing something special for someone else helps the helper feel better about him- or herself.

5. Have the adult working with the children write out a list of each child's strengths to help the adult form a more positive conception of the children. Encourage the adult to capitalize on these strengths whenever possible to promote success in each child's life.

6. Ask the children to write down ten positive things about themselves—friendly, can play ball well, can repair a bicycle, can play the

piano, and so on. Help the children find ways to use their positive attributes to increase positive feelings about themselves.

7. Supportive counseling with significant adults in the child's life will often help these adults to understand the child and the inappropriate behaviors that often result from poor self-concepts. Instruction in effective parenting may be helpful. Books such as Ginott's *Between Parent and Child* (1965) and Gordon's *Parent Effectiveness Training* (1970), discussions, role playing, and parent groups are effective for helping adults understand and relate to children.

8. Have the child list situations that he or she finds uncomfortable or difficult. Discuss ways of behaving in these situations and role play new behaviors. Encourage the child to try the new behaviors in realistic situations and report the results to you.

9. Use active listening (see Chapter 4). Teach the child problem-solving skills; being able to solve one's own problems builds confidence in self.

10. Involve the child in group activities at home and school. Encourage the child to join organizations such as the Scouts, church group, or a club in which he or she will feel accepted and achieve success. Adults should avoid encouraging participation in groups requiring skills that the child does not possess. Give responsibilities or tasks in school and in the home at which the child can feel success. Avoid drudgery jobs.

11. Use a contract with rewards for attempting new behaviors. Rehearse and practice the new behaviors in a safe atmosphere before they are tried in a real-life situation.

12. Help the child change thoughts of "I can't" to "I will try." Examine what would be the worst thing to happen if the child attempted the task (see Chapter 14 for discussion of cognitive restructuring). Encourage positive thinking.

13. Accept no excuses for poor behavior. Avoid being judgmental and criticizing. Ask the child what *can* be accomplished and negotiate a contract or a new contract if the first one was not successful (see Contracting, Chapter 14).

14. Children with poor self-concepts often benefit from assertiveness training (see Assertiveness Training, Chapter 14).

15. Use diaries, drawings, incomplete sentences, fantasy games, storytelling, and play therapy as an aid to understanding the child's feelings and thoughts (see Play Therapy and Storytelling, Chapter 14).

16. Find an appropriate model or buddy for the child. Ask the child to describe the liked behaviors of the model. Rehearse and practice these behaviors with the child.

17. Examine the family constellation (Dreikurs, Grunwald, & Pepper, 1971). Often poor self-concepts are formed when children are compared to older or younger siblings and feel that they do not measure up.

18. *Guidance Activities for Counselors and Teachers* (Thompson & Poppen, 1979) offers two chapters on group techniques for improving

self-concept, including several variations of strengths assessment. Also, *100 Ways to Enhance Self-Concept in the Classroom* (Canfield & Wells, 1976) is an excellent resource for helping counselors work with difficult children.

CHEATING

Our present school system and society strongly encourage competition and high grades, values that can contribute to cheating. Students cheat for a variety of reasons, the main one possibly being the pressure to achieve. School personnel and parents can place less emphasis on competition and more on cooperation with others and competition with self. School personnel and parents can also let students know that they expect honesty.

1. Determine the type of pressures the child may be encountering. Talk with the child and significant adults about their expectations for the child. Often parents and teachers place unrealistic pressures on children to excel in school, sports, or other areas. If this is the problem, consult with the adults and cooperatively plan ways to reduce the stress.

2. Determine the goal of the cheater (see Goals of Misbehavior, Chapter 7). Is the child trying to impress someone, earn recognition, please parents or teachers, or cover up a learning problem?

3. Talk with the cheating children concerning their study habits and preparation for work. Building better study skills may increase self-confidence and reduce cheating.

4. Encourage teachers to hold class discussions with students on cheating, exploring ways to reduce cheating and drawing up guidelines for consequences should the problem occur. A film, story, or hypothetical example may stimulate a rewarding discussion. Combine your discussion with a sociodrama, role play, or puppet play about cheating (see role playing in Thompson & Poppen, 1979, pp. 69–74).

5. Consult with teachers about reducing temptations to cheat by arranging classroom desks or tables to separate students.

6. Children are often asked by their friends to cheat, and many have trouble knowing how to handle the situation without losing a friend. A group or family discussion focusing on the problem with a question such as "What would you do if your best friend asked you for the answer to a question during a test?" may help children find an alternative to cheating or helping their friends to cheat.

7. Consult with the teacher about testing procedures. Could an open-book test be given? Could the teacher use alternative forms of the test? Is the teacher in the room and monitoring the test at all times?

8. If a child is caught cheating, remove the child's paper quietly and confront the child privately. Tell the child what you saw and discuss what consequences should be imposed. Ask that a plan be made to solve the present cheating problem and to prevent cheating in the future.

9. Refrain from accusing a child of cheating unless there is proof.

Do not attempt to force a confession. Avoid name calling, scolding, lecturing, moralizing, and preaching.

10. Place more emphasis on cooperative behavior and less on competition in interactions with the child. Stress competing with self rather than competing with another person.

11. Dreikurs (1968) suggests that, if two students are caught giving each other help on a test, each student should be given half of the score. They will soon realize the effect of cheating on their grades.

12. Relaxation and systematic desensitization may help a cheating child if the behavior is the result of anxiety or test phobia (see Relaxation and Systematic Desensitization, Chapter 14). Suspend competitive and punitive grading practices that create test anxiety.

13. De-reflection may be an effective technique for helping the cheating child with a fear of tests or fear of failure (see Chapter 11).

14. Contract with the child to avoid cheating in the future. Clearly define cheating behavior and the consequences of the behavior (see Contracting, Chapter 14).

TRUANCY

Truancy is considered a deliberate absence from school without a valid reason. Truants are generally telling the school that they prefer to be elsewhere. Children who do not achieve well or who have other learning problems are often truant because they find school an unpleasant place. It is easier to avoid the situation than to face failure, rejection, or embarrassment.

1. The reasons for truancy may be difficult to pinpoint. Determine the motive for the behavior (see Goals of Misbehavior, Chapter 7). Is the child experiencing learning problems, failure, or rejection? Does the child receive encouragement to attend school and find learning relevant? Determine the time sequence when truancy seems to occur most often. Is the truancy related to family problems or needs?

2. Personal interest from school personnel may be an effective reinforcer. Actively listen to the child for clues about what is happening in the child's life (see Chapter 4). Many students respond to special attention in the form of invitations from the teacher, other school personnel, or peers to come to school and participate in the activities.

3. Look over the truant's class schedule and academic progress. Determine if the classes are too difficult or the assignments beyond the child's capabilities. Are there other ways of learning in which the child might feel more success and find more relevance?

4. Check into the home situation. Could the truancy be the result of a lack of proper clothing or lunch money, or baby-sitting responsibilities or other job requirements? Enlist the cooperation of the parents and devise a system for keeping in touch with them concerning days present and absent.

5. Hold a group or family discussion about truancy. Discuss with the truant children how their presence or absence in school is helping or hurting them in reaching their immediate or long-term goals. Work with them to make a plan to avoid truancy in the future.

6. Contract with the student to attend school the next day. Continue to renegotiate the contract, increasing days in attendance in a step-by-step manner. Include a clause in the contract making the child responsible for all work missed. Rewards and/or penalties for attendance and nonattendance may be worked out cooperatively with the child (see Contracting, Chapter 14).

7. Older students serving as peer counselors may be helpful in devising ways to keep truant children in school. The attention of the older student will also serve as a reinforcer for attending school.

8. Involve the child in school activities that require his or her presence—for example, handling audio-visual equipment or physical education equipment, room responsibilities, or a responsibility in a group project of interest.

9. Refrain from using critical and sarcastic comments such as "Glad to see you made it today," or "If you had been here, you would have had the assignment." Avoid scolding, lecturing, punishing, and preaching. Concentrate on the positive behaviors of the child. School must become a pleasant place for truant children if their behavior is to be changed.

10. Whenever possible, allow the children choices in arranging their daily school activities and learning. Adjustments may also be made in the curricula to reflect the children's individual abilities and achievement levels.

11. For children who see little relevance in school life, hold a discussion of "What does it take to make it through life?" Ask the children to imagine themselves as adults in their jobs or daily activities. Discuss what abilities and skills they will need in order to make it in their imagined adult world.

12. Out-of-school suspension for truancy is seldom effective. The child who is consistently truant does not want to be in school, and suspension is no punishment. Seek ways to make school a pleasant and rewarding place.

13. Krumboltz and Thoresen (1976) report a case study in which an adolescent boy was encouraged to return to school and remain in attendance through the use of three techniques. He was first asked to visualize his future and what he would like to be and do in the future if he did not go back to school. His future plans and the reasons that he should return to school were discussed with the counselor. Next, the counselor asked him to look at the self that tries to make us do what we really want to and the other self that interferes and keeps us from accomplishing those goals. Behavioral rehearsal was used to help the young person imagine going back to school and to practice coping with the problems

that would arise. A behavioral contract was drawn up with his family and the school authorities, placing responsibility for the boy's behavior on him and outlining contingencies and reinforcements.

CARELESSNESS IN WORK AND WITH PROPERTY

One of the more common complaints heard among teachers and parents is that children are careless with school property, books, the completion of assigned work, personal property such as coats and sweaters, and other possessions. Lecturing, scolding, preaching, and nagging are seldom effective in changing their habits. Children need to learn responsibility for their own actions and possessions, and that an adult will not always be present to assume responsibility for them. Dreikurs, Grunwald, and Pepper (1971) emphasize that children should assume responsibility for property, for property rights, and for their actions in order to learn respect for property.

1. Determine the reason for the carelessness. Is the behavior due to a lack of interest or motivation? Could the carelessness be an attempt to cover up a learning or emotional problem or an attempt to get back at parents for some real or imagined wrong? Actively listen to the child for clues that may indicate the motivation for carelessness (see Chapter 4).

2. If the child is careless, the work can be redone until it is correct. Lost items or property can be paid for with time or work. Forgotten items such as lunches and tennis shoes should not be hurriedly brought by parents. The logical consequence of carelessness, forgetting, or losing is that the child must assume responsibility—redo the work, replace the property, or do without the forgotten items (see Logical Consequences, Chapter 14).

3. Praise and reinforce responsible behavior—for example, "The paper was well written," or "You did a good job cleaning out the basement." Consistently give attention to acceptable behavior.

4. Help the careless child find a model who behaves in a mature and responsible manner. Pair the child with the model for activities. Ask the child to observe the model's behaviors for several days. Discuss the behaviors of the model with the careless child. Role play and rehearse these behaviors. Make a plan for the child to try the new learning.

5. Carelessness may be due to a lack of understanding. Give clear and specific instructions to the child for proper preparation of work and other activities. Have the careless child write down the instructions in order to eliminate forgetting and mistakes.

6. If carelessness with homework assignments is a problem, ask the child to write down all assignments and take them home. Talk with parents to gain their cooperation in checking assigned work each night. Discontinue the procedure when the child begins to assume responsi-

bility for homework. The parent should be available to assist the child but not do the homework for the child.

7. If the problem seems to be due to inability to cope with the amount of work or responsibility assigned, reduce the requirements for a period of time, requiring quality rather than quantity. Gradually work up to the point where the child meets the expected criteria (see Contracting, Chapter 14).

8. Carelessness may reflect a difference in cultural values. The child's environment may not place a great value on achievement or the possession of property. Hold a group discussion focusing on the value of property and assuming responsibility for oneself. Help the children to identify acts of carelessness and their consequences, and make a plan for avoiding careless acts.

UNDERACHIEVEMENT

Underachievement is usually defined as a discrepancy between the child's ability and actual achievement. It may be related to poor self-concept, cultural deprivation, lack of family involvement and encouragement, peer pressures, learning or emotional problems, physical illness, or a lack of interest in school subjects and content.

1. Try to determine the causes contributing to underachievement. Become a "child watcher" and use active listening to try to understand the child (see Chapter 4). Underachievement is often related to physical problems or other learning difficulties; therefore, a psychological evaluation and checkup with a physician may provide some insight into the problem.

2. Assess the academic level at which the child is performing and assist the teachers to build learning and class assignments from this base. Much of new learning is based on old learning; the child must be able to accomplish prerequisite skills before achieving success in new ones. Once the weak link in the chain of learning is identified—a past school experience, physical health, cultural background, or any other factor—counseling can begin, and instructional materials can be designed to promote success.

3. Contract with the child to complete at least a small amount of work each day. Build in rewards for progress. The completion of two problems or questions is better than no progress. Renegotiate the contract periodically, increasing the amount of work expected (see Contracting, Chapter 14).

4. Try peer teaching or peer tutoring. Students who are in an upper grade can tutor students in lower grades. They can also be helpful to peers having trouble in areas of their strengths. Both children will learn and benefit from the relationship.

5. Capitalize on an area of interest or ability by relating the assignment to that interest or ability. Situations in math, writing, spelling,

and other subjects can often be related to the child's interests, hobbies, and skills.

6. Team teaching may be helpful. Two or more teachers are often able to generate more ideas to stimulate the child. The child may also be able to cooperate with one teacher more than with another.

7. Avoid lecturing, nagging, scolding, and threatening the child. Encouragement and a positive attitude will produce better results. See Poor Self-Concept (earlier in this chapter) for additional ideas.

8. Vary school activities from physical to quiet in order to prevent fatigue and boredom. Involve the child in arranging the day's work. Children are likely to cooperate and complete assigned tasks if they have been a part of the planning.

9. Teachers can consult with underachieving children for alternative ideas for completing learning objectives. Since children learn in different ways, the child may be the best consultant for determining methods for achieving learning objectives.

10. Special arrangements can be made for testing or for completing other class assignments. For example, if the child has problems in reading or writing, oral testing, tape recorders, or typewriters could be used.

11. Help the child find an admired friend and model. Ask the child to talk with the model about study habits and to observe the model's methods for studying. Contract with the child to practice these procedures (see Chapter 14). Allow the two children to work and study together as much as possible.

12. Check on study skills, test-taking procedures, place and time for studying. A contract incorporating a schedule for studying specific subjects at certain times and places will help the child plan study time more wisely and develop discipline for studying. (A study habits survey has been suggested by Thompson and Poppen, 1979.)

13. If the underachievement is related to parental pressures, counsel with the parents about how to decrease this pressure. Plan with them for methods to reinforce studying without pressuring the child. Assist parents and the child to determine an appropriate place and time to study. Make a plan to avoid or cope with things that might interfere with study times (small siblings, telephone calls, peers).

14. When homework assignments are not completed at home, the logical consequence is for the child to complete the work during free time at school (see Logical Consequences, Chapter 14). Avoid nagging, scolding, or lecturing.

15. Focus on and reinforce improvements in work. Past faults and failures should be forgotten; emphasize the positive—for example: "Jimmy, you did a part of your homework assignment, and it was done very well. I wonder if you would be willing to work on these two additional questions."

16. It is better for the parent/child relationship if parents do not teach or tutor their own children. If asked by the child for help, a parent

may provide assistance; however, someone outside the family will be a more effective teacher or tutor.

17. For children with special learning problems, plan a consultation session with all resource persons and teachers involved. Cooperatively draw up a learning plan with role and objectives of each professional clearly defined.

18. Underachievers usually respond best to a structured environment for learning. Research by Laport and Nath (1976) indicates that underachievers need specific, hard goals. They found that children who were simply told to do their best set low goals and achieved below their maximum abilities. Give directions for assignments very clearly. A check or reward system may be used for completed work. Learning contracts may be helpful to the underachiever. Some underachievers will require additional time to complete all assignments; continue to encourage their completion.

DAYDREAMING

Daydreaming is not always bad; it sometimes clears confusion, solves problems, or is creative in other ways. However, excessive daydreaming or daydreaming at the wrong times—in school—can affect the child's academic progress. Adlerian theory would suggest that daydreaming children are striving for superiority. These children have no faith in their abilities to achieve success in the real world; therefore, they create fantasies in which they are always great or superior.

1. Periodic eye contact between the child and the adult may help to decrease daydreaming. If it is difficult to make eye contact with the child, a light touch on the shoulder should bring the child back to reality.

2. Interrupt children's fantasies by calling them by name. Avoid embarrassing the children by asking them to answer a question they obviously have not heard.

3. Try the techniques of incomplete sentences, storytelling, diary, or play therapy to learn more about the child and the possible reason for the daydreaming.

4. Channel daydreaming into constructive channels by having the child write out the daydream. The writing could be incorporated into a learning exercise.

5. Write out a contract with the daydreamers for completion of assigned work (see Chapter 14). Contract for only the amount of work the children feel they can accomplish. Renegotiate contracts for additional work in a step-by-step plan.

6. Tape an index card to the child's desk. When the child is working on a task, place a check on the card and give verbal reinforcement for the accomplishment. A contract may be made with the child to earn rewards or privileges for a certain number of checks. Ignore the daydreaming; reward on-task behavior.

7. Plan the child's environment and schedule, varying activities from quiet to physical. Assess the day's schedule to determine if activities are interesting, relevant, and appropriate for the child's level of maturity, interest, and ability.

8. Find the child a friend who will encourage participation in groups and other activities. Encourage the teacher to include the daydreamer in group activities and projects. Counsel with the parents to plan for ways to reduce daydreaming at home and encourage participation in activities.

9. Often children retreat to a daydream world because the real one is too painful. Determine if the child is having learning, social, emotional, or physical problems. A psychological evaluation and physical examination may be helpful.

10. Daydreaming may be related to poor self-concept. Consult Poor Self-Concept (earlier in this chapter) for additional ideas for working with these children.

SHYNESS AND WITHDRAWAL

Shyness and withdrawal are attempts to avoid participation in one's surroundings. The child may fear the situation, fear failure or criticism, lack self-confidence, or fear embarrassment or humiliation. It is also possible that the child is physically ill. Unfortunately, shy and withdrawn children are usually ignored because they make little trouble compared to the attention-seeking child.

1. Try to determine the underlying cause for the reserved behavior. Use diaries, puppets, role playing, incomplete sentences, drawing, storytelling, play therapy, or any similar technique to try to understand the child better. Children will often express their feelings through these means when they will not verbalize them.

2. Work on developing trust and good rapport with the child. Try active listening to increase understanding of the child (see Chapter 4).

3. Have the shy child help another student through peer teaching or peer tutoring. Capitalize on any interest or ability to promote sharing and participation.

4. Involve shy or withdrawn children in small-group activities or projects with other children they like. Often a shy child will talk in small groups. Encourage and reinforce these attempts to participate. Send them on errands with another child. A sociogram may help to determine other liked children.

5. Give the withdrawn children responsibilities such as carrying messages, feeding the fish, watering plants, handing out supplies, or helping the school secretary answer the phone and take messages. Avoid drudgery jobs and asking the children to perform tasks that may embarrass them (speaking in front of the class).

6. Make a list with the withdrawn children of things they would like to be able to do—for example, join a group of friends, speak to a

particular person, play a game. Have the children select one thing on their list and set a goal to accomplish this behavior. Use behavior rehearsal to help the children practice certain responses or behaviors. Contract with the children to try these new behaviors (see Behavior Rehearsal and Contracting, Chapter 14).

7. Avoid embarrassing shy children by teasing them about their shyness or by calling on them to "perform" in front of a group without first discussing and arranging the activity with them. One technique for encouraging a child to participate in class is to plan a question and answer with the child. The teacher asks the question in class and the child agrees to answer with the response. When the child feels comfortable answering rehearsed questions, a contract is made with the child and teacher that the teacher will call on the child only when he or she volunteers to answer. Ask the child to volunteer at least a certain number of times per week. Renegotiate periodic contracts, encouraging participation in a step-by-step progression.

8. Find a model for the shy child. Ask the child to observe the model for several days and list liked behaviors. Role play, rehearse, and contract with the child to try the new behaviors.

9. Withdrawn or shy children may benefit from assertiveness training (see Chapter 14). Have the children list situations in which they would like to be more assertive. Discuss possible ways of meeting the situation. Practice the new behaviors with the children both individually and in small groups.

10. Keat (1972) suggests that a broad spectrum of techniques be used with the withdrawn child, such as: (a) building a relationship of trust, understanding, and confidence; (b) using the techniques of assertiveness training; (c) behavioral rehearsal with the counselor role playing the behavior and then the client rehearsing the behavior; (d) relaxation exercises such as breathing exercises, isometrics, and deep muscle relaxation techniques; (e) motor coordination training (if necessary); or (f) cognitive restructuring. These techniques are described in Chapter 14.

11. Zimbardo (1977) points out that shyness does have its advantages. The child can be selective in relationships; it offers the opportunity to observe the situation cautiously; the shy person will never be considered obnoxious or overly aggressive; and the shy person may be considered to be a good listener. If the child decides to change the behavior, Zimbardo suggests five steps: (a) understand self; (b) understand the reason for the shyness; (c) build self-esteem; (d) develop social skills; and finally, (e) help others overcome their shyness. Gestalt counseling techniques are often used to help a child look at weaknesses as secret strengths. For example, "Being shy helps me by _____." Behavioral counseling strategies are also designed to look at the pay-offs of seemingly unhelpful behaviors.

12. See Poor Self-Concept section of this chapter for other ideas to encourage more participation in learning and interpersonal situations.

EXCESSIVE TENSION AND ANXIETY

A little tension and anxiety may motivate a child, but excessive tension and anxiety interfere with learning and performance. Excessive tension and anxiety may be situational or a chronic condition. The symptoms include continued restlessness and movement, nail biting, tics, frequent blinking, rapid breathing, repeated throat clearing, and similar somatic complaints.

School-related tension and anxiety

1. Tell highly anxious children they have a right to fail (see De-reflection, Chapter 11). Take away the pressure to excel and to be perfect. This technique may ease the anxiety and allow further exploration of conditions causing the anxiety.

2. Highly anxious children function better with a teacher who is warm and understanding but also organized and structured. Suggest that teachers use teaching techniques such as behavioral objectives and learning contracts so that highly anxious students will know exactly what is expected of them.

3. Consult with the child's parents and teachers. Determine if the anxiety is a result of pressures and perfectionistic expectations. If so, work with the children and adults to encourage more realistic expectations.

4. Teachers and parents may help to decrease tension and anxiety in children by talking quietly to them about relaxing—for example, "Relax your neck; relax your shoulders." Deep breathing exercises may also help the child relax. See Relaxation Techniques (Chapter 14) for a detailed description of these techniques.

5. Avoid overemphasizing the importance of success on a test or task. Many adults cause anxiety in their efforts to impress the child with the importance of doing well.

6. If the child is highly anxious about tests, use the "study buddy" system. Pair the child with a capable student who is willing to help. Developing better study skills may help to reduce anxieties related to school.

7. Encourage teachers to de-emphasize tests and to allow the child to demonstrate learning in other ways, such as oral tests, oral reports, projects, and papers.

8. Look over the child's school work and academic progress. Anxiety is often related to learning disabilities.

General anxiety

1. Some tension and anxiety may be related to fear of the unknown—for example, going to new places or being placed in new situations. A thorough explanation of the feared situation and/or a visit to a feared place with a trusted person may reduce situational anxiety.

2. Talk with anxious children and agree on methods such as physical activity, talking, or writing for release of these feelings. When the children become highly anxious or tense, they could be allowed to signal the teacher or another adult and proceed to carry out the plan previously discussed. Counselors may suggest that the anxious children come to their office when they experience intense feelings.

3. Diaries, autobiographies, drawing, puppets, and other forms of play therapy may assist in determining the causes for the anxious feelings (see Play Therapy, Chapter 14).

4. Children will have less anxiety about situations if they feel competent. Discuss with the child the reasons for the anxiety and ways of handling the situations, and rehearse the situations.

5. Relaxation methods and desensitization have been found to be effective methods of reducing tension and anxiety (see Relaxation Techniques, Chapter 14).

6. Refer the child to a medical specialist for an examination if the anxiety appears to be extremely debilitating.

DISTRACTIBILITY—SHORT ATTENTION SPAN

Being able to focus one's attention on the task to be done and ignore irrelevant stimuli in the environment is necessary for learning school material and new behaviors. Although attention span and the amount of distractibility vary with the child and the situation, these learning problems seem to be appearing with increasing frequency in today's classrooms.

1. Determine if the child is actually distracted very easily and has a short attention span. The child's inattention may be the result of some other reason, such as the nature of the work the child is asked to do (boring or too difficult); noisy or more interesting surroundings (windows, TV, pictures, bulletin boards); or fatigue or physical illness.

2. Record the time when distractions and inattention seem most frequent. Rearrange the environment or schedule. Vary quiet activities with more physical ones. Limit overstimulation and distractors. Interesting bulletin boards, teachers' clothing and jewelry, mobiles, and brightly colored pictures can be distracting.

3. Use seating arrangements or some method of screening the distractible child from excessive stimuli. Consider small carrels or "offices." Bookcases, movable screens, or even large moving cartons that have been painted or decorated can be used to reduce stimuli.

4. Contract for the completion of short assignments. Talk with the distractible children about the amount of work they feel they can accomplish—two math problems, one paragraph of English. Write a realistic contract to assure success. Continue to renegotiate the contract, increasing the assignments as the distractibility decreases.

5. Recommend that highly distractible children be checked by a medical specialist to determine if the behavior is a medical problem.

6. Shorten teaching time and study periods and schedule the periods more frequently. Visual aids, games, and other teaching aids may add interest and maintain attention.

7. Acker, Oliver, Carmichael, and Ozerkevich (1975) report a case study of a 10-year-old boy whose attention span and on-task activity were increased by rewarding the whole class for the boy's on-task behavior. Periodic observations of behavior were made, and points were earned for appropriate behaviors. These points were exchanged for class privileges such as trips to the museum. The decisions about how to "spend" the points were made by the boy and the whole class. The researchers suggest that the boy's peers tended to ignore off-task behavior, which resulted in an increase in on-task behavior.

8. Douglas (1972) contends that more time needs to be spent in teaching children to "stop, look, and listen." She thinks that a short attention span is like impulsiveness; therefore, methods should be implemented to decrease impulsiveness and improve attentiveness and reflectiveness—for example, techniques for teaching reflective strategies and games requiring impulse control.

9. Develop the ability to raise or lower your voice, place your hand on the child's shoulder, catch the child's eye, and other techniques to catch the distractible child's attention and direct it back to the task.

IMMATURITY AND DEPENDENT BEHAVIOR

Dependency may be the result of overprotective or critical parents, who have told their children in many ways that they are not capable of functioning or thinking for themselves. Immature or dependent children usually do not achieve well in school because they are not ready to learn the subject matter presented. They may have trouble with interpersonal relationships because of their immature behavior and often become social isolates or discipline problems; alternatively, they may choose their friends from a younger group.

1. Work with the parents on strategies to help them trust the child's abilities and potentials. Suggest methods to develop independent behaviors. Books such as *Between Parent and Child* (Ginott, 1965) and *Parent Effectiveness Training* (Gordon, 1970) may help parents to understand their children's development and abilities.

2. Have the children identify areas in which they would like to be more independent or behaviors they would like to change. Discuss these situations and alternative ways of behaving with the children, and rehearse the situations until the children feel comfortable with the new behaviors.

3. Encourage and praise attempts to become more mature and independent. Ask the child to do jobs or assume responsibilities in the

home and classroom to increase feelings of confidence. Avoid assigning drudgery jobs.

4. Have the children select a model and observe the model's behaviors for several days. Pair the children with mature models for group activities. Ask them to keep a list of the model's behaviors they particularly like. Rehearse the behaviors the children would like to acquire until they feel confident.

5. Encourage immature or dependent children to join groups such as Little League, Boy or Girl Scouts, clubs, or church groups. The children will need support and encouragement to take the first steps and continued counseling to learn social skills for good relationships in the groups.

6. Give the children as many choices as possible—for example, whether to complete the reading or the math assignment, or whether to wear a blue shirt or a red shirt.

7. Learn about the child's abilities, interests, and hobbies. Have the child peer teach or tutor another student in one of these areas of expertise to build self-confidence. Both children will benefit from the teaching and the relationship.

8. Work with immature or dependent children to teach them problem-solving techniques. Counsel with parents and teachers to encourage these children to attempt to solve their own problems with adult guidance rather than depending on others for solutions.

9. Avoid reinforcing dependent behaviors. Encourage immature children to make decisions and accept responsibilities within their capabilities. Reinforce efforts toward more mature behavior with praise and encouragement.

10. Use active listening to help immature and dependent children to express their fears and other feelings (see Chapter 4). Help them to develop realistic goals and to make a systematic plan for attaining these goals.

PERFECTIONISTIC BEHAVIOR

Compulsive and overly perfectionistic children usually perform their tasks and assignments well and therefore often "overachieve." The behavior can become inhibiting to everyday functioning; for example, the child takes too much time to complete assignments and feels that everything must be absolutely perfect. Perfectionistic behavior is often accompanied by symptoms of anxiety.

1. Perfectionistic children usually perform best in a well-structured situation, where rules and expectations are clearly defined. Clearly explain all instructions and utilize teaching methods such as behavioral objectives and learning contracts to reduce anxiety concerning expectations.

2. Talk with parents and teachers to determine if pressures and

expectations placed on the child are too great. Perfectionistic children often have perfectionistic adults for models. Counsel with adults about normal growth and development and the behaviors that can be expected of the child.

3. Involve the children in individual and group activities that do not require perfect performance. Techniques such as creative drawing or writing de-emphasize perfection and also allow the child to express feelings.

4. Encourage the child to relax. Teach the child breathing exercises and other relaxation techniques (see Relaxation Exercises, Chapter 14). Encourage the child to change "internal self-talk" to recognize that perfection in all areas is not essential (see Chapters 6 and 14 for discussion of cognitive restructuring). "Should's" and "have to's" can be changed to "It might be better if's." For example, "It might be better if I make all 'A's,' but that is not required for me to be a good person."

5. Use negative rehearsal to help perfectionistic children be less rigid. Observe a situation in which the child appears to be very perfectionistic. Role play the same situation with the children, encouraging behavior that is less than perfect. Discuss with the children what would happen if they were not 100% perfect in the situation. Make a plan with the children to decrease compulsiveness.

6. Give an allotted amount of time for the children to finish a task. Place a timer within the child's sight. When the timer rings, review the child's progress. If sufficient progress has not been made, contract with the child to set a new goal the next time.

7. The overly perfectionistic child may be compensating for feelings of inadequacy. See Poor Self-Concept section of this chapter for further suggestions for working with these children.

8. See Excessive Tension and Anxiety section of this chapter for additional ideas for working with perfectionistic children.

SCHOOL PHOBIA

School phobia may grow out of unpleasant or embarrassing experiences in school, failure in school, fear of separation from the security of home and parents, fear of the unknown, or other experiences that may have associated bad feelings with school.

1. Actively listen to try to understand the phobic child's underlying feelings and to establish a feeling of trust and security (see Chapter 4).

2. The child can be desensitized by being brought to school by a parent and staying for a short period of time, such as 15 minutes the first day, 20 minutes the second day, 25 minutes the third day. Continue in this manner until the child can remain in school a full day.

3. The desensitization procedure may be used with rewards. Write out a contract with the child to provide a reward for staying in school

a certain amount of time, for example, 30 minutes (see Chapter 14). Renegotiate the contract for longer periods of time as the child is able to stay in school an increasing length of time.

4. If one parent is reinforcing the child's anxiety about school, suggest that the other parent or another adult bring the child to school. A parent may unconsciously be encouraging school phobia by conveying his or her own anxiety to the child verbally or nonverbally (for example, "Now, you call me if you get afraid while you are in school" or becoming more nervous and irritable as they approach school).

5. Avoid placing the child in any situation that may increase fear or cause embarrassment. Explain all new situations and expectations clearly. Role playing expected behaviors may help the child feel more confident about meeting the new situation.

6. School phobia may be related to learning difficulties. Review the child's academic progress and provide needed help. Children who find school an unpleasant place because they continually fail often become phobic.

7. Ask the teacher to involve phobic children in pleasant group projects and activities. The more pleasure the children derive from school, the more they will want to attend. Successful learning, good peer relationships, pleasant teachers and other school personnel and activities can be positive reinforcers.

8. Allow phobic children to phone home occasionally or at specific intervals if they feel fearful or insecure. Make arrangements with the parents so that they will be there to answer and to reassure the child.

9. Many parents include something from home in the child's lunchbox or with books—a picture or some favorite object, for instance.

10. Relaxation and desensitization procedures may be necessary for the extremely phobic child (see Relaxation Exercises and Systematic Desensitization, Chapter 14).

11. Blanco (1972) suggests that counselors work with parents, encouraging them to (a) make persistent and continued efforts to get the child to school daily, even for a short period of time; (b) seek family counseling if the child is extremely anxious and phobic; (c) have the child visit classes, playgrounds, and other areas prior to entering school; (d) get the child off to school in a natural way without tearful goodbyes or overemphasis on parting; (e) enlist the aid of a pediatrician if psychosomatic ailments occur. The pediatrician should be aware of the phobic problem if it occurs with any frequency.

12. Rutter (1975) outlines some areas of questioning that may help the counselor to understand the phobic child. He suggests the following questions: (a) What is the child like when not at school—temperamentally, socially, and so forth? (b) Does the child's refusal to go to school vary with the planned curriculum or activities for that day? (c) Does the child's refusal to go to school vary with what is occurring in

the home—when there is illness, unhappiness, arguments, mother beginning a new job, a new baby?

13. See other ideas for working with the phobic child under Excessive Tension and Anxiety, earlier in this chapter.

REFERENCES

Acker, L., Oliver, P., Carmichael, J., and Ozerkevich, M. Interpersonal attractiveness and peer interaction during behavioral treatment of the target child. *Canadian Journal of Behavioral Science*, 1975, 7, 262–273.

Blanco, R. *Prescription for children with learning and adjustment problems.* Springfield, Ill.: Charles C Thomas, 1972.

Canfield, J., and Wells, H. C. *100 ways to enhance self-concept in the classroom.* Englewood Cliffs, N. J.: Prentice-Hall, 1976.

Douglas, V. Stop, look and listen: The problem of sustained attention and impulse control in hyperactive and normal children. *Canadian Journal of Behavioral Science*, 1972, 4, 259–282.

Dreikurs, R. *Psychology in the classroom* (2nd ed.). New York: Harper & Row, 1968.

Dreikurs, R., Grunwald, B., and Pepper, F. *Maintaining sanity in the classroom.* New York: Harper & Row, 1971.

Ginott, H. *Between parent and child.* New York: Macmillan, 1965.

Gordon, T. *Parent effectiveness training.* New York: Peter H. Wyden, 1970.

Keat, D. Broad-spectrum behavior therapy with children: A case presentation. *Behavior Therapy*, 1972, 3, 454–459.

Krumboltz, J., and Thoresen, C. *Counseling methods.* New York: Holt, Rinehart and Winston, 1976.

Laport, R., and Nath, R. Roles of performance goals in prose learning. *Journal of Educational Psychology*, 1976, 3, 260–264.

Rutter, M. *Helping troubled children.* New York: Plenum Press, 1975.

Schaefer, C., and Millman, H. *Therapy for children: A handbook of effective treatments for problem behavior.* San Francisco: Jossey-Bass, 1977.

Thompson, C., and Poppen, W. *Guidance activities for counselors and teachers.* Monterey, Calif.: Brooks/Cole, 1979.

Zimbardo, P. *Shyness.* Reading, Mass.: Addison-Wesley, 1977.

CHAPTER

18

COUNSELING CHILDREN WITH SPECIAL NEEDS AND PROBLEMS

Chapter 1 described some of the difficulties inherent in our complex present-day society—difficulties with which our children must cope during their major years of growth and development. Counselors obviously cannot supply all the answers to these problems; however, several concerns seem to be pressing and frequently seen by counselors. It is the purpose of this chapter to suggest methods for working with children with these special needs and problems. The suggestions should be incorporated into a caring and accepting counseling atmosphere and modified to meet the unique needs of the child and the presenting concern. The reader may wish to refer to Chapters 16 and 17 for special procedures for handling problem behaviors that may accompany these societal problems. The following problems will be considered: child abuse, divorce, alcoholism, and cultural barriers.

CHILD ABUSE

Congress has defined *child abuse* as the "physical or mental injury, sexual abuse, negligent treatment or maltreatment of a child under the age of 18 by a person who is responsible for the child's welfare under circumstances which indicate the child's health or welfare is harmed or threatened" (U.S. Department of Health, Education and Welfare, 1975, p. 1). The description of child abuse in state laws varies from general to specific definitions that include starvation, malnutrition, and failure to thrive (Caskey & Richardson, 1975). Because of these varied definitions, and because a large number of child abuse cases are not reported, it is difficult to determine the incidence of the problem; however, some estimates range up to or more than 1 million children each year. According to the National Center on Child Abuse and Neglect, the number of child abuse cases reported in 1978 does not begin to reveal the actual incidence of abuse. There may be as many as 3 million children abused yearly in the United States.

Griggs and Gale (1977) found that every state has passed or rewritten a child abuse law during the past few years. According to these authors, such legislation protects the child by requiring doctors, teachers, or other helping professionals to report abuse to the proper authorities; it protects parents from false accusations; and it protects the person reporting the suspected abuse from possible damage suits. Most state laws include provisions allowing for criminal prosecution of persons failing to report known cases of child abuse.

Several hypotheses have been advanced to explain the causes of child abuse. Green (1978) feels that unmet parental dependency needs, impulsivity, poor self-concept, high defensiveness, and a projection of negative parental feelings and perceptions onto the child can result in child abuse. Starr states that we can only understand child abuse by considering "the characteristics of the abused child in interaction with parental psychological factors, the manner in which the parents were themselves reared by their parents, social stresses on the family, and our cultural acceptance of violence" (1979, p. 873).

The first priority of society is usually to punish the offender. As with many crimes, the victim tends to be forgotten once medical attention is given for the physical problems and the child is removed from the care of the abuser. The traditional method in child abuse cases has been to help the parents to understand themselves and their feelings and to find more constructive means of handling their feelings. Several researchers (Glass, 1970; Green, 1978; Reiner & Kaufman, 1969) believe that abusing parents lack the characteristics necessary for rewarding human relationships: they have not been loved; they feel hurt and rejected; and thus they cannot give the love, care, warmth, and tenderness necessary for good parenting. The treatment, therefore, should be counseling to improve the self-concept and relationship skills of the parents. Obviously, it is quite important first to assure the physical safety of the child and then to attempt to persuade abusing parents to seek treatment—usually group counseling or parent training classes. However, the child, too, needs counseling help. Very little literature in counseling has focused on meeting the needs of the abused child.

Abused children may be recognized by a variety of symptoms. Some may be referred to counselors because they are aggressive and have behavioral problems; they model the abusive behavior of their parents.

Others may be referred because they are extremely withdrawn, isolated, or have academic or social problems. Recently, doctors have identified a new syndrome—emotional dwarfism—which is indicative of child abuse: bizarre eating, drinking, sleeping, and social behavior; impaired intellectual growth; and an inability to respond to people and to painful stimuli. With proper care, these children can begin to grow rapidly again and catch up to normal developmental levels.

Abused children are not easy clients. They have learned not to trust themselves, other people, or their environment. The world and the people in it are inconsistent and hurt them. It is safer to withdraw from this painful world and not chance relationships. Building friendship and trust may be a difficult step. Counselors should be prepared to become totally involved with the children in order to prove that people can be trusted and to have their caring tested by the child. Counselors will need to be adult models, demonstrating consistent and positive ways of behaving and interacting to the children.

Abused children may also benefit from group counseling with peers serving as models. Participation in a group will encourage the children to share their feelings and will provide the friendship, acceptance, and support they desperately need. Group counseling can provide the setting for the children to role play and rehearse new and more constructive ways of behaving without negative consequences. Individual counseling, used in conjunction with group counseling, will allow the children a time to share more private feelings. Activities to strengthen the self-concept may be integrated into both individual and group counseling. Behavior modification techniques can help children control their behavior (see Contracting, Chapter 14) and change inappropriate behavior. Counselors, teachers, and parents will need to be involved in order to provide a consistent and predictable environment for the children.

Hefler and Kempe (1976) suggest that counselors may want to provide an environment designed to stimulate growth and development. Many abused children are deprived of environmental stimulation in their early years and may develop specific lags in motor, speech, cognitive, perceptual, or other learning skills. The possibility of such deprivation and remedial sources, such as day-care centers or stimulating school environments, should be investigated.

Elkind (1980) points out that young children in Piaget's concrete operations stage (age 7–11) will say their parents are good parents even though they are abusive. Their view of reality is that their parents are kind and loving; they cannot verbalize their feelings because of their view of the world. This is a cognitive assumption (not a behavioral one) that often interferes with counseling children of abusive parents. Elkind suggests that play therapy is the counseling method most useful in helping children express their feelings.

Child abuse appears to involve a family network of destructive interactional patterns and faulty personality development. Counseling with the entire family to overcome individual problems or stresses and to improve family relationships would seem to be the most appropriate procedure for working with the abuser and the abused.

Families in which an incident of abuse has occurred may feel fear and anxiety about what other people will think and do if the attack is discovered, or they may fear another attack. Generalized fear, anxiety, and distrust of people may follow the attack and result from the emotional trauma. In addition, they may be convinced that this is a family problem and should be kept within the family. They may also fear punishment for the offender (Slager-Jorne, 1978).

Counseling with children who have been sexually abused requires extra consideration, understanding, and support. Often the children are initially unable to discuss the problem with the counselor because of intense feelings of guilt, feelings that somehow they provoked the attack. They may feel worthless and ashamed of having been used or abused in such a manner, and feel that perhaps they could have done something to prevent the attack. Kristal (1977) points out that often it is not the sexual act itself, but parental overreaction or a painful court experience that causes the most trauma.

One avenue for helping children to deal with the intense feelings accompanying abuse is bibliocounseling (see Chapter 14). Carefully selected books that portray the problem realistically but offer children positive approaches for coping can be therapeutic as well as opening the door for discussion of the problem. Similarly, play therapy may allow children who are unable to verbalize an opportunity to express their feelings. Individual counseling is indicated to provide support and assistance in dealing with feelings. Counselors will want to be extremely cautious about placing abused children in a group situation, especially if the abuse has been sexual and the trauma is very recent.

Counselors working with abused children must be prepared to provide understanding and support for all persons involved in the problem, even the abuser (Slager-Jorne, 1978). The abuser is acting out of feelings of worthlessness and rejection and the inability to form satisfying relationships. It is a natural reaction to feel anger and antipathy toward the accused attacker of a child; however, these feelings must be recognized and resolved if counselors are to relate to the family in a helpful and effective manner (Kristal, 1977).

CHILDREN OF DIVORCE

The incidence of divorce is increasing rapidly in American society. The number of children affected by divorce each year ranges in the millions, with estimates that, by the early 1980s, approximately 50 percent of all school-age children will be touched in some way by divorce. Hetherington (1979) estimates that 40% to 50% of the children born in the 1970s will live in a single-parent home at some time during their lives.

Divorce causes drastic changes in family relationships and therefore is quite painful and traumatic to all involved (Salk, 1978). Adults frequently seek help to cope with the hurt associated with divorce through individual and group counseling or through organized helping groups such as Parents without Partners. Adults express concern about the children affected by divorce, but for the most part little direct help is given to help the children understand their feelings and adjust to the changes occurring in their lives (Kessler & Bostwick, 1977). Gardner (1976) suggests that divorce itself does not necessarily cause psychopathology in children, but parents may contribute to psychopathological disorders. The children may model the behavior of one or both parents, or the parents may be free from psychiatric problems themselves but may manage the children in such a way as to produce psychological problems.

Hetherington (1979) points out that some children experience serious problems in development as a result of the trauma of divorce, while others cope well with this stress and emerge as well-adjusted individuals. The long-term problems appear to be related to sustained turmoil and disruption of the quality of life in the household.

Older children may react to a divorce with anger, hostility, or depression. Because of their limited cognitive abilities, younger children are usually left with a vague and confused understanding of what caused such a drastic change in the family. Unmet dependency needs may result in feelings of abandonment. Because many parents are reluctant to talk with their children about divorce, the children may never fully understand the cause of the family break. Consequently, many children feel guilty, fantasizing that something they did caused the divorce. Others may feel ashamed, hurt, rejected, isolated, abandoned, or distrustful of adults who might hurt them again. Parents are often too involved in their own hurts during divorce to be aware of their children's erroneous beliefs or are unable to give enough of themselves to meet the children's needs for love and support.

Hozman and Froiland (1977) write that children go through the same stages as their parents in their emotional response to divorce: denial, anger, bargaining, depression, and acceptance. Children may first decide not to accept reality and instead to live in a safer fantasy world. The authors present a case study in which supportive counseling was used effectively to help a child through this stage. During the anger stage, the child may strike out at all who resemble parents—for instance, teachers and other school personnel. Hozman and Froiland describe how a counselor used play therapy to help a child in this stage by allowing him to verbalize his anger and by finding constructive physical outlets for his anger. Group counseling was used also to help the child feel less alone.

When denial and anger do not produce the desired results, the child may try to "bargain" with parents, God, or others to make a deal for the desired outcome. Hozman and Froiland demonstrate how reality therapy, with its emphasis on responsibility for one's own behavior, may help the child in this stage. When children discover they cannot change reality, depression may occur. Counseling strategies suggested for this stage were an exploration of feelings of present and future accomplishments. Hozman and Froiland state that "Acceptance comes when the child learns that there is an objective reality that exists, and while not liking that reality, he or she must admit that it is actual" (1977, p. 532). Children may or may not need counseling during the acceptance stage, but every effort should be made to see that they have learned behaviors that will help them cope. Hozman and Froiland feel that when this model is utilized in working with children of divorce, and when counselors "devise individualized experiences for the children, the child will in fact not be forgotten in the divorce" (p. 533).

Children face a variety of stresses during and after the time of divorce. The family income may decrease, and often mothers who had been at home have to go to work; many are unskilled and must accept low-paying jobs. There may be conflict between the parents, with the children being used by one or both parents. Children may be torn by conflicting loyalties, or they may learn to manipulate the parents in an effort to get their way. Appropriate role models may not be available to encourage sex-role identification. The lack of a role model of the opposite sex can deter the development of satisfactory heterosexual relationships. Children of divorced parents may be asked to assume the role of the absent parent and to fulfill physical or emotional responsibilities beyond their maturity level.

An additional stress that many children experience when their parents divorce is a feeling of abandonment. Mothers and fathers are supposed to love one another, and it may appear logical to children that, if parents can "abandon" one another, then they can abandon children they are also supposed to love. The children may develop a distrust of adults who try to show caring for them, fearing that they will be hurt again.

Gardner (1976) cautions that one parent should never make excuses if the other appears to be uninterested in the child by seldom visiting, writing, or sharing in the child's life and activities. The child will recognize the excuse as untruthful and will learn to be distrustful of this parent also. Gardner advocates being very honest with children about the behavior of the missing parent.

Inasmuch as the number of children affected by divorce is increasing, counselors may consider the use of peer counselors to help a child going through turmoil caused by a divorce. Other children who have experienced divorce can understand the child's feelings and perhaps offer suggestions or describe how they handled a similar situation.

Filmed vignettes depicting what happens to a family when divorce occurs may act as a stimulus for discussing feelings and ways of reacting, coping, and behaving (Magid, 1977). Books about divorce also help children to understand what has happened to their family and provide a stimulus for discussion of feelings and behaviors.

Wilkinson and Bleck (1977) describe a group counseling method called Children's Divorce Group (CDG). These counseling groups consist of eight 45-minute sessions for upper-grade elementary students. Group activities include introductions, agreeing on rules for the group, activities focused on feelings, drawing the family, and problem-solving techniques integrating role playing and puppets. The authors state that responses from children participating in the group activities were extremely positive. All felt that they had learned something about themselves and others and believed that the group had made a difference in their lives.

As in counseling with any problem in which values, beliefs, and attitudes may affect the counselor's objectivity, counselors may want to assess their feelings about divorce and their potential reactions to both the parents and the child. Children who are the victims of divorce have been hurt by adults they trusted and will be quick to detect uneasiness, anxiety, or insincerity in the counselor's behavior.

CHILDREN OF ALCOHOLICS

Probably the "special" children who receive the least attention and support in our society are the children of alcoholic parents. The little research that has been conducted with these children indicates they usually do not achieve well academically and are especially prone to long-lasting emotional or behavioral problems (Triplett & Arneson, 1978). Inasmuch as the number of alcoholics is rising, the number of children affected directly or indirectly by this problem is likely to increase also.

The children of alcoholic parents frequently do not have their physical or psychological needs met in the family. Money needed for food and shelter may be spent on alcohol; but even if there is money, the parents may not be attentive to the child's physical needs because of their preoccupation with alcohol. The child's need for love, belonging, and security cannot be met by parents who have lost control over their lives and frequently dislike themselves for their behavior. Seixas (1977) states that alcoholism damages all family relationships and impairs functioning in both the alcoholic and the nonalcoholic. The children of alcoholics receive little or very inconsistent attention and consequently feel confused and rejected.

Hecht agrees with the view that the pattern of relationships in alcoholic families is faulty. He states that "structure and limits are necessary for children to grow successfully; they have to understand rules and regulations, cause and effect. But the child of the alcoholic learns that rules are to be broken, family patterns are unreliable, and few things can be counted on" (1977, p. 198). Triplett and Arneson (1978) write that, because of inconsistent family patterns, children learn to distrust their parents, and this distrust generalizes to the relationship they have with other adults. In an earlier study, Cork (1969), too, noted this distrust of adults and lack of involvement in adult relationships. However, early identification and intervention can be helpful in preventing pathological development in the children (Hecht, 1977).

The literature contains few suggestions for counseling with the children of alcoholic parents. A counselor can only surmise appropriate counseling strategies from a description of the lives and characteristics of the children.

Probably a major problem counselors will face is identifying the children of alcoholic parents. They may have behavior problems, they may be having trouble academically or socially, or they may be suffering with the "family secret" in silence and withdraw from the world. The parents will be extremely reluctant to admit there could be a family problem contributing to the child's presenting problem. Because many of the children do not think they can trust adults, they usually will not voluntarily talk about alcoholism. It will require time, patience, understanding, and consistency on the part of the counselor in order to develop a supportive counseling relationship based on trust. Individual and group procedures to enhance self-esteem may assist the child with feelings of rejection and insecurity. Play therapy may help children to act out feelings about their parents or themselves that they are unable to verbalize.

Group procedures following the pattern of Children's Divorce Groups (Wilkinson & Bleck, 1977), as described in the previous section, can be a helpful technique for exploring children's feelings about alcoholic parents and about themselves, and for promoting a feeling of belonging. In addition, the groups can provide a safe atmosphere for exploring more appropriate ways of behaving and for role playing or rehearsing new behaviors.

Suggestions for handling the specific behavior problems are given in Chapters 16 and 17. The children of alcoholic parents will need consistent role models as their parents are inconsistent, depending on their sobriety. They may be harsh and punitive while drinking and extremely tolerant and giving while sober. Their guilt over their drinking can make them easy prey for a child's manipulations. Counselors will want to be aware of their behavior as role models and encourage interaction with other appropriate adult models.

Obviously, the parents should be encouraged to seek help with their problem and with their parenting skills, although typical alcoholics will deny their problem and its effect on the children. The resources of organizations such as Alcoholics Anonymous, Alanon, and Alateen can be extremely helpful. Counselors, too, can utilize the skills of trained alcoholism counselors as consultants. The latter use family intervention strategies and help children understand the condition.

As with any case in which values may interfere with counseling objectivity, counselors need to examine their feelings about both the child and the family. Alcoholism is a family problem that affects all members differently but which requires the counselor to be understanding of the family structure and interactions.

COUNSELING WITH CHILDREN ABOUT DEATH AND DYING

Death has been a taboo subject for discussion in our society. When asked about death or dying, most adults try to find ways of avoiding the subject or excuse themselves by expressing their inadequacy to discuss such a subject with young people. A survey conducted by Rosenthal and Terkelson (1978) reported that counselor and counselor educator respondents thought school counselors should be trained to work in this area; however, there are few programs designed to provide the relevant knowledge and skills. Only recently have we begun to realize that talking about death may help all of us to accept it as a part of life and to cope with the feelings that accompany death. Every child will be affected by the death of pets or grandparents, or perhaps an even closer loss of parents or siblings. Counselors need to be prepared to help children accept the reality of death as a part of life. In order to work effectively with children on the issue of death, counselors must first examine their own attitudes toward death. A counselor in conflict will not be able to provide the support and understanding needed by the child.

Children have trouble understanding death for many reasons. As Piaget points out, children are limited in understanding by the stage of their cognitive development. Young children are unable to understand the finality and irreversibility of death; they feel that they are immortal. As children grow, they begin to question death and its causes. It may be recognized as inevitable and final, but it is still difficult for the child to comprehend the process. Children often feel that only old people die. As children approach adolescence, they become interested in death from a religious or philosophical point of view (Kastenbaum & Aisenberg, 1976; Kavanaugh, 1972).

Many factors in the child's environment may encourage faulty concepts concerning death. The mass media often portray death violently. Adults in the child's life may react negatively to death. Often they attempt to "protect" the child from death by refusing to discuss the subject and by hiding their own feelings. It may be difficult for children to understand adult reactions. They may think they caused or contributed to the death in some way or decide that death is a punishment for something "bad" they have done. Unfounded fears and anxieties can arise out of these misunderstandings. Euphemistic explanations often cause misconceptions in children. If told that the person is "only asleep" or that "God has called her," children can learn to fear sleep or fear that God will call them away from their world.

For the most part, children have difficulty learning effective ways of handling death. Adults may not provide the answers needed or demonstrate appropriate behaviors. Unresolved grief can result in mental illness (Bendiksen & Fulton, 1975) or difficulties in marriage or with the law (Markusen, & Fulton, 1971). The child can experience fear or generalized anxiety, guilt or responsibility for the death, fear of being abandoned, or fear of again loving someone they could possibly lose.

From her work with terminally ill patients, Kübler-Ross (1969) has defined the stages that most patients and their families will go through in facing death. The first reaction is denial—"This is not happening to me." Second, the patient and family will experience anger over the situation—"Why did this have to happen to me and not to somebody else?" Third, there will be a stage of bargaining. The person may try to make a bargain with God to be a better person if He will let them or their loved one live. When the inevitability of death must be faced and the pressures become a harsh reality, depression commonly occurs. When these feelings can be worked through successfully, a quiet acceptance of death can be achieved.

Following are several guidelines for helping children who are coping with death or a dying loved one.

1. Someone close to the child can explain death realistically and as a natural process. Words and concepts appropriate to the child's age and level of understanding should be carefully chosen (Hammond, 1980a; Kavanaugh, 1972; Simpson, 1979).

2. Children should be allowed to talk freely, ask questions, and express their emotions. Through these expressions, adults can learn more about the child's conceptions, fears, or anxieties (Hammond, 1980a; Kavanaugh, 1972; Simpson, 1979). Ryerson (1977) cautions that questions may have a hidden meaning and suggests that it is important to determine the intent of the question before responding.

3. Avoid encouraging children to stifle their grief and "be brave." Expression of emotions is a healthy way of coping with grief and can facilitate the healing process (Hammond, 1980a; Simpson, 1979).

4. Children losing a close loved one will need a tremendous amount of support and reassurance that they will not be abandoned by those surviving. A child will need extra amounts of time and "tender, loving care" (Kavanaugh, 1972; Simpson, 1979).

5. Children who are old enough should decide whether or not to attend the funeral service. The service can provide an opportunity for them to further communicate their thoughts or feelings (Grollman, 1967; Simpson, 1979).

6. When discussing religious beliefs as they relate to death, adults must remember that children may have trouble with concepts such as heaven and eternity. Children taught in Sunday school that God loves them cannot understand why God would "take away" or "call" someone they need and love (Linn & Schwarz, 1958).

7. Education about death can be integrated into daily life through discussion of the subject at appropriate times during the life of the child (for instance, when a pet dies) or through group discussions and group guidance. Children should not be "protected" from the facts of death (Kavanaugh, 1972; Simpson, 1979). Teachers can use the study of animal development to show students that death is a natural process (Ryerson, 1977).

8. Bibliocounseling can be helpful in helping a child understand death; however, books should be carefully selected by adults and followed up with a discussion in order to clarify misconceptions that may occur. Hammond (1980a) was so moved by her experience in counseling two children whose mother had died that she wrote a children's picture book on death, *When My Mommy Died* (Hammond, 1980b). She suggests two clinical books: *A Child's Parent Dies* (Furman, 1974) and *Children of Parting Parents* (Tessman, 1978). She recommends *Learning to Say Goodbye When a Parent Dies* (LeShan, 1976) for junior high school-age children. Additional references and suggested readings are listed at the end of this chapter.

9. Ryerson (1977) suggests that counseling activities with children include reading and discussing fairy tales or stories that include non-threatening references to death; role playing a situation in which one child comforts another or a visit to a nursing home; using puppets to reenact a familiar story depicting death; drawing a picture of the family or a situation that includes the person who died; or play therapy activities.

COUNSELING WITH CHILDREN FROM DIFFERENT CULTURES

The child who enters the counselor's office may be black, white, native American, Asian, Mexican, or from a number of other cultures or subcultures. The counselor is most often Caucasian and middle class. How can these two uniquely different individuals eliminate the cultural barriers and form the facilitative relationship necessary for effective counseling?

For counseling to be effective, most researchers would agree, the essential ingredients of understanding and respect must be present. Counselors attempt to understand the world of the child as the child perceives it, and they have faith in the child's ability to grow and fulfill his or her potential, given the proper support and guidance. In theory, counselors respect each person's uniqueness and potential. In practice, however, barriers may consciously or unconsciously interfere with this facilitative counseling relationship. Many counselors seem unaware of the cultural differences that exist between themselves and their clients. In fact, Lewis suggests that counselors may "unconsciously make their own tastes or demands for excellence and perfection the measure of goodness, pronouncing all that is broadly different from them imperfect and low or of secondary value" (1976, p. 28). On the other hand, some counselors have the tendency to overcompensate for the cultural difference. In their efforts to be fair and understanding, these counselors may lose their objectivity and effectiveness (Lewis, 1976).

Smith suggests that increased research on counseling minorities may have led to even greater stereotyping: "In an effort to sensitize others to the situations of members of a particular racial group, we sometimes ignore individual differences—defeating the very goals we set out to accomplish" (1977, p. 390). She defines stereotypes as methods "that people use for refusing to deal with each other on an individual basis" (1977, p. 390), an accusation that hits at the very core of the counselor's philosophy and ethical responsibility.

There is research to indicate that clients are treated differentially on the basis of their racial and group affiliation (Yamamoto, James, Bloombaum, & Hattem, 1967; Yamamoto, James, & Palley, 1968). Smith (1977) proposes that, if counselors select their helping technique on the basis of the client's race or socioeconomic class, they are treading in dangerous waters. She suggests that counselors use whatever technique is appropriate to help any client become productive and self-fulfilling.

Sue (1977) states that cultural, class, and language factors discriminate against the culturally different and suggests that a "culturally competent counselor" is one who is knowledgeable of cultural and class factors and is able to use differential counseling approaches that are consistent with the client's lifestyle. Sue also advocates that counselors examine what they do in counseling (the process) and the goals they hold for their clients to determine their appropriateness for the client and his or her culture.

Wrenn (1976) found that many of the values of different cultures are appropriate concerns for the counselor working with children—specifically, respect for authority figures, the values of past adult experiences, the role of women in the culture, and attitudes toward sexuality.

1. *Respect for authority figures.* Cultures vary in the degree to which children are allowed to respond to or question the authority of adults. Whereas a counselor might suggest to an American child that she discuss a conflict with her parents, this behavior could be considered highly disrespectful in some homes.

Moreover, within our culture there are subcultures that are rebellious or distrustful toward all authority figures. The counselor may be considered to be a part of the prevailing "establishment," and the child will view this supposedly accepting and nonjudgmental person with a great deal of suspicion.

2. *The value of adults' past experiences.* Because of the rapid and complex changes in American society during the past several years, many young people today do not consider the experiences of their elders as relevant and meaningful for their lives. Wrenn found this idea prevalent in many of the other countries he studied and suggests that coun-

selors should be careful about citing their past experiences to children. The emphasis should be on what the *clients* can do to solve the problem under the present circumstances. They should aim for a solution that will agree with the client's values, not necessarily the counselor's values.

3. *The role of women in the culture.* The current emphasis in the United States is on equal rights and respect for women. However, other cultures may not view the woman's role as equal; many have not made significant progress toward equal educational and occupational opportunities nor equal rights.

Counselors, too, need to become aware of their own views toward a woman's place in the world. Some unconsciously guide their female child clients toward traditional roles and encourage traditional socialization processes.

4. *Attitudes toward sexuality.* According to Wrenn's (1976) study, most young people in the United States consider sexual activity as a normal part of their life. He found that eight of the sixteen countries studied agreed with this idea. Wrenn cautions counselors to be aware of their own attitudes toward sexual behavior and toward homosexuality, and not to allow their attitudes to interfere with the counseling relationship. Attitudes toward sexuality may not affect cross-cultural counseling in particular, but they may interfere in any counseling relationship.

Wrenn also discusses cultural differences in attitudes toward work and leisure, the culture's emphasis on economic and personal security, and attitudes toward occupational choices. These areas would be of prime importance to counselors working with older youth who are making important choices concerning their careers and vocations.

Sue and Sue (1977) suggest that three cultural barriers may hinder cross-cultural counseling: language barriers, class-bound values, and culture-bound values.

1. *Language barriers.* Much traditional counseling has placed emphasis on the establishment of rapport through verbal and nonverbal communication. Children from other cultures or subcultures may be disadvantaged in their ability to communicate their thoughts or feelings accurately. Counselors often are not familiar with the informal language or slang of other cultures. The meaning of body language, such as eye contact or personal space, varies from culture to culture. These factors may make communication between the counselor and child extremely difficult and lead to misconceptions and misunderstandings.

2. *Class-bound values.* Sue and Sue (1977) point out that class-bound values may hinder counseling because of conflicting attitudes and different expectations from counseling. Some of the areas of concern investigated by Wrenn (1976) could be a part of this barrier (attitudes toward women, sexuality, work, education).

3. *Culture-bound values.* Cultures hold differing attitudes, values, beliefs, mores, and customs. Counselors can consciously or unconsciously communicate that these differences are inferior or a handicap to be overcome.

Sue (1978, p. 451) lists the characteristics of a culturally effective counselor as:

1. Understanding his or her own values and philosophy concerning the nature of people and their behavior, realizing that others may differ
2. Recognizing that "no theory of counseling is politically or morally neutral"
3. Understanding that sociological and political forces external to the person have shaped culturally different persons
4. Being able to view the world as the client does, avoiding being "culturally encapsulated"
5. Being truly eclectic, drawing on techniques and methods of counseling appropriate to the culture and lifestyle of the client

Stimulated by Sue's discussion, Arredondo-Dowd and Gonsalues proposed a "counselor training program with a specialization in bilingual-multicultural education ... [requiring] specific attitudes, skills, and competencies based on the interdisciplinary philosophies of counseling, bilingual education, and multicultural education" (1980, p. 657). They recommend that direct cultural competencies, linguistic competencies, and pedagogical competencies be included in counselor training to prepare culturally effective counselors. Pointing to the present multicultural-bilingual American culture, the increasing numbers of immigrants and refugees, the fact that counselors have expressed a feeling of need in this area, and the involvement of counselors in federal training programs to develop better bilingual programs, the authors suggest strongly that counselors must act now in order to meet the future more efficiently.

Several strategies have been studied to help counselors eliminate those barriers that may be present in cross-cultural counseling. Counselors have been encouraged to become more aware of the differing cultures in an effort to understand their clients better. Counselor education programs have been suggested to recruit and train minority counselors. A number of peer counselor programs have been successful in meeting the needs of culturally different children. Because of similarity of background, perspective, experience, and personality, peers are often able to build trust and rapport when others have failed.

As with counseling with other social concerns of children, counselors may first need to examine their own attitudes, stereotypes, prejudices, and feelings toward cultural groups in order to assure that counseling is as effective as possible.

SUMMARY

Children with unique social problems present special challenges to counselors. It is our belief that counselors can effectively handle these challenges if:

1. They have respect for individuals and a deep belief in the worth of persons and their ability to solve their own problems.
2. They know and understand themselves and their attitudes, values, and beliefs.
3. They continue diligently to seek knowledge and refine their counseling skills in order to reach their full potential as effective helpers.

SUGGESTED READING FOR CHILDREN[1]

Abandonment

Byars, Betsy. *The house of wings*. Illustrated by Daniel Schwartz. New York: Viking Press, 1972 (142 pages). A wounded crane and the care an old man gives it teach Sammy to love the grandfather whom he couldn't understand before. Ages 10–12.[3]

Clymer, Eleanor. *Luke was there*. New York: Holt, Rinehart & Winston, 1973 (74 pages). Julius and his brother Danny are sent to a children's home when their mother has to be hospitalized. Already abandoned by his father, uncle, and stepfather, Julius is further upset when Luke, counselor at the home, has to leave. Ages 8–12.[1]

Karl, Jean E. *Beloved Benjamin is waiting*. New York: Dutton, 1978 (150 pages). Hounded by a gang of kids after her mother's disappearance leaves her on her own, Lucinda hides in the abandoned caretaker's house in the local cemetery where she makes contact with intelligent beings from another galaxy. Ages 11 and up.[5]

O'Dell, Scott. *Island of the blue dolphins*. Boston: Houghton Mifflin, 1960 (184 pages). The Island of St. Nicolas is a harsh rock that looms far off the California coast. It was on this bleak and lonely place, according to history, that an Indian girl spent eighteen years alone during the 1800s. This novel tells her story—a story of the courage and self reliance, and acceptance of fate that transformed an ordeal into an uplifting experience. Ages 10 and up.[2]

Sachs, Marilyn. *The bears' house*. Illustrated by Louis Glanzman. Garden City, N.Y.: Doubleday, 1971 (82 pages). Fran Ellen's real home is a sad place—no father, a sick mother, and no money. But she also has an imaginary home—the doll house her teacher brought to school. Here in her dream home, all her wishes come true. Ages 10–12.[3]

Adoption/Foster homes

Caines, Jeannette F. *Abby*. Pictures by Steven Kellogg. New York: Harper & Row, 1973 (32 pages). Pre-school Abby enjoys her special place in the family as the adopted child. Ages 3–7.[5]

[1]Sincere appreciation and gratitude is given to Margaret Sumner, Learning Resources Center, Austin Peay State University, Clarksville, Tennessee; and to Elenor Brown and Flo Plemmons, Linden Elementary School, Oak Ridge, Tennessee, for their diligent efforts in combining this list of suggested readings for children.

Cameron, Eleanor. *A spell is cast.* Illustrated by Beth and Joe Krush. Boston: Little, Brown, 1964 (271 pages). A Junior Literary Guild selection. Cory Winterslow, visiting her stepmother's family in California, believes she is alone in the world because she was never legally adopted by her stepmother after her parents' death, and she desperately wants to belong. A tidal wave, among other things, makes her desire a reality. Ages 10–12.[2]

Daringer, Helen F. *Adopted Jane.* Illustrated by Kate Seredy. New York: Harcourt Brace Jovanovich, 1947 (225 pages). Against the background of the early 1900s the story of Jane, an orphan from the James Ballard Memorial Home, is unfolded. She spends a summer visiting two different families, with both of whom she is happy, both of whom want to adopt her. Jane makes a happy, though not an easy choice. 10–12 years.[2]

Doss, Helen (Grigsby). *Family nobody wanted.* Boston: Little, Brown, 1954 (267 pages). A dozen years ago Carl Doss, a Methodist minister, and his wife Helen adopted a baby boy. Now they have a dozen children—all adopted, although considered unadoptable because of mixed racial parentage. The author tells how these children all fitted into one happy family. 9–12 years.[2]

Fitzgerald, John. *Me and my little brain.* New York: Dial Press, 1971 (137 pages). This first-person narrative humorously and somewhat fancifully depicts a boy's acceptance of his newly adopted brother and an orphan's adjustment to the death of his parents and brother. The four-year-old's anguish after witnessing the death of his family is vividly portrayed, making it easy for the reader to sympathize with him. Ages 9–12.[3]

Haywood, Carolyn. *Primrose Day.* New York: Harcourt Brace Jovanovich, 1942 (200 pages). Merry Primrose Ramsay, an English girl of seven, comes to America. This is the story of her trip on the boat, of her new home with Aunt Helen and Jerry, and of school, where things are at first difficult. 10–12 years.[2]

Paterson, Katherine. *The great Gilly Hopkins.* 1st ed. New York: Thomas Y. Crowell, 1978 (148 pages). An eleven-year-old foster child tries to cope with her longings and fears as she schemes against everyone who tries to be friendly. Ages 11 and up.[4]

Terris, Susan. *Whirling rainbows.* Garden City, N.Y.: Doubleday, 1974 (153 pages). A 13-year-old adopted Jewish girl of American Indian heritage seeks to find her real self at summer camp. 9–12 years.[5]

Warren, Mary P. *Walk in my moccasins.* Illustrated by Victor Mays. Philadelphia: Westminster Press, 1966 (157 pages). Story about the adjustment problems faced by five Sioux children adopted by a Montana teacher and his wife. 10–12 years.[2]

Child abuse

Byars, Betsy. *The pinballs.* New York: Harper & Row, 1977 (136 pages). Three children of diverse backgrounds are placed with the Masons, who have taken care of many other foster children, and begin to help one another accept things as they are. Ages 11 and up.[6]

Hunt, Irene. *The lottery rose.* New York: Scribner's, 1976 (185 pages). Georgie Burgess, a victim of child abuse, is sent to live in a home for boys, where he learns to replace suspicion with trust and friendship. Ages 11 and up.[4]

Smith, Doris Buchanan. *Tough Chauncey.* Frontispiece by Michael Eagle. West Caldwell, N.J.: Morrow, 1974 (222 pages). Abused and neglected by his family, a "tough" 13-year-old sees running away as the only solution until a friend opens his eyes to an alternative. Ages 11 and up.[5]

Death

Ball, Zachary, pseud. *Bristle Face.* New York: Holiday House, 1962. Death of pet. Orphan. Parent/parents: substitute. Running away. A story about a homeless boy's affection for a dog that attaches itself to him and the way in which boy and dog find a home with a kind-hearted man. The setting is in the rural South (Mississippi) at the turn of the century. Ages 10 and up.[2]

Borack, Barbara. *Someone small.* Pictures by Anita Lobel. New York: Harper & Row, 1969 (32 pages). Death of pet. Sibling: new baby. A little girl resents her baby sister and asks for a bird of her own. She gets the bird and plays and plays with it. As it gets older, so does her baby sister, who is now fun to play with. Then the bird dies, and the little girl learns that her sister can also share sad times. Written in rhymed sentences. Ages 4–7.[2]

Brown, Margaret W. *Dead bird.* Illustrated by Remy Charlip. Scott, W. R., 1958. Death: funeral. In finding a dead bird, still warm but dead, a little girl and her playmates meet death for the first time. Ages 4–7.[2]

Cleaver, Vera & Bill. *Where the lilies bloom.* Illustrated by Jim Spanfeller. Philadelphia: Lippincott, 1969 (174 pages). Death: of father. Family: unity. Promise: keeping. Resourcefulness. This is the story of a young Appalachian girl's attempt to preserve the dignity and independence of her family in the face of frightening odds. Her father's death posed a very real problem for Mary Call Luther who had promised to bury him secretly to save the cost of an undertaker and preacher. She had also promised to take care of the family, to prevent them from becoming charity cases, and to stand in the way of her "cloudy-headed" older sister's marriage. Ages 11 and up.[2]

Corbin, William, pseud. *Golden Mare.* New York: Coward, McCann & Geoghegan, 1959. Death: of pet. Cardiac conditions. Courage, meaning of. Pets: love for. Twelve-year-old Robin Daveen had rheumatic fever as a young child. The disease left him with a severely damaged heart. Because of his heart condition, Robin's physical activities are limited to riding a gentle old mare named Magic around the corral and shooting his .22 calibre rifle at tin cans. Ages 9–12.[1]

Fenton, Edward. *Duffy's rocks.* New York: Dutton, 1974 (198 pages). An Irish-Catholic boy growing up in the Pittsburgh area in the 1930s painfully searches for his identity. Ages 12 and up.[5]

Greene, Constance C. *Beat the turtle drum.* Illustrated by Donna Diamond. New York: Viking Press, 1976 (119 pages). Sustained by her parents and friends, Kate recalls and grieves for her younger sister, Joss, suddenly dead at eleven. Ages 11 and up.[6]

Kaplan, Bess. *The empty chair.* New York: Harper & Row, 1975 (243 pages). After her mother's death and her father's remarriage, Becky feels that she must fight against growing to love her stepmother because of loyalty to her mother and fear of her mother's angry ghost. Ages 11 and up.[6]

Little, Jean. *Home from far.* Illustrated by Jerry Lazare. Boston: Little, Brown, 1965 (145 pages). A Junior Literary Guild selection. When Jenny Macgregor's twin brother Michael is killed, her parents take in as foster children a boy Michael's age and his younger sister. How Jenny and the boy courageously try to adjust to the new life forced upon them makes up this story. Ages 10–12.[2]

Mann, Peggy. *There are two kinds of terrible.* Garden City, N.Y.: Doubleday, 1977 (132 pages). After his beloved mother dies of cancer, a boy must learn to relate to his father who has withdrawn into his own shell of suffering. Ages 10 and up.[4]

Paterson, Katherine. *Bridge to Terabithia.* Illustrated by Donna Diamond. New York: Thomas Y. Crowell, 1977 (128 pages). The life of a ten-year-old boy in rural Virginia expands when he becomes friends with a newcomer who subsequently meets an untimely death trying to reach their hideaway, Terabithia, during a storm. Ages 10 and up.[4]

Shecter, Ben. *Someplace else.* New York: Harper & Row, 1971 (167 pages). Young Arnie Shiffman didn't like his new neighborhood at all—too many tough gangs, tramps, and, even worse, that pest, Gloria. Then he met Elliot, the best stink-bomb-maker on the block, and Houdini, the wonder dog. Ages 10–12.[3]

Smith, Doris Buchanan. *A taste of blackberries*. Illustrated by Charles Robinson. New York: Thomas Y. Crowell, 1973 (58 pages). Jamie's antics and exuberance make him special to everyone, and especially to his best friend. When Jamie dies, his friend must cope with his grief and guilt. Ages 9–12.[3]

Viorst, Judith. *The tenth good thing about Barney*. New York: Atheneum, 1971. A little boy saddened by the death of his cat thinks of nine good things about Barney to say at his funeral. Ages 6–9.

White, E. B. *Charlotte's Web*. New York: Harper & Row, 1952. The story of a little girl who could talk to animals, but especially the story of the pig, Wilbur, and his friendship with Charlotte, the spider, who could not only talk but write as well. Ages 8–12.[1]

Divorce

Bawden, Nina. *The runaway summer*. Philadelphia: Lippincott, 1969 (185 pages). When a young girl's parents are divorced, she is sent to live with relatives where her growing resentment and hostility create a difficult situation. Ages 9–12.[3]

Berger, Terry. *A friend can help*. Milwaukee, Wisc.: Raintree Publishers, 1974. A narrator, a grade-school child, has been living with only her mother for some time because her parents are divorced. She visits a friend and tells her she feels sad because she misses her dad. She feels better to be able to talk to a child. Ages 3–7.[1]

Berger, Terry. *How does it feel when your parents get divorced?* Photographs by Miriam Shapiro. New York: J. Messner, 1977 (62 pages). Discusses problems and emotions young people experience when parents divorce, the family separates, and life styles change.[4]

Blue, Rose. *A month of Sundays*. Illustrated by Ted Lewin. New York: Watts, 1972 (60 pages). When ten-year-old Jeffrey's parents decided to get a divorce, it was one of those things that happens to everyone. Jeff hated the idea of moving to New York City, where his mother would work. The school was strange, the kids seemed funny, and almost all the sights and sounds of the city were unfamiliar. Ages 9–10.[3]

Cleaver, Vera & Bill. *Ellen Grae*. Illustrated by Ellen Raskin. Philadelphia: Lippincott, 1967 (89 pages). Ellen Grae, a happy, unrealistic girl who loves to tell tall tales, must accept the challenge of maturity when her friend Ira tells her his tragic secret. Ages 9–12.[2]

Enright, Elizabeth. *Saturdays*. New York: Harcourt, Brace & Co., 1941, (175 pages). Four motherless children with an understanding father and a housekeeper evolve a scheme for taking turns on successive Saturdays in spending their allowances. Ages 9–12.[2]

Gardner, Richard. *The boys and girls book about divorce;* with an introduction for parents; foreword by Louise Bates Ames; illustrated by Alfred Lowenheim. New York: Science House, 1970 (159 pages). The author's "discussion of common childhood fears and worries attendant on divorce is designed to help the child understand his disquieting thoughts and feelings and to face his problems realistically." Ages 9–12.[2]

Goff, Beth. *Where is daddy? The story of a divorce*. Illustrated by Susan Perl. Boston: Beacon Press, 1969. This story about the psychological crisis of a child whose parents are divorced was written by a psychiatric social worker as an aid in the treatment of children in these circumstances. Ages 4–8.[6]

Greene, Constance. *A girl called Al.* New York: Viking Press, 1969 (127 pages). The narrator is a forthright, good-humored child whose family life is stable and secure. Her best friend Al, whose parents are divorced, proudly tries to be a non-conformist to hide the hurt and loneliness. Ages 11 and up.

Lexau, Joan M. *Emily and the klunky baby and the next door dog.* New York: Dial Press, 1972. Ages 5–8.

Lexau, Joan M. *Me day.* Pictures by Robert Weaver. New York: Dial Press, 1971. Rafer, the son of divorced parents, wakes up elated on the morning of his birthday. As the day progresses and Rafer hears nothing from his divorced father, his spirits go down. When he is sent on a mysterious errand, a surprise awaits him that makes his birthday a happy one. Ages 7–8.[3]

Mann, Peggy. *My dad lives in a downtown hotel.* Illustrated by Richard Cuffari. Garden City, N.Y.: Doubleday, 1973 (92 pages). A young boy is convinced that his parents' separation is his fault. Ages 9–12.[5]

Newfield, Marcia. *A book for Jodan.* Illustrated by Diane de Groat. New York: Atheneum, 1975. When Jodan learns that her parents are separating, she wonders what can be done to keep them together. Ages 9–12.[5]

Norris, Gunilla B. *Lillan.* Illustrated by Nancie Swanberg. New York: Atheneum, 1968 (136 pages). For Lillan, her parents' divorce brings a lot of unpleasant changes, such as Mama going to work, and having to rent out the best part of their apartment. There is also the nagging fear that Papa's going could lead to Mama's going as well. This story, set in Sweden, points up the problems Lillan has to face before she grows up. Ages 9–12.[2]

Sachs, Marilyn. *Veronica Ganz.* Illustrated by Louis Glanzman. Garden City, N.Y.: Doubleday, 1968 (156 pages). Veronica Ganz, the bully of Grade 8B, meets her match in little Peter Wedemeyer until she discovers a secret weapon. Ages 9–12.[2]

Family

Brenner, Barbara Johnes. *A year in the life of Rosie Bernard.* Illustrated by Joan Sandin. New York: Harper & Row, 1971 (179 pages). When motherless Rosie Bernard arrived in Brooklyn in 1932, she was scared. Coming to live with nine relatives she had never met before was not easy, but she soon became fast friends with her three cousins, especially Peter. Ages 9–11.

Brink, Carol R. *Caddie Woodlawn: A frontier story.* New York: Macmillan, 1935. Eleven-year-old Caddie Woodlawn is considered to be a tomboy by her family. During the 1860s, this is a change in gender role. The reader is treated to scenes of a strongly knit family in which the Woodlawn children are guided and disciplined by loving and concerned parents. Ages 9–12.[1]

Burch, Robert Joseph. *Simon and the game of chance.* Illustrated by Fermin Rocker. New York: Viking Press, 1970 (128 pages). Thirteen-year-old Simon's father sermonized against everything Simon wanted to do—from joining the basketball team to getting a Saturday job. This story tells how, through family tragedy, Simon and his father discovered that they shared more than either of them had suspected. Ages 10–12.[2]

Byars, Betsy. *The cartoonist.* Illustrated by Richard Cuffari. New York: Viking Press, 1978 (119 pages). In the face of his mother's insensitivity and his grandfather's self-absorption, Alfie draws cartoons in his own special attic room, until events force him to defend and come out of his private world. Ages 10–12.[6]

Byars, Betsy. *Go and hush the baby.* Illustrated by Emily A. McCully. New York: Viking Press, 1971. Will tries to quiet his crying baby brother by singing "For he's a jolly good baby," playing games, and telling stories. Ages 3–6.[3]

Byars, Betsy. *The midnight fox*. Illustrated by Ann Grifalconi. New York: Viking Press, 1968 (157 pages). Tom hated the idea of spending the summer on his relatives' farm. But after he saw a black fox there, he enjoyed the days he spent watching her—until she stole a turkey and his uncle set out to kill her. Ages 9–12.[2]

Byars, Betsy. *The TV kid*. Illustrated by Richard Cuffari. New York: Viking Press, 1976, (123 pages). To escape failure, boredom, and loneliness, a young boy plunges with all his imagination into the world of television. Ages 9–12.[6]

Byars, Betsy. *Trouble River*. Illustrated by Rocco Negri. New York: Viking Press, 1969 (158 pages). Dewey Martin and his grandmother must make their way down the Trouble River on a homemade raft to escape the danger of hostile Indians. They find the raft hard to navigate on the river, but they persevere and eventually reach Hunter City and safety. Ages 9–12.[2]

Carlson, Natalie Savage. *The half sisters*. Pictures by Thomas di Grazia. New York: Harper & Row, 1970 (163 pages). It is the summer of Luvvy Savage's twelfth birthday and she has high hopes that when her half sisters arrive home from boarding school they will recognize how grown-up she has become. Ages 10–12.[3]

Carroll, Ruth (Robinson) & Latrobe. *Tough Enough*. New York: Henry Z. Walck, Inc., 1954. Beanie's family thought the puppy was a real nuisance, till Tough Enough had a chance to prove his worth during a flash flood. Ages 8–10.[2]

Cleary, Beverly. *Ramona and her father*. Illustrated by Alan Tiegreen. West Caldwell, N.J.: Morrow, 1977 (186 pages). The family routine is upset during Ramona's year in second grade when her father unexpectedly loses his job. Ages 8–11.[5]

Cleary, Beverly. *Ramona and her mother*. West Caldwell, N.J. Morrow, 1979 (208 pages). Ramona finally realizes her mother loves her for herself—even though Ramona is having a hard time being seven-and-a-half. Ages 8–11.[5]

Cleaver, Vera. *Where the lilies bloom*. Philadelphia: Lippincott, 1969, (174 pages). Death: of father. Family: unity. Promise: keeping. Resourcefulness. This is the story of a young Appalachian girl's attempt to preserve the dignity and independence of her family in the face of frightening odds. Her father's death posed a very real problem for Mary Call Luther who had promised to bury him secretly to save the cost of an undertaker and preacher. She had also promised to take care of the family, to prevent them from becoming charity cases, and to stand in the way of her "cloudy-headed" older sister's marriage. Ages 11 and up.[2]

Coles, Robert. *Dead end school*. Illustrated by Norman Rockwell. Boston: Little, Brown, 1968 (100 pages). Basing his story on actual events, the author relates the experiences of Jim, a Black boy who is moved from one ghetto school to another. Ages 11 and up.[2]

Cone, Molly Lamken. *Annie, Annie*. Boston: Houghton Mifflin, 1969 (112 pages). Annie's parents allow her to make all her own decisions. She misunderstands their policy, feels that they don't really care about her, and rebels by taking a live-in job with the Sigbys, where there are rules for everything. All Annie has to do is what she's told and she loves it—at first, that is. Ages 10–13.[2]

Cone, Molly Lamken. *A promise is a promise*. Illustrated by John Gretzer. Boston: Houghton Mifflin, 1964 (153 pages). This is the story of a Jewish family and of Ruthy Morgen, an impulsive girl who has troubles with dates, older brothers, best friends, sharp-tongued neighbors and two forlorn cats. Ages 11–13.[2]

Danziger, Paula. *The cat ate my gymsuit*. New York: Dell, 1974. Marcy Lewis thinks of herself as a frump. She is encouraged to think for herself by a new

English teacher, and thereby brings about changes in the family. Ages 11 and up.

Fox, Paula. *Blowfish live in the sea.* New York: Bradbury Press, 1970 (pages 116). Carrie's half brother Ben has long felt rejected by his father until, on a strange visit in Boston, he is able to see that his father really needs him. Ages 11 and up.[5]

Fox, Paula. *Portrait of Ivan.* Illustrated by Saul Lambert. New York: Bradbury Press, 1969 (131 pages). There are two portraits of Ivan. One, commissioned by his father, is a painter's likeness. The other is a puzzle, which only Ivan can complete after journeying a thousand miles. Ages 11 and up.[2]

Friis, Babbis. *Kristy's courage.* Trn. from the Norwegian by Lise Sømme McKinnon. Illustrated by Charles Geer. New York: Harcourt Brace Jovanovich, 1965 (159 pages). Scarred in an automobile accident and treated thoughtlessly in a new school, Kristy seeks help at the hospital, and emerges as a plucky little girl. Ages 8–10.[2]

Hautzig, Esther. *The endless steppe; growing up in Siberia.* New York: Thomas Y. Crowell, 1968 (243 pages). The author describes the five terrible years during World War II her family spent in Siberia after they were declared capitalists by the Russians and deported there from their native Poland. Ages 11 and up.[2]

Hoban, Russell. *The sorely trying day.* Pictures by Lillian Hoban. New York: Harper & Row, 1964. Father came home feeling tired and weary. His whole household was in an uproar. The more he tried to unravel the quarrel, the more misbehavior he discovered. Only when a mouse finally admitted that he was at the root of it all, did each of the culprits admit his share in the general upheaval—and apologize. Ages 3–7.[2]

Hoff, Syd. *Irving and me.* New York: Harper & Row, 1967 (226 pages). This story relates the adventures and mishaps that happen to thirteen-year-old Artie Granick, a homesick displaced Brooklynite, "when he seeks companionship and excitement in his new home town in Florida." How Artie learns to value his own abilities and succeeds in finding true friendship is told. Ages 12 and up.[2]

Johnson, Annabel Jones & Edgar. *The grizzly.* Pictures by Gilbert Riswold. New York: Harper & Row, 1964 (160 pages). David's father Mark who is separated from David's mother takes him on a weekend fishing trip. The intrusion of a giant mother grizzly, who chases David up a tree, then turns on Mark and injures him, and finally puts their pickup truck out of commission, forces David to take charge. He finds resources in himself that he never dreamed he had. And there is even a hope that David, his mother, and father can become a family again. Ages 10–13.[2]

Kingman, Lee. *The year of the raccoon.* Boston: Houghton Mifflin, 1966 (246 pages). Although his two brothers are outstanding and gifted, Joey, 14, has to satisfy himself with being average—a drifter, his father calls him. But what is wrong, he wonders, with taking time to notice and enjoy the world about him—and his pet raccoon. Ages 11–up.[3]

Lasker, Joe. *He's my brother.* Chicago: Whitman, 1973 (40 pages). A young boy describes the experiences of his slow learning younger brother at school and at home. Ages 4–9.[5]

L'Engle, Madeleine Franklin. *Meet the Austins.* New York: Vanguard Press, 1960. Vicky Austin is 12 years old when Maggy arrives to live with the Austin family. Maggy's father has been killed in an airplane explosion and her guardian asks the Austins to care for Maggy for a while. Maggy, spoiled and willful, changes her behavior as she feels the love within the family. Ages 11–13.[1]

Lenski, Lois. *Blue Ridge Billy*. Philadelphia: Lippincott, 1946. Billy's feelings of love, respect, and loyalty for his family and his joy in music are clearly drawn. Ages 9–12.[1]

Lenski, Lois. *Strawberry girl*. Philadelphia: Lippincott, 1945 (193 pages). Awarded the Newbery medal, 1946. Life among Florida Crackers is here told in the story of Birdie Boyer, the warm-hearted little girl, whose industrious family makes its living by raising strawberries, thus arousing the bitter enmity of the Slaters, who are proud, lazy neighbors. Ages 9–11.[2]

Lexau, Joan M. *Striped ice cream*. Illustrated by John Wilson. Philadelphia: Lippincott, 1968 (95 pages). This is the story of Becky, a little Black girl who wanted striped ice cream for her birthday but was afraid her family's budget wasn't big enough for such a special treat. Ages 8–11.[2]

Lexau, Joan M. *The trouble with Terry*. Illustrated by Irene Murray. New York: Dial Press, 1962 (149 pages). Fifth grader Terry blamed her family for her own failures until she did some straight thinking about the advantages of being a girl instead of a tomboy. Ages 8–11.[2]

Little, Jean. *Spring begins in March*. Illustrated by Lewis Parker. Boston: Little, Brown, 1966 (156 pages). Failing in school and deprived of a room of her own by an unwelcome grandmother, Meg despairs until her seemingly indifferent crippled sister helps her face reality and herself. Ages 10–12.[2]

Little, Jean. *Home from far*. Illustrated by Jerry Lazare. Boston: Little, Brown, 1965 (145 pages). (A Junior Literary Guild selection.) When Jenny Macgregor's twin brother Michael is killed, her parents take in as foster children a boy Michael's age and his younger sister. How Jenny and the boy courageously try to adjust to the new life forced upon them makes up this story. Ages 10–12.[2]

Lord, Beman. *Rough ice*. Pictures by Arnold Spilka. New York: Henry Z. Walck, Inc., 1963 (64 pages). Because his father had been a big hockey star, Eddie put off admitting that a weak ankle was forcing him to play only goalie in the Pee Wee Hockey League. Then came an exciting practice game and to Eddie's chagrin and relief the truth was out. Ages 8–11.[2]

Maddock, Reginald. *The dragon in the garden*. Boston: Little, Brown, 1968. Jimmy has a good relationship with both of his parents, particularly his father, and is able to talk to them about his problems. In this story he adjusts to the difference between the sheltered life he has lived with his parents and the cruelty that he sometimes encounters in the world around him. Ages 10–13.[1]

Neville, Emily Cheney. *It's like this, cat*. New York: Harper & Row, 1963. This is a humorous and lively first-person account of a middle-class boy growing up in New York City. Although the problems he encounters are not particularly serious, they are familiar to many teenage boys. Ages 11 and up.[1]

Norris, Gunilla Brodde. *If you listen*. New York: Atheneum, 1971. Lisa's family has arrived at their summer home and Lisa feels that it will be "just another cage" for her because "no one listens to anyone else in this family." Ages 10 and up.[1]

Norris, Gunilla Brodde. *A time for watching*. New York: Knopf, 1969. Joachim, a ten-year-old Swedish boy, has an insatiable desire to see what makes machines work but does not think of others when he takes the various mechanisms apart. His father comes to realize that it is curiosity that motivates his son. Ages 8–10.[1]

Norris, Gunilla Brodde. *A feast of light*. New York: Knopf, Inc., 1967. Nine-year-old Ulla feels lonely in America and wants to return to Sweden. She is befriended by a woman she calls her American grandmother. A close family relationship helps Ulla through a difficult period of adjustment.[1]

O'Hara, Mary, pseud. *My friend Flicka*. Philadelphia: Lippincott, 1941. Ten-year-old Ken is given a filly he names Flicka. His father has given him the horse reluctantly because he thinks Ken does not act responsibly. Ken nurses Flicka through a grave illness. Family relationships and the lack of understanding between father and son are realistically portrayed. Ages 11–up.[1]

Parkinson, Ethelyn M. *Today I am a ham.* Nashville, Tenn.: Abingdon, 1969. Fourteen-year-old Eric Crane cannot measure up to his father's expectations. He receives satisfaction—and eventually his parent's recognition—as he pursues a hobby in which he experiences success. Ages 9–12.[1]

Perl, Lila. *Me and fat Glenda.* Somers, Conn.: Seabury Press, 1972 (192 pages). Sara Mayberry, a normal, intelligent 11-year-old, tries to fit unobtrusively into her new neighborhood despite the neighbors' reaction to her slightly off-beat parents. Her only friend turns out to be fat Glenda, the neighborhood misfit, whom no one else likes. Ages 9–12.[3]

Perl, Lila. *That crazy April.* Somers, Conn.: Seabury Press, 1974 (188 pages). A month of crazy and often upsetting events, including a hapless fashion show, causes an 11-year-old to question her own outlook and role as a girl. Ages 10–12.[5]

Phipson, Joan, pseud. *The family conspiracy.* New York: Harcourt Brace Jovanovich, 1962. The six Barker children are concerned about their mother's health. She needs an operation and their father has urged her to have it. The mother knows the family cannot pay for the surgery. All the children find jobs and eventually manage to earn the sum necessary for their mother's surgery. The family lives in Australia. Ages 10–13.[1]

Rawlings, Marjorie (Kinnan). *The yearling.* Decorations by Edward Shenton. New York: Scribner's, 1938 (428 pages). A simple story of simple (but by no means incomplex) people living in the scrub regions near the St. John River in Florida. The period is the decades after the Civil War. This is a boy's book, or rather it is a book about a world in which the important happenings are part of a boy's life and have to be understood by him. Ages 12 and up.[2]

Rodgers, Mary. *Freaky Friday.* New York: Harper & Row, 1972 (145 pages). When Annabel woke up in the morning, she found that she had turned into her mother! She spends the day in her mother's body and learns that "When you're grown-up, people don't tell you what to do, you have to tell yourself, which is sometimes much more difficult." Ages 10–13.[3]

Sachs, Marilyn. *Amy and Laura.* Illustrated by Tracy Sugarman. Garden City, N.Y.: Doubleday, 1966 (189 pages). Sisters Amy and Laura learn a lot about both the good and bad parts of life when they must face changes at home and in school upon Mama's return from the hospital. Ages 9–12.[2]

Sachs, Marilyn. *Dorrie's book.* Drawings by Anne Sachs. Garden City, N.Y.: Doubleday, 1975 (136 pages). An only child relates the trials and tribulations she experiences when her mother has triplets. Ages 11–13.[6]

Sachs, Marilyn. *Marv.* Illustrated by Louis Glanzman. Garden City, N.Y.: Doubleday, 1970 (160 pages). The story of Marv, doodler, dreamer, builder, who, with his useless contraptions, tries to win the approval of his formidable older sister. Ages 10–12.[3]

Sachs, Marilyn. *A pocket full of seeds.* Illustrated by Ben Stahl. Garden City, N.Y.: Doubleday, 1973 (137 pages). During World War II, a young Jewish girl returns from an overnight visit with a friend to find her family gone. Ages 10–12.[5]

Sachs, Marilyn. *The truth about Mary Rose.* Illustrated by Louis Glanzman. Garden City, N.Y.: Doubleday, 1973 (160 pages). The aunt for whom Mary Rose was named had died thirty years ago while trying to save her brother from a fire, or so Mary Rose believed until she overheard her Uncle Stanley's version of what happened that night. Ages 10–13.[3]

Sandberg, Inger. *Come on out Daddy!* New York: Delacorte Press, 1969. This book deals with the conflict between a child's desire to play with his parent and the parent's need to finish his work. The father is sympathetic as he explains why he cannot change jobs. The illustrations are a combination of drawings and montages. Ages 4–7.[1]

Sonneborn, Ruth A. *Friday night is papa night.* Illustrated by Emily A. McCully. New York: Viking Press, 1970. Because Pedro's father is unable to come home during the week, each Friday night supper is a special occasion. When he doesn't arrive one evening, the children are brokenhearted. Ages 5–8.[3]

Vestly, Anne Catharine. *Hello, Aurora.* Tr. from the Norwegian by Eileen Amos. U.S. edition adapted by Jane Fairfax. Illustrated by Leonard Kessler. New York: Thomas Y. Crowell, 1974 (135 pages). A young girl whose mother works as a lawyer while her father cares for the family struggles to ignore the neighborhood gossip about her family arrangement. Ages 8–11.[6]

Wilder, Laura (Ingalls). *By the shores of Silver Lake.* Illustrated by Garth Williams. New York: Harper & Row, 1939. Dakota in the early days of the railroads is the background for this true story of American life. Contains a description of a railroad building camp seen through the eyes of Laura at the age of 13. Ages 8–11.[2]

Friendship—Sense of belonging

Brandenberg, Franz. *Nice new neighbors.* Illustrated by Aliki. New York: Greenwillow Books, 1977 (56 pages). The Fieldmouse children find a way to make new friends when they move to a new house. Ages 6–9.[4]

Bulla, Clyde Robert. *Shoeshine girl.* Illustrated by Leigh Grant. New York: Thomas Y. Crowell, 1975 (84 pages). Determined to earn some money, 10-year-old Sara Ida gets a job at a shoeshine stand. Ages 9–11.[5]

Byars, Betsy. *After the goat man.* Illustrated by Ronald Himler. New York: Viking Press, 1974 (126 pages). An overweight boy gains the insight and strength to overcome his problems through his search for Goat Man. Ages 9–11.[5]

Byars, Betsy. *The 18th emergency.* Illustrated by Robert Grossman. New York: Viking Press, 1973 (126 pages). As he thinks of ways to elude the school bully, Mouse recalls his friend Ezzie's 17 solutions to jungle emergencies, but finds that his own plight calls for a different kind of solution. Ages 9–11.[3]

Cunningham, Julia. *Come to the edge.* New York: Pantheon, 1977 (79 pages). After he is befriended by a sign painter, a confused runaway finds trust and a purpose for living. Ages 11–13.[3]

Delton, Judy. *Two is company; story.* Pictures by Giulio Maestro. New York: Crown, 1976 (47 pages). Bear becomes jealous when Duck, his best friend, makes friends with Chipmunk, who is new in the neighborhood. Ages 5–7.[6]

Duvoisin, Roger. *Petunia's treasure.* New York: Knopf, 1975. When Petunia finds a treasure chest on the bottom of the river she discovers the burdens that accompany new-found wealth. Ages 5–7.[5]

Freschet, Berniece. *Elephant and friends.* Illustrated by Glen Rounds. New York: Scribner's, 1978. Elephant's friends join together to help repay his wisdom and kindness. Ages 6–9.

Garrigue, Sheila. *Between friends.* New York: Bradbury Press, 1978 (160 pages). After moving from California to Massachusetts 11-year-old Jill is eager to make new friends. Ages 11–13.[4]

Greene, Bette. *Philip Hall likes me. I reckon maybe.* Pictures by Charles Lily. New York: Dial Press, 1974 (135 pages). Ages 10–13.

Hoffman, Phyllis. *Steffie and me.* Pictures by Emily Arnold McCully. New York:

Harper & Row, 1970 (32 pages). A story told by a little girl about her friendship with Stephanie. They are partners at school, best friends and neighbors, and they both plan to marry Bruce. Ages 6–8.[3]

Iwasaki, Chihiro. *Will you be my friend?* New York: McGraw-Hill, 1970. Allison is anxious to ask the new boy next door to be her friend until she begins to think of him as a troublemaker. Ages 3–5.[6]

Lystad, Mary. *That new boy.* Pictures by Emily McCully. New York: Crown, 1973. The boy who moves in across the street wears funny clothes and glasses and George doesn't think that he is the kind of boy that he can make friends with—until he meets him. Ages 6–7.[3]

McNulty, Faith. *Mouse and Tim.* Pictures by Marc Simont. New York: Harper & Row, 1978. A boy and a mouse describe their relationship during the months they spend together. Ages 8–10.[4]

Mannheim, Grete. *The two friends.* New York: Knopf, 1968. Illustrated with photographs. When Jenny started school everything seemed so new. Even with older sister Selma there to help her, Jenny was frightened. But very soon she began to make friends and she discovered that everything, in school and out, is more fun when you have a special friend to share it with. Ages 6–8.

Marshall, James. *George and Martha encore.* Boston: Houghton Mifflin, 1973 (46 pages). In five brief episodes two hippopotamuses reinforce their friendship. Ages 3–7.

Neville, Emily Cheney. *The Seventeenth-Street gang.* Pictures by Emily McCully. New York: Harper & Row, 1966 (148 pages). A story set in New York City. When a boy named Hollis moves to their block, Ivan, Junior, C.C., Louise, Toby, and Minnow decide that he's not their type and, egged on by Minnow, unite to torment him. Louise is the first to realize that Hollis isn't at all bad, and gradually the others accept him too. Minnow holds out, however, and finds herself ostracized from the Seventeenth-Street gang. Ages 10–13.[2]

Orgel, Doris. *Next door to Xanadu.* Pictures by Dale Payson. New York: Harper & Row, 1969 (160 pages). Set in Brooklyn, this is a story about a lonely, overweight little girl whose attempts to find a best friend lead to a better understanding of herself. Ages 9–11.

Paterson, Katherine. *Bridge to Terabithia.* Illustrated by Donna Diamond. New York: Thomas Y. Crowell, 1977, (128 pages). The life of a ten-year-old boy in rural Virginia expands when he becomes friends with a newcomer who subsequently meets an untimely death trying to reach their hideaway, Terabithia, during a storm. Ages 10–13.[4]

Perl, Lila. *Me and fat Glenda.* Somers, Conn.: Seabury Press, 1972 (192 pages). Sara Mayberry, a normal, intelligent 11-year-old, tries to fit unobtrusively into her new neighborhood despite the neighbors' reaction to her slightly off-beat parents. Her only friend turns out to be fat Glenda, the neighborhood misfit, whom no one else likes. Ages 9–12.[3]

Sachs, Marilyn. *Peter and Veronica.* Illustrated by Louis Glanzman. Garden City, N.Y.: Doubleday, 1969 (174 pages). The unlikely friendship of Peter Wedemeyer and gawky, bullying Veronica Ganz faces its severest test when plans for Peter's Bar Mitzvah uncover the prejudices of both families. New York City in 1941 is the setting for this story. Ages 10–12.[2]

Sharmat, Marjorie Weinman. *Sophie and Gussie.* Pictures by Lillian Hoban. New York: Macmillan, 1973 (64 pages). Four tales capture the charming antics of two squirrels. Ages 6–8.[6]

Viorst, Judith. *Rosie and Michael.* Illustrated by Lorna Tomei. New York: Atheneum, 1974 (39 pages). Two friends tell what they like about each other. Ages 4–7.[5]

Relationships with older generation

Blue, Rose. *Grandma didn't wave back.* New York: Watts, 1972 (62 pages). A ten-year-old girl learns to accept the fact that her grandmother is growing senile and must be sent to a nursing home. Ages 8–11.

Borack, Barbara. *Grandpa.* Pictures by Ben Shecter. New York: Harper & Row, 1967 (32 pages). A picture book in which a little girl tells with love about her grandfather, a grandfather who hides in the same place every time, makes her friends laugh—and always stops tickling when she asks him to. Ages 3–6.[2]

Buckley, Helen Elizabeth. *Grandfather and I.* Pictures by Paul Galdone. New York: Lothrop, 1959. (A Junior Literary Guild selection.) Ages 4–7.

Buckley, Helen Elizabeth. *Grandmother and I.* Pictures by Paul Galdone. New York: Lothrop, 1961. Companion volume: *Grandfather and I.* This story describes the joys of being with one's grandmother, especially when there are problems to be faced and troubles to overcome. Ages 4–7.[2]

Byars, Betsy. *The house of wings.* Illustrated by Daniel Schwartz. New York: Viking Press, 1972 (142 pages). A wounded crane and the care an old man gives it teach Sammy to love the grandfather whom he couldn't understand before. Ages 10–12.[3]

Coutant, Helen. *First snow.* Pictures by Vo-Dinh. New York: Knopf, 1974 (30 pages). Grandmother and a first snow help a little Vietnamese girl understand how death can be accepted as part of life. Ages 7–9.[5]

Greene, Constance C. *The unmaking of Rabbit.* New York: Viking Press, 1972 (125 pages). Paul wants friends more than anything, but when a gang of boys from school tell him that to become a member he will have to steal, he decides that a clear conscience is worth more than friends. Ages 10–13.[3]

Miles, Miska. *Annie and the old one.* Illustrated by Peter Parnall. Boston: Little, Brown, 1971 (48 pages). When Annie's grandmother says that she will return to Mother Earth when the new rug is taken from the loom, Annie tries to stop the rug's growth. Ages 6–9.[3]

Orgel, Doris. *The mulberry music.* Pictures by Dale Payson. New York: Harper & Row, 1971 (130 pages). When Libby's Grandma Liza becomes seriously ill, Libby can't see her and, in a panic, she defies her parents, hospital rules, and locked doors. Her search for Grandma Liza gives her better understanding of herself, and shows her how love survives death. Ages 10–12.[3]

Single parents

Agle, Nan Hayden. *Susan's Magic.* Somers, Conn.: Seabury Press, 1973. Susan Prescott, a fourth grader, wishes that her divorced father would return home. In her loneliness she creates a fantasy world that often brings her trouble. Ages 9–12.[1]

Anckarsvärd, Karin. *Doctor's boy.* Tr. from the Swedish by Annabelle MacMillan. Illustrated by Fermin Rocker. New York: Harcourt Brace Jovanovich, 1965 (156 pages). Orig. publ. 1963 in Sweden. In horse-and-buggy days, the life of a rural Swedish doctor, with long distances to travel, was not an easy one. But to ten-year-old Jon, who was determined to follow his father's profession, making calls with him after school or on weekends was the most exciting part of life. Ages 9–11.[2]

Bonham, Frank. *Durango Street.* New York: Dutton, 1965 (190 pages). Rufus Henry, a Black teenager who had just moved to the Durango Housing Project, knew that he would have to join a gang (and risk revoking his parole) in order to survive. Then Alex Robbins became their police-sanctioned sponsor and things began to look better. Ages 11–up.[2]

Buckley, Peter & Jones, Hortense. *William, Andy and Ramón.* New York: Holt, Rinehart & Winston, 1966 (70 pages). The story of William, Andy and Ramón who live in the same apartment building and are friends. Ages 6–8.[3]

Clymer, Eleanor. *My brother Stevie.* New York: Holt, Rinehart & Winston, 1967 (76 pages). Annie Jenner, a 12-year-old living with her grandmother, is overwhelmed by the responsibility of caring for her difficult younger brother. When she is befriended by an understanding teacher, however, she gains new strength to cope with her dilemma. Ages 8–11.[2]

Harmon, A. W. *Base hit.* Philadelphia: Lippincott, 1970. Hank Howell doesn't play baseball as well as his father expects. Hank dreads every game. His friend's father helps Hank, and helps Hank's father see what he is doing. Ages 9–12.[1]

Keith, Harold Verne. *The runt of Rogers School.* Philadelphia: Lippincott, 1971. Fifth grader Benni Robinson and his mother have just moved to Texas from Oklahoma. Bennie's father died recently, and his mother has taken a new job with a Texas oil company. Bennie is short and faces many humiliations before he comes into his own. Ages 9–12.[1]

Konigsburg, E. L. *About the B'nai Bagels.* New York: Atheneum, 1969 (172 pages). Mark had three worries: his Bar Mitzvah performance, his best friend who found another best friend, and his performance as a member of the B'nai B'rith Little League team. Ages 10–13.[2]

La Farge, Phyllis. *Joanna runs away.* Pictures by Trina Schart Hyman. New York: Holt, Rinehart & Winston, 1973 (55 pages). Almost without meaning to, a little girl tries to make her special daydream about the vegetable man's cart horse come true. Ages 7–9.[5]

Lenski, Lois. *Blue Ridge Billy.* Philadelphia: Lippincott, 1946. Billy's feelings of love, respect, and loyalty for his family and his joy in music are clearly drawn. Ages 9–12.[1]

Lexau, Joan. *The trouble with Terry.* Illustrated by Irene Murray. New York: Dial Press, 1962 (149 pages). Fifth grader Terry blamed her family for her own failures until she did some straight thinking about the advantages of being a girl instead of a tomboy. Ages 8–11.[2]

Simon, Shirley. *Best friend.* New York: Lothrop, 1964. Jenny has always followed the lead set by her best friend, Dot. When their friendship falls apart, Jenny discovers resources that she did not know she had. She also finds it is very nice to have several friends. Ages 9–12.[1]

Smith, Doris Buchanan. *Tough Chauncey.* Frontispiece by Michael Eagle. West Caldwell, N.J.: Morrow, 1974 (222 pages). Abused and neglected by his family, a tough 13-year-old sees running away as the only solution until a friend opens his eyes to an alternative. Ages 11 and up.[5]

Stanek, Muriel. *I won't go without a father.* Chicago: Whitman, 1972. Steve is envious of children who have fathers and does not want to go to his school's open house. He fears he will be considered different. Ages 8–10.[1]

Wagner, Jane. *J.T.* New York: Van Nostrand Reinhold, 1969 (64 pages). J.T., a constant worry to his anxious mother since his father has left, is running from neighborhood toughs when he finds a badly wounded one-eyed alley cat. J.T. cares for the cat and gains the understanding of the adults in his life. Ages 8–10.[1]

Zolotow, Charlotte (Shapiro). *A father like that.* Pictures by Ben Shecter. New York: Harper & Row, 1971 (32 pages). A small boy tells his mother what he would like a father to be. Ages 4–6.[5]

Notes and sources

Note: Annotations were taken from the following catalog cards as well as *The Bookfinder: A Guide to Children's Literature about the Needs and Problems of Youth Aged 2–15* published by the American Guidance Service.

1. Sharon Spredemann Dreyer, *The Bookfinder: A Guide to Children's Literature about the Needs and Problems of Youth Aged 2–15*, (Circle Pines, Minn.: American Guidance Service, Inc., 1977), 1030
2. Catalog card annotation (Bronx, New York: H. W. Wilson Company)
3. Catalog card annotation (New York, New York: School Library Journal)
4. Catalog card annotation (Williamsport, Penn.: Brodart Company)
5. Catalog card annotation (Burnsville, Minn.: Catalog Corporation of America)
6. Catalog card annotation (Commerce, Georgia: Baker and Taylor Company)

REFERENCES

Arredondo-Dowd, P. M., and Gonsalues, J. Preparing culturally effective counselors. *Personnel and Guidance Journal*, 1980, *58*, 657–661.

Bendiksen, R., and Fulton, R. Death and the child: An anterospective test of the child bereavement and later behavior disorder hypothesis. *Omega*, 1975, *6*, 45–49.

Caskey, Q., and Richardson, I. Understanding and helping child abusing parents. *Elementary School Guidance and Counseling*, March 1975, pp. 196–207.

Cork, M. R. *The forgotten child.* Toronto: Alcoholism and Drug Addiction Research Foundation, 1969.

Elkind, D. Child development and counseling. *Personnel and Guidance Journal*, 1980, *58*, 353–355.

Furman, E. *A child's parent dies.* New Haven, Conn.: Yale University Press, 1974.

Gardner, R. A. *Psychotherapy with children of divorce.* New York: Aronson, 1976.

Gelles, R. J. Violence toward children in the United States. *American Journal of Orthopsychiatry*, 1978, *48*, 580–592.

Glass, M. C. Who would abuse a child? *Social Scope*, 1970, *36*, 580–592.

Green, A. H. Child abuse. In B. B. Wolman, J. Egan, and A. O. Ross (Eds.), *Handbook of treatment of mental disorders in childhood and adolescence.* Englewood Cliffs, N.J.: Prentice-Hall, 1978.

Griggs, S., and Gale, P. The abused child: Focus for counselors. *Elementary School Guidance and Counseling*, 1977, *11*, 189–194.

Grollman, E. *Explaining death to children.* Boston: Beacon Press, 1967.

Hammond, J. M. A parent's suicide: Counseling the children. *The School Counselor*, 1980, *27*, 385–388. (a)

Hammond, J. *When my mommy died.* Ann Arbor, Mich.: 1980. (b)

Hecht, M. A cooperative approach toward children from alcoholic families. *Elementary School Guidance and Counseling*, 1977, *11*, 197–203.

Hefler, R., and Kempe, C. H. *Child abuse and neglect: The family and community.* Cambridge, Mass.: Ballinger, 1976.

Henning, J. S., and Oldham, J. T. Children of divorce: Legal and psychological crises. *Journal of Clinical Child Psychology*, 1977, *6*, 55–59.

Hetherington, E. M. Divorce: A child's perspective. *American Psychologist*, 1979, *34*, 851–858.

Hozman, T. L., and Froiland, D. J. Children: Forgotten in divorce. *Personnel and Guidance Journal*, 1977, *55*, 530–533.

Kastenbaum, R., and Aisenberg, R. *The psychology of death*. New York: Springer, 1976.

Kavanaugh, R. E. *Facing death*. Los Angeles: Nash, 1972.

Kessler, S., and Bostwick, S. H. Beyond divorce: Coping skills for children. *Journal of Clinical Child Psychology*, 1977, *6*, 38–41.

Kristal, H. F. *The role of the school in child abuse and neglect*. Washington, D.C.: American School Counselor Association, 1977.

Kübler-Ross, E. *On death and dying*. New York: Macmillan, 1969.

LeShan, E. *Learning to say goodbye when a parent dies*. New York: Macmillan, 1976.

Lewis, S. Black counselor educators use peer counseling. *Journal of Non-white Concerns in Personnel and Guidance*, 1976, *5*, 23–28.

Linn, L., and Schwarz, L. *Psychiatry and religious experience*. New York: Random House, 1958.

Magid, K. M. Children facing divorce: A treatment program. *Personnel and Guidance Journal*, 1977, *55*, 534–536.

Markusen, E., and Fulton, R. Childhood bereavement and behavior disorders: A critical review. *Omega*, 1971, *2*, 107–117.

Newberger, E. H., and Bourne, R. The medicalization and legalization of child abuse. *American Journal of Orthopsychiatry*, 1978, *48*, 593–607.

Reiner, B. S., and Kaufman, I. *Character disorders in parents of delinquents*. New York: Family Service Association of America, 1969.

Rosenthal, N., and Terkelson, C. Death education and counseling: A survey. *Counselor Education and Supervision*, 1978, *18*, 109–114.

Ryerson, M. Death education and counseling for children. *Elementary School Guidance and Counseling*, 1977, *11*, 165–174.

Salk, L. *What every child would like parents to know about divorce*. New York: Harper & Row, 1978.

Seixas, J. Children from alcoholic families. In N. J. Estes and M. E. Heinemann (Eds.), *Development, consequences and interventions*. St. Louis, Mo.: C. V. Mosby, 1977.

Simpson, M. *The facts of death*. Englewood Cliffs, N.J.: Prentice-Hall, 1979.

Smith, E. Counseling black individuals: Some stereotypes. *Personnel and Guidance Journal*, 1977, *55*, 390–397.

Slager-Jorne, P. Counseling sexually abused children. *Personnel and Guidance Journal*, 1978, *10*, 103–105.

Starr, R. H., Jr. Child abuse. *American Psychologist*, 1979, *34*, 872–878.

Sue, D. W. Counseling the culturally different: A conceptual analysis. *Personnel and Guidance Journal*, 1977, 55, 422–425.

Sue, D. W. Counseling across cultures. *Personnel and Guidance Journal*, 1978, *56*, 451.

Sue, D. W., and Sue, D. Barriers to effective cross-cultural counseling. *Journal of Counseling Psychology*, 1977, *24*, 420–429.

Tessman, L. *Children of parting parents*. New York: Aronson, 1978.

Triplett, J. L., and Arneson, S. W. Children of alcoholic parents: A neglected issue. *The Journal of School Health*, December 1978, pp. 596–599.

U.S. Department of Health, Education and Welfare. *Child abuse and neglect: A report on the status of research*. Washington, D.C.: U.S. Government Printing Office, 1975.

Wilkinson, G. S., and Bleck, R. T. Children's divorce groups. *Elementary School Guidance and Counseling*, 1977, *11*, 204–213.

Wrenn, C. G. Values and counseling in different countries and cultures. *The School Counselor*, 1976, *24*, 6–14.

Yamamoto, J., James, Q. C., Bloombaum, M., and Hattem, J. Racial factors in patient selection. *American Journal of Psychiatry*, 1967, *124*, 630–636.

Yamamoto, J., James, Q. C., and Palley, J. Cultural problems in psychiatric therapy. *Archives of General Psychiatry*, 1968, *19*, 45–49.

CHAPTER
19

COUNSELING WITH EXCEPTIONAL CHILDREN

THE SITUATION OF EXCEPTIONAL CHILDREN

Exceptional children are those who are different in some way from their peers. They deviate from what is considered to be normal or average in physical appearance, learning abilities, or behavior. They may be exceptionally gifted or they may be exceptionally handicapped in their abilities to learn or to function in life. Unfortunately, many societies throughout history have not readily accepted handicapped or disabled persons but have viewed them as evil omens, demons, or even witches. Some have felt that handicapped children were God's punishment for the sins of the parents. Many native American tribes murdered their handicapped children; others worshipped them as gods, loving and protecting them. During the Middle Ages especially, a mentally or physically defective person was often seen as possessed by evil spirits.

Though all of us deviate from the "average" to some degree—in height or weight, introversion or extroversion, the amount of happiness or sadness in our lives, and so on—myths concerning exceptional individuals still pervade our "enlightened" society today. They continue to be stereotyped, shunned, rejected, pitied, "hidden in the closet," or wrongfully institutionalized. Much of our society still provides no medical, psychological, or educational help for exceptional children and continues to segregate them from the "normal" population. Buscaglia states:

> Though they may not be aware of it at the time, the infant born with
> a birth defect and the adult who is crippled later in life, will be limited

not so much by the actual disability as much as by society's attitude regarding the disability. It is society, for the most part, that will define the disability as a handicap and it is the individual who will suffer from this definition. (1975, p. 11)

Until recently, counseling with the exceptional child has been limited to assessment, assigning a vague diagnosis, and perhaps suggesting a prognosis. Parents and children have been left to cope with the developmental and adjustment problems as best they could. Usually, no thorough explanation of the condition has been given to the parents or children. They have not been told what to expect in the future in terms of learning, social, or behavior problems. Nor have the parents and children been counseled to help them adjust to and cope with the handicapping condition. Doctors, nurses, teachers, and counselors have been inadequately prepared to meet and to work with the problems presented by being "different" in a society that has little tolerance for and understanding of the different.

Being a special child presents problems to both the parents and the special child. Parents are confused about the disability. They have fears concerning their child's present and future life. They may experience feelings of guilt (Did I cause this?), self-pity (Why did it have to happen to me?), or even self-hate. Having special children causes financial burdens for medical specialists, diagnostic tests, special schools or teachers, special therapies. Having special children causes a strain on personal resources and family relationships. Often the children must have extra attention and care. The time and energy required may take away the time and pleasure that could be derived from relationships with husband or wife, other children, or friends.

What will happen to the special child when he or she grows up? Will this child be self-supporting and able to find happiness; or will the child be rejected by the world, require institutionalization, or possibly become a criminal? These and many other worries, frustrations, fears, and questions plague the parent of the exceptional child.

What are the personal thoughts and concerns of the special child? From an early age, the children begin to realize they are different in some manner. This difference is often interpreted to mean "not as good as" other children. They cannot ride a bike like the kid next door; they look different from the child down the street; they do not understand jokes or what is going on in their surroundings; they are not accepted by the gang and are called *weirdo*, *dumb*, *retard*, or a multitude of other hurtful names. Even gifted children bear the burden of nicknames like *weirdo* or *brain* and may feel rejection because of their exceptionality. The same messages are sometimes subtly conveyed to the children by parents and other significant adults. From verbal and nonverbal signals and interactions, the children are soon assured by the world that being different means being odd, inferior, or worthless.

Growth and maturity bring special problems to both child and parents. Upon entering school, some exceptional children have academic problems. These may be compensated for by withdrawing from the school world physically or psychologically, or the children may become behavior problems. After all, it is better that others think "I do not want to learn" than "I cannot learn." Social relationships may be a disaster; peers often do not understand the exceptionality. No one discusses exceptionalities with other children because society is uncomfortable with the idea of difference. This lack of understanding interferes in friendship, and classmates tend to isolate, reject, and taunt the special child. School can be a very painful place.

At home, things may not be much better, especially at report card time and when the notes come home from the teacher or principal: "Johnny is not doing well in school. He must study harder"; "Johnny is misbehaving in class. We simply cannot tolerate disruptive behavior." No one seems to understand that these learning and behavior problems may have underlying causes. Since most parents are ego involved with their child's academic achievement, pressure may be put on the child to study harder or behave more appropriately. Perhaps Johnny has been working very hard but still cannot quite achieve up to expectations of parents and school. He may decide "What is the use? I cannot please them no matter how hard I try." Society may have lost the opportunity for helping Johnny become a productive citizen and happy adult unless someone intervenes.

Progress toward helping exceptional or handicapped children become accepted members of society has been slow. In the 1800s the first steps were made toward recognizing the needs of the handicapped by the establishment of the first schools for the deaf and blind. In the mid-1930s, the Crippled Children Act was passed by Congress, authorizing financial aid to families of the orthopedically handicapped. President Franklin D. Roosevelt, a victim of polio and handicapped himself, undoubtedly gave impetus to this legislation. President John F. Kennedy, who had a mentally retarded sister, urged that attention be given to the developmental disabilities of children, including mental retardation and learning disabilities. In 1961, a President's Panel on Mental Retardation was established, and in 1963 a National Institute of Child Health and Human Development was founded.

The "child advocacy" movement of the late 1960s and early 1970s resulted in the formation of the National Center for Child Advocacy. During the 1970s and 1980, legislative appropriations and federal committees and agencies increased. In 1975, President Ford signed the Education for All Handicapped Children Act, Public Law 94–142. This law provides that all handicapped children shall receive free educational experiences designed to meet their particular needs. It describes specific procedures for identification and placement, and for designing educational programs for children with certain handicapping conditions. President Jimmy Carter appointed a triple amputee to head the Veterans Administration in an effort to increase public awareness of the handicapped. The launching of the Soviet satellite Sputnik in the 1950s spurred a search for talented children, but in more recent years gifted children have not received as much attention as those with learning, social, or behavioral disabilities. However, President Reagan's proposed budget cuts may reduce federal money and services for all exceptional persons in the coming years. Exceptional children are beginning to come out of the closet, but the steps continue to be slow and painful.

Traditionally, exceptional children have been the responsibility of special educators. Counselors have apparently not seen themselves as trained to meet the needs of exceptional children and have felt that this was a domain they should not enter (Gowan, 1972). However, a contradiction begins to emerge when we consider the philosophy of counseling. Counselors purport to have a deep caring and respect for *all* individuals and their needs. They are committed to the idea that each person is a unique individual and capable of reaching his or her potential. It seems somewhat inconsistent for counselors to be uninvolved with this very large population of today's children. Counseling literature suggests many ways for counseling with the developmental and behavioral problems of children, but there has been little research conducted in the area of counseling with the special problems of exceptional children.

Ohlsen's (1977) definition of counseling has been in print a number of years:

> . . . an accepting, trusting, and safe relationship in which clients learn to discuss openly what worries and upsets them, to define precise behavioral goals to acquire essential social skills, and to develop the courage and self-confidence to implement desired new behaviors. They can learn to make future plans, to appraise their progress toward their goals, to cope with conflict, and to enrich the various facets of their lives—such as family, politics, recreation, religion, and work. (p. 1)

The present authors have defined counseling as a therapeutic relationship, a problem-solving process, a reeducation, and a method for changing behavior. Counseling has also been discussed as a method for helping children cope with developmental problems and as a preventive process. Who more than exceptional children, constantly faced with rejection and failure, need an accepting relationship, someone to listen, assistance in setting present and future goals, guidance for improving interpersonal relationships and, perhaps most important, help in building a strong self-concept and confidence. Counseling with the exceptional child requires no magic formula; however, it does require counselor dedication to the philosophy that all individuals are unique and capable of growth to reach their potential.

METHODS FOR COUNSELING WITH EXCEPTIONAL CHILDREN

Some of the recent literature has been devoted to the topic of counseling the exceptional child. However, the results of much of this research are inconclusive, many studies contain methodological problems, and many of the articles are opinion or suggested methods of counseling without research to support their efficacy. A number of articles focus on counseling with the parents of exceptional children. Some research suggests methods for counseling with children who have learning disabilities or behavioral disorders. Few suggestions are made for counseling with the mentally retarded, physically disabled, or gifted (see Leigh, 1975). The suggestions for counseling exceptional children contained in this chapter are a combination of the most helpful research and opinion published in the current literature. As is true with most counseling methods, the counseling strategies should be incorporated into a positive and accepting counseling relationship.

In order to understand the world of the exceptional child, counselors will need to have a basic knowledge of the handicapping condition. What are the symptoms and general characteristics of a child with this exceptionality? What are the child's limitations? What are the child's strengths and potentials? All children have some developmental and psychological needs in common, but are there other needs specific to the exceptional condition that must be considered? The counselor does not need to become an expert in the teaching techniques of special education, but knowledge of the needs and characteristics of these children is necessary for effective counseling.

Perhaps a primary concern of the counselor working with exceptional children should be the child's self-concept. Gowan (1972) writes that a great part of the counselor's job should focus on changing low self-concepts. He suggests that in many instances just having someone to listen to the problem helps the child to cope with the situation. Being listened to may begin the process of changing the child's evaluation of self and promote feelings of self-worth.

The self-concept of a person begins to form early in life and is determined by the feedback of significant persons in the child's world. In daily interactions, parents, friends, teachers, and peers send verbal and nonverbal messages to children about their worth and abilities. Exceptional children often receive negative messages about their worth. Parents may feel guilty or overprotective; friends and peers may pity them or see them as a burden; teachers may resent having to work with them. "Normal" people feel uncomfortable with "different" children for a variety of reasons. Since most exceptional children experience some type of rejection and failure, it is not surprising that many have negative self-concepts.

Lombana (1980) suggests using bibliocounseling in school guidance activities to overcome stereotypes and negative attitudes toward the handicapped and to provide accurate information about children who are different. She suggests that children should read stories about a handicapped young person and then discuss such topics as the characteristics of a child with this condition, how the child coped with the problem or could cope, reactions of friends and family, and problems and successes. Books and material suggested by Lombana are included in the suggested readings at the end of this chapter.

In attempts to diagnose and find help for a child with special problems, the child as a person is sometimes forgotten in the proliferation of testing, diagnosing, and planning. Though these procedures are designed to aid the child, they may increase self-doubts and fears. Testing, diagnosing, and planning are necessary, but they cannot replace a good relationship—one in which the child feels free to express fears, anxieties, doubts, and insecurities. Being listened to is being respected. It may begin the process of developing or restoring a more positive self-evaluation. Building better self-concepts includes helping exceptional children to see themselves as people who can and do perform and accomplish goals. Unfortunately, most people tend to focus on the child's limitations, rather than emphasizing the child's strengths and what can be done.

Wright (1974) suggests strategies for coping with an exceptionality rather than succumbing to it:

1. Emphasize what the children can do.
2. Evaluate as worthwhile areas of life in which the children can perform.
3. Encourage the children to play an active part in deciding on their life's role.
4. Show an appreciation of the achievements of the children, even though they may fall short of some standard.
5. Assure the children that the negative aspects of their lives are manageable rather than overwhelming.
6. Discuss with the children ways in which the disabilities may be overcome, removed, or compensated for with aids or new skills and behaviors.
7. Assist the children to find ways to live satisfactorily with their limitations, even though they are a hindrance.

A good self-concept is essential for a happy life, success in friendships, career choices, marriage, and all relationships. Counseling can begin by helping the child feel good about him- or herself and others. (See Poor Self-Concept, Chapter 17, for specific ideas for improving self-concept.)

CATEGORIES OF EXCEPTIONALITY

A controversy exists over the categorizing or labeling of children as *learning disabled, mentally retarded, deaf,* and so on. Hobbs (1975) points out that children who are so categorized may be permanently stigmatized, rejected, or prevented from developing in a healthy manner. There is the possibility these children will be assigned to inferior educational programs, institutionalized, or sterilized because of poor diagnoses; this is especially true of minority children. Minority children, those most often categorized or labeled as exceptional, are often the very children who need special attention or educational services to encourage their achievement. Furthermore, classification of a child can encourage the behaviors characteristic of the label. Nevertheless, Hobbs points out, classification is necessary to obtain services for exceptional children. Children who do not neatly fit categories may have trouble obtaining diagnostic services and treatment. Thus, in spite of its problems, classification and labeling are essential. Hobbs advocates better safeguards to decrease the detrimental effects of categorization. He concludes that exceptional children have the same needs as other children and should be treated no differently unless their behavior warrants such treatment.

Haring (1978) categorizes exceptional children in the following ways:

1. Sensory handicaps, including children with hearing and vision impairment
2. Mental deviations, including the gifted as well as the mentally retarded
3. Communication disorders, such as speech and language disorders
4. Learning disabilities
5. Behavior disorders
6. Health impairments, including neurological defects, orthopedic conditions, diseases such as muscular dystrophy and sickle cell anemia, birth defects, and developmental disabilities

There are a multitude of ways to classify children with problems. It is beyond the scope of this chapter to discuss each exceptionality individually; therefore, what is included is a general discussion of the gifted, mentally retarded, learning disabled, and physically handicapped, and children categorized as having behavioral disorders. These conditions seem to be the most generally recognized exceptionalities and the conditions counselors are most apt to encounter daily.

The gifted

Much of the discussion so far has focused on children who have disabilities or some handicapping condition. However, children who are gifted are also considered to be exceptional, and they, too, face unique problems related to their exceptionality. The current definition of the gifted as used by the U.S. Office of Education (1972) is:

> Gifted and talented children are those identified by professionally qualified persons who, by virtue of outstanding abilities, are capable of high performance. These are children who require differentiated educational programs in order to realize their contribution to self and society.
>
> Children capable of high performance include those with demonstrated achievement and/or potential ability in any of the following areas, singly or in combination: (1) General intellectual ability;

(2) Specific academic aptitude; (3) Creative or productive thinking; (4) Leadership ability; (5) Visual and performing arts; and (6) Psychomotor ability. (Cited by Haring, 1978, p. 389)

This definition is important for not only its emphasis on intellectual performance but its recognition that children are gifted in other areas—leadership, arts, physical abilities. On the basis of this definition, approximately 3% to 5% of the population is considered to be gifted or talented.

It is difficult to describe all the characteristics of a person considered to be gifted. Lewis Terman attempted to define the gifted in his studies during the early 1930s. He dispelled many of the myths concerning the gifted, but his studies focused primarily on the academically gifted. The characteristics he identified do not seem adequate to describe the gifted or talented child of today. Because the definition of giftedness covers many different areas, it seems unfair to rely on a restrictive list of traits that could screen out a gifted student. Haring (1978) suggests that it might be more appropriate to identify gifted students directly through appropriate school programs.

When the Soviets launched Sputnik in 1957, Americans became very concerned with the "space race," and very interested in identifying gifted children and encouraging their growth and progress academically. Less emphasis was placed on helping the gifted socially and emotionally; it was thought that the bright could solve most any problem and find their way without help. Forgotten was the possibility that the bright child could have problems in relationships with friends because of advanced intellectual interests; that this child needed help in making career choices because of the wide range of available opportunities; and that the child could have knowledge beyond his or her years but lack physical or developmental abilities. The pressures placed on the gifted child by parents, teachers, peers, and society were not recognized.

Colangelo and Zaffrann (1979) write that behavioral techniques of counseling will help gifted individuals interested primarily in mastery and integration of new material. They suggest a client-centered counseling approach for the gifted who are more interested in exploration and creativity. These writers point out that the primary tasks of the counselor are: (1) to enhance learning opportunities; (2) to help children (and significant others) understand themselves, their potentials, and their limitations; and (3) to guide the children in developing good social relationships.

Gowan (1972) writes that the counselor for the gifted should be permissive, intraceptive, nondirective, and a good role model for the children. He points out that the gifted are independent and want to solve problems themselves; therefore, they need a counselor who will allow them this freedom. Gowan also warns counselors that overinvolvement with the gifted child may interfere with objectivity and that the halo effect can blur problem areas (that is, one or two outstanding characteristics can influence judgments about the total person). If the counselor identifies too strongly with the bright child and his or her achievements, areas of possible concern can be ignored.

Behavioral disorders

There is some problem in defining an emotionally disturbed child or one considered to have a behavioral disorder. Most labels, criteria, and definitions are vague, although valid and reliable assessments may indicate emotional problems. Behavior indicative of emotional problems can vary according to social and cultural expectations; what is considered normal by one group may appear deviant to another.

Consideration should be given to the possibility that the disturbance or behavior could be due to physiological causes or environmental factors. Children are expected to learn what is acceptable behavior and unacceptable behavior from socialization agents such as parents and schools. "Right" and "wrong" are taught through a system of rewards and punishments meted out by adults. Children depend less on these external reinforcements as the conscience or internal control develops. Because of individual differences, children vary in reaction to this training and their willingness to adapt to adult standards.

Behavior considered to be abnormal and an indication of emotional problems is usually persistent, frequent, and inappropriate to the situation. Most definitions of behavioral disorders or emotional disturbance refer to symptoms such as an inability to maintain satisfactory relationships and/or inappropriate behaviors or feelings for the situation. More severe symptoms include pervasive moods of depression, extreme withdrawal over an extended period of time, and symptoms of psychotic disorders such as schizophrenia or autism. Emotional disturbance or behavioral disorders may also be classified by degree. The more severe cases usually are treated in an institution, while children with milder problems continue to be educated in the public school and function in the everyday environment (Haring, 1978). Though definitions and estimates of the problem vary greatly, the U.S. Office of Education estimates that about 2% of our children are emotionally disturbed. The prognosis for mildly disturbed children is excellent. The future for the more severely disturbed is not as bright; they may not be able to function independently in life. For the purpose of this section, only mildly disturbed children will be considered.

Emotionally disturbed children need love and understanding, but they also need a counselor who can provide security and stability. The counselor who is effective with the emotionally disturbed is able to detect and reflect the feelings and frustrations of the children, discuss these feelings, and decide how to manage them effectively. Much of the success achieved from working with the emotionally disturbed has been due to the relationship between adult and child as well as the technique used. Emotionally disturbed children have often experienced inconsistency in their relationships. They are often suspicious of adults because of past experiences with hurtful people. The counselor of emotionally disturbed children needs to be strong enough to place consistent limits on the children, requiring them to assume responsibility for their behavior.

In order to bring consistency and stability to the life of the emotionally disturbed child, expected and appropriate behaviors can be discussed with the child. At the time of the discussion, it is often helpful to write out what is considered to be inappropriate and the consequences of this behavior. Expected behaviors can be defined by methods such as contracting. The counselor, parents, teachers, and all significant people in the child's life must be willing to set limits and consistently maintain the rules. Behavior modification techniques emphasizing positive reinforcement have been found to be very effective with the emotionally disturbed. Relaxation exercises, talking therapy, physical activities, writing, drawing, or games may be scheduled into the child's day to provide outlets for tension and other emotions. Changes in the environment, expectations, stimulation, and conflicts should be reduced whenever and wherever possible. Peer groups can be used as effective reinforcers and to provide models for appropriate behavior.

Hawke and Lesser (1978) suggest that the counselor of a child whose behavior is antisocial assess the child's present functioning and explore relationships and interactions. The authors state that "management must be related to a careful formulation of the needs and capacities of the child, his family, and society, and the resulting plan must be one that is realistically available and likely to be implemented and followed through by the participants" (p. 233).

The tasks of the counselor of a child with a behavioral disorder can be summarized as: (1) forming a counseling relationship with the child that includes well-defined responsibilities and limits; (2) working to change the image and expectations of the child through counseling and consultation with family and other significant people in the child's world; (3) individual and group counseling to deal with feelings and behaviors, teach social skills, and improve academic performance.

The learning disabled

The newest and most controversial category in the area of exceptional children is the learning disabled (L.D.). Equally controversial are the various definitions of learning disabilities that have been proposed. The National Advisory Committee on Handicapped Children has defined a learning disability as follows:

> Children with special learning disabilities exhibit a disorder in one or more of the basic psychological processes involved in understanding or using spoken or written languages. These may be manifested in disorders of listening, thinking, talking, reading, writing, spelling or

arithmetic. They include conditions which have been referred to as perceptual handicaps, brain injury, minimal brain dysfunction, dyslexia, developmental aphasia, etc. They do not include learning problems which are due primarily to visual, hearing, or motor handicaps, to mental retardation, emotional disturbance, or to environmental disadvantage. (1968, p. 4)

Tarver and Hallahan (1976) list the ten characteristics of the L.D. child most cited in the literature: hyperactivity, perceptual-motor impairments, emotional lability, general coordination deficits, disorders of attention, impulsivity, disorders of memory, disorders of language, specific learning problems in certain academic areas, equivocal neurological signs. Behavioral disparities or a wide range of performance abilities also may indicate the presence of a learning disability. Estimates of the incidence of learning disabilities in children 18 years and younger range from 3% to 40%, depending on the definition used and authority cited.

Just as in counseling with other exceptional children, the counselor begins by recognizing and reflecting the feelings of the L.D. child. Because their characteristics tend to create an unstable world, these children have often experienced failure, rejection, isolation, and confusion. Perceptions of their world change; their visual perception plays tricks on them; their impulsivity causes them trouble with authority figures; they may have communication difficulties because of poor auditory or language skills; they are often clumsy and awkward. These and the other behaviors that accompany their disability do not endear them to teachers, parents, or peers, and emotional problems often result.

One of the tasks of a counselor working with an L.D. child may be to coordinate diagnostic services in order to pinpoint the child's specific strengths and weaknesses and plan an educational program based on these findings. A typical diagnostic evaluation will include physical, educational, and psychological assessments and perhaps the opinions of other specialists, such as speech pathologists or ophthalmologists. This data must be shared with all those working with the child in order for a well organized plan for remediation to be developed and for services not to overlap or be omitted.

Emotional problems, due primarily to feelings of failure and worthlessness, often compound the learning problems of L.D. children. Hawke and Lesser (1978) suggest that some children may respond to special teaching techniques, realistic expectations, and reduced pressures; others may need more specific help in dealing with the feelings of failure and discouragement. Individual or group counseling must be considered an essential part of any program planned for L.D. children. The authors further state that it may be necessary to involve the child and the entire family in counseling in order to deal with the feelings and reactions of all family members. Behavior modification procedures, implemented both in the home and in school, have proven very effective in helping

L.D. children as they provide structure and stability in a world of tur-moil. Relaxation training may help L.D. children cope with tensions and anxieties. Talking therapy can provide an outlet for expression of pent-up feelings and exploration of doubts. The counselor's job is build-ing an improved self-concept, helping the children to learn social skills, assisting the children in learning to cope with environmental demands, and guiding the children in planning ways to realize their potential.

In recent years, drugs have been used by medical specialists to con-trol the attention, distractibility, and behavior of L.D. children. The use of drugs is very controversial, and the counselor would be involved only in observing the effect of the drug and reporting these effects to the parents. Other therapies, such as diet control, megavitamins, and motor training, have been advocated by some professionals. These, too, are still highly controversial. Most have little research support for their use in helping L.D. children.

Dillard, Kinnison, and Caldwell (1978) list five tasks for the coun-selor of an L.D. child:

1. Be a catalyst in changing the reputation of the child from negative to positive through frequent consultation with teachers, parents, and the child.
2. Facilitate communication between teachers, student, and par-ents.
3. Use guidance programs as an aid to counseling.
4. Provide individual or group counseling.
5. Allow the child to be a team member in the planning of the educational process.

These authors suggest that the resource room teacher be a student advocate, teaching social and survival skills to L.D. children, and that the teacher develop contracts for academic achievement, behaviors, attitudes, and so on. These would seem to be equally important tasks for counselors as well.

Rudolph (1978a) summarizes the tasks of counselors with L.D. chil-dren as follows:

1. Recognizing the characteristics of learning disabilities, including those that may be masked by behaviors such as withdrawal or acting out
2. Becoming familiar with the assessment instruments used to determine learning disabilities in order to be able to understand and communicate to others these children's learning problems
3. Coordinating the activities of the professionals (resource teach-ers, school psychologists, medical doctors, special therapists) working with L.D. children
4. Counseling and consulting with parents in order to promote understanding and facilitate growth
5. Counseling with L.D. children, who have their unique learning, social, or emotional problems

6. Counseling and consulting with school personnel in order to promote their understanding of L.D. children's learning, social, and/
   or behavioral problems

The mentally retarded child

The most commonly accepted definition of the mentally retarded
is one developed by the American Association on Mental Deficiency:

> Mental retardation refers to significantly subaverage general intel-
> lectually functioning existing concurrently with deficits in adaptive
> behavior, and manifested during the developmental period. (Grossman,
> 1973, p. 11)

The behavior and potentials of the mentally retarded will depend
on the severity of the condition. A mildly retarded individual can be
educated in the regular classroom with some special help. Vocational
skills, independent living skills, and work-study programs are often a
part of the educational plan. Mildly retarded individuals may be able
to live independent lives and hold jobs, and some have satisfactory
marriages and relationships with others.

The moderately retarded child is usually educated in a self-con-
tained classroom, with instruction concentrated on taking care of personal needs, performing daily tasks, and getting along with others.
Supervision in work or in the performance of other activities is usually
necessary.

Severely or profoundly retarded individuals usually are institutionalized and require constant care and supervision. Many are confined to
bed and cannot care for even their most basic needs. Recent studies
indicate that the severely or profoundly retarded do respond to behavior
modification techniques for learning and improving behavior.

The counseling techniques included in this section are geared to
mildly or moderately retarded children, the groups most likely to face
societal problems and pressures. These children have physical and psychological needs similar to those of other children, but the added handicap of their exceptionality interferes with their adjustment. Hawke
points out that

> the problems of mentally retarded children stem primarily from the
> deficits in intellectual and cognitive ability implicit in the diagnosis.
> In addition, these children are subject to stresses and emotional and
> social problems similar to, or even greater than, those experienced by
> children of normal and superior cognitive ability. The retardation, how-
> ever, limits their ability to deal effectively with these problems. (1978,
> p. 265)

The counselor can concentrate efforts on promoting self-reliance
and self-esteem, and teaching appropriate standards, values, and behavior. Peer feedback and peer modeling can be highly effective counseling
techniques. Group counseling can help the child learn and rehearse
effective ways of behaving. Behavior modification techniques such as

the token system or contingency contracting have been found to work effectively with the mentally retarded.

Counselors will need to work with the parents and other significant people in the child's life to help them understand and encourage the child's abilities. Special attention can be focused on teaching the child independent living skills as well as personal/social skills. The child and parents will also need guidance and assistance in planning for the child's educational and vocational future.

Studies about the value of counseling and psychotherapy for the mentally retarded are inconclusive; however, it seems obvious that the counselor could provide valuable services in the area of personal/social development and in helping the family to deal effectively with adjustment and behavior problems.

The physically handicapped child

Professionals, parents, and educators cannot agree on one definition to cover the children with disabilities or handicaps such as visual and hearing impairments, diabetes mellitus, epilepsy, muscular dystrophy, cerebral palsy, and other physical disabilities and health problems. Many children are multihandicapped, and some conditions have overlapping symptoms. It would, of course, help counselors understand the world of the child if they were aware of the characteristics, physical problems, symptoms, and prognoses of the physically handicapped child. Counselors will also want to know the child's strengths. Lack of knowledge and fear of the unknown can produce fear and apprehension in the counselor, which can be sensed by the child.

The counselor working with the physically handicapped needs to be able to work with all agencies, professionals, parents, and other significant persons in the child's life. Coordinating services, rearranging physical environments, removing barriers and inconveniences, and securing special equipment and materials may be only the first step to meeting the needs of the physically handicapped. The counselor should focus on building feelings of self-worth and healthy attitudes. The children may need to be encouraged to express and recognize their feelings toward the disability, helped to learn social/personal skills, counseled in the area of independent living, and assisted in making vocational plans for the future. More important than the physical limitation is the fact that each child is a unique individual and has capabilities and potential; it is the counselor's role to facilitate growth toward reaching this potential.

Summary

The tasks of the counselor who is working with any exceptional children might include the following:

1. Working toward an understanding of the child's specific exceptionality and the unique social, learning, or behavioral problems that may accompany this exceptionality

2. Counseling for the enhancement of self-concept
3. Facilitating adjustment to exceptionality
4. Coordinating the services of other professionals or agencies working with the exceptional child
5. Helping the significant people in the child's life (parents and teachers especially) to understand the exceptionality, the child's strengths and limitations, and the child's special problems
6. Assisting in the development of effective and independent living skills
7. Encouraging recreational skills and hobbies
8. Teaching personal/social skills
9. Assisting in educational planning and possibly securing needed educational aids and equipment for the child
10. Parent counseling
11. Acquiring a knowledge of and working relationship with professional and referral agencies

The ethical code and guidelines for the counselor working with an exceptional child are best summarized by Buscaglia (1975). He reminds us that children should be allowed to be their own person, unique and individual; these children are *people* first, and that they have the same needs (love, self-actualization, and so on) and the same rights (even to fail) as other children. He suggests that it is our responsibility to listen, encourage, and facilitate their growth by supplying guidance and other resources. We must allow them to be themselves and to make choices about their lives without imposing our ideas, values, and attitudes on them. Buscaglia ends his summarization by reminding us: "And this above all—remember that the disabled need the best *you* possible. In order for them to be themselves, growing, free, learning, changing, developing, experiencing persons—*you* must be all of these things. You can only teach what you are. If you are growing, free to learn, change, develop and experience, you will allow *them* to be" (1975, pp. 20–21).

COUNSELING WITH THE PARENTS OF EXCEPTIONAL CHILDREN

Maes states that "exceptional children, their families, and teachers frequently experience stress beyond that of more typical children and the adults associated with them" (1978, p. 4). There is a social stigma attached to being different. Parents are never prepared to face the reality that their child is handicapped or exceptional in some way. The counselor must be concerned with the feelings and reactions of the parents toward the child for the effectiveness of the counselor's work depends to a great extent on the dynamics of the home environment. Many studies indicate that in some situations parent counseling may be more beneficial than direct therapy or remediation with the child (see Leigh, 1975). Parents, too, must make the adjustments demanded by the child's exceptional condition, and it is important that the counselor see parents in order to facilitate this adjustment.

Many parents are able to accept and adjust to their child's condition in a healthy manner, while others, even though they love their child, may have trouble dealing with their feelings and the situations.

Parents may experience a range of emotions: grief, shock and disbelief; fear and anxiety about the child's future; helplessness because they cannot change the condition; and disappointment because theirs is not the perfect child they expected. They may resent the child because of the burdens placed on the family by the disability. Whatever the feeling, the counselor needs to assist the parents to work through these feelings. Parents are the main support system for the children, and they must be free to accept and support the child in his or her growth and development.

Parents of exceptional children who are gifted do not experience the shame, guilt, or helplessness that parents of other exceptionalities may feel. However, they may find it difficult to cope with the creativity, advanced intellectual development, and precociousness of their child and wish their child were ordinary. Finding adequate and stimulating educational facilities may be frustrating and possibly financially draining.

Gardner (1973) points out several ways parents may react when they learn of their child's learning disability. Mental retardation, emotional disturbance, or a physical handicap may provoke similar reactions. Frequently, parents deny the reality of the problem. As a part of this denial, they may go "doctor shopping," looking for a specialist who will deny the diagnosis or provide a miracle cure. It is not unreasonable to obtain a second or third opinion from doctors; however, after having been taken from doctor to doctor for a period of time, the child may become convinced and fearful that something is terribly wrong.

Parents may have a tendency to overprotect children with disabilities from a world that is cold and hurtful. They may be overwhelmed with pity and express this feeling by becoming a servant to the child's needs. Some become martyrs, giving up their lives and their needs to devote themselves totally to the child. The children of overprotective parents get the idea that they are not capable of doing anything for themselves because their parents have never allowed them the opportunity.

Parents often need to work through their own guilt feelings about the exceptionality. Mothers often feel that a handicap is the result of something they did while pregnant, such as horseback riding, tennis, or a fall. The problem of the child may be seen as a consequence or punishment for the parent's wrong behavior.

Shame concerning the exceptionality may be the parents' primary reaction. "What will other people think?" Parents are often afraid that other people will gossip, accuse, or ridicule. Parents continue to carry vague uncertainties about the causes of disabilities and may suspect that neighbors are blaming them for "bad genes," poor health care, ignorance, or other shameful reasons for the disability.

Counseling tasks for the counselor working with the parents of exceptional children could include:

1. Encouraging and helping parents gain knowledge about their child's exceptionality, the prognosis, and the child's strengths and limitations
2. Assisting the parents in working through feelings and attitudes that may inhibit the child's progress
3. Advising parents concerning state, federal, or community resources available for education, medical, emotional, or financial assistance
4. Assisting the parents to set realistic expectations for their child
5. Encouraging the parents to view their child as a unique individual with rights and potentials and the ability to make choices about his or her own life

There are excellent books available to help both children and parents understand the characteristics of an exceptionality and the future of children with a particular exceptionality. The books of R. A. Gardner contain a section written to the parents about the disability and a section written for the children to explain the disability in terms they can understand. Some books to help children understand some of these exceptionalities (mental retardation, giftedness, and physical handicaps) are listed at the end of this chapter.

Parent groups are probably one of the better ways of helping parents of exceptional youngsters. Through sharing, the parents learn that others have the feelings and problems they are experiencing. They realize that they are not alone in their plight; many other parents have children who are different. Parents not only share their feelings in groups, they also share methods for problem solving. The particular crisis one set of parents is facing may have been experienced by others, and the solution can be discussed. Parent groups provide an atmosphere of understanding, acceptance, and support; they reassure troubled parents that they are not alone and that others care.

COUNSELING WITH THE TEACHERS OF EXCEPTIONAL CHILDREN

Maes (1978) has pointed out that not only exceptional children and their families experience greater stress than typical children and their parents; the teachers of exceptional children also experience stress beyond that of a typical teacher. In a recent survey of attitudes toward the exceptional student (Rudolph, 1978b), it was found that a high percentage of those school personnel questioned were concerned or apprehensive about having exceptional or handicapped children in their class-rooms. Specific concerns of the classroom teachers centered around their competence to meet the educational and personal needs of the child and the teaching time that exceptional children might require, limiting their ability to work with other children. Counselors can give help indirectly to the exceptional child by helping teachers and other school personnel to relieve tensions and pressures. Listening and reflecting teachers' feelings and concerns, helping them to understand the nature of the disability and the child's strengths and limitations, and assisting them in planning classroom management procedures may be an important part of the counseling methods for helping the exceptional child.

The needs of special children and their families have been ignored for too many years. Stereotypes and societal attitudes must be changed. Further research is needed to help us counsel special children more effectively. Money and resources are needed to provide means for helping the children become productive citizens. Exceptional children can learn, can enjoy life, can be independent and productive, and can fulfill their individual potential whether they are exceptionally gifted or handicapped. Exceptional children are unique individuals just as "normal" children are unique. They have the same rights to respect and growth as other children and the same needs. The challenge is there for counselors.

SUGGESTED READING FOR CHILDREN[1]

Mentally handicapped

Byars, Betsy. *Summer of the swans.* New York: Viking Press, 1970. The tragedy of mental retardation and the pain of adolescence are presented in the story of Sara and Charlie, her retarded brother.

Cleaver, Vera and Bill Cleaver. *Me too.* Philadelphia: Lippincott, 1973. Twelve-year-old Lydia is bright and intelligent; her twin sister Lorna has a mental age of five. Lydia's efforts to educate Lorna fail, but she learns to understand the "exceptional" status of her sister.

Friis-Baastad, Babbis. *Don't take Teddy.* New York: Scribner's, 1976. Mikkel, a Norwegian boy, tries to protect his older retarded brother from the police by taking him away on a nightmarish journey.

Konigsburg, E. L. *George.* New York: Atheneum, 1970. Ben manages to hide his schizophrenic symptoms until he enters the sixth grade, when his alter ego, George, begins to speak out loud.

Lasker, Joe. *He's my brother.* Chicago: Whitman, 1974. The home and school experiences of a slow-learning boy are described by his brother.

Little, Jean. *Take wing.* Boston: Little, Brown, 1968. Laurel knows something is wrong with her younger brother although her parents refuse to admit it. Eventually, the family is forced to acknowledge that James is retarded.

[1]Sincere appreciation is expressed to Margaret Sumner, Learning Resources Center, Austin Peay State University, Clarksville, Tennessee, for her diligent efforts in compiling this list of suggested readings for children.

Melton, David. *A Boy called hopeless*. Independence, Mo.: Independence Press, 1976. Mary Jane tells the story of how her family loved and worked with her younger brother Jeremiah who was declared mentally retarded by the doctors.

Platt, Kin. *Hey dummy!* Radnor, Pa.: Chilton, 1971. Neil befriends a brain-damaged boy. When his friend is later accidentally killed, Neil goes into a deep mental shock, and his behavior and speech patterns become similar to his friend's.

Wrightson, Patricia. *A racecourse for Andy*. New York: Harcourt Brace Jovanovich, 1968. Andy, a likable retarded boy, "buys" the local racetrack from a tramp. The adults are amused, but his concerned friends try to protect him.

Physical handicaps

Branfield, John. *Why me?* New York: Harper & Row, 1973. An adolescent girl who is a diabetic comes to terms with her handicap by caring for a dog who has diabetes too.

Cunningham, Julia. *Burnish me bright*. New York: Pantheon, 1970. A mute orphan learns the skill of pantomime, which helps him to survive in a French village.

Garfield, James. *Follow my leader*. New York: Viking Press, 1957. Eleven-year-old Jimmy is blinded by an exploding firecracker. He communicates his feelings as he learns to adjust to life in a dark world.

Killilea, Marie. *Wren*. New York: Dell, 1968. A family faces difficulties not only in helping a baby who has cerebral palsy but in helping an older sister understand and accept her sister's condition.

Litchfield, Ada B. *A button in her ear*. Chicago: Whitman, 1976. Using a very positive approach to a physical handicap, Angela explains to her parents, teachers, and peers how she came to get a hearing aid and how it helps her.

Little, Jean. *Mine for keeps*. Boston: Little, Brown, 1962. When Sally, a cerebral palsy victim, returns home from a school for the handicapped, her family has to learn to give love but not to help too much.

Norris, Gunilla Brodde. *The top step*. New York: Atheneum, 1970. A young boy who has been told he will outgrow the effects of asthma anxiously waits for that day to arrive.

Robinson, Veronica. *David in silence*. Philadelphia: Lippincott, 1966. David's handicap of deafness causes fear, anger, and confusion in those around him.

Southall, Ivan. *Let the balloon go*. New York: St. Martin's, 1968. A 12-year-old boy with a mild spastic condition learns to be truly free to grow in his own way.

Stein, Sara Bonnett. *About handicaps: An open family book for parents and children together*. New York: Walker, 1974. The relationship between Joe and his friend Matthew is strengthened as Matthew's father helps him to understand Joe's handicap. Photographs and separate text for adults are included.

The gifted

Conford, Ellen. *And this is Laura*. Boston: Little, Brown, 1977. Laura thinks she is the only member of her family who isn't extraordinary in some way until she discovers her ability to see into the future.

Cresswell, Helen. *Absolute zero*. New York: Macmillan, 1978. The Bagthorpe family concentrates on winning contests. This story is a humorous portrayal of a whole family with special gifts.

Danziger, Paula. *The cat ate my gymsuit.* New York: Dell, 1974. Marcy and her gifted classmates were bored and frustrated with one substitute teacher after another until the arrival of Ms. Finney, who proved equal to the situation.

Greene, Constance. *A girl called Al.* New York: Viking Press, 1969. Al, an individualistic, independent girl, proudly describes herself as a nonconformist. She and her classmates gradually learn to understand each other.

Gripe, Maria. *Hugo and Josephine.* New York: Dell, 1969. Six-year-old Hugo is a remarkably refreshing child, totally independent and direct. He opens up a new world for his friend Josephine and changes his teacher's ideas about education.

Konigsburg, E. L. *Father's arcane daughter.* New York: Atheneum, 1976. A wealthy, overprotected brother and sister cannot make use of their gifts until a long-lost sister appears and opens the door to a world of new ideas for them.

Rodgers, Mary. *Freaky Friday.* New York: Harper & Row, 1972. An intelligent 13-year-old turns into her mother and, through conferences with school personnel, gains a better understanding of herself and her school problems.

Rogers, Pamela. *The rare one.* Nashville, Tenn.: Nelson, 1973. A sensitive young English boy adjusts to a new family situation and discovers that wisdom does not necessarily accompany intellectual giftedness.

Sebestyen, Ouida. *Words by heart.* Boston: Little, Brown, 1979. This is the story of a young black girl who has a "magic mind" and her courage in trying to make a better life for her family and herself.

Wojciechowska, Mia. *Don't play dead before you have to.* New York: Harper & Row, 1970. Teenaged Byron needs money for a car, so he babysits an unusually intelligent 5-year-old boy. As they become friends, they help each other with the problems of growing up.

REFERENCES

Buscaglia, L. *The disabled and their parents: A counseling challenge.* Thorofare, N. J.: Charles B. Slack, 1975.

Colangelo, N., and Zaffrann, R. T. Special issues in counseling the gifted. *Counseling and Human Development,* 1979, *11,* 1–12.

Dillard, J. M., Kinnison, L. R., and Caldwell, B. Some developmental concerns and strategies in counseling learning disabled adolescents. *Counseling and Human Development,* 1978, *10,* 1–5.

Gardner, R. *MBD: The family book about minimal brain dysfunction.* New York: Aronson, 1973.

Gowan, J. The guidance of exceptional children. In J. Gowan, G. Demos, and C. Kohaska (Eds.), *The guidance of exceptional children: A book of readings.* New York: David McKay, 1972.

Grossman, H. J. (Ed.). *Manual on terminology and classification in mental retardation* (rev. ed.). Washington, D.C.: American Association on Mental Deficiency, 1973.

Haring, N. G. (Ed.). *Behavior of exceptional children* (2nd ed.). Columbus, Ohio: Charles E. Merrill, 1978.

Hawke, W. A. Psychiatric aspects of mental retardation. In P. D. Steinhauer and Q. Rae-Grant (Eds.), *Psychological problems of the child and his family.* New York: Macmillan, 1978.

Hawke, W., and Lesser, S. P. The child with a learning disorder. In P. D. Steinhauer and Q. Rae-Grant (Eds.), *Psychological problems of the child and his family.* New York: Macmillan, 1978.

Hobbs, N. *The futures of children.* San Francisco: Jossey-Bass, 1975.

Leigh, J. What we know about counseling the disabled and their parents: A review of the literature. In L. Buscaglia (Ed.), *The disabled and their parents: A counseling challenge.* Thorofare, N.J.: Charles B. Slack, 1975.

Lombana, J. H. Fostering positive attitudes toward handicapped students: A guidance challenge. *The School Counselor,* 1980, *27,* 176–182.

Maes, W. Counseling for exceptional children. *Counseling and Human Development,* 1978, *10,* 1–11.

National Advisory Committee on Handicapped Children. *Special education for handicapped children: First annual report.* Washington, D.C.: U.S. Department of Health, Education and Welfare, 1968.

Ohlsen, M. *Group counseling* (2nd ed.). New York: Holt, Rinehart and Winston, 1977.

Prescott, M. R., and Iselin, K. L. W. Counseling parents of a disabled child. *Elementary School Guidance and Counseling,* 1978, *12,* 170–177.

Rudolph, L. The counselor's role with the learning disabled child. *Elementary School Guidance and Counseling,* 1978, *12,* 162–169.(a)

Rudolph, L. B. *Perceptions of exceptional individuals: How are they viewed in the world?* Unpublished manuscript, Austin Peay State University, Clarksville, Tennessee, 1978. (b)

Tarver, S., and Hallahan, D. P. Children with learning disabilities: An overview. In J. M. Kauffman and D. P. Hallahan (Eds.), *Teaching children with training disabilities: Personal perspectives.* Columbus, Ohio: Charles E. Merrill, 1976.

U.S. Office of Education. *Education of the gifted and talented.* Washington, D.C.: Subcommittee on Labor and Public Welfare, U.S. Senate, 1972.

Wright, B. A. An analysis of attitudes—Dynamics and effects. *New Outlook for the Blind,* 1974, *68,* 108–118.

CHAPTER

20

LEGAL AND ETHICAL CONSIDERATIONS FOR COUNSELORS

THE PROFESSION OF COUNSELING

At the present time, counseling is seeking to identify itself as a profession. One mark of a profession is its ability to set standards for the training and practice of its members. The American Personnel and Guidance Association (APGA) is encouraging state organizations to seek licensure (or some type of credentialing) for counselors in private practice. The American Psychological Association (APA) has supported licensure for psychologists for many years, and most states have a law regulating the practice of psychology. Both APGA and APA have codes of ethics to guide and govern members (APGA, 1981; APA, 1981). These codes have become a part of the counselor and/or psychologist licensure laws in various states. Unfortunately, unless these codes are a part of law regulating the practicing psychologist or counselor, the provisions are unenforceable.

A code of ethics provides practitioners with a standard to assist in judging appropriate behavior in counseling situations. Ethical codes are only "statements of principles, which must be interpreted and applied to a particular context" (Stude & McKelvey, 1979, p. 453).

McGowan and Schmidt (1962) attempt to explain the need for standards or guidelines. They suggest that codes of ethics (1) assist professionals to decide what they should do when situations of conflict arise; (2) help to clarify the counselor's responsibilities to self and the client;

(3) give some assurance that the members' practices will not be harmful to the profession; (4) give some guarantee that the counselor's services will give "sensible regard" to social codes and community expectations; and (5) give the counselor some protection of professional freedom and integrity.

Early literature concerning the ethical behavior of counselors was directed mainly toward providing additional guidelines and interpretations of ethical behavior. Research studies in the early 1970s suggested that many counselors were engaging in questionable ethical practices (Paradise, 1978). Van Hoose and Kottler (1977) state that in recent years the helping professions have gained prominence in the United States and have assumed increasing responsibility for the social problems that exist in our society, yet they are concerned that some current practices within the profession threaten its survival. They fear that the ethical issues of counseling are too often ignored. Van Hoose and Kottler contend that professional codes of ethics are designed not to protect the public from untrained or incompetent practitioners but to protect the profession from interference by the government or legislative bodies, from "the self-destruction of internal bickering" (1977, p. 8), and from the public (threat of malpractice).

LAWS AND ETHICS

Counselors need to be aware of the ethical codes of their profession; they must also be aware of laws, interpretations of these laws by local authorities, and court decisions that may affect their practice. Counselors working with children need to be knowledgeable about the rights of minors and the rights of parents concerning their children.

The first legal responsibility counselors incur is to communicate honestly their competencies, skills, methods, and other conditions of counseling (Van Hoose & Kottler, 1977). Counselors working in agencies or institutions usually have their credentials reviewed when they are employed, but they are still obligated to discuss these conditions with their clients. These conditions provide a basis for the unwritten contract between counselor and client.

Laws and their application vary from state to state and from city to city. It probably would be helpful to counselors to discuss potential conflicts with their immediate supervisor, juvenile authorities, or other professionals. For example, what is the responsibility of counselors to children and parents when they are asked for information concerning birth control, pregnancy in underage girls, venereal disease, or drug or alcohol use.

Burgum and Anderson (1975) list four possible areas in which a counselor may become a defendant in a criminal case: (1) accessory to a crime after the fact; (2) encouraging illegal abortions; (3) coconspirator in civil obedience; and (4) contributing to the delinquency of a minor.

Their article will provide counselors with a more thorough understanding of possible dangerous situations and methods for handling these conflicts.

Wagner (1981) conducted a survey of school counselors to determine the attitudes of elementary, middle, and secondary school counselors toward confidentiality. The counselors surveyed (347 elementary, 423 middle school, and 426 secondary counselors) viewed the limits of confidentiality as being set by their counseling setting as well as the age, maturity, and problem of the child. They did agree that informal discussion of a child's problem with a person not involved was a violation of confidentiality. Elementary counselors were the least stringent about maintaining confidentiality, followed by middle school counselors; secondary counselors were the most stringent. Counselors in elementary schools were more likely to inform parents and authorities about illegal behavior such as drug possession or sales; secondary counselors were least likely to inform. Wagner points out that these findings parallel the counselor's perceived responsibility to parents. They also seem to reflect the counselor's assessment of the child's age, cognitive level, and maturity level. The movement of a child toward adolescence and increasing independence from the family apparently encourages counselors to work with the individual rather than bring in individuals responsible for his or her care—parents or guardians.

School counselors may be faced with legal questions concerning medical treatment of minors (for example, in case of V.D.), the rights of minors in abortion issues, drug counseling, and the rights of married or unmarried pregnant girls in school. Talbutt (1980) has published an enlightening article on these issues, citing court rulings, which may be of assistance to school counselors. He has attempted to address several issues related to the rights of minors. Important points brought out by the article include some of the following:

1. Recent Supreme Court decisions have favored the right of a minor to have an abortion without parents' consent; however, some states have rejected this ruling. If states are in conflict with the Supreme Court decision, the latter would take precedence. The issue of the right of a minor to have an abortion is extremely volatile. Counselors are urged to make themselves knowledgeable about state and federal laws concerning the issue and to follow closely changes in the law. Talbutt quotes Burgum and Anderson cautioning counselors that recent decisions do not "affect the civil liability of a counselor who may . . . have negligently interfered with parents' rights to advise a minor . . ." (cited in Talbutt, 1980, p. 403). Counselors are also cautioned not to assume medical or psychological skills they do not possess.

2. Every state has a law dealing with child abuse. Some states levy fines for failure to report child abuse; in others, counselors could be found guilty of a misdemeanor (in addition to civil liability) if they fail

to report child abuse. Since state laws vary, counselors have a responsibility to check legal regulations in their states.

3. Talbutt (1980) refers to the American School Counselors Association's (1976) position paper on the counselor's responsibilities in drug counseling. The statement suggests that school counselors respect individuals' rights while helping them to assume responsibility; focus their counseling on the individual's concerns rather than the abuse of drugs; refer the client for appropriate services; and respect the parents' rights—all while abiding by ASCA professional ethics and staying within the limits of local, state, and federal laws. The accomplishment of these guidelines may be difficult since there are no clear-cut answers in every case; laws vary, and ethics and laws conflict at times.

Talbutt (1980) also discusses the rights of married students and unmarried pregnant women, as well as labeling of potential drug abusers. These issues seem more appropriate for literature on counseling with adolescents; interested readers are referred to Talbutt's article for discussion of these topics.

Talbutt raises important questions about the legal responsibilities of counselors, pointing out that we have no well-defined answers. At this time, the best protection for counselors seems to be a thorough knowledge of local, state, and federal laws, trends, and court decisions.

An additional area of concern to counselors, and one that may present a conflict between laws, is confidentiality. States with laws regulating the practice of psychology and counseling usually provide for privileged communication between client and counselor similar to the relationship of lawyer and client. However, the federal Family Rights and Privacy Act gives parents and students of legal age the right to inspect their records (Burcky & Childers, 1976). Counselors need to be aware of the types of records kept in institutional files. They may not be able to maintain confidentiality if the parents of underage children request access to such files. A personal file may be kept for confidential notes as personal files do not fall under this law. However, files that have been seen by *anyone*, including office file clerks or secretaries, or which have been discussed with anyone in the process of decision making, are no longer considered personal notes. Van Hoose and Kottler point out that "counselors and psychotherapists have a right to collect information about a client in order to provide proper treatment, but they also have a responsibility to use this information wisely; if they do not, then they must be prepared to be held ethically and legally accountable for abuse of a privilege" (1977, p. 85).

Maintaining confidentiality may also present a violation of ethical codes. The counselor is charged with keeping information discussed in a counseling relationship confidential unless "there is clear and imminent danger to the client or others" (APGA Ethical Standard, Section B, No. 4, 1981). The counselor must then directly intervene, consulting with other professionals whenever possible. The APA standard states essentially the same principle regarding confidentiality. Stude and McKelvey suggest that "knowing when a client's confidential revelation gives rise to a responsibility on the part of the counselor to effect public disclosure, under penalty of personal liability, is difficult even for the courts" (1979, p. 454). Counselors must be aware that in some instances their efforts to maintain confidentiality may violate the law. In these difficult situations, the helping person may want to seek consultative assistance from other professionals or from the ethics committees of professional organizations such as APA or APGA.

In court cases in states where counselors and psychologists (or other helpers) are not protected by a licensure law providing for privileged communication, they have no recourse except to reveal the information if subpoenaed. Most states have a licensure law providing privileged communication for psychologists; however, only six states (Alabama, Arkansas, Florida, Idaho, Texas, and Virginia) presently have such laws for counselors. Some courts, more tolerant than others, will allow the counselor to share the privileged information with the judge in private to determine if it is information necessary to the proceeding or if public disclosure would be too hurtful to those involved, such as children who are a part of the case.

Davis (1980) is especially concerned about maintaining confidentiality in group counseling. She points out that leaders in the field of group counseling, such as Gazda (1978), have asserted that confidentiality is essential to the development of trust within the group. Meyers and Smith (1977) found that, when confidentiality was not assured in a group situation, self-disclosure was reduced. Davis, however, found that group members do discuss what occurs in the group process with others; "soliciting assurances of confidentiality may not be realistic" (1980, p. 201). She suggests that group leaders need to give accurate information about confidentiality in order that members may decide how much information they want to disclose during group counseling.

Counselors may find other conflicts between the ethical guidelines of their profession and local, state, and federal laws. For example, should a counselor reveal to parents that their minor daughter is pregnant? Is maintaining confidentiality in this case interference with the parents' right to advise a minor? Burgum and Anderson (cited in Talbutt, 1980) suggest that counselors can be liable in such a case. Situations such as this require the counselor to be knowledgeable of ethical and legal regulations and then weigh the consequences of the considered resolution. Before these situations occur (should they ever), it would be helpful if counselors had talked with their immediate supervisors and with local and state authorities to determine their views on the role of the counselor in working with potentially controversial issues. The reader is referred to the chapter on counseling children with special concerns (Chapter 18) for some assistance in dealing with these cases. There may be times when counselors risk legal repercussions for following ethical standards. The choice must be made by the counselor in the light of the circumstances.

TEST YOUR ETHICAL BEHAVIOR

Although an understanding of ethical and legal issues is of utmost importance to those working in the helping professions, there seems to be a serious lack of training, research, and knowledge in the area. As a test of your general understanding of ethical and legal issues, it is suggested that you consider the following situations, describing methods and procedures you would use in handling the incident. Then check your answers with the APA (1981) and APGA (1981) standards cited (see Appendixes A and B) and our comments. For many situations, there will be no *right* solution; the final answer will depend on your counseling setting, the philosophy of your supervisor, the interpretation of the law by your local or state authorities, potential advantages or disadvantages of the solution, and the risks to the counselor and client. In these situations, *our comments are only our interpretation and not necessarily the right answer.*

Situation 1

Your colleague informs you that he has spent 22 years in school preparing for a career in counseling, and he intends to do little reading in the future, do no research, and attend only an occasional professional meeting. His feeling is that nothing new is ever presented and that such activities are a waste of time that could be better spent helping people. Is this attitude and behavior ethical? Why or why not?

Answer: Section A, No. 1 and 2, APGA; Principle 2c, APA

Comments. The standards state that professionals have obligations to "maintain the highest levels of professional services . . ." and improve themselves and their professional practice. This person has an ethical obligation to continue his professional development in order to more effectively spend time helping people. Since research in counseling methods is ongoing and society is presenting clients with ever-changing conflicts, the counselor who does not participate in continuing education will become ineffective very soon.

Situation 2

A recent graduate of a counseling training program has been offered a job in an institution with very strict discipline codes. The philosophy of the institution states that children are basically selfish and unrestrained and that they must be taught socially acceptable behavior by severe and restrictive methods. The counselor does not agree with this philosophy but accepts the job with the intention of changing the attitudes of the administration. Is this ethical behavior? Why or why not?

Answer: Section A, No. 2, APGA; Section B, No. 14, APGA; Principle 3d, APA; Principle 6c, APA

Comments.   The philosophy of the counselor should be in agreement with that of the employing institution. However, the acceptance of the institution's philosophy concerning the nature of children would violate the basic assumption of counselors that people are unique and have worth, dignity, and potential. The counselor has an obligation to honestly discuss her philosophy with the institution before employment and attempt to arrive at some agreement. If no agreement can be reached, the counselor should seriously consider not accepting the position (even though jobs are scarce!). To work under the conditions described would reduce the effectiveness of the counselor and could be considered unethical practice.

Situation 3

A cocounselor noticed a male counselor "fondling" a young girl he had been working with for several weeks. (This particular behavior was not classified as sexual abuse.) The child's father had recently died, and she seemed to be seeking male attention to make up for her loss. The fellow counselor reported the behavior to the head administrator immediately. Was this ethical behavior? Why or why not?

Answer: Section A, No. 3, APGA; Principle 7g, APA

Comments.   The cocounselor could have approached the male counselor and discussed this concern with him before reporting it to the head administrator. It is possible the cocounselor misperceived the situation. If doubt concerning the male counselor's behavior is not resolved, a report to the administrator is appropriate. Local, state branch, division, or association ethical committees should be contacted if the cocounselor continues to notice inappropriate contact with the child.

Situation 4

A mother whose child has been diagnosed as having childhood schizophrenia comes to you for help. She has heard that you are an excellent counselor. She does not like the child's present therapist and wants you, a counselor, to also work with the child. What is your obligation?

Answer: Section A, No. 4, APGA; Section B, No. 3, APGA; Principle 2, Introduction and 2a, APA; Principle 7b, APA

Comments.   Two issues are present in this situation. You must assess your competencies to determine if working with a schizophrenic child is within the range of your qualifications. Secondly, a counselor does not work with the client of another counselor without the knowledge and permission of the first counselor.

Situation 5

You are working as a counselor for an institution that prohibits you from accepting remuneration for services other than your salary. A client offers you free use of his fishing lodge for a month during the summer for working with him in an additional service capacity. Is this ethical behavior? Why or why not?

Answer: Section A, No. 2, APGA; Principle 6, Introduction and 6d, APA

Comments.   Although the use of a fishing lodge is not money, it has a monetary value and is considered remuneration. The use of the lodge is not given as a gift, but is contingent on the additional services provided; thus to accept the use of the lodge would violate your agreement with the institution for which you worked. Since, under the ethical standards of the APGA, counselors agree to follow the policies of their employing institutions, this would be inappropriate. APA suggests that all parties should be informed of differences and commitments.

Situation 6

You are asked to appear on a local television show to give general suggestions and guidelines to parents concerning methods for disciplining children. Would you accept? Why or why not?

Answer: Section A, No. 6, APGA; Principle 4, Introduction and 4k, APA

Comments.   A counselor may ethically provide *general* factual, current, and relevant information concerning methods for disciplining children (for example, an explanation of logical consequences for unacceptable behavior).

Situation 7

A colleague counseling with parent groups subtly suggests during the counseling sessions that children grow up to be better adjusted if mothers perform the traditional roles of "mothering" and fathers behave as "masters" of the household. Is this appropriate behavior? Why or why not?

Answer: Section A, No. 8, APGA; Principle 1f, APA; Principle 2f, APA

Comments.   This behavior could be meeting the counselor's personal needs to maintain traditional sexual roles, or it could be the unconscious result of socialized sexual stereotyping. Nevertheless, the counseling behavior is inappropriate and unethical. Personal biases could unduly influence the group participants.

Situation 8

Mr. Jones brings his 12-year-old son to your office. He angrily tells you that he has caught this boy engaging in homosexual play, and he wants you to straighten him out. He will not have a homosexual son! What is your reply?

Answer: Section A, No. 8, APGA; Section B, Introduction, APGA; Preamble, APA

Comments.   You might tell Mr. Jones that you will be glad to work with his son if the boy would like counseling; however, your primary obligation is to the son and his choice of lifestyle. You can help him explore the advantages and disadvantages of homosexual and hetero-sexual lifestyles, but the choice is his. Perhaps Mr. Jones also needs to know that this could be curiosity concerning sex that is normal for the child's developmental level.

Situation 9

You are conducting a children's group counseling session. One very outspoken child, Jamie, begins to point out all the wrong behaviors of another child, Rachel. Soon, other members join in with Jamie to tell Rachel what they dislike about her behavior. The group criticisms are very realistic, and the young girl does need to work on these areas, so you decide to let the group criticism proceed in order to let her hear the feedback of her peers. Is this ethical or unethical behavior? Why?

Answer: Section B, No. 1, APGA; Preamble, APA

Comments.   Although in some instances peer feedback is helpful in changing children's behavior, this appears to be a potentially destruc-tive situation. Too much criticism can be dangerous psychologically and increase problems rather than helping to solve them. Excessive group criticism can cause feelings of worthlessness and even self-destructiveness. The welfare of the child must be protected. A better method would be to handle problem behaviors one at a time in the group (and individually if necessary) at a rate conducive to building positive self-esteem as well as positive change.

Situation 10

Your 12-year-old counselee's mother demands to know what you and her daughter have been discussing during your individual sessions. She asserts that, since the child is a minor, under the Family Rights and Privacy Act she has the right to see your records. What would you do?

Answer: Section B, No. 5, APGA; Principle 5, Introduction and 5a, 5d, APA

Comments.   The mother has a right to see institutional records but not your personal notes. In order to be considered "personal," the records cannot have been seen by anyone (including typists or file clerks) or discussed with anyone in consultation. You also could tell the mother that you had promised the child that what she said to you would be confidential, but that with the girl's permission you would be glad to talk with her about your sessions, or you would be glad to see mother and daughter together to discuss her request further. (See Chapter 13 for a discussion of notes and records.)

Situation 11

You are an instructor at a large university teaching counseling practice. You have a videotape of a session between a counselor trainee and client from a class taught two years ago that would help to demonstrate a particular counseling method. What are your responsibilities with regard to showing this videotape for instructional purposes?

Answer: Section B, No. 6, APGA; Principle 5b, APA

Comments.   All references to names or other identifying information should be erased from the tape. The tape should be made so that only the counselor is visible. The client should have his or her back to tape or be completely out of the picture. A permission slip signed by the client, or by a legal representative if the client is a child, to use the tape for training sessions will further protect the instructor.

Situation 12

You have been working with a difficult client for one year. You have reached the point at which you feel you are not helping this client and would like to discuss the case with someone to seek advice about your professional duty. What is your ethical duty?

Answer: Section B, No. 9 and 10, APGA; Principle 2f, APA; Principle 6e, APA

Comments.   You have the right to consult another professional who is not involved in the situation concerning your difficult client. Describe only the presenting problem, keeping the client's identity confidential. If you are convinced you cannot help the client further, you are obligated to seek an appropriate referral source for the client. If the client refuses referral, the counselor is not obligated to continue the counseling.

Situation 13

Your supervisor approaches you to counsel with his son, age 10, who is also the best friend of your son. What is your response? Why?

Answer: Section B, No. 11, APGA; Principle 6a, APA

Comments.   The counselor can reflect the supervisor's concern for his son and suggest a counseling source. Explain that the son could be uncomfortable talking to you because of the relationship between you and his father and the friendship of the two young people. Ethical standards suggest that you counsel with people with whom you have a close relationship only when there is no other counseling source available and the situation demands intervention.

Situation 14

A young client, age 13, tells you she is pregnant. You suspect sexual abuse by her father. What is your obligation?

Answer: Section B, No. 4, APGA; Principle 5, Introduction, APA; Principle 5d, APA

Comments.   Most states have laws requiring people suspecting or having knowledge of child abuse to report the incident. Reports can be made anonymously in some states. People possessing such knowledge and failing to report it to the proper authorities may become criminally liable. See Chapter 18 for additional information on dealing with child abuse. This case also presents a medical concern—a 13-year-old pregnant girl. Counselors will need to check their institutional, local, and state laws about the medical rights of minors if the young girl does not want to reveal the suspected pregnancy to her parents. Refer to Talbutt's (1980) article discussed previously in this chapter.

Situation 15

A 10-year-old boy reports to you that he has been smoking marijuana. He needs your help to stop. You are working with him to modify this behavior. Since marijuana is illegal, are you obligated to report the *use?*

Answer: Section B, No. 4, APGA; Principle 5, Introduction, APA; Principle 5d, APA

Comments.   *Before* such incidents occur, it would be helpful to talk with your immediate supervisor and local authorities to determine their view of your role. You must also deal with the question of whether the *use* could be potentially dangerous to the child and whether *use* is illegal in your state. Obviously, reporting such incidences will decrease the confidence of your clients and interfere with relationships in the future. On the other hand, not reporting the incident may place you in danger of being criminally or civilly liable as discussed earlier. If you decide the incident should be reported, it would be helpful to inform the child client you must report this to the proper authorities and assure him you will be there to help him through the situation. There is no clear-cut or "good" answer to this situation.

Situation 16

The 10-year-old in Situation 15 tells you he is selling marijuana and intends to continue since he sees nothing wrong with marijuana. He feels the laws are "stupid." What would you do?

Answer: Section B, No. 4, APGA; Principle 5, Introduction, APA; Principle 5d, APA

Comments. Essentially the same comments apply as in Situation 15; however, the counselor is faced with a more serious problem when the sale of drugs is involved. Most states view the sale of marijuana as a more serious offense than use, and the counselor would probably be in a more serious situation for not reporting the sale. Again, there is no "good" answer. Counselors are encouraged to discuss the situation with their supervisor and authorities before it occurs.

Situation 17

Marcie, age 9, is upset about her parents' divorce. She threatens suicide and tells you she has planned to take her mother's tranquilizers tonight. You discuss the situation with her at length. When she is ready to leave, you still have fears she may try suicide. What would you do?
Answer: Section B, No. 4, APGA; Principle 5, Introduction, APA; Principle 5d, APA

Comments. Because of the *possible* danger of suicide, the counselor should call Marcie's parents or other significant family members. Marcie should not be left alone at any time until the conflict has been resolved. The counselor will want to tell Marcie of the break in confidentiality before calling her family and the reason for breaking confidentiality.

Situation 18

A salesman from a reputable testing firm demonstrates a new, inexpensive, brief-form IQ test. The test can be easily administered and quickly scored. He claims it can help you with your testing and can assist in diagnosis of exceptionalities. When you ask about the reliability and validity of the test, he tells you that studies are still being conducted in this area. You are under pressure to complete numerous diagnostic evaluations of children in order that they may receive special help, and this short, inexpensive test would cut your work by one-third. What would you do?
Answer: Section C, No. 2, APGA; Principle 8c, APA

Comments. The counselor is responsible for choosing appropriate instruments that have established validity and reliability. The APGA standards point out that legal and ethical questions may arise when tests are used for educational placement and related counseling activities.

Situation 19

A researcher using a battery of tests tells you he is going to mislead the subjects about what kind of tests they are taking and avoid interpretation of the results because it will bias his research. Is this ethical behavior? Why or why not?

Answer: Section C, No. 1, APGA; Section C, No. 8, APGA; Section D, No. 5, APGA; Principle 8a, APA; Principle 9d, e, h, APA

Comments. The researcher should make the participants aware of the nature of the tests and provide a full interpretation of the results. If deception is required, there must be adequate justification, and the participants should be given a full explanation as soon as possible.

Situation 20

You are asked to administer a national test such as the ACT, NTE, or GRE. Your coworker suggests that it is ridiculous to follow the instructions word-by-word as the administrator's manual requires. The coworker suggests that you shorten the testing time by giving instructions in your own words and timing the subtests by when most subjects finish. What would you do?

Answer: Section C, No. 5, APGA; Principle 8, Introduction, APA

Comments. To ensure validity, the tests must be given under the same conditions as those used in the standardization. Following the directions as stated is essential; any change in procedure should be reported to the test company or scorer.

Situation 21

A friend is being required to take the MMPI for admission to a counseling program. You have copies of the MMPI booklet stacked on your shelf. He asks to look one over, and perhaps make a photocopy, in order to study for this test. Are there unethical procedures involved in this situation?

Answer: Section C, No. 6, 11, APGA; Principle 8, Introduction, APA

Comments. You are violating ethical standards by not having the tests secured. Prior knowledge of the test obtained by looking it over or obtaining a copy would invalidate the results and is also considered unethical.

Situation 22

A university professor requires all students enrolled in his experimental psychology class to participate in a research project in order that they may learn more about the techniques of research. Is this behavior ethical? Why or why not?

Answer: Section D, No. 6, APGA; Principle 9f, APA

Comments. APGA states that participation should be voluntary unless it can be shown that no harmful effects will occur as a result of involuntary participation. APA cautions that the participants' freedom of choice must be protected, especially in situations where the investigator has a position of power over the participant. The interpretation of the authors is that requiring participation in the situation is unethical behavior.

Situation 23

A researcher published an article knowing that it contained a small error in statistics. He felt that the error was insignificant and therefore would not be harmful in any way or unethical. Is this unethical behavior? Why or why not?

Answer: Section D, No. 8, APGA; Principle 1a, APA

Comments.   The behavior is unethical. Even a "small error" may be misleading in interpreting results.

Situation 24

Research on the effectiveness of different counseling methods indicated one method to be highly ineffective compared to others. In order to protect the reputation of a colleague, the researcher did not show the data about the ineffective method, but reported only results that showed some effectiveness. Was this appropriate reporting? Why or why not?

Answer: Section D, No. 13, APGA; Principle 1a, APA

Comments.   The results on the ineffective method should be reported. To withhold or suppress unfavorable results is unethical.

It is difficult to recommend specific answers to the situations above because situations, people, and laws vary. References are given to APA and APGA codes of ethics to aid readers in formulating a resolution. It is hoped that readers will be stimulated to read the ethical standards thoroughly and consider the issues in the light of presenting situations and regulations.

The foregoing situations are by no means all of the ethical and legal situations encountered in counseling. Other situations and their resolutions for study may be found in the casebooks prepared by APGA and APA. These were intended only to give readers some indication of their own ethical knowledge and practices. Should uncertainty arise concerning interpretations of ethical practices, counselors have the option of consulting other professionals or local, state, or national professional ethics committees.

REFERENCES

APA (American Psychological Association). *Ethical principles of psychologists.* Washington, D.C.: APA, 1981.

APGA (American Personnel and Guidance Association). *Ethical standards.* Washington, D.C.: APGA, 1981.

ASCA (American School Counselors Association). Position statements. *The School Counselor*, 1976, *23*, 281–288.

Burcky, W. D., and Childers, J. H., Jr. Buckley Amendment: Focus of a professional dilemma. *The School Counselor*, 1976, *23*, 162–164.

Burgum, T., and Anderson, S. *The counselor and the law*. Washington, D.C.: American Personnel and Guidance Association, 1975.

Davis, K. Is confidentiality in group counseling realistic? *Personnel and Guidance Journal*, 1980, *58*, 197–201.

Gazda, S. M. *Group counseling: A developmental approach* (2nd ed.). Boston: Allyn & Bacon, 1978.

McGowan, J. F., and Schmidt, L. D. *Counseling: Reading in theory and practice*. New York: Holt, Rinehart and Winston, 1962.

Meyers, R. G., and Smith, S. R. A crisis in group therapy. *American Psychologist*, 1977, *32*, 638–643.

Paradise, L. V. What price ethics: New research directions in counselor ethical behavior. *Counseling and Values*, 1978, *23*, 2–7.

Stude, E. W., and McKelvey, J. Ethics and the law: Friend or foe? *Personnel and Guidance Journal*, 1979, *57*, 453–456.

Talbutt, L. Medical rights of minors: Some answers and unanswered legal questions. *School Counselor*, 1980, *27*, 403–406.

Van Hoose, W. H., and Kottler, J. A. *Ethical and legal issues in counseling and psychotherapy*. San Francisco: Jossey-Bass, 1977.

Wagner, C. Confidentiality and the school counselor. *Personnel and Guidance Journal*, 1981, *51*, 305–310.

APPENDIX A
ETHICAL STANDARDS[1]

PREAMBLE

The American Personnel and Guidance Association is an educational, scientific, and professional organization whose members are dedicated to the enhancement of the worth, dignity, potential, and uniqueness of each individual and thus to the service of society.

The Association recognizes that the role definitions and work settings of its members include a wide variety of academic disciplines, levels of academic preparation and agency services. This diversity reflects the breadth of the Association's interest and influence. It also poses challenging complexities in efforts to set standards for the performance of members, desired requisite preparation or practice, and supporting social, legal, and ethical controls.

The specification of ethical standards enables the Association to clarify to present and future members and to those served by members, the nature of ethical responsibilities held in common by its members.

The existence of such standards serves to stimulate greater concern by members for their own professional functioning and for the conduct of fellow professionals such as counselors, guidance and student personnel

[1](Approved by Executive Committee upon referral of the Board of Directors, January 17, 1981.)

workers, and others in the helping professions. As the ethical code of the Association, this document establishes principles that define the ethical behavior of Association members.

Section A: General

1. The member influences the development of the profession by continuous efforts to improve professional practices, teaching, services, and research. Professional growth is continuous throughout the member's career and is exemplified by the development of a philosophy that explains why and how a member functions in the helping relationship. Members must gather data on their effectiveness and be guided by the findings.

2. The member has a responsibility both to the individual who is served and to the institution within which the service is performed to maintain high standards of professional conduct. The member strives to maintain the highest levels of professional services offered to the individuals to be served. The member also strives to assist the agency, organization, or institution in providing the highest caliber of professional services. The acceptance of employment in an institution implies that the member is in agreement with the general policies and principles of the institution. Therefore the professional activities of the member are also in accord with the objectives of the institution. If, despite concerted efforts, the member cannot reach agreement with the employer as to acceptable standards of conduct that allow for changes in institutional policy conducive to the positive growth and development of clients, then terminating the affiliation should be seriously considered.

3. Ethical behavior among professional associates, both members and nonmembers, must be expected at all times. When information is possessed that raises doubt as to the ethical behavior of professional colleagues, whether Association members or not, the member must take action to attempt to rectify such a condition. Such action shall use the institution's channels first and then use procedures established by the state Branch, Division, or Association.

4. The member neither claims nor implies professional qualifications exceeding those possessed and is responsible for correcting any misrepresentations of these qualifications by others.

5. In establishing fees for professional counseling services, members must consider the financial status of clients and locality. In the event that the established fee structure is inappropriate for a client, assistance must be provided in finding comparable services of acceptable cost.

6. When members provide information to the public or to subordinates, peers or supervisors, they have a responsibility to ensure that the content is general, unidentified client information that is accurate, unbiased, and consists of objective, factual data.

7. With regard to the delivery of professional services, members should accept only those positions for which they are professionally qualified.

8. In the counseling relationship the counselor is aware of the intimacy of the relationship and maintains respect for the client and avoids engaging in activities that seek to meet the counselor's personal needs at the expense of that client. Through awareness of the negative impact of both racial and sexual stereotyping and discrimination, the counselor guards the individual rights and personal dignity of the client in the counseling relationship.

Section B: Counseling relationship

This section refers to practices and procedures of individual and/or group counseling relationships.

The member must recognize the need for client freedom of choice. Under those circumstances where this is not possible, the member must apprise clients of restrictions that may limit their freedom of choice.

1. The member's *primary* obligation is to respect the integrity and promote the welfare of the client(s), whether the client(s) is (are) assisted individually or in a group relationship. In a group setting, the member is also responsible for taking reasonable precautions to protect individuals from physical and/or psychological trauma resulting from interaction within the group.

2. The counseling relationship and information resulting therefrom be kept confidential, consistent with the obligations of the member as a professional person. In a group counseling setting, the counselor must set a norm of confidentiality regarding all group participants' disclosures.

3. If an individual is already in a counseling relationship with another professional person, the member does not enter into a counseling relationship without first contacting and receiving the approval of that other professional. If the member discovers that the client is in another counseling relationship after the counseling relationship begins, the member must gain the consent of the other professional or terminate the relationship, unless the client elects to terminate the other relationship.

4. When the client's condition indicates that there is clear and imminent danger to the client or others, the member must take reasonable personal action or inform responsible authorities. Consultation with other professionals must be used where possible. The assumption of responsibility for the client(s) behavior must be taken only after careful deliberation. The client must be involved in the resumption of responsibility as quickly as possible.

5. Records of the counseling relationship, including interview notes, test data, correspondence, tape recordings, and other documents, are to be considered professional information for use in counseling and they should not be considered a part of the records of the institution or agency in which the counselor is employed unless specified by state statute or regulation. Revelation to others of counseling material must occur only upon the expressed consent of the client.

6. Use of data derived from a counseling relationship for purposes of counselor training or research shall be confined to content that can be disguised to ensure full protection of the identity of the subject client.

7. The member must inform the client of the purposes, goals, techniques, rules of procedure and limitations that may affect the relationship at or before the time that the counseling relationship is entered.

8. The member must screen prospective group participants, especially when the emphasis is on self-understanding and growth through self-disclosure. The member must maintain an awareness of the group participants' compatibility throughout the life of the group.

9. The member may choose to consult with any other professionally competent person about a client. In choosing a consultant, the member must avoid placing the consultant in a conflict of interest situation that would preclude the consultant's being a proper party to the member's efforts to help the client.

10. If the member determines an inability to be of professional assistance to the client, the member must either avoid initiating the counseling relationship or immediately terminate that relationship. In either event, the member must suggest appropriate alternatives. (The member must be knowledgeable about referral resources so that a satisfactory referral can be initiated.) In the event the client declines the suggested referral, the member is not obligated to continue the relationship.

11. When the member has other relationships, particularly of an administrative, supervisory and/or evaluative nature with an individual seeking counseling services, the member must not serve as the counselor but should refer the individual to another professional. Only in instances where such an alternative is unavailable and where the individual's situation warrants counseling intervention should the member enter into and/or maintain a counseling relationship. Dual relationships with clients that might impair the member's objectivity and professional judgment (e.g., as with close friends or relatives, sexual intimacies with any client) must be avoided and/or the counseling relationship terminated through referral to another competent professional.

12. All experimental methods of treatment must be clearly indicated to prospective recipients and safety precautions are to be adhered to by the member.

13. When the member is engaged in short-term group treatment/ training programs (e.g., marathons and other encounter-type or growth groups), the member ensures that there is professional assistance available during and following the group experience.

14. Should the member be engaged in a work setting that calls for any variation from the above statements, the member is obligated to consult with other professionals whenever possible to consider justifiable alternatives.

Section C: Measurement and evaluation

The primary purpose of educational and psychological testing is to provide descriptive measures that are objective and interpretable in either comparative or absolute terms. The member must recognize the need to interpret the statements that follow as applying to the whole range of appraisal techniques including test and nontest data. Test results constitute only one of a variety of pertinent sources of information for personnel, guidance, and counseling decisions.

1. The member must provide specific orientation or information to the examinee(s) prior to and following the test administration so that the results of testing may be placed in proper perspective with other relevant factors. In so doing, the member must recognize the effects of socioeconomic, ethnic and cultural factors on test scores. It is the member's professional responsibility to use additional unvalidated information carefully in modifying interpretation of the test results.

2. In selecting tests for use in a given situation or with a particular client, the member must consider carefully the specific validity, reliability, and appropriateness of the test(s). *General* validity, reliability and the like may be questioned legally as well as ethically when tests are used for vocational and educational selection, placement or counseling.

3. When making any statements to the public about tests and testing, the member must give accurate information and avoid false claims or misconceptions. Special efforts are often required to avoid unwarranted connotations of such terms as *IQ* and *grade equivalent scores.*

4. Different tests demand different levels of competence for administration, scoring, and interpretation. Members must recognize the limits of their competence and perform only those functions for which they are prepared.

5. Tests must be administered under the same conditions that were established in their standardization. When tests are not administered under standard conditions or when unusual behavior or irregularities occur during the testing session, those conditions must be noted and the results designated as invalid or of questionable validity. Unsupervised or inadequately supervised test-taking, such as the use of tests through the mails, is considered unethical. On the other hand, the use of instruments that are so designed or standardized to be self-administered and self-scored, such as interest inventories, is to be encouraged.

6. The meaningfulness of test results used in personnel, guidance, and counseling functions generally depends on the examinee's unfamiliarity with the specific items on the test. Any prior coaching or dissemination of the test materials can invalidate test results. Therefore, test security is one of the professional obligations of the member. Conditions that produce most favorable test results must be made known to the examinee.

7. The purpose of testing and the explicit use of the results must be made known to the examinee prior to testing. The counselor must ensure

that instrument limitations are not exceeded and that periodic review and/or retesting are made to prevent client stereotyping.

8. The examinee's welfare and explicit prior understanding must be the criteria for determining the recipients of the test results. The member must see that specific interpretation accompanies any release of individual or group test data. The interpretation of test data must be related to the examinee's particular concerns.

9. The member must be cautious when interpreting the results of research instruments possessing insufficient technical data. The specific purposes for the use of such instruments must be stated explicitly to examinees.

10. The member must proceed with caution when attempting to evaluate and interpret the performance of minority group members or other persons who are not represented in the norm group on which the instrument was standardized.

11. The member must guard against the appropriation, reproduction, or modifications of published tests or parts thereof without acknowledgment and permission from the previous publisher.

12. Regarding the preparation, publication and distribution of tests, reference should be made to:

a. *Standards for Educational and Psychological Tests and Manuals*, revised edition, 1974, published by the American Psychological Association on behalf of itself, the American Educational Research Association and the National Council on Measurement in Education.

b. The responsible use of tests: A position paper of AMEG, APGA, and NCME. *Measurement and Evaluation in Guidance*, 1972, *5*, 385–388.

c. "Responsibilities of Users of Standardized Tests," APGA, *Guidepost*, October 5, 1978, pp. 5–8.

Section D: Research and publication

1. Guidelines on research with human subjects shall be adhered to, such as:

a. *Ethical Principles in the Conduct of Research with Human Participants*, Washington, D.C.: American Psychological Association, Inc., 1973.

b. Code of Federal Regulations, Title 45, Subtitle A, Part 46, as currently issued.

2. In planning any research activity dealing with human subjects, the member must be aware of and responsive to all pertinent ethical principles and ensure that the research problem, design, and execution are in full compliance with them.

3. Responsibility for ethical research practice lies with the principal researcher, while others involved in the research activities share ethical obligation and full responsibility for their own actions.

4. In research with human subjects, researchers are responsible for the subjects' welfare throughout the experiment and they must take all

reasonable precautions to avoid causing injurious psychological, physical, or social effects on their subjects.

5. All research subjects must be informed of the purpose of the study except when withholding information or providing misinformation to them is essential to the investigation. In such research the member must be responsible for corrective action as soon as possible following completion of the research.

6. Participation in research must be voluntary. Involuntary participation is appropriate only when it can be demonstrated that participation will have no harmful effects on subjects and is essential to the investigation.

7. When reporting research results, explicit mention must be made of all variables and conditions known to the investigator that might affect the outcome of the investigation or the interpretation of the data.

8. The member must be responsible for conducting and reporting investigations in a manner that minimizes the possibility that results will be misleading.

9. The member has an obligation to make available sufficient original research data to qualified others who may wish to replicate the study.

10. When supplying data, aiding in the research of another person, reporting research results, or in making original data available, due care must be taken to disguise the identity of the subjects in the absence of specific authorization from such subjects to do otherwise.

11. When conducting and reporting research, the member must be familiar with, and give recognition to, previous work on the topic, as well as to observe all copyright laws and follow the principles of giving full credit to all to whom credit is due.

12. The member must give due credit through joint authorship, acknowledgment, footnote statements, or other appropriate means to those who have contributed significantly to the research and/or publication, in accordance with such contributions.

13. The member must communicate to other members the results of any research judged to be of professional or scientific value. Results reflecting unfavorably on institutions, programs, services, or vested interests must not be withheld for such reasons.

14. If members agree to cooperate with another individual in research and/or publication, they incur an obligation to cooperate as promised in terms of punctuality of performance and with full regard to the completeness and accuracy of the information required.

15. Ethical practice requires that authors not submit the same manuscript or one essentially similar in content, for simultaneous publication consideration by two or more journals. In addition, manuscripts published in whole or in substantial part, in another journal or published work should not be submitted for publication without acknowledgment and permission from the previous publication.

Section E: Consulting

Consultation refers to a voluntary relationship between a professional helper and help-needing individual, group or social unit in which the consultant is providing help to the client(s) in defining and solving a work-related problem or potential problem with a client or client system. (This definition is adapted from Kurpius, DeWayne. Consultation theory and process: An integrated model. *Personnel and Guidance Journal*, 1978, 56.)

1. The member acting as consultant must have a high degree of self-awareness of his-her own values, knowledge, skills, limitations, and needs in entering a helping relationship that involves human and-or organizational change and that the focus of the relationship be on the issues to be resolved and not on the person(s) presenting the problem.

2. There must be understanding and agreement between member and client for the problem definition, change goals, and predicated consequences of interventions selected.

3. The member must be reasonably certain that she/he or the organization represented has the necessary competencies and resources for giving the kind of help that is needed now or may develop later and that appropriate referral resources are available to the consultant.

4. The consulting relationship must be one in which client adaptability and growth toward self-direction are encouraged and cultivated. The member must maintain this role consistently and not become a decision maker for the client or create a future dependency on the consultant.

5. When announcing consultant availability for services, the member conscientiously adheres to the Association's *Ethical Standards*.

6. The member must refuse a private fee or other remuneration for consultation with persons who are entitled to these services through the member's employing institution or agency. The policies of a particular agency may make explicit provisions for private practice with agency clients by members of its staff. In such instances, the clients must be apprised of other options open to them should they seek private counseling services.

Section F: Private practice

1. The member should assist the profession by facilitating the availability of counseling services in private as well as public settings.

2. In advertising services as a private practitioner, the member must advertise the services in such a manner so as to accurately inform the public as to services, expertise, profession, and techniques of counseling in a professional manner. A member who assumes an executive leadership role in the organization shall not permit his/her name to be used in professional notices during periods when not actively engaged in the private practice of counseling.

The member may list the following: highest relevant degree, type and level of certification or license, type and/or description of services, and other relevant information. Such information must not contain false, inaccurate, misleading, partial, out-of-context, or deceptive material or statements.

3. Members may join in partnership/corporation with other members and/or other professionals provided that each member of the partnership or corporation makes clear the separate specialties by name in compliance with the regulations of the locality.

4. A member has an obligation to withdraw from a counseling relationship if it is believed that employment will result in violation of the *Ethical Standards*. If the mental or physical condition of the member renders it difficult to carry out an effective professional relationship or if the member is discharged by the client because the counseling relationship is no longer productive for the client, then the member is obligated to terminate the counseling relationship.

5. A member must adhere to the regulations for private practice of the locality where the services are offered.

6. It is unethical to use one's institutional affiliation to recruit clients for one's private practice.

Section G: Personnel administration

It is recognized that most members are employed in public or quasi-public institutions. The functioning of a member within an institution must contribute to the goals of the institution and vice versa if either is to accomplish their respective goals or objectives. It is therefore essential that the member and the institution function in ways to (a) make the institution's goals explicit and public; (b) make the member's contribution to institutional goals specific; and (c) foster mutual accountability for goal achievement.

To accomplish these objectives, it is recognized that the member and the employer must share responsibilities in the formulation and implementation of personnel policies.

1. Members must define and describe the parameters and levels of their professional competency.

2. Members must establish interpersonal relations and working agreements with supervisors and subordinates regarding counseling or clinical relationships, confidentiality, distinction between public and private material, maintenance, and dissemination of recorded information, work load and accountability. Working agreements in each instance must be specified and made known to those concerned.

3. Members must alert their employers to conditions that may be potentially disruptive or damaging.

4. Members must inform employers of conditions that may limit their effectiveness.

5. Members must submit regularly to professional review and evaluation.

6. Members must be responsible for inservice development of self and/or staff.

7. Members must inform their staff of goals and programs.

8. Members must provide personnel practices that guarantee and enhance the rights and welfare of each recipient of their service.

9. Members must select competent persons and assign responsibilities compatible with their skills and experiences.

Section H: Preparation standards

Members who are responsible for training others must be guided by the preparation standards of the Association and relevant Division(s). The member who functions in the capacity of trainer assumes unique ethical responsibilities that frequently go beyond that of the member who does not function in a training capacity. These ethical responsibilities are outlined as follows:

1. Members must orient students to program expectations, basic skills development, and employment prospects prior to admission to the program.

2. Members in charge of learning experiences must establish programs that integrate academic study and supervised practice.

3. Members must establish a program directed toward developing students' skills, knowledge, and self-understanding, stated whenever possible in competency or performance terms.

4. Members must identify the levels of competencies of their students in compliance with relevant Division standards. These competencies must accommodate the para-professional as well as the professional.

5. Members, through continual student evaluation and appraisal, must be aware of the personal limitations of the learner that might impede future performance. The instructor must not only assist the learner in securing remedial assistance but also screen from the program those individuals who are unable to provide competent services.

6. Members must provide a program that includes training in research commensurate with levels of role functioning. Para-professional and technician-level personnel must be trained as consumers of research. In addition, these personnel must learn how to evaluate their own and their program's effectiveness. Graduate training, especially at the doctoral level, would include preparation for original research by the member.

7. Members must make students aware of the ethical responsibilities and standards of the profession.

8. Preparatory programs must encourage students to value the ideals of service to individuals and to society. In this regard, direct financial remuneration or lack thereof must not influence the quality of service

rendered. Monetary considerations must not be allowed to overshadow professional and humanitarian needs.

9. Members responsible for educational programs must be skilled as teachers and practitioners.

10. Members must present thoroughly varied theoretical positions so that students may make comparisons and have the opportunity to select a position.

11. Members must develop clear policies within their educational institutions regarding field placement and the roles of the student and the instructor in such placements.

12. Members must ensure that forms of learning focusing on self-understanding or growth are voluntary, or if required as part of the education program, are made known to prospective students prior to entering the program. When the education program offers a growth experience with an emphasis on self-disclosure or other relatively intimate or personal involvement, the member must have no administrative, supervisor, or evaluating authority regarding the participant.

13. Members must conduct an educational program in keeping with the current relevant guidelines of the American Personnel and Guidance Association and its Divisions.

APPENDIX B
ETHICAL PRINCIPLES
OF PSYCHOLOGISTS
(1981 REVISION)[1,2]

This version of the Ethical Principles of Psychologists (formerly entitled: Ethical Standards of Psychologists) was adopted by the American Psychological Association's Council of Representatives on January 24, 1981. The Ethical Principles of Psychologists (1981 Revision) contains both substantive and grammatical changes in each of the nine ethical principles which comprised the Ethical Standards of Psychologists previously adopted by the Council of Representatives in 1979, plus a new tenth principle entitled: Care and Use of Animals. Inquiries concerning the Ethical Principles of Psychologists should be addressed to the Administrative Officer for Ethics; American Psychological Association; 1200 Seventeenth Street, N.W.; Washington, D.C. 20036.

[1]Approved by the Council of Representatives (January 1981).
[2]These Ethical Principles apply to psychologists, to students of psychology and others who do work of a psychological nature under the supervision of a psychologist. They are also intended for the guidance of non-members of the Association who are engaged in psychological research or practice.

PREAMBLE

Psychologists respect the dignity and worth of the individual and strive for the preservation and protection of fundamental human rights. They are committed to increasing knowledge of human behavior and of people's understanding of themselves and others and to the utilization of such knowledge for the promotion of human welfare. While pursuing these objectives, they make every effort to protect the welfare of those who seek their services and of the research participants that may be the object of study. They use their skills only for purposes consistent with these values and do not knowingly permit their misuse by others. While demanding for themselves freedom of inquiry and communication, psychologists accept the responsibility this freedom requires: competence, objectivity in the application of skills, and concern for the best interests of clients, colleagues, students, research participants and society. In the pursuit of these ideals, psychologists subscribe to principles in the following areas: 1. Responsibility, 2. Competence, 3. Moral and Legal Standards, 4. Public Statements, 5. Confidentiality, 6. Welfare of the Consumer, 7. Professional Relationships, 8. Assessment Techniques, 9. Research with Human Participants, and 10. Care and Use of Animals.

Acceptance of membership in the American Psychological Association commits the member to adherence to these principles.

Psychologists cooperate with duly constituted committees of the American Psychological Association, in particular, the Committee on Scientific and Professional Ethics and Conduct, by responding to inquiries promptly and completely. Members also respond promptly and completely to inquiries from duly constituted state association ethics committees and professional standards review committees.

Principle 1: Responsibility

In providing services, psychologists maintain the highest standards of their profession. They accept responsibility for the consequences of their acts and make every effort to insure that their services are used appropriately.

a. As scientists, psychologists accept responsibility for the selection of their research topics and the methods used in investigation, analysis, and reporting. They plan their research in ways to minimize the possibility that their findings will be misleading. They provide thorough discussion of the limitations of their data, especially where their work touches on social policy or might be construed to the detriment of persons in specific age, sex, ethnic, socioeconomic or other social groups. In publishing reports of their work, they never suppress disconfirming data, and they acknowledge the existence of alternative hypotheses and explanations of their findings. Psychologists take credit only for work they have actually done.

b. Psychologists clarify in advance with all appropriate persons and agencies the expectations for sharing and utilizing research data. They avoid relationships which may limit their objectivity or create a conflict of interest. Interference with the milieu in which the data are collected is kept to a minimum.

c. Psychologists have the responsibility to attempt to prevent distortion, misuse, or suppression of psychological findings by the institution or agency of which they are employees.

d. As members of governmental or other organizational bodies, psychologists remain accountable as individuals to the highest standards of their profession.

e. As teachers, psychologists recognize their primary obligation to help others acquire knowledge and skill. They maintain high standards of scholarship by presenting psychological information objectively, fully, and accurately.

f. As practitioners, psychologists know that they bear a heavy social responsibility because their recommendations and professional actions may alter the lives of others. They are alert to personal, social, organizational, financial, or political situations and pressures that might lead to misuse of their influence.

Principle 2: Competence

The maintenance of high standards of competence is a responsibility shared by all psychologists in the interest of the public and the profession as a whole. Psychologists recognize the boundaries of their competence and the limitations of their techniques. They only provide services and only use techniques for which they are qualified by training and experience. In those areas in which recognized standards do not yet exist, psychologists take whatever precautions are necessary to protect the welfare of their clients. They maintain knowledge of current scientific and professional information related to the services they render.

a. Psychologists accurately represent their competence, education, training, and experience. They claim as evidence of educational qualifications only those degrees obtained from institutions acceptable under the Bylaws and Rules of Council of the American Psychological Association.

b. As teachers, psychologists perform their duties on the basis of careful preparation so that their instruction is accurate, current, and scholarly.

c. Psychologists recognize the need for continuing education and are open to new procedures and changes in expectations and values over time.

d. Psychologists recognize differences among people, such as those that may be associated with age, sex, socioeconomic, and ethnic backgrounds. When necessary, they obtain training, experience, or counsel to assure competent service or research relating to such persons.

e. Psychologists responsible for decisions involving individuals or policies based on test results have an understanding of psychological or educational measurement, validation problems, and test research.

f. Psychologists recognize that personal problems and conflicts may interfere with professional effectiveness. Accordingly, they refrain from undertaking any activity in which their personal problems are likely to lead to inadequate performance or harm to a client, colleague, student, or research participant. If engaged in such activity when they become aware of their personal problems, they seek competent professional assistance to determine whether they should suspend, terminate, or limit the scope of their professional and/or scientific activities.

Principle 3: Moral and legal standards

Psychologists' moral and ethical standards of behavior are a personal matter to the same degree as they are for any other citizen, except as these may compromise the fulfillment of their professional responsibilities, or reduce the public trust in psychology and psychologists. Regarding their own behavior, psychologists are sensitive to prevailing community standards and to the possible impact that conformity to or deviation from these standards may have upon the quality of their performance as psychologists. Psychologists are also aware of the possible impact of their public behavior upon the ability of colleagues to perform their professional duties.

a. As teachers, psychologists are aware of the fact that their personal values may affect the selection and presentation of instructional materials. When dealing with topics that may give offense, they recognize and respect the diverse attitudes that students may have toward such materials.

b. As employees or employers, psychologists do not engage in or condone practices that are inhumane or that result in illegal or unjustifiable actions. Such practices include but are not limited to those based on considerations of race, handicap, age, gender, sexual preference, religion, or national origin in hiring, promotion, or training.

c. In their professional roles, psychologists avoid any action that will violate or diminish the legal and civil rights of clients or of others who may be affected by their actions.

d. As practitioners and researchers, psychologists act in accord with Association standards and guidelines related to the practice and to the conduct of research with human beings and animals. In the ordinary course of events psychologists adhere to relevant governmental laws and institutional regulations. When federal, state, provincial, organizational, or institutional laws, regulations, or practices are in conflict with Association standards and guidelines, psychologists make known their commitment to Association standards and guidelines, and wherever possible work toward a resolution of the conflict. Both practitioners and researchers are concerned with the development of such legal and quasi-legal regulations as best serve the public interest, and they work toward changing existing regulations that are not beneficial to the public interest.

Principle 4: Public statements

Public statements, announcements of services, advertising, and promotional activities of psychologists serve the purpose of helping the public make informed judgments and choices. Psychologists represent accurately and objectively their professional qualifications, affiliations, and functions, as well as those of the institutions or organizations with which they or the statements may be associated. In public statements providing psychological information or professional opinions or providing information about the availability of psychological products, publications, and services, psychologists base their statements on scientifically acceptable psychological findings and techniques with full recognition of the limits and uncertainties of such evidence.

a. When announcing or advertising professional services, psychologists may list the following information to describe the provider and services provided: name, highest relevant academic degree earned from a regionally accredited institution, date, type and level of certification or licensure, diplomate status, APA membership status, address, telephone number, office hours, a brief listing of the type of psychological services offered, an appropriate presentation of fee information, foreign languages spoken, and policy with regard to third-party payments. Additional relevant or important consumer information may be included if not prohibited by other sections of these Ethical Principles.

b. In announcing or advertising the availability of psychological products, publications, or services, psychologists do not present their affiliation with any organization in a manner that falsely implies sponsorship or certification by that organization. In particular and for example, psychologists do not state APA membership or fellow status in a way to suggest that such status implies specialized professional competence or qualifications. Public statements include, but are not limited to, communication by means of periodical, book, list, directory, television, radio, or motion picture. They do not contain: (i) a false, fraudulent, misleading, deceptive, or unfair statement; (ii) a misinterpretation of fact, or a statement likely to mislead or deceive because in context it makes only a partial disclosure of relevant facts; (iii) a testimonial from a patient regarding the quality of a psychologist's services or products; (iv) a statement intended or likely to create false or unjustified expectations of favorable results; (v) a statement implying unusual, unique, or one-of-a-kind abilities; (vi) a statement intended or likely to appeal to a client's fears, anxieties, or emotions concerning the possible results of a failure to obtain the offered services; (vii) a statement concerning the comparative desirability of offered services; (viii) a statement of direct solicitation of individual clients.

c. Psychologists do not compensate or give anything of value to a representative of the press, radio, television, or other communication medium in anticipation of or in return for professional publicity in a news item. A paid advertisement must be identified as such, unless it is apparent from the context that it is a paid advertisement. If communicated to the public by use of radio or television, an advertisement shall be prerecorded and approved for broadcast by the psychologist, and a recording of the actual transmission shall be retained by the psychologist.

d. Announcements or advertisements of "personal growth groups," clinics, and agencies give a clear statement of purpose and a clear description of the experiences to be provided. The education, training, and experience of the staff members are appropriately specified.

e. Psychologists associated with the development or promotion of psychological devices, books, or other products offered for commercial sale make reasonable efforts to insure that announcements and advertisements are presented in a professional, scientifically acceptable, and factually informative manner.

f. Psychologists do not participate for personal gain in commercial announcements or advertisements recommending to the public the purchase or use of proprietary or single-source products or services when that participation is based solely upon their identification as psychologists.

g. Psychologists present the science of psychology and offer their services, products, and publications fairly and accurately, avoiding misrepresentation through sensationalism, exaggeration, or superficiality. Psychologists are guided by the primary obligation to aid the public in developing informed judgments, opinions, and choices.

h. As teachers, psychologists insure that statements in catalogs and course outlines are accurate and not misleading, particularly in terms of subject matter to be covered, bases for evaluating progress, and the nature of course experiences. Announcements, brochures, or advertisements describing workshops, seminars, or other educational programs accurately describe the audience for which the program is intended as well as eligibility requirements, educational objectives, and nature of the materials to be covered. These announcements also accurately represent the education, training, and experience of the psychologists presenting the programs, and any fees involved.

i. Public announcements or advertisements soliciting research participants in which clinical services or other professional services are offered as an inducement, make clear the nature of the services as well as the costs and other obligations to be accepted by the participants of the research.

j. Psychologists accept the obligation to correct others who represent that psychologist's professional qualifications, or associations with products or services, in a manner incompatible with these guidelines.

k. Individual diagnostic and therapeutic services are provided only in the context of a professional psychological relationship. When personal advice is given by means of public lecture or demonstration, newspaper or magazine articles, radio or television programs, mail, or similar media, the psychologist utilizes the most current relevant data and exercises the highest level of professional judgment.

l. Products that are described or presented by means of public lectures or demonstrations, newspaper or magazine articles, radio or television programs, or similar media meet the same recognized standards as exist for use in the context of a professional relationship.

Principle 5: Confidentiality

Psychologists have a primary obligation to respect the confidentiality of information obtained from persons in the course of their work as psychologists. They reveal such information to others only with the consent of the person or the person's legal representative, except in those unusual circumstances in which not to do so would result in clear danger to the person or to others. Where appropriate, psychologists inform their clients of the legal limits of confidentiality.

a. Information obtained in clinical or consulting relationships, or evaluative data concerning children, students, employees, and others, are discussed only for professional purposes and only with persons clearly concerned with the case. Written and oral reports present only data germane to the purposes of the evaluation and every effort is made to avoid undue invasion of privacy.

b. Psychologists who present personal information obtained during the course of professional work in writings, lectures, or other public forums either obtain adequate prior consent to do so or adequately disguise all identifying information.

c. Psychologists make provisions for maintaining confidentiality in the storage and disposal of records.

d. When working with minors or other persons who are unable to give voluntary, informed consent, psychologists take special care to protect these persons' best interests.

Principle 6: Welfare of the consumer

Psychologists respect the integrity and protect the welfare of the people and groups with whom they work. When there is a conflict of interest between a client and the psychologist's employing institution, psychologists clarify the nature and direction of their loyalties and responsibilities and keep all parties informed of their commitments. Psychologists fully inform consumers as to the purpose and nature of an evaluative, treatment, educational or training procedure, and they freely acknowledge that clients, students, or participants in research have freedom of choice with regard to participation.

a. Psychologists are continually cognizant of their own needs and of their potentially influential position vis-a-vis persons such as clients, students, and subordinates. They avoid exploiting the trust and dependency of such persons. Psychologists make every effort to avoid dual relationships which could impair their professional judgment or increase the risk of exploitation. Examples of such dual relationships include but are not limited to research with and treatment of employees, students, supervisees, close friends, or relatives. Sexual intimacies with clients are unethical.

b. When a psychologist agrees to provide services to a client at the request of a third party, the psychologist assumes the responsibility of clarifying the nature of the relationships to all parties concerned.

c. Where the demands of an organization require psychologists to violate these Ethical Principles, psychologists clarify the nature of the conflict between the demand and these principles. They inform all parties of psychologists' ethical responsibilities, and take appropriate action.

d. Psychologists make advance financial arrangements that safeguard the best interests of and are clearly understood by their clients. They neither give nor receive any remuneration for referring clients for professional services. They contribute a portion of their services to work for which they receive little or no financial return.

e. Psychologists terminate a clinical or consulting relationship when it is reasonably clear that the consumer is not benefiting from it. They offer to help the consumer locate alternative sources of assistance.

Principle 7: Professional relationships

Psychologists act with due regard for the needs, special competencies, and obligations of their colleagues in psychology and other professions. They respect the prerogatives and obligations of the institutions or organizations with which these other colleagues are associated.

a. Psychologists understand the areas of competence of related professions. They make full use of all the professional, technical, and administrative resources that serve the best interests of consumers. The absence of formal relationships with other professional workers does not relieve psychologists of the responsibility of securing for their clients the best possible professional service nor does it relieve them of the obligation to exercise foresight, diligence, and tact in obtaining the complementary or alternative assistance needed by clients.

b. Psychologists know and take into account the traditions and practices of other professional groups with whom they work and cooperate fully with such groups. If a person is receiving similar services from another professional, psychologists do not offer their own services directly to such a person. If a psychologist is contacted by a person who is already receiving similar services from another professional, the psychologist carefully considers that professional relationship and proceeds with caution and sensitivity to the therapeutic issues as well as the client's welfare. The psychologist discusses these issues with the client so as to minimize the risk of confusion and conflict.

c. Psychologists who employ or supervise other professionals or professionals in training accept the obligation to facilitate the further professional development of these individuals. They provide appropriate working conditions, timely evaluations, constructive consultation and experience opportunities.

d. Psychologists do not exploit their professional relationships with clients, supervisees, students, employees, or research participants sexually or otherwise. Psychologists do not condone nor engage in sexual harrassment. Sexual harrassment is defined as deliberate or repeated comments, gestures, or physical contacts of a sexual nature that are unwanted by the recipient.

e. In conducting research in institutions or organizations, psychologists secure appropriate authorization to conduct such research. They are aware of their obligation to future research workers and insure that host institutions receive adequate information about the research and proper acknowledgement of their contributions.

f. Publication credit is assigned to those who have contributed to a publication in proportion to their professional contribution. Major contributions of a professional character made by several persons to a common project are recognized by joint authorship, with the individual who made the principal contribution listed first. Minor contributions of a professional character and extensive clerical or similar nonprofessional assistance may be acknowledged in footnotes or in an introductory statement. Acknowledgement through specific citations is made for unpublished as well as published material that has directly influenced the research or writing. A psychologist who compiles and edits material of others for publication publishes the material in the name of the originating group, if appropriate, with his/her own name appearing as chairperson or editor. All contributors are to be acknowledged and named.

g. When psychologists know of an ethical violation by another psychologist, and it seems appropriate, they informally attempt to resolve the issue by bringing the behavior to the attention of the psychologist. If the misconduct is of a minor nature and/or appears to be due to lack of sensitivity, knowledge, or experience, such an informal solution is usually appropriate. Such informal corrective efforts are sensitive to any rights to confidentiality involved. If the violation does not seem amenable to an informal solution, or is of a more serious nature, psychologists bring it to the attention of the appropriate local, state, and/or national committee on professional ethics and conduct.

Principle 8: Assessment techniques

In the development, publication, and utilization of psychological assessment techniques, psychologists make every effort to promote the welfare and best interests of the client. They guard against the misuse of assessment results. They respect the client's right to know the results, the interpretations made and the bases for their conclusions and recommendations. Psychologists make every effort to maintain the security of tests and other assessment techniques within limits of legal mandates. They strive to assure the appropriate use of assessment techniques by others.

a. In using assessment techniques, psychologists respect the right of clients to have a full explanation of the nature and purpose of the techniques in language that the client can understand, unless an explicit exception to this right has been agreed upon in advance. When the explanations are to be provided by others, the psychologist establishes procedures for insuring the adequacy of these explanations.

b. Psychologists responsible for the development and standardization of psychological tests and other assessment techniques utilize established scientific procedures and observe the relevant APA standards.

c. In reporting assessment results, psychologists indicate any reservations that exist regarding validity or reliability because of the circumstances of the assessment or the inappropriateness of the norms for the person tested. Psychologists strive to insure that the results of assessments and their interpretations are not misused by others.

d. Psychologists recognize that assessment results may become obsolete. They make every effort to avoid and prevent the misuse of obsolete measures.

e. Psychologists offering scoring and interpretation services are able to produce appropriate evidence for the validity of the programs and procedures used in arriving at interpretations. The public offering of an automated interpretation service is considered as a professional-to-professional consultation. The psychologist makes every effort to avoid misuse of assessment reports.

f. Psychologists do not encourage or promote the use of psychological assessment techniques by inappropriately trained or otherwise unqualified persons through teaching, sponsorship, or supervision.

Principle 9: Research with human participants

The decision to undertake research rests upon a considered judgment by the individual psychologist about how best to contribute to psychological science and human welfare. Having made the decision to conduct research, the psychologist considers alternative directions in which research energies and resources might be invested. On the basis of this consideration, the psychologist carries out the investigation with respect and concern for the dignity and welfare of the people who participate, and with cognizance of federal and state regulations and professional standards governing the conduct of research with human participants.

a. In planning a study, the investigator has the responsibility to make a careful evaluation of its ethical acceptability. To the extent that the weighing of scientific and human values suggests a compromise of any principle, the investigator incurs a correspondingly serious obligation to seek ethical advice and to observe stringent safeguards to protect the rights of human participants.

b. Considering whether a participant in a planned study will be a "subject at risk" or a "subject at minimal risk," according to recognized standards, is of primary ethical concern to the investigator.

c. The investigator always retains the responsibility for insuring ethical practice in research. The investigator is also responsible for the ethical treatment of research participants by collaborators, assistants, students, and employees, all of whom, however, incur similar obligations.

d. Except for minimal risk research, the investigator establishes a clear and fair agreement with the research participants, prior to their participation, that clarifies the obligations and responsibilities of each. The investigator has the obligation to honor all promises and commitments included in that agreement. The investigator informs the participant of all aspects of the research that might reasonably be expected to influence willingness to participate, and explains all other aspects of the research about which the participant inquires. Failure to make full disclosure prior to obtaining informed consent requires additional safeguards to protect the welfare and dignity of the research participant. Research with children or participants who have impairments which would limit understanding and/or communication, requires special safeguard procedures.

e. Methodological requirements of a study may make the use of concealment or deception necessary. Before conducting such a study, the investigator has a special responsibility to: (i) determine whether the use of such techniques is justified by the study's prospective scientific, educational, or applied value; (ii) determine whether alternative procedures are available that do not utilize concealment or deception; and (iii) insure that the participants are provided with sufficient explanation as soon as possible.

f. The investigator respects the individual's freedom to decline to participate in or to withdraw from the research at any time. The obligation to protect this freedom requires careful thought and consideration when the investigator is in a position of authority or influence over the participant. Such positions of authority include but are not limited to situations when research participation is required as part of employment or when the participant is a student, client, or employee of the investigator.

g. The investigator protects the participants from physical and mental discomfort, harm, and danger that may arise from research procedures. If risks of such consequences exist, the investigator informs the participant of that fact. Research procedures likely to cause serious or lasting harm to a participant are not used unless the failure to use these procedures might expose the participant to risk of greater harm, or unless the research has great potential benefit and fully informed and voluntary consent is obtained from each participant. The participant should be informed of procedures for contacting the investigator within a reasonable time period following participation should stress, potential harm, or related questions or concerns arise.

h. After the data are collected, the investigator provides the participant with information about the nature of the study and attempts to remove any misconceptions that may have arisen. Where scientific or humane values justify delaying or withholding information, the investigator incurs a special responsibility to monitor the research and to assure that there are no damaging consequences for the participant.

i. Where research procedures result in undesirable consequences for the individual participant, the investigator has the responsibility to detect and remove or correct these consequences, including long-term effects.

j. Information obtained about the research participant during the courses of an investigation is confidential unless otherwise agreed upon in advance. When the possibility exists that others may obtain access to such information, this possibility, together with the plans for protecting confidentiality, is explained to the participant as part of the procedure for obtaining informed consent.

Principle 10: Care and use of animals

An investigator of animal behavior strives to advance our understanding of basic behavioral principles and/or to contribute to the improvement of human health and welfare. In seeking these ends, the investigator insures the welfare of the animals and treats them humanely. Laws and regulations notwithstanding, the animal's immediate protection depends upon the scientist's own conscience.

a. The acquisition, care, use, and disposal of all animals is in compliance with current federal, state or provincial, and local laws and regulations.

b. A psychologist trained in research methods and experienced in the care of laboratory animals closely supervises all procedures involving animals and is responsible for insuring appropriate consideration of their comfort, health, and humane treatment.

c. Psychologists insure that all individuals using animals under their supervision have received explicit instruction in experimental methods and in the care, maintenance, and handling of the species being used. Responsibilities and activities of individuals participating in a research project are consistent with their respective competencies.

d. Psychologists make every effort to minimize discomfort, illness, and pain to the animals. A procedure subjecting animals to pain, stress, or privation is used only when an alternative procedure is unavailable and the goal is justified by its prospective scientific, educational, or applied value. Surgical procedures are performed under appropriate anesthesia; techniques to avoid infection and minimize pain are followed during and after surgery.

e. When it is appropriate that the animal's life be terminated, it is done rapidly and painlessly.

Name Index

Subject Index